# Teacher Edition

## ZANER-BLOSER

# STRATEGIES
## for Writers

### Level B – Recommended for Grade 2 and Above

## Authors

**Leslie W. Crawford, Ed.D.**
Georgia College & State University

**Rebecca Bowers Sipe, Ed.D.**
Eastern Michigan University

**Robert C. Calfee, Ph.D.**
University of California, Riverside

## Consulting Author

**Barry Sneed**
Master Teacher
Perry Local Schools
Perry, Ohio

*ZB*

**Zaner-Bloser**

# Rubric Based Instruction ᴸᴹ

Zaner-Bloser proudly presents a strategic and innovative approach to writing instruction that makes it easier to improve students' writing. **Strategies for Writers** is a complete writing program that features rubric-based instruction.

## Rubric Based Instruction ™ is Writing Instruction for Students

- **Rubric**-based instruction is logical and effective, so students always know what's expected and what to do.

- The writing process is taught with special emphasis on prewriting and revising, so students are guided smoothly through these challenging areas.

- Specific types of writing are modeled in an upbeat, conversational way throughout, so students are engaged and eager to write.

- Grammar is taught in conjunction with writing, so students learn how grammar is best applied to writing.

# STRATEGIES for Writers

## for Teaching Writing

- Instruction is **Rubric**-based, so teaching is focused and learning becomes more independent.

- Complete writing instruction is provided in one program, so it's easy for teachers to teach the writing process, different types of writing, and grammar.

- Units are self-contained, so they can be taught in any order.

- A School-Home Connection Blackline Master is provided in every unit, so teachers can easily communicate with families.

## and Writing Assessment

- Assessment is **Rubric**-based, so students know exactly what they need to do to succeed.

- Instruction supports major national, state, and NCTE standards, so students learn the skills necessary to succeed in writing assessment.

- Global rubrics that can be used as pretest and posttest rubrics are available in the Teacher Edition Appendix.

**Wherever your students' writing skills are, Strategies for Writers will take them to the next step!**

**Rubric Based Instruction**

# The Authors

## Leslie W. Crawford, Ed.D.

**Co-author of *Strategies for Writers***

Dr. Crawford is an honored language arts educator and Fulbright Scholar who has contributed to many educational publications. In addition to co-authoring *Strategies for Writers*, Dr. Crawford is also co-author of Zaner-Bloser's *9 Good Habits for All Readers*.

Dr. Crawford received his Doctorate in Education from the University of California, Berkeley. He was Dean of the John H. Lounsbury School of Education at the Georgia College & State University from 1996 to 2001 and is currently a professor of Early Childhood and Middle Grades Education at the same university.

## Robert C. Calfee, Ph.D.

**Co-author of *Strategies for Writers***

Dr. Calfee is a cognitive psychologist who earned his degrees at UCLA and did post-graduate work at Stanford University where he later served as a professor in the Committee on Language, Literacy, and Culture and the Committee on Psychological Studies. He is presently Dean of the Graduate School of Education, University of California, Riverside.

Dr. Calfee has authored numerous critical papers and several books, including *The Reading-Writing Connection* and *Teach Our Children Well*.

## Rebecca B. Sipe, Ed.D.

**Co-author of *Strategies for Writers***

Dr. Sipe is a highly respected authority on the teaching of language arts, including writing and grammar. She is an NCTE chair, lectures and holds workshops nationally, and has published numerous articles.

Dr. Sipe began her career in education as a classroom teacher and received her Doctorate in Education from Boston University. She is currently Assistant Professor of English Education at Eastern Michigan University.

## Barry Sneed, *Master Teacher*

Mr. Sneed holds a Master of Education in Curriculum and Instruction from Cleveland State University. A classroom teacher for eleven years, Mr. Sneed is a recipient of the Milken Family Foundation's National Educator Award, a children's book author, and a frequent speaker at Ohio's Kindergarten-Primary Conferences and elementary schools. Mr. Sneed currently teaches first grade for Perry Local Schools in Perry, Ohio.

## Lee Bromberger, *Assessment Specialist*

Mr. Bromberger received his Master of Arts, English, from Marquette University and is currently the K–12 Language Arts Curriculum Co-Chair at Mukwonago High School in Wisconsin. He is known for his research on the correlation of writing standards to assessment, which he presented at the NCTE national convention in 2001. Mr. Bromberger has also authored various publications on writing and grammar.

# The Program Components

**Student Edition** contains the step-by-step writing instruction students need, modeled in an upbeat, conversational way throughout the program.

**Poster Pack includes 10 grade level rubrics that are found in the Student Edition.**

**Teacher Edition** gives complete guidelines that make writing instruction easy for teachers.

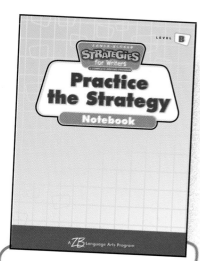

**Practice the Strategy Notebook** provides guided practice for the strategies being taught in the unit.
Pages may be reproduced.

**Transparencies** include tools to focus classroom instruction, including blank graphic organizers and writing models for proofreading and grammar instruction.

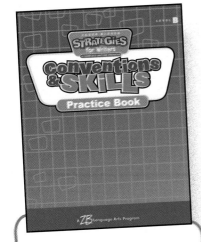

**Conventions & Skills Practice Book Student Edition** provides students with complete conventions and skills instruction for their level.

**Conventions & Skills Practice Book Teacher Edition** is fully annotated and easily makes conventions and skills instruction an important part of the program.

Level B book covers shown.

The **Strategies for Writers Sing-Along CD** features fun songs to help students learn the writing process. Songs include "The Writing Process Hokey Pokey."

## is Writing Instruction for Students

# Rubric-Based Instruction Helps Students Succeed

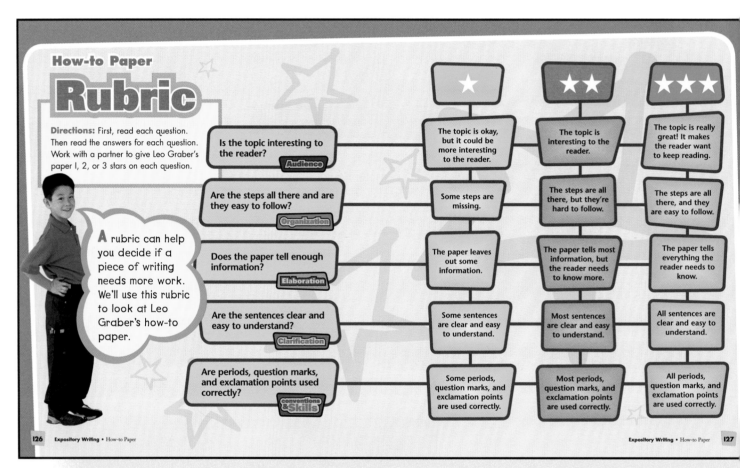

Level B rubric shown.

Students succeed when they have clear guidelines and expectations for their writing. **Strategies for Writers** provides clear guidelines because the rubric is central to its instructional plan.

- The **Rubric** in each chapter is specific to the type of writing and strategies being taught.

- In the beginning of each chapter, the **Rubric** is introduced and the students are taught how to use it by applying it to a model.

- Throughout the chapter, the strategies being taught support the points of the **Rubric**.

- In the **Practice the Strategy Notebook**, the same **Rubric** appears again for students to evaluate their own writing.

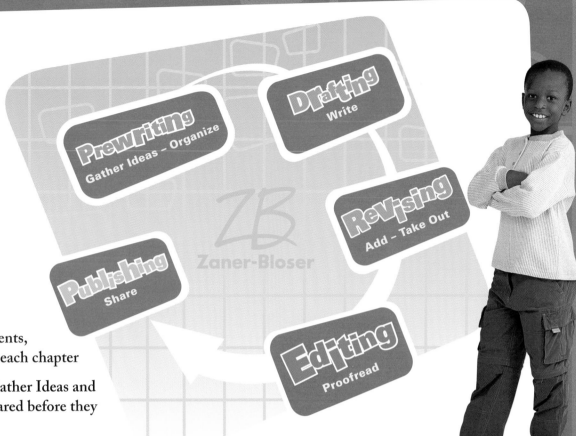

## The Writing Process in
**Strategies for Writers**...

- Uses writing partners that walk students, step-by-step, through the process in each chapter

- Has two strategies for prewriting (Gather Ideas and Organize), so students are well prepared before they begin writing

- Has two strategies for revising (Add and Take Out) that give students clear guidelines for improvement

- Is successful in teaching students that writing is a recursive process, so they are continually encouraged to improve

## Conventions & Skills in
**Strategies for Writers**...

*are taught on three different levels:*

 A short lesson on the Editing page of each chapter focuses on one skill.

 For students who need further instruction, a complete lesson is provided in the back of the Student Edition for the same skill introduced on the Editing page.

 50 grade-level appropriate lessons (a full year's worth of instruction) are available in the **Conventions & Skills Practice Book.**

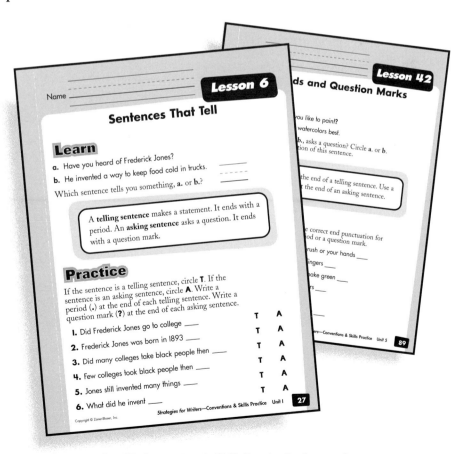

Level B **Conventions & Skills Practice Book** pages shown.

# The Student Edition

An engaging, step-by-step instructional plan empowers students to take their writing to the next step.

## Model

Student writing partners in each chapter walk students, step-by-step, through an entire writing process to create a specific type of writing.

> **C**onversational text throughout the Student Edition engages students and makes learning fun.

> **A** variety of graphic organizers helps students organize their information.

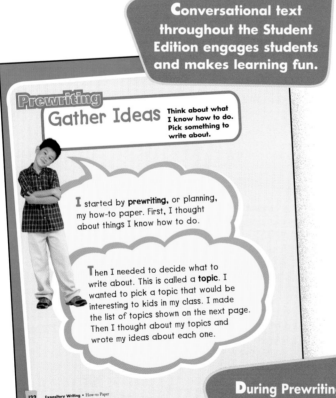

> **D**uring Prewriting, writing partners model the prewriting strategies of gathering ideas and organizing information.

Level B Student Edition pages shown.

### Prewriting
### Gather Ideas
Think about what I know how to do. Pick something to write about.

I started by **prewriting,** or planning, my how-to paper. First, I thought about things I know how to do.

Then I needed to decide what to write about. This is called a **topic.** I wanted to pick a topic that would be interesting to kids in my class. I made the list of topics shown on the next page. Then I thought about my topics and wrote my ideas about each one.

132  Expository Writing • How-to Paper

### Prewriting
### Organize
Decide on the steps. Use an order chain to put the steps in the right order.

The next step in prewriting is to **organize.** I talked with my writing partner, Joe, about the steps to make a jigsaw puzzle.

Then I used an order ___ to organize my steps. ___ order chain is on the ___ page.

#### Order ___
An **order chain** h___ of a how-to pape___ to last.

134  Expository Writing • How-to Paper

**Topic: How to Make a Jigsaw Puzzle**

| | |
|---|---|
| **First Step** | Find a picture in a magazine and cut it out. |
| **Next Step** | Cut a piece of heavy paper the same size as the picture. |
| **Next Step** | Paste the picture on the heavy paper. |
| **Next Step** | Wait for the paste to dry. Draw two wavy lines across and two wavy lines down the back of the paper. |
| **Last Step** | Cut the picture apart on the lines. |

Read Tai's order chain again. Do you think he covered all the steps? Talk about the order chain with a partner.

Stop and Go! Try this yourself on page 100 in the **Practice Notebook!** the Strategy

Expository Writing • How-to Paper  135

T8

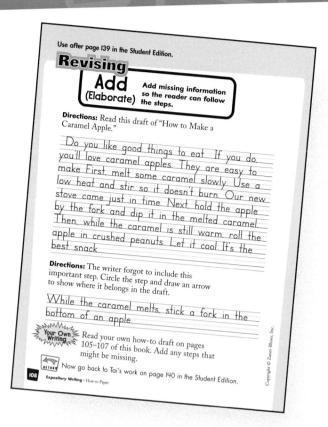

Use after page 135 in the Student Edition.

**Prewriting**

**Organize** Decide on the steps. Use an order chain to put the steps in the right order.

**Directions:** Copy the circled steps from page 100 on the order chain below. Make sure they are in the right order.

**Topic:** How to Make a Caramel Apple

First Step

Next Step

Next Step

Next Step

Last Step

Go to **Your Own Writing** pages 102–103 in this book.

Expository Writing • How-to Paper  101

## Guided Practice

After each step is modeled, students are directed to their **Practice the Strategy Notebook** to practice.

Use after page 139 in the Student Edition.

**Revising**

**Add (Elaborate)** Add missing information so the reader can follow the steps.

**Directions:** Read this draft of "How to Make a Caramel Apple."

Do you like good things to eat If you do you'll love caramel apples They are easy to make First melt some caramel slowly Use a low heat and stir so it doesn't burn Our new stove came just in time Next hold the apple by the fork and dip it in the melted caramel Then, while the caramel is still warm, roll the apple in crushed peanuts Let it cool It's the best snack

**Directions:** The writer forgot to include this important step. Circle the step and draw an arrow to show where it belongs in the draft.

While the caramel melts, stick a fork in the bottom of an apple

**Your Own Writing** Read your own how-to draft on pages 105–107 of this book. Add any steps that might be missing.

Now go back to Tai's work on page 140 in the Student Edition.

108  Expository Writing • How-to Paper

Level B **Practice the Strategy Notebook** pages shown.

Use after page 137 in the Student Edition.

**Your Own Writing**

**Drafting**

**Write** Use my order chain. Write sentences that tell the steps in correct order.

**Directions:** Use the lines on these pages to write a draft of your own how-to paper. Follow the order chain you filled in on pages 102–103 to tell the steps of your how-to paper in the right order.

Expository Writing • How-to Paper  105

Level B **Practice the Strategy Notebook** page shown.

## Apply to your own writing

After students practice the strategy, they can immediately apply the strategy to their own work. Then, they are directed back to their Student Edition to go on to the next step.

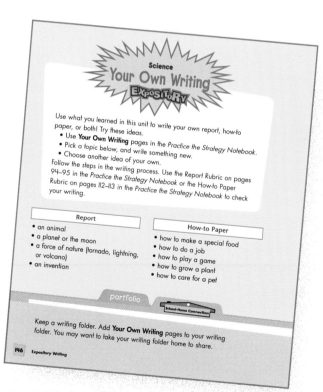

**Science**

**Your Own Writing**

**EXPOSITORY**

Use what you learned in this unit to write your own report, how-to paper, or both! Try these ideas.
• Use **Your Own Writing** pages in the *Practice the Strategy Notebook*.
• Pick a topic below, and write something new.
• Choose another idea of your own.

Follow the steps in the writing process. Use the Report Rubric on pages 94–95 in the *Practice the Strategy Notebook* or the How-to Paper Rubric on pages 112–113 in the *Practice the Strategy Notebook* to check your writing.

| Report |
| --- |
| • an animal |
| • a planet or the moon |
| • a force of nature (tornado, lightning, or volcano) |
| • an invention |

| How-to Paper |
| --- |
| • how to make a special food |
| • how to do a job |
| • how to play a game |
| • how to grow a plant |
| • how to care for a pet |

*portfolio*

**School-Home Connection**

Keep a writing folder. Add **Your Own Writing** pages to your writing folder. You may want to take your writing folder home to share.

146  Expository Writing

Level B Student Edition page shown.

At the end of each unit, writing prompts help students apply the writing strategies to other content areas.

# Rubric Based℠ Instruction in Teaching Writing

## The Teacher Edition

A complete, step-by-step guide makes it easy for teachers to improve students' writing.

**T**ips from a master classroom teacher are provided for classroom activities designed to improve students' writing and communication skills.

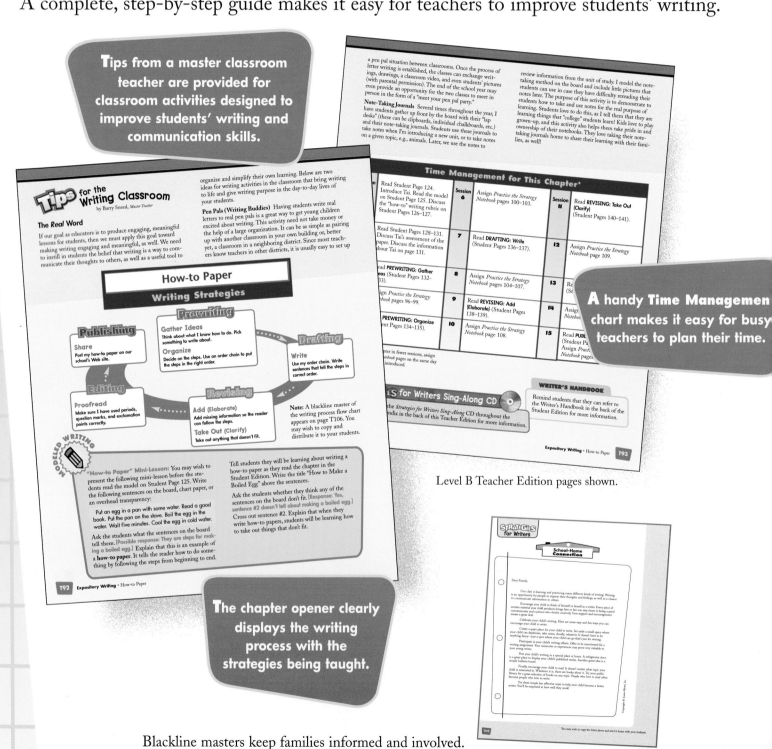

**A** handy **Time Management** chart makes it easy for busy teachers to plan their time.

Level B Teacher Edition pages shown.

**T**he chapter opener clearly displays the writing process with the strategies being taught.

Blackline masters keep families informed and involved.

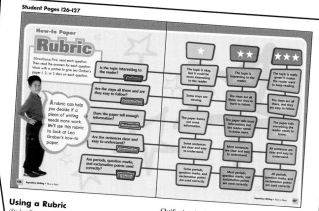

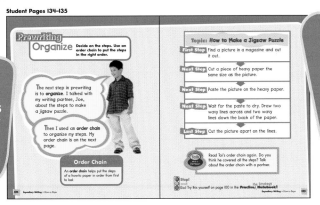

**Teaching suggestions are provided to help meet the needs of every student.**

**The rubric is introduced early in each chapter, so teaching is focused and students know from the start what is expected of them.**

**The Teacher Edition is fully annotated and student pages are clearly displayed, so it's easy for teachers to stay organized.**

**Clear instructions are provided for teachers to guide their students, step-by-step, through the writing process.**

**Practice the Strategy Notebook assignments are highlighted and clearly described.**

Level B Teacher Edition pages shown.

# Rubric Based Instruction

# in Writing Assessment

The **Rubric** provides clear guidelines for students to assess other students' writing, for students to assess their own writing, and for teachers to assess students' writing.

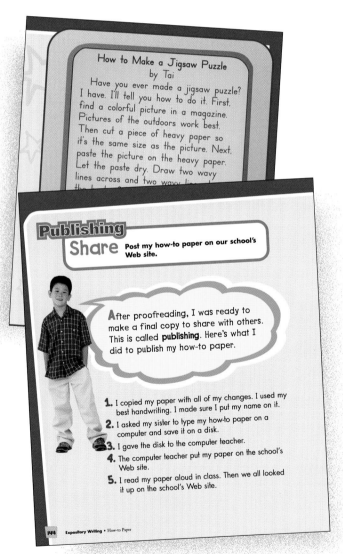

Level B Student Edition pages shown.

Level B rubric shown.

Global rubrics that can be used as pretest and posttest rubrics are available in the Teacher Edition Appendix.

During the publishing step of the writing process, students use the **Rubric** to assess both the writing partner's writing and any of their own writing that was developed within the chapter.

# Standardized Test-Taking

**Strategies for Writers** supports students' success on the
**Terra Nova Basic Battery** by developing students' abilities
in these key areas:

* Demonstrate an understanding of topic sentences.
* Demonstrate an understanding of concluding sentences.
* Demonstrate an understanding of connective and transitional words
  and phrases.
* Demonstrate an understanding of supportive statements.
* Demonstrate an understanding of sequence of ideas.
* Demonstrate an understanding of relevance of information.
* Focus on a topic and develop an organized response.

**Strategies for Writers** supports students' success on the
**Stanford 9 Achievement Test** by developing students'
abilities in these key areas:

* Demonstrate an understanding of the descriptive writing mode.
* Demonstrate an understanding of the narrative writing mode.
* Demonstrate an understanding of the expository writing mode.
* Demonstrate an understanding of the persuasive writing mode.
* Produce writing that has clear and coherent paragraphs that develop a
  central idea.
* Produce writing that shows evidence of considering audience and purpose.
* Produce writing that is developed by progressing through the writing process
  (i.e., prewriting, drafting, revising, and editing successive versions).
* Produce writing that demonstrates grade-level appropriate knowledge of
  grammar, usage, and mechanics.

**Strategies for Writers** supports students' success on the
**ITBS (Iowa Tests of Basic Skills)** by developing students'
abilities in these key areas:

* Produce writing that demonstrates an understanding of capitalization.
* Produce writing that demonstrates an understanding of punctuation.
* Produce writing that demonstrates an understanding of usage and expression.

# NCTE/IRA Standards

**Strategies for Writers** aligns with these NCTE/IRA Standards:

**Students** adjust their use of spoken, written, and visual language (e.g., conventions, style, vocabulary) to communicate effectively with a variety of audiences and for different purposes.

**Students** employ a wide range of strategies as they write and use different writing process elements appropriately to communicate with different audiences for a variety of purposes.

**Students** apply knowledge of language structure, language conventions (e.g., spelling and punctuation), media techniques, figurative language, and genre to create, critique, and discuss print and non-print texts.

**Students** conduct research on issues and interests by generating ideas and questions and by posing problems. They gather, evaluate, and synthesize data from a variety of sources (e.g., print and non-print texts, artifacts, people) to communicate their discoveries in ways that suit their purpose and audience.

**Students** use a variety of technological and information resources (e.g., libraries, databases, computer networks, video) to gather and synthesize information and to create and communicate knowledge.

**Students** use spoken, written, and visual language to accomplish their own purposes (e.g., for learning, enjoyment, persuasion, and the exchange of information).

# Table of Contents

# Table of Contents

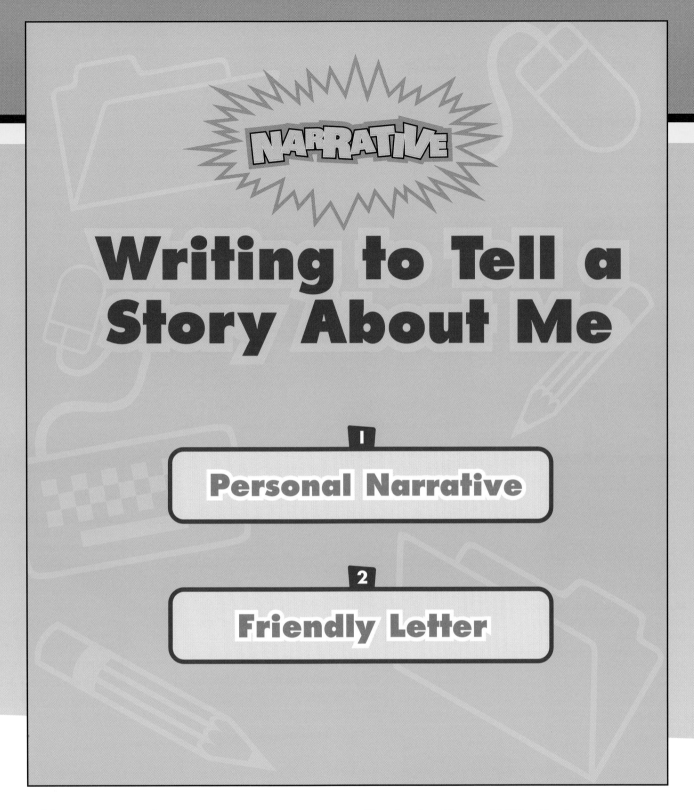

# NARRATIVE

# Writing to Tell a Story About Me

**1 Personal Narrative**

**2 Friendly Letter**

## Defining Writing to Tell a Story

Explain to students that people write for different reasons. As an example, read the following sentence aloud or write it on the board:

• My first swimming lesson was hard.

Ask students what they think this sentence is about. [Response: a swimming lesson] Then ask students what kind of writing this sentence could begin. [Response: a story] Explain that people sometimes write stories about themselves. They tell about what they did or about what happened to them. Sometimes, they tell their stories in books; sometimes, they tell their stories in letters to their family or friends.

## Books to Share With Students

For excellent examples of narrative writing, you may wish to share these books with your students:

• *Owl Moon* by Jane Yolen
• *No Jumping on the Bed* by Tedd Arnold
• *Danny and the Dinosaur* by Syd Hoff
• *Two Bad Ants* by Chris Van Allsburg
• *When I Go Camping with Grandma* by Marion Dane Bauer

You may also wish to use some of the titles from Zaner-Bloser Literacy.

## Tips for the Writing Classroom
by Barry Sneed, *Master Teacher*

### Taking Risks, *Write* from Day One...

The start of the school year is always challenging. Establishing the daily routines for the writing classroom is an integral part of early preparations. While some teachers believe they must ease into writing over time, I have always felt that diving in head first works best. Helping students realize that writing is all around us, and that during the coming year they can expect to become better, stronger writers than they were last year, makes writing exciting and desirable, not something that is labored and frightening. Here are a few ideas for establishing writing routines in the classroom:

**Journal Writing** Start journal writing on Day 1 by having students draw a picture about themselves, their families, or something they like. Ask them to label the picture or write a few words or a sentence about it. This provides you with a concrete writing sample for each child and a glimpse of the range of the levels of students in your room.

## Personal Narrative
### Writing Strategies

### Prewriting

**Gather Ideas**
Make a list of interesting topics. Pick one.

**Organize**
Make a storyboard to tell what happened.

### Drafting

**Write**
Use my storyboard. Write sentences to tell what happened first, next, and last.

### Revising

**Add (Elaborate)**
Add time-order words to show how one event follows the other.

**Take Out (Clarify)**
Take out sentences that don't help tell what happened.

### Editing

**Proofread**
Make sure I start each sentence with a capital letter and end it with a period.

### Publishing

**Share**
Add my story to the class album.

**Note:** A blackline master of the writing process flow chart appears on page T106. You may wish to copy and distribute it to your students.

### MODELED WRITING

**Personal Narrative Mini-Lesson:** You may wish to present the following mini-lesson before the students read the model on Student Page 11. Write the following on the board, chart paper, or an overhead transparency:

> I was in a class play. First, I read the play. Then I chose my part. Next, I learned my lines and practiced them. Then I helped make my costume. My cousin is an actor. Finally, it was opening night.

Ask the students what the sentences on the board tell them. [Possible responses: story events about what someone did; a story in order] Explain that a **personal narrative** tells about something the writer did or about something that happened to the writer. Tell students they will be learning more about writing a personal narrative as they read the chapter in the Student Edition. They will see a model of this kind of writing and learn and practice some strategies for writing their own personal narrative. Write the title "My Class Play" above the sentences. Ask the students whether they think any of the sentences on the board don't fit. [Response: Yes, the sixth sentence doesn't tell about the class play.] Cross out the sixth sentence. Explain to students that when they write a personal narrative, they will also learn how to take out sentences that don't help tell what happened.

**Edit a Sentence a Day** Write a sentence on the board before the students arrive. As they arrive, they should take out their "Morning Writing Paper" and write the sentence, correcting mistakes they find. Then go over the sentence with the class. Allow volunteers to come up and make corrections. Incorporate proofreading marks as they are learned throughout the year.

**Daily Morning Letter** Each morning before students arrive write a short letter (in friendly letter format) to the class, either on the front board or on large chart paper. Upon arrival, have students either correct the letter or simply have them respond to the letter in writing. This can be used to reinforce the friendly letter format, as well as to review daily

skills or conventions. It is also a great classroom management tool for establishing a student routine upon arrival into the classroom, as students know what to do and are often excited to see what message each day's letter contains!

**Sample Letter:**

October 5

dear class

today we have an assembly about animals. We will not have math this morning, so please do page 25 in your books for math practice when you finish editing this letter.

thanks

mr. sneed

## Time Management for This Chapter*

| Session | | Session | | Session | |
|---|---|---|---|---|---|
| **1** | Introduce the genre. Introduce Kyle on Student Page 10. Read the model on Student Page 11. Discuss the rubric on Student Pages 12–13. | **6** | Read **PREWRITING: Organize** (Student Pages 20–21). | **11** | Assign *Practice the Strategy Notebook* pages 15–17. |
| **2** | Read Student Pages 14–17. Discuss Kyle's assessment of the model. Discuss the information about Kyle on Student Page 17. | **7** | Assign *Practice the Strategy Notebook* pages 10–11. | **12** | Read **REVISING: Add (Elaborate)** (Student Pages 24–25). Assign *Practice the Strategy Notebook* page 18. Tell students to use this strategy in their own writing. |
| **3** | Read **PREWRITING: Gather Ideas** (Student Pages 18–19). | **8** | Assign *Practice the Strategy Notebook* pages 12–13. | **13** | Read **REVISING: Take Out (Clarify)** (Student Pages 26–27.) Assign *Practice the Strategy Notebook* page 19. |
| **4** | Assign *Practice the Strategy Notebook* pages 6–7. | **9** | Read **DRAFTING: Write** (Student Pages 22–23). | **14** | Read **EDITING: Proofread** (Student Pages 28–29). Assign *Practice the Strategy Notebook* pages 20–21. |
| **5** | Assign *Practice the Strategy Notebook* pages 8–9. | **10** | Assign *Practice the Strategy Notebook* page 14. | **15** | Read **PUBLISHING: Share** (Student Pages 30–31). Assign *Practice the Strategy Notebook* pages 22–23. |

* To complete the chapter in fewer sessions, assign the *Practice the Strategy Notebook* pages on the same day each strategy is introduced.

## STRATEGIES for Writers Sing-Along CD

You may wish to use the *Strategies for Writers Sing-Along* CD throughout the chapter. See the Appendix in the back of this Teacher Edition for more information.

## WRITER'S HANDBOOK

Remind students that they can refer to the Writer's Handbook in the back of the Student Edition for more information.

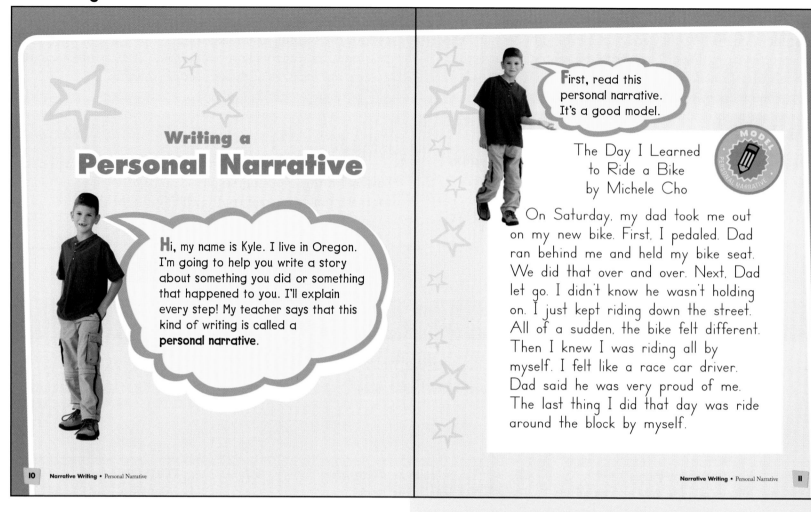

Writing a
# Personal Narrative

Hi, my name is Kyle. I live in Oregon. I'm going to help you write a story about something you did or something that happened to you. I'll explain every step! My teacher says that this kind of writing is called a **personal narrative**.

First, read this personal narrative. It's a good model.

The Day I Learned to Ride a Bike
by Michele Cho

On Saturday, my dad took me out on my new bike. First, I pedaled. Dad ran behind me and held my bike seat. We did that over and over. Next, Dad let go. I didn't know he wasn't holding on. I just kept riding down the street. All of a sudden, the bike felt different. Then I knew I was riding all by myself. I felt like a race car driver. Dad said he was very proud of me. The last thing I did that day was ride around the block by myself.

10    **Narrative Writing** • Personal Narrative      **Narrative Writing** • Personal Narrative    11

## Introduce the Genre:
### Personal Narrative

*(Student Pages 10–11)*

Read Kyle's words on Student Page 10 with the students. Tell them that he is going to show them how to write a personal narrative. Tell them that they will read Kyle's work as a class. At each step, they will have a chance to talk with a partner. Then they will practice using the same strategies to write their own personal narratives. Ask the students to think of an important day or experience in their own life. [Possible responses: the day I got a new pet; the day we moved; the day I started second grade]

## Read the Model:
### Personal Narrative

Read the model story on Student Page 11. Ask what makes the story a good example of a personal narrative. [Possible responses: It tells about something that happened in the writer's life. It's interesting. It's written in a clear order.] As you read the model with the students, point out that the model may contain words that the students do not know. Work with the students to choose and add high-frequency words from the model to your room's Word Wall, if you currently use one.

## Meeting Students' Needs:
### Second-Language Learners

Pair second-language learners with English-speaking students. Ask the partners to take turns telling one story about themselves. You may wish to assign a specific topic, such as the first day of second grade. Explain to students that they may use pictures, symbols, or hand gestures to tell their stories. You may wish to call on volunteers to model telling a story about themselves to the entire class, in English and in another language.

### Students Who Need Extra Help

You may wish to use a part of the day to reteach a part of the chapter to students who need extra help. Ask the students to state in their own words what they think Kyle is doing in the Student Edition. Reinforce students' understanding and fill in gaps wherever necessary. You may wish to use conferencing as a time to make sure all students are comfortable with the skills and concepts that are being covered.

### Gifted Students

Challenge students who are exceeding your expectations by encouraging them to expand on their writing. For example, students could be encouraged to add dialogue to their personal narrative.

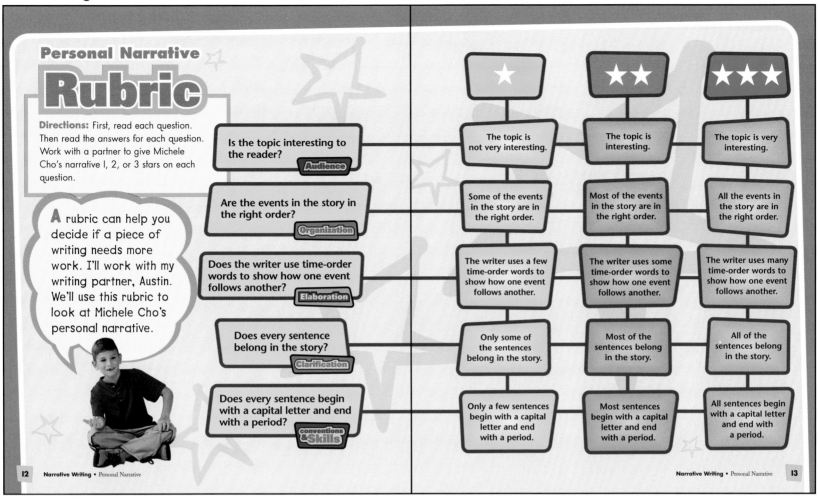

## Using a Rubric

Use the text on Student Pages 14–16 to model the use of a rubric for evaluating a piece of writing. Explain that a *rubric* is a tool for deciding how a piece of writing can be made better. The rubric on these pages will be used to check the model personal narrative. Point out that the rubric helps writers focus on important parts of the writing, such as the topic of the story, how the story is organized, and whether sentences are written correctly.

Read the information in the boxes on Student Page 13 with the students. Take a few moments to explain the relationship between the number of stars and the information in the boxes. Explain that the answer boxes show how well the paper scores on the questions on Student Page 12. Some problems are expected, and the paper can still receive one star. Fewer problems mean that a paper will get two stars. No problems mean that a paper will get three stars. Remind students that this story is a model, so it probably will receive a high score in all areas.

## Discuss the Personal Narrative Rubric

*(Student Pages 12–13)*

Read the questions on Student Page 12 with the students. Explain that writers use these questions to write a good personal narrative. Discuss each question with the students.

**Audience: Is the topic interesting to the reader?** Readers enjoy a story about something that interests them.

**Organization: Are the events in the story in the right order?** A story should tell things in the order in which they happened.

**Elaboration: Does the writer use time-order words to show how one event follows another?** Words like *first, next, then,* and *last* help readers follow the order of the story.

**Clarification: Does every sentence belong in the story?** Sentences that don't belong in a story are confusing to the reader.

**Conventions & Skills: Does every sentence begin with a capital letter and end with a period?** Capital letters and periods help readers understand where new sentences begin and end.

Have students evaluate the model personal narrative with a partner, using the Personal Narrative Rubric on Student Pages 12–13. Ask partners to share their evaluations with the whole group.

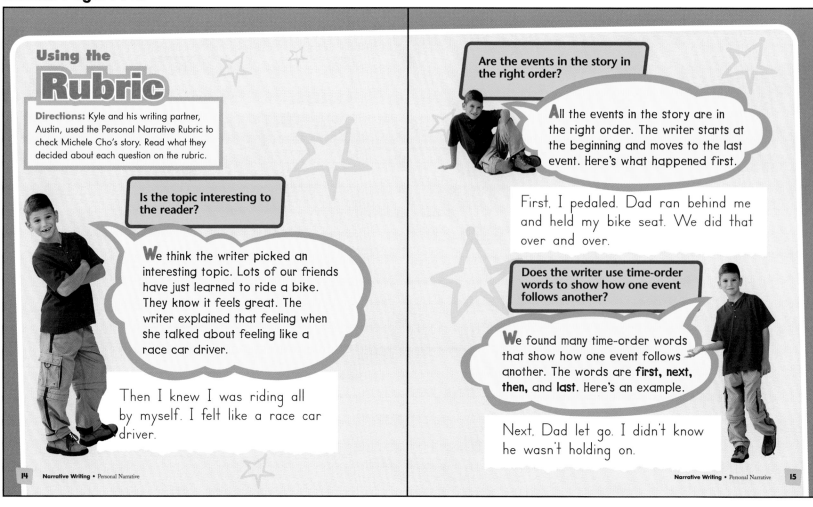

## Using the Rubric to Study the Model

*(Student Pages 14–16)*

Explain to students that now they can see how Kyle and his writing partner, Austin, are going to use the questions on the rubric to evaluate the personal narrative on Student Page 11. You may also wish to use the Writing Model to Introduce the Rubric Transparency.

Read Kyle's words on Student Pages 14–16. Ask the students if they agree that learning how to ride a bike is an interesting topic. Read the sentences from the model paper shown on Student Page 14. Explain that these sentences help make the topic interesting by telling how the writer felt. Ask students whether they agree that the story tells everything in the right order. Were they able to follow the order of events? You may wish to go back to the model story on Student Page 11 and ask students to find the words *first, next, then,* and *last.* Help students see how these words show time order and help the reader follow the story without getting confused. Ask students if they agree with Kyle that every sentence belongs in the story. Then remind students that a capital letter and a period help readers know where a new sentence begins and ends.

## A Few Words About Rubrics

by Rebecca Sipe, *Program Author*

What are rubrics and why are they important to teachers? Rubrics are a way to help define clearly the qualities in student writing. Though teachers may choose to emphasize different traits, rubrics frequently address areas such as **audience, organization, elaboration, clarification,** and **conventions and skills**. Each area will be broken down into levels (1 star, 2 stars, and 3 stars), and each level will describe the writer's demonstration of proficiency with that area.

When teachers and students work with a rubric, we can use it to talk with students about the strengths and weaknesses of their papers and to show them how to improve their work.

We've all heard that teachers can't agree on how to evaluate or assess writing. That just isn't true. When we take time to consciously identify the traits and levels of quality reflected in student writing, it is easy for teachers—as well as parents and students—to reach agreement on assessment.

## Working With a Partner Mini-Lesson:
### Read Your Writing to Your Partner

Help students understand how to work with a partner effectively by giving them some basic tips. You may wish to write these on chart paper and post them where students can readily see them.

Tell students that when they are working with a partner, they should **read their writing to their partner** rather than having their partner read it alone. This helps the writer hear his or her own work. It also helps the listener understand how the writer means the words to be read. **Note:** You may wish to give students a copy of the Working with a Partner Checklist on page T166.

**Model the Tip** Model this tip for the students by acting out a mock conference with a volunteer. You may wish to ask a student to act as your writing partner or enlist the help of a parent volunteer or a teacher's aid. Prepare a piece of your own writing and read it aloud to your partner. Then, ask the partner to read his or her paper aloud to you. Remind students to listen carefully as partners read their writing.

## Kyle:
### Writer of a Personal Narrative

*(Student Page 17)*

Read Kyle's words to the students and the information about Kyle to learn more about him. Be sure students understand that Kyle will write his own personal narrative in this chapter. Review the information given about him. Discuss what Kyle might write about in his personal narrative, based on his interests and hobbies.

Point out that Kyle will go through the steps in the writing process (Prewriting, Drafting, Revising, Editing, and Publishing). At each stage, Kyle will use a good writing strategy and explain how he used it. Students should watch for key words, including, **Gather, Organize, Write, Add (Elaborate), Take Out (Clarify), Proofread,** and **Share,** to follow the strategies Kyle uses as he goes through the writing process.

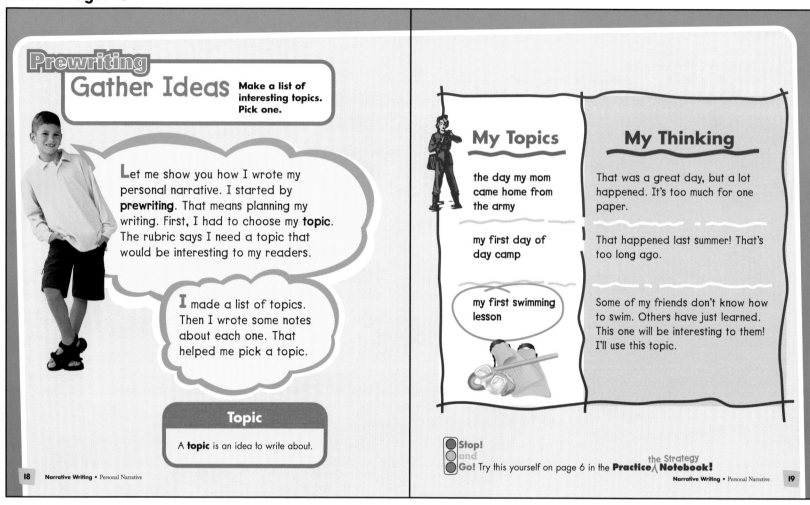

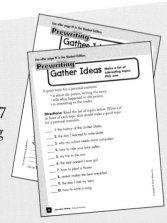

# Prewriting Gather Ideas

**Strategy: Make a list of interesting topics. Pick one.**

*(Student Pages 18–19)*

Read Kyle's words on Student Page 18. Then read aloud and discuss the definition of *topic*. Explain to the students that in this section Kyle tells how he went about writing his personal narrative. He starts by explaining how he chose his topic. Ask the students how Kyle decided on his topic. [**Possible response: He wanted to write something his classmates would want to read about.**]

Point out Kyle's list of possible topics on Student Page 19. Discuss Kyle's reasons for choosing his first swimming lesson rather than any of the other topics. Ask the students if they agree with Kyle's thinking.

## the Strategy Practice Notebook!

*Practice the Strategy Notebook* pages 6–7 provide additional practice in selecting a topic for another personal narrative. After students have completed this activity, you may wish to have them share their responses.

## the Strategy Practice Notebook!

*Practice the Strategy Notebook* pages 8–9 provide an opportunity for students to select a topic for their own personal narrative. You may wish to assign these pages now or after students have completed this chapter in the Student Edition. You may wish to save students' *Your Own Writing* pages and add them to their Work-in-Progress Portfolios.

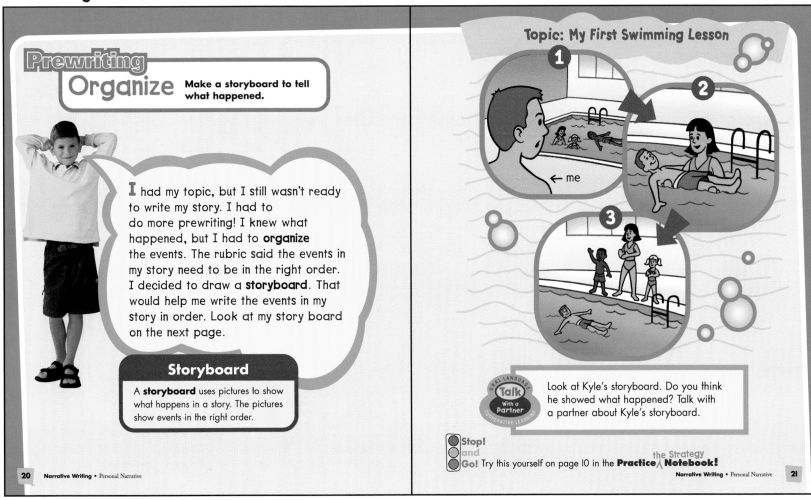

# Prewriting Organize

**Strategy: Make a storyboard to tell what happened.**

*(Student Pages 20–21)*

Read Kyle's words on Student Page 20 with the students. Explain that before he starts writing, Kyle needs to organize his information. He has to decide the order in which things happen in his story.

Direct students' attention to Kyle's storyboard on Student Page 21. Explain that a storyboard is a good way to organize what happens in a personal narrative because it shows things in order. It also helps the writer to be sure to tell all the important things that happened.

**ORAL LANGUAGE Talk With a Partner COOPERATIVE LEARNING**

Encourage the students to discuss Kyle's storyboard with their partners. Ask the students if Kyle's storyboard seems complete. Does the storyboard tell what happened? Does it show all the important events? Are the events in order? You may wish to discuss the partners' findings as a large group activity, as well.

**Note:** A storyboard transparency is provided in the *Strategies for Writers Transparencies*.

## the Strategy Practice Notebook!

*Practice the Strategy Notebook* pages 10–11 provide additional practice in using a storyboard to organize events for a personal narrative. After students have completed this activity, you may wish to have them share their storyboard with a writing partner.

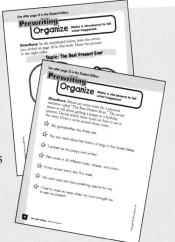

## the Strategy Practice Notebook!

*Practice the Strategy Notebook* pages 12–13 provide an opportunity for students to create a storyboard for their own personal narrative. You may wish to assign these pages now or after students have completed this chapter in the Student Edition.

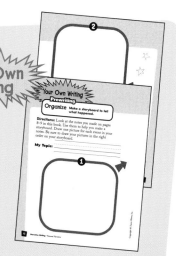

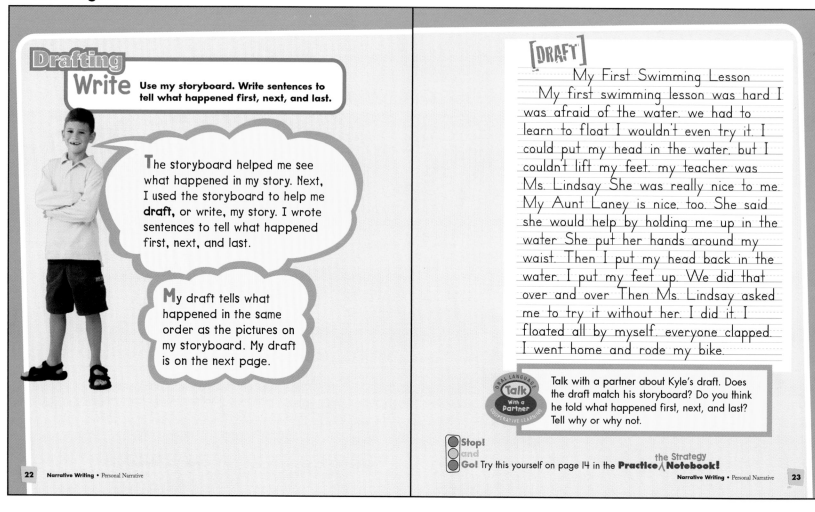

**Drafting Write** Use my storyboard. Write sentences to tell what happened first, next, and last.

The storyboard helped me see what happened in my story. Next, I used the storyboard to help me **draft,** or write, my story. I wrote sentences to tell what happened first, next, and last.

My draft tells what happened in the same order as the pictures on my storyboard. My draft is on the next page.

[DRAFT]

My First Swimming Lesson

My first swimming lesson was hard I was afraid of the water. we had to learn to float I wouldn't even try it. I could put my head in the water. but I couldn't lift my feet. my teacher was Ms. Lindsay She was really nice to me. My Aunt Laney is nice. too. She said she would help by holding me up in the water She put her hands around my waist. Then I put my head back in the water. I put my feet up. We did that over and over Then Ms. Lindsay asked me to try it without her. I did it. I floated all by myself. everyone clapped. I went home and rode my bike.

Talk With a Partner: Talk with a partner about Kyle's draft. Does the draft match his storyboard? Do you think he told what happened first, next, and last? Tell why or why not.

Stop! and Go! Try this yourself on page 14 in the **Practice the Strategy Notebook!**

22 **Narrative Writing** • Personal Narrative

23 **Narrative Writing** • Personal Narrative

---

**Drafting Write**

**Strategy: Use my storyboard. Write sentences to tell what happened first, next, and last.**

*(Student Pages 22–23)*

Discuss the term *draft* with the students. Explain that a draft is an early form of a paper. In a draft, writers don't worry about mistakes. The important thing is to get their ideas down on paper. They know they will have a chance to go back and fix mistakes later. Read Kyle's draft with the students. Ask them whether they think Kyle wrote what happened first, next, and last in the right order.

Encourage the students to discuss Kyle's draft with their partner. Does the draft tell what happened? What important events does it name? Are the events in order?

**the Strategy Practice the Notebook!**

*Practice the Strategy Notebook* page 14 provides additional practice in looking at a draft and in locating the key events in order based on a storyboard. After students have completed this activity, you may wish to have them share their responses.

**the Strategy Practice the Notebook!**

*Practice the Strategy Notebook* pages 15–17 provide an opportunity for students to write a draft of a personal narrative by following the events they have already drawn on their storyboard on pages 12–13. After students have finished writing, you may wish to have them read their drafts to a partner or share their drafts in a large-group activity. You may wish to assign these pages now or after students have completed this chapter in the Student Edition.

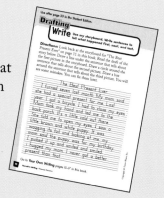

Your Own Writing

**T26 Narrative Writing** • Personal Narrative

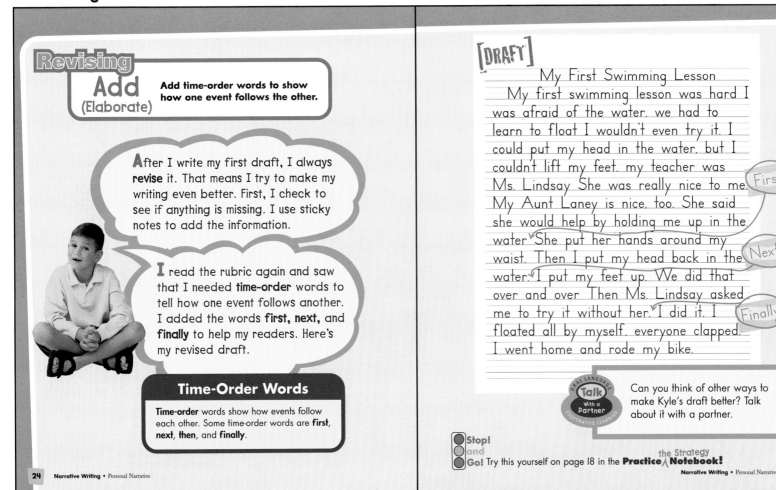

# Revising Add (Elaborate)

**Strategy: Add time-order words to show how one event follows the other.**

*(Student Pages 24–25)*

Read aloud the definition of the term *time-order words* and discuss it with the students. Then read Kyle's words on Student Page 24 with the students. Explain the term *revise*. Tell students that to revise means to "change." When writers revise their work, they change what they say or how they say it to make their writing even better. Explain that one kind of revising is adding information.

**Note:** *Strategies for Writers* employs the term **Elaborate** in grades 3–8. You may wish to explain to students that *elaborate* means "to add."

Explain that Kyle uses a colored pencil to make changes. This helps him to see his changes better, so he can be sure to include them when he writes his final copy. **Note:** You may wish to give students their own colored pencils to revise and edit their writing.

Read Kyle's revised draft on Student Page 25 with the students. Ask students how Kyle's revisions have made his paper even better. **[Possible responses: Adding words that tell time order makes the events easier to follow. These words help readers understand what is happening when.]**

## Spelling Strategies:
### Spell the Word Syllable by Syllable

Before students begin the Editing portion of the chapter, you may wish to remind them that checking spelling is an important part of editing their writing. Encourage students to use several strategies to figure out the spelling of new or hard words. One strategy they can use is to **spell the word syllable by syllable**. Students are likely to find that breaking a long word into parts will make spelling the word much easier.

Encourage the students to talk with a partner about Kyle's revisions. Did the changes make Kyle's story better? What other changes could Kyle have made?

### the Strategy
### Practice Notebook!

*Practice the Strategy Notebook* page 18 provides additional practice in revising a draft by adding missing time-order words. After students have completed this activity, remind them to use this strategy to revise their own personal narrative.

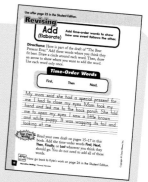

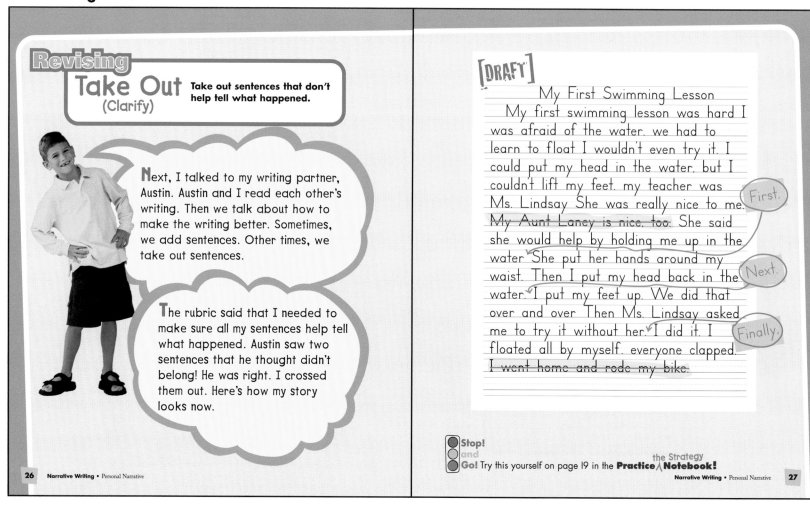

## Revising Take Out (Clarify)

**Strategy: Take out sentences that don't help tell what happened.**

*(Student Pages 26–27)*

Read Kyle's words on Student Page 26 with the students. Explain that another kind of revising is taking out things that don't fit. Read Kyle's revised draft on Student Page 27 with the students. Point out that Kyle took out the sentence "My Aunt Laney is nice, too" because it didn't belong. He did the same with the last sentence in his draft. Ask students why these sentences didn't fit. [Possible responses: The story is not about Aunt Laney. Riding a bike doesn't have anything to do with Kyle's swimming lesson.]

**Note:** *Strategies for Writers* employs the term **Clarify** in grades 3–8. You may wish to explain that *clarify* means "to make clear," usually by taking out what's unnecessary.

## Tips for Successful Conferencing:
### Open-Ended Discussions

Conferencing can be challenging, especially at the beginning of the school year. You may want to hold very short conferences while the rest of the class is engaged in individual work. Engage them in an open-ended discussion about writing and to reassure students that there are no "right answers." You may wish to choose some questions from this list:

- Do you like to write? (Why? Why not?)
- What kinds of writing do you like to do?
- How did you decide what to write about?
- What are some things you've done that were fun? Which of these could you write about?
- Is there anything you'd like to ask about writing?

### the Strategy
**Practice Notebook!**

*Practice the Strategy Notebook* page 19 provides additional practice in revising a draft by taking out sentences that don't fit. After students have completed this activity, remind them to use this strategy to revise their own personal narrative.

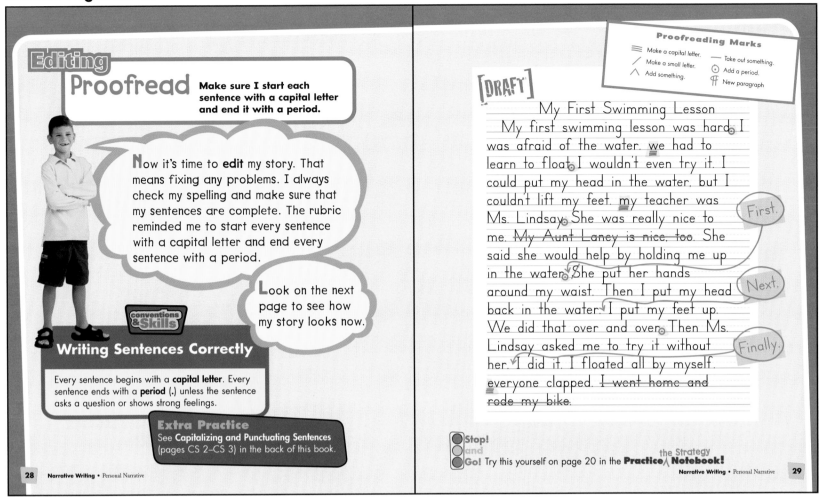

## Editing Proofread

**Strategy: Make sure I start each sentence with a capital letter and end it with a period.**

*(Student Pages 28–29)*

Explain to students that editing is another step in the writing process. Editing is different from revising. When writers edit, they fix grammar and spelling mistakes. Tell students that to *proofread* means to read their paper and look for mistakes.

Read Kyle's words on Student Page 28 with the students. Remind them that Kyle always checks his spelling and makes sure his sentences are complete. Tell students that Kyle is now going to fix any mistakes in starting sentences with a capital letter and ending them with a period. Read the rules for capitalizing and punctuating sentences on Student Page 28 with the students.

Point out the proofreading symbols chart on Student Page 29 to the students. Explain that these symbols help writers remember what corrections they made, so they can include those corrections in their final copy.

Read Kyle's edited draft on Student Page 29 with the students. Ask them if Kyle made all the necessary corrections. You may wish to use the corresponding Writing Model for Proofreading Practice Transparency.

## Extra Practice: Conventions & Skills

### Student Edition

If your students need more practice in starting a sentence with a capital letter and ending it with a period, you may wish to assign Student Pages CS 2–CS 3.

### Conventions & Skills Practice

For more targeted practice related to this skill, see these lessons in the optional *Conventions & Skills Practice Book*:

Lesson 1: What Is a Sentence?

Lesson 6: Sentences That Tell

Lesson 41: Capitalizing the First Word in a Sentence

Lesson 47: Writing Sentences Correctly

### Practice the Strategy Notebook!

*Practice the Strategy Notebook* pages 20–21 provide additional practice in editing a draft by correcting errors in starting sentences with a capital letter and ending them with a period. After students have completed this activity, remind them to use this strategy to edit their own personal narrative.

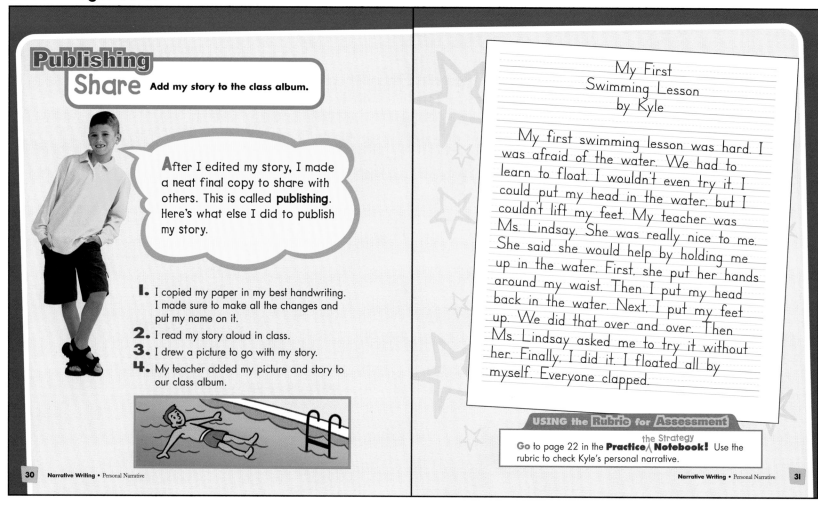

## Publishing Share · Add my story to the class album.

**A**fter I edited my story, I made a neat final copy to share with others. This is called **publishing**. Here's what else I did to publish my story.

**1.** I copied my paper in my best handwriting. I made sure to make all the changes and put my name on it.

**2.** I read my story aloud in class.

**3.** I drew a picture to go with my story.

**4.** My teacher added my picture and story to our class album.

30 · Narrative Writing • Personal Narrative

---

My First
Swimming Lesson
by Kyle

My first swimming lesson was hard. I was afraid of the water. We had to learn to float. I wouldn't even try it. I could put my head in the water, but I couldn't lift my feet. My teacher was Ms. Lindsay. She was really nice to me. She said she would help by holding me up in the water. First, she put her hands around my waist. Then I put my head back in the water. Next, I put my feet up. We did that over and over. Then Ms. Lindsay asked me to try it without her. Finally, I did it. I floated all by myself. Everyone clapped.

**USING the Rubric for Assessment**

**Go** to page 22 in the **Practice Notebook!** Use the rubric to check Kyle's personal narrative. *(the Strategy)*

Narrative Writing • Personal Narrative · 31

---

## Publishing Share

**Strategy: Add my story to the class album.**

*(Student Pages 30–31)*

Read Kyle's words on Student Page 30 with the students. Explain that publishing is the process of finishing a piece of writing to share it with others. Once writers are finished revising and editing their writing, they may publish it. They make a final copy of their writing, being sure to include all the changes they made.

Explain to students that there are many ways to share published writing. Kyle's class is making a class album, so his teacher will add his story to the other students' stories in the album. Other publishing options include creating a class book, sharing the stories during "author day," or reading the stories aloud to another class. Read the final copy of Kyle's personal narrative on Student Page 31 with the students.

Encourage the students to talk with a partner about how Kyle shared his story. Was it a good way to share writing? How else could Kyle have shared his writing?

## Using a Rubric

*Practice the Strategy Notebook* pages 22–23 provide a rubric for assessing Kyle's final personal narrative. Encourage students to work with a partner to evaluate Kyle's story by using this rubric. After students have completed the activity, you may wish to have them share the results in a large-group activity.

Dear Family,

Our class is beginning a writing program called *Strategies for Writers*. This program was developed to help students become better writers by using good writing strategies at each step of the writing process. Here is how the program works.

*Strategies for Writers* has six units. Each of the first five units teaches one kind of writing—to give information, to tell a story about myself, to describe, to tell a story about someone else, and to persuade. Each unit contains two chapters, so that students can experience a variety of writing genres. The sixth unit teaches how to take a writing test.

*Strategies for Writers* provides students with several tools to become successful writers. First, each chapter contains several writing models. The first model is an excellent example of the type of writing presented in the chapter. The second model develops throughout the chapter as a student guide "writes" and explains the steps he or she took to write this model. The third model is in the *Practice the Strategy Notebook* to reinforce what the students have learned in the Student Edition.

The second tool in *Strategies for Writers* is the rubric. A rubric is a set of expectations. A specific rubric is presented at the beginning of each chapter. The student guide explains how to use the rubric to write and to evaluate writing. The rubric is presented again in the *Practice the Strategy Notebook* so that students can use it to evaluate the model in the Student Edition as well as their own writing. This takes the guesswork out of what makes a good paper.

A third important tool is the writing process. *Strategies for Writers* makes the writing process clear and easy to follow. Each step in the process—prewriting, drafting, revising, editing, and publishing—is presented by the student guide. Students see how the student guide goes through the steps of the writing process to compose a paper. Then, the students practice the steps by working on a practice model in the *Practice the Strategy Notebook*. Finally, students apply the steps by writing their own paper.

A fourth tool for writers in *Strategies for Writers* is the presentation of good writing strategies at each step of the writing process. The student guide explains one strategy for each step, including how to make lists and take notes, how to organize information, how to write a good draft, how to make revisions, how to proofread for mistakes, and how to publish the final copy.

Finally, *Strategies for Writers* teaches grammar and mechanics as part of writing. Each chapter focuses on a specific convention or skill, such as complete sentences, punctuation, and parts of speech. Additional practice with grammar and mechanics is available in the back of the Student Edition and in the separate *Conventions and Skills Practice Book*.

As you can see, *Strategies for Writers* is a complete writing program. Our class is looking forward to becoming better writers as we learn together.

You may wish to copy the letter above and send it home with your students.

# Tips for the Writing Classroom

by Barry Sneed, *Master Teacher*

## Think Outside the Desk!

As you think about writing, you may wonder how something so complex can be made appealing and exciting to children. First, a child must believe he or she is a writer, regardless of the child's current level of skill. Everyone wishes to communicate, and children are eager to accept writing as a way of doing it as long as we encourage their efforts. By accepting all works, showing interest and pride, and providing guidance, a teacher can help students build the desire, excitement, and skills necessary to become successful writers. To achieve this, I recommend setting up a writing area in the classroom that will provide children with both choice and ownership in the process and product. Then be sure to provide the time for them to use that writing area.

Start by choosing an area in the room and make a sign or banner designating it as **The Writing Center**. Stock it with a variety of paper. Grade-appropriate writing paper should

---

# Friendly Letter

## Writing Strategies

### Prewriting

**Gather Ideas**
Think about who will read my friendly letter and what I want to say.

**Organize**
Make a storyboard to tell what happened.

### Drafting

**Write**
Use my storyboard. Write sentences to tell what happened first, next, and last.

### Revising

**Add (Elaborate)**
Add details to make my letter more interesting.

**Take Out (Clarify)**
Take out sentences that don't help tell what happened.

### Editing

**Proofread**
Make sure I wrote all five parts of my friendly letter correctly.

### Publishing

**Share**
Address an envelope. Ask an adult to help me mail my letter.

**Note:** You may wish to copy and distribute the Friendly Letter Form on page T46.

---

## MODELED WRITING

**Friendly Letter Writing Mini-Lesson:** You may wish to present the following mini-lesson before the students read the model on Student Page 33. Write the following on the board or on chart paper:

> 12 Main Street
> New York, NY 12345
> June 3, 20—
>
> Dear Travis,
>     We went to the zoo today. I like the circus, too. First, we saw the polar bear. Then we saw the lions. Last, we saw the birds. It was a great day.
>                 Your pal,
>                 Kate

Ask the students what the writing on the board tells them. [Possible response: It's a letter about going to the zoo.] Explain that this kind of writing is called a **friendly letter**. Tell students they will be learning about writing a friendly letter as they read the chapter in the Student Edition. They will see a model of this kind of writing and learn and practice strategies for writing their own friendly letters. Ask the students whether they think any of the sentences on the board don't fit. [Response: Yes, sentence #2 tells about the circus, not about the zoo.] Cross out sentence #2. Explain to students that in this chapter they will also learn to take out sentences that don't belong.

always be a choice, but also provide drawing paper, colored paper of varying sizes and shapes (a great tie-in to math and helps recycle scraps), fancy lined paper (with lines forming triangles, pyramids, or diamonds), and even paper with different textures. Change the selection monthly, or put out special themed or holiday papers as appropriate. When children have a choice in the paper they choose, they are encouraged to make wise and creative choices to meet their writing needs.

Provide students with 20–30 minutes of uninterrupted writing time daily. Equip each child with a two-pocket folder to hold a small dictionary, a list of writing topics, and the child's writings until the weekly writing conference with the teacher. (See "Tips for the Writing Classroom," Unit 2, Chapter 2, for information on the Super Readers/Writer's Workshop.)

Finally, allow students choice in where and how they write. Students love to write on the floor, on a lap desk or clipboard, under a table, at their desk, or at the teacher's desk. They may choose to write alone or with others. As long as you set the expectation that writing must occur, allowing students choice in where and how to write empowers them and builds their love for the process.

## Time Management for This Chapter*

| Session 1 | Introduce Rachel. Read the model on Student Page 33. Discuss the friendly letter rubric on Student Pages 34–35. | Session 6 | Assign *Practice the Strategy Notebook* pages 28–31. | Session 11 | Read **REVISING: Take Out (Clarify)** (Student Pages 48–49). |
|---|---|---|---|---|---|
| 2 | Read Student Pages 36–39. Discuss Rachel's assessment of the model. Discuss the information about Rachel on Student Page 39. | 7 | Read **DRAFTING: Write** (Student Pages 44–45). | 12 | Assign *Practice the Strategy Notebook* page 37. |
| 3 | Read **PREWRITING: Gather Ideas** (Student Pages 40–41). | 8 | Assign *Practice the Strategy Notebook* pages 32–35. | 13 | Read **EDITING: Proofread** (Student Pages 50–51). |
| 4 | Assign *Practice the Strategy Notebook* pages 24–27. | 9 | Read **REVISING: Add (Elaborate)** (Student Pages 46–47). | 14 | Assign *Practice the Strategy Notebook* pages 38–39. |
| 5 | Read **PREWRITING: Organize** (Student Pages 42–43). | 10 | Assign *Practice the Strategy Notebook* page 36. | 15 | Read **PUBLISHING: Share** (Student Pages 52–53). Assign *Practice the Strategy Notebook* pages 40–41. |

* To complete the chapter in fewer sessions, assign the *Practice the Strategy Notebook* pages on the same day each targeted strategy is introduced.

## STRATEGIES for Writers Sing-Along CD

You may wish to use the *Strategies for Writers Sing-Along* CD throughout the chapter. See the Appendix in the back of this Teacher Edition for more information.

## WRITER'S HANDBOOK

Remind students that they can refer to the Writer's Handbook in the back of the Student Edition for more information.

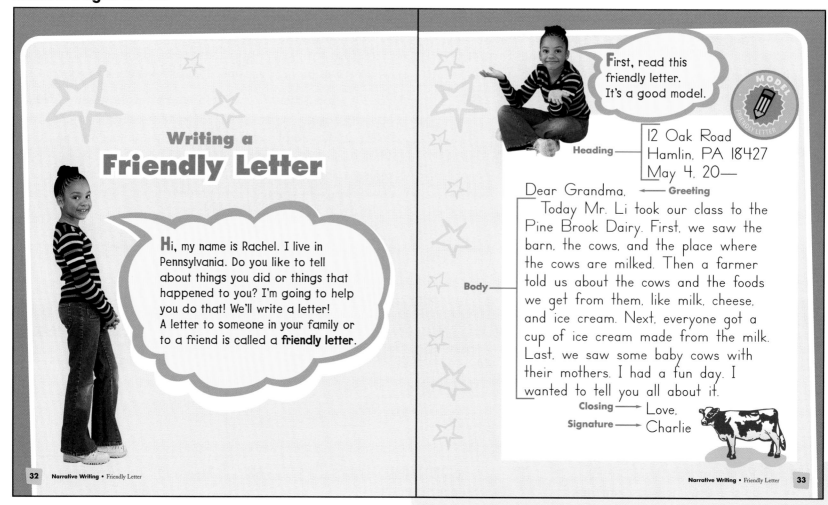

**Writing a Friendly Letter**

Hi, my name is Rachel. I live in Pennsylvania. Do you like to tell about things you did or things that happened to you? I'm going to help you do that! We'll write a letter! A letter to someone in your family or to a friend is called a **friendly letter**.

First, read this friendly letter. It's a good model.

**Heading**
12 Oak Road
Hamlin, PA 18427
May 4, 20—

Dear Grandma, ← **Greeting**

**Body**
Today Mr. Li took our class to the Pine Brook Dairy. First, we saw the barn, the cows, and the place where the cows are milked. Then a farmer told us about the cows and the foods we get from them, like milk, cheese, and ice cream. Next, everyone got a cup of ice cream made from the milk. Last, we saw some baby cows with their mothers. I had a fun day. I wanted to tell you all about it.

**Closing** → Love,
**Signature** → Charlie

32 **Narrative Writing** • Friendly Letter

**Narrative Writing** • Friendly Letter 33

# Introduce the Genre:
## Friendly Letter

*(Student Pages 32–33)*

Read Student Page 32 with the students. Explain that the student in their book is going to show them how to write a friendly letter that tells a story. Tell them that they will read Rachel's work as a class and they will have a chance to talk about it with a partner. Then they will practice using the same strategies to write their own friendly letter. Ask the students to think of examples of stories they could tell in a friendly letter. [Possible responses: a story about a trip, holiday, party, or other special day; a story about losing, finding, or making something]

# Read the Model:
## Friendly Letter

Read the model of a friendly letter on Student Page 33. Ask what makes the letter a good example of a friendly letter. [Possible responses: It tells a good story. It's interesting. It looks like a letter.] As you read the model with the students, point out that the model may contain words that students do not know. You may wish to add these words to your Word Wall and encourage students to refer to the Word Wall as they proofread their own letters for spelling.

# Meeting Students' Needs:
## Second-Language Learners

Make sure that students know what a dairy is. Point to clues that will help students with vocabulary words, such as the word *barn*. You might wish to create a semantic map with the word *dairy* at its center, and help students name and cluster related concepts, such as *cows, barn, silo,* and so on. Then have students work in small groups to reread and discuss the letter. Encourage them to ask questions about any words or ideas they do not understand.

## Students Who Need Extra Help

Reread the first sentence of the letter aloud with students. Ask them to predict what a class would do or see on a visit to a dairy. Discuss the food products that come from cows, such as milk, cheese, and ice cream. Write these words on the board and review strategies for decoding them. Then encourage students to form pictures in their minds of what they see as they read the letter.

## Gifted Students

Challenge students to find places where they might add extra details to the letter. Remind them that the extra details must make sense in the letter and make the letter more interesting.

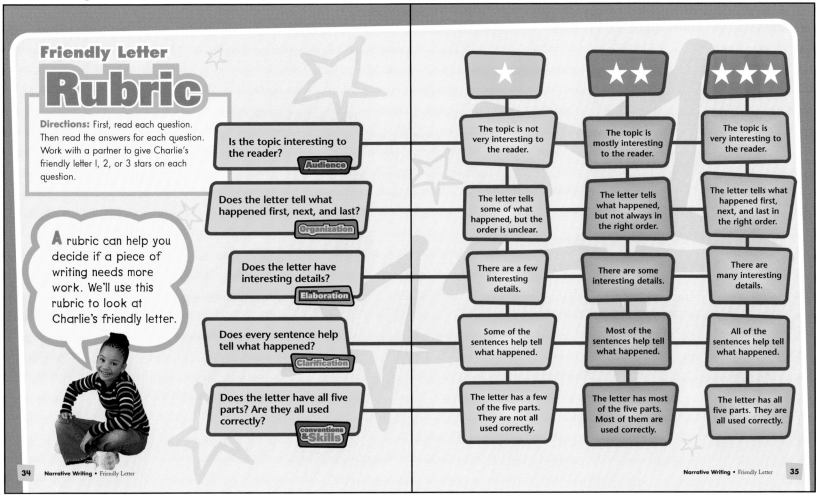

## Using a Rubric

Use the text on Student Pages 36–38 to model the use of a rubric for evaluating a piece of writing. For more information on using a rubric, please see page T21.

## Discuss the Friendly Letter Rubric

*(Student Pages 34–35)*

Read the questions on Student Page 34 with the students. Explain that these questions are what writers use to write a good friendly letter. Discuss each question with the students.

**Audience: Is the topic interesting to the reader?** The person who receives the letter will want to read a story about something that is interesting to him or her.

**Organization: Does the letter tell what happened first, next, and last?** The letter writer should begin with the first event, tell what happens next, and end with the last event.

**Elaboration: Does the letter have interesting details?** To make the letter interesting to the reader, the writer should give details that help the reader see or feel what the writer saw or felt.

**Clarification: Does every sentence help tell what happened?** If the letter has sentences that don't help tell what happened, the story can become confusing.

**Conventions & Skills: Does the letter have all five parts? Are they all used correctly?** All five parts of the letter should appear in their right place, capitalized and punctuated correctly.

Have students evaluate the model friendly letter with a partner, using the Friendly Letter Rubric on Student Pages 34–35. Ask partners to share their evaluations with the whole group.

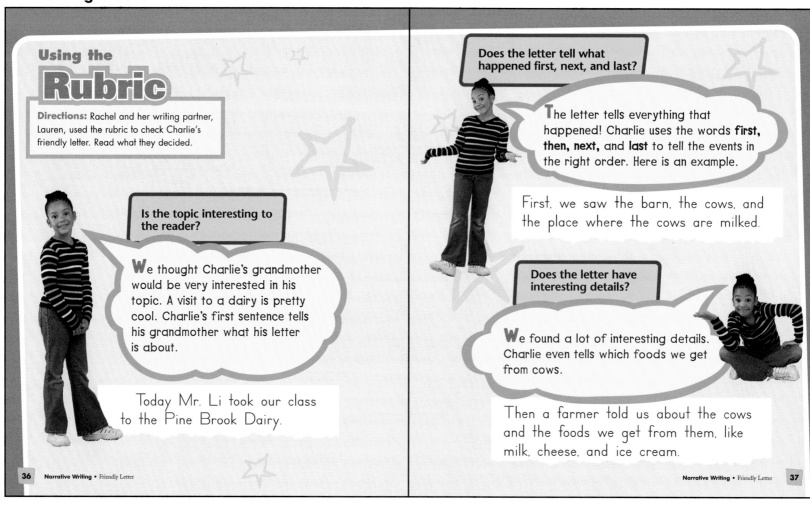

## Using the Rubric to Study the Model

*(Student Pages 36–38)*

Read Rachel's words on Student Page 36. Ask the students whether they agree that Charlie's grandmother would be interested in his topic. Read the example sentence aloud. Ask the students whether they agree that it starts the letter in a way that helps the reader know what the letter is about.

Read Student Page 37 with the students. Did the letter tell them what happened first, next, and last? Point out to students the word *First* in the sentence from the model friendly letter. Ask students if they agree that the letter has interesting details. Point out the specific words *milk, cheese,* and *ice cream* in the model sentence to explain the more general word *foods*.

Read Student Page 38 with the students. Ask students if they agree with Rachel that every sentence belongs in the letter. Remind students that they will be learning about the five parts of a friendly letter as they read and discuss the chapter.

## From Rubrics to Letter Grades

If your district uses letter grades for assessment, you may use the rubric in the Student Edition to determine an appropriate letter grade for each student. An efficient way to do this is to assign a point value from the rubric to a letter grade.

- Three stars equal 3 points, or an **A**.
- Two stars equal 2 points, or a **B**.
- One star equals 1 point, or a **C**.

To score a paper as a whole, add the student's score for each writing element (i.e. each question on the rubric) and divide by 5 (the number of elements.)

You may also wish to score each element individually and focus on the student's growth with that element over time.

**Example:** A student earned the following:

| | |
|---|---|
| Audience—2 stars | (2 points) |
| Organization—3 stars | (3 points) |
| Elaboration—2 stars | (2 points) |
| Clarification—3 stars | (3 points) |
| Conventions & Skills—1 star | (1 point) |
| Total | 11 points ÷ 5 = 2.2 (B) |

**Note:** You may wish to round up to the next highest whole number or down to the next lowest whole number.

## Working With a Partner Mini-Lesson:
### Speak in a Soft Voice

Help students understand how to work with a partner effectively by giving them some basic tips. You may wish to post these tips in a visible spot in your room.

Tell students that when they are working with a partner, they should **speak in a soft voice**. Remind them that everyone else is working with a partner or concentrating on writing or reading at the same time.

**Model the Tip** Model the kind of soft voice students should use to work with a partner, and give students a chance to practice it. Ask a volunteer to act as your "partner." Read your paper to your "partner" in a quiet voice but loudly enough for the partner to hear you. Ask the partner whether he/she heard you. Then ask the rest of the students whether they heard you. Explain that when working with a partner, students should speak softly enough not to be heard by the rest of the class but loudly enough to be heard by their partner. You may wish to give students a copy of the Working With a Partner Sheet on page T166.

## Rachel:
### Writer of a Friendly Letter

*(Student Page 39)*

Read Rachel's words to the students and the information about Rachel to learn more about her. Be sure students understand that Rachel will write her own friendly letter in this chapter. Review the information given about her. Discuss what Rachel might write about in her friendly letter, based on her interests.

Point out that Rachel will go through the steps in the writing process (Prewriting, Drafting, Revising, Editing, and Publishing). At each stage, Rachel will use a good writing strategy and explain how she used it. Students should watch for key words, including **Gather, Organize, Write, Add (Elaborate), Take Out (Clarify), Proofread,** and **Share,** to follow the strategies Rachel uses as she goes through the writing process.

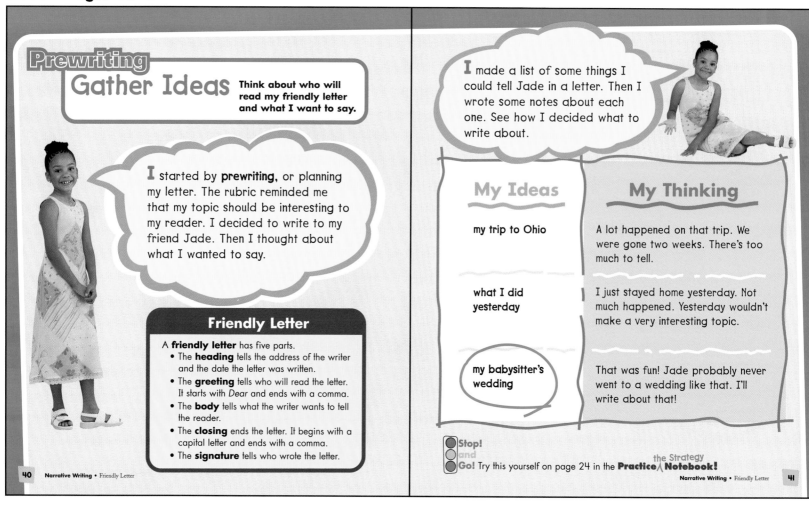

# Prewriting  Gather Ideas

**Strategy: Think about who will read my friendly letter and what I want to say.**

*(Student Pages 40–41)*

Read aloud and discuss the five parts of a friendly letter on Student Page 40. Then read Rachel's words.

Explain to the students that in this section Rachel tells how she went about writing her friendly letter. She starts by explaining how she chose her topic. Ask the students how Rachel decided on her audience and her topic. [Possible responses: She wanted to write to her friend. Her topic should interest the person who will read the letter.]

Point out Rachel's list of possible topics on Student Page 41. Discuss Rachel's reasons for choosing her babysitter's wedding rather than either of the other choices. Ask the students if they agree with Rachel's thinking.

Ask the students about what kinds of weddings they have attended. Tell them that there are many differnt kinds of weddings. Explain that Rachel's babysitter's wedding is in the Jewish tradition.

## the Strategy Practice the Notebook!

*Practice the Strategy Notebook* pages 24–25 provide additional practice in selecting a topic for another friendly letter. After students have completed this activity, you may wish to have them share their responses.

## the Strategy Practice the Notebook!

*Practice the Strategy Notebook* pages 26–27 provide an opportunity for students to select someone to write to and a topic for their own friendly letter. You may wish to assign these pages now or after students have completed this chapter in the Student Edition. You may wish to save students' *Your Own Writing* pages and add them to their Work-in-Progress Portfolios.

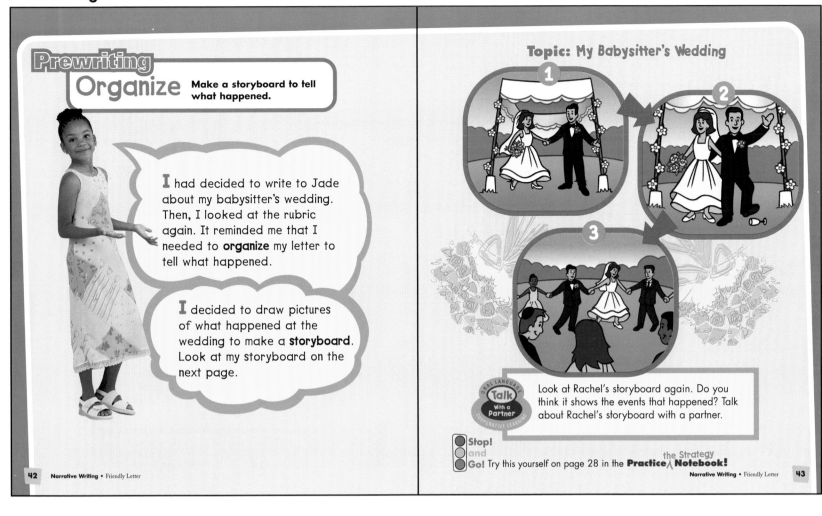

## Prewriting Organize

**Strategy: Make a storyboard to tell what happened.**

*(Student Pages 42–43)*

Read Rachel's words on Student Page 42 with the students. Explain that before she starts writing, Rachel needs to organize her information. She has to decide how her letter can tell things in the right order. Explain that a storyboard is a good way to start organizing a friendly letter because it shows events in order. It also allows the writer to see if any important things that happened are missing or out of order. Direct students' attention to Rachel's storyboard.

Encourage the students to discuss Rachel's storyboard with their partner. Ask if Rachel's storyboard seems complete. Will the events make a good story? You may also wish to discuss the findings with the class.

**Note:** A storyboard transparency is provided in the *Strategies for Writers Transparencies*.

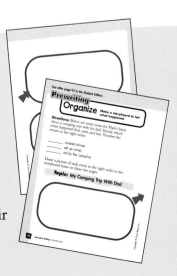

### Practice the Strategy Notebook!

*Practice the Strategy Notebook* pages 28–29 provide additional practice in using a storyboard to organize events for a story in a friendly letter. After students have completed this activity, you may wish to have them share their storyboard with a writing partner.

### Practice the Strategy Notebook!

*Practice the Strategy Notebook* pages 30–31 provide an opportunity for students to list key elements in their story and to create a storyboard for their own friendly letter. You may wish to assign these pages now or after students have completed this chapter in the Student Edition.

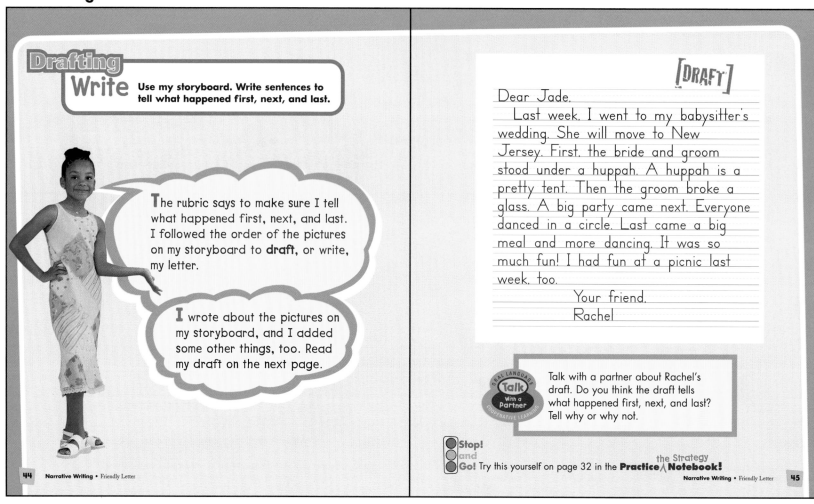

**Drafting Write** Use my storyboard. Write sentences to tell what happened first, next, and last.

The rubric says to make sure I tell what happened first, next, and last. I followed the order of the pictures on my storyboard to **draft**, or write, my letter.

I wrote about the pictures on my storyboard, and I added some other things, too. Read my draft on the next page.

[DRAFT]

Dear Jade,
    Last week, I went to my babysitter's wedding. She will move to New Jersey. First, the bride and groom stood under a huppah. A huppah is a pretty tent. Then the groom broke a glass. A big party came next. Everyone danced in a circle. Last came a big meal and more dancing. It was so much fun! I had fun at a picnic last week, too.
            Your friend,
            Rachel

Talk With a Partner

Talk with a partner about Rachel's draft. Do you think the draft tells what happened first, next, and last? Tell why or why not.

Stop! and Go! Try this yourself on page 32 in the Practice the Strategy Notebook!

44 Narrative Writing • Friendly Letter

45 Narrative Writing • Friendly Letter

---

# Drafting Write

**Strategy:** Use my storyboard. Write sentences to tell what happened first, next, and last.

*(Student Pages 44–45)*

Discuss the term *draft* with the students. Explain that a draft is an early form of a paper. In a draft, writers don't worry about mistakes. The important thing is to get ideas down on paper. Writers know that they will have a chance to go back and fix mistakes later. Read Rachel's draft with the students. **Note:** The word *huppah* is pronounced /**hoop•**uh/.

Remind students that a story needs to tell what happens first, next, and last. Ask the students whether Rachel was clear about the order of events.

Talk With a Partner

Encourage the students to identify the events in the wedding and the order in which they are told. Students should name what comes first, next, and last. [Possible responses: The bride and groom standing under the huppah comes first. Breaking the glass and the party are next. Last are the big meal and dancing.] Also ask students to find the words *first, then, next,* and *last* in the story. [Responses: *First* is in the third sentence. *Then* and *next* appear in the middle of the letter. *Last* appears near the end of the letter.]

**Practice the Strategy Notebook!**

*Practice the Strategy Notebook* page 32 provides practice in using a storyboard to write sentences to tell what happened. After students have completed this activity, you may wish to have them read their draft to a partner or share their draft in a large-group activity.

**Your Own Writing**

**Practice the Strategy Notebook!**

*Practice the Strategy Notebook* pages 33–35 provide practice in writing a draft of their own friendly letter by following the steps in the storyboard they drew on pages 30–31. After students have completed this activity, you may wish to have them read their draft to a partner or share their draft in a large-group activity. You may assign these pages now or after students have completed this chapter in the Student Edition.

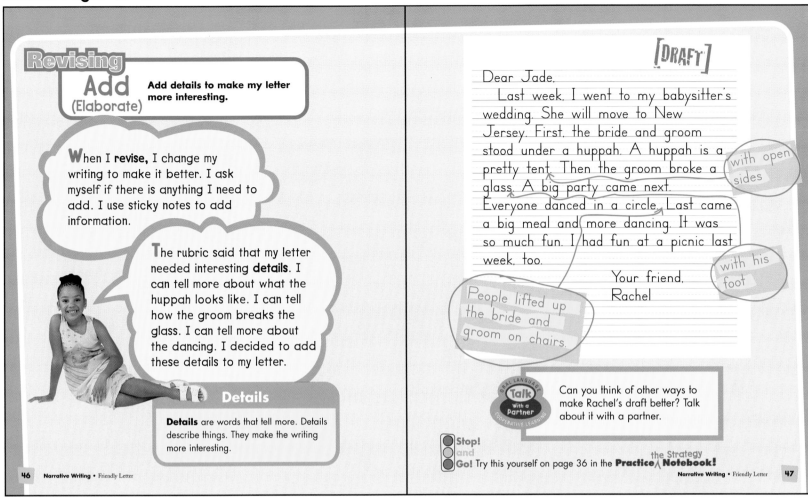

## Revising Add (Elaborate)

**Strategy: Add details to make my letter more interesting.**

*(Student Pages 46–47)*

Read aloud the definition of the term *details* on Student Page 46 and discuss it with the students. Then read Rachel's words. Explain the term *revise* to students. Tell them that it means "to change." When writers revise their work, they change what they say or how they say it. They do that to make their writing better. Explain that one kind of revising is adding details. **Note:** *Strategies for Writers* employs the term **Elaborate** in grades 3–8. You may wish to explain to students that *elaborate* means to "to add."

Read Rachel's revised draft on Student Page 47 with the students. Ask students how Rachel's revisions have made her letter even better. [**Possible responses: The details make the letter more interesting. They help the reader understand more about the wedding.**]

Encourage students to talk with a partner about Rachel's revisions. Did the changes improve her letter? What other changes could Rachel have made?

## Tips for Successful Conferencing:
### Conferencing Parameters

Conferencing can be a very important tool for developing young writers. Here are some parameters for writing conferences:

• Keep time limits. Short conferences are best.

• Be encouraging, but be genuine. Don't overdo the praise.

• Keep the focus on what the writer can accomplish rather than on things that are "wrong."

• Limit the scope of the conference. If you focus on just one or two things, you may accomplish far more than you would by taking on too much.

### the Strategy
### Practice Notebook!

*Practice the Strategy Notebook* page 36 provides additional practice in revising a friendly letter draft by adding interesting details. After students have completed this activity, remind them to use this strategy to revise their own friendly letter.

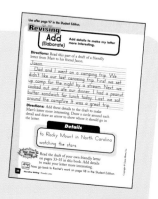

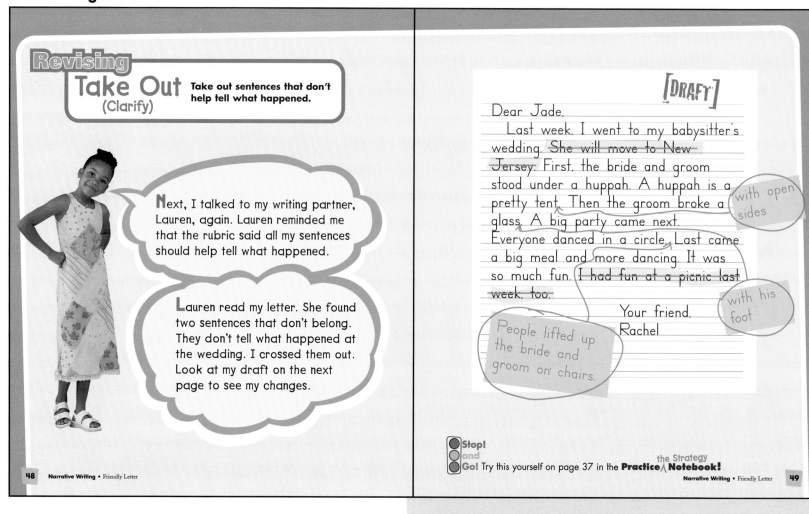

Stop! and Go! Try this yourself on page 37 in the **Practice the Strategy Notebook!**

## Revising Take Out (Clarify)

**Strategy: Take out sentences that don't help tell what happened.**

*(Student Pages 48–49)*

Read Rachel's words on Student Page 48 with the students. Explain that another kind of revising is taking out sentences that don't help tell the story. Read Rachel's revised draft on Student Page 49 with the students. Point out that Rachel took out the sentence "She will move to New Jersey" because it doesn't belong in her letter. Ask students why it needs to be taken out. [**Possible response: It doesn't help tell what happened at the wedding.**] Repeat with "I had fun at a picnic last week, too." **Note:** *Strategies for Writers* employs the term **Clarify** in grades 3–8. You may wish to explain to students that *clarify* means "to make clear," usually by taking out what is not necessary.

## Spelling Strategies:
### Use Phonics

Before students begin the Editing portion of the chapter, you may wish to remind them that checking spelling is an important part of editing their writing. Encourage students to use several different strategies to figure out the spelling of new or hard words.

One strategy is to **use phonics**. Many of the words students are unsure of can be spelled correctly by sounding them out while writing them.

### Practice the Strategy Notebook!

*Practice the Strategy Notebook* page 37 provides additional practice in revising a draft by taking out sentences that don't help tell what happened. After students have completed this activity, remind them to use this strategy to revise their own friendly letter.

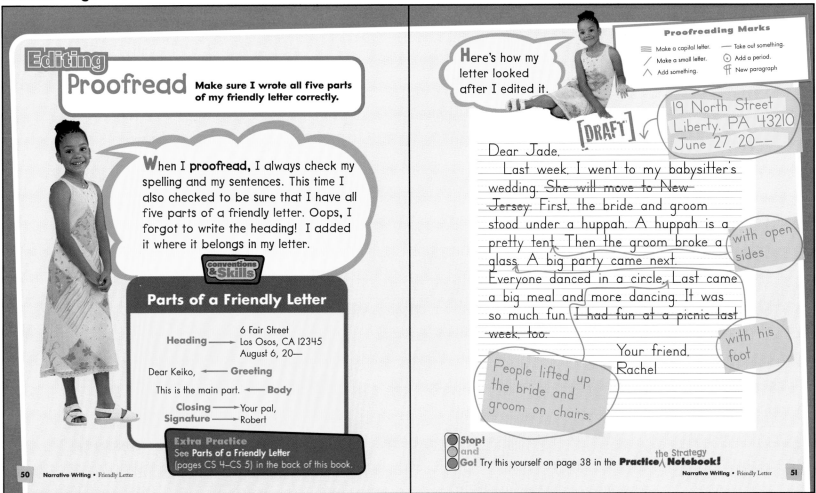

# Editing Proofread

**Strategy: Make sure I wrote all five parts of my friendly letter correctly.**

*(Student Pages 50–51)*

Read Rachel's words on Student Page 50 to the students. Remind students that Rachel always checks her spelling and sentences. Tell students that Rachel is now going to fix mistakes in writing the parts of a friendly letter. Remind students that using a pencil that writes in a different color helps writers see their changes better. **Note:** You may wish to give students their own colored pencils to edit their writing.

Read the parts of a friendly letter at the bottom of Student Page 50 with the students. Call attention to the various uses of capital letters and commas.

Point out the Proofreading Symbols Chart on Student Page 51 to the students. Explain that these symbols help writers remember which corrections they made, so they can include those corrections in their final copy.

Read Rachel's edited draft on Student Page 51 with the students. Ask them if Rachel made all the necessary corrections. You may wish to use the corresponding Writing Model for Proofreading Practice Transparency.

**Note:** You may wish to copy and give students the Friendly Letter Form on page T46.

## Extra Practice: Conventions & Skills
### Student Edition

If your students need more practice in writing the parts of a friendly letter, you may wish to assign Student Pages CS 4–CS 5.

## Conventions & Skills Practice

For more targeted practice related to this skill, see these lessons in the optional *Conventions & Skills Practice Book*:

Lesson 41: Capitalizing the First Word in a Sentence

Lesson 43: Periods and Exclamation Points

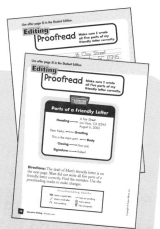

### the Strategy
**Practice Notebook!**

*Practice the Strategy Notebook* pages 38–39 provide additional practice in editing a draft by correcting errors in the parts of a friendly letter. After students have completed this activity, remind them to use this strategy to edit their own friendly letters.

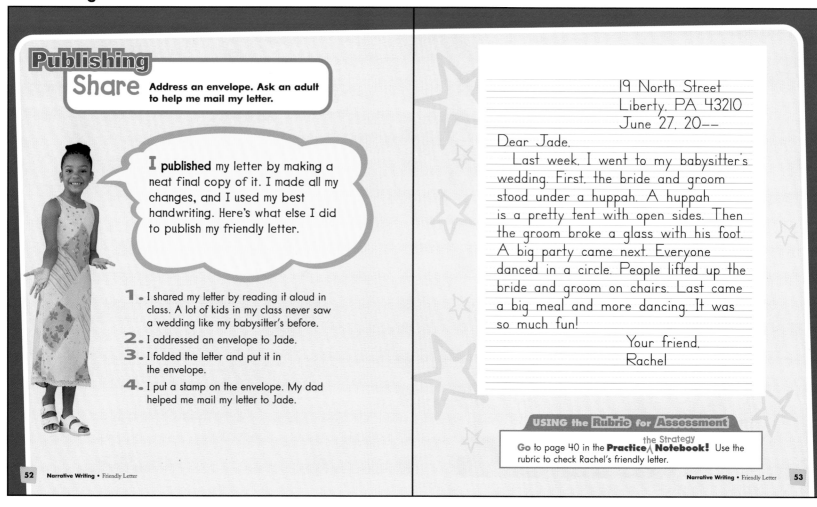

## Publishing Share

**Strategy: Address an envelope. Ask an adult to help me mail my letter.**

*(Student Pages 52–53)*

Read Rachel's words on Student Page 52 with the students. Explain that publishing is the process of finishing a piece of writing to share it with others. Once writers are finished revising and editing their writing, they may publish it. They make a final copy of their writing, being sure they include all the changes they made. Remind students that there are many ways to share published writing. Another publishing option is to send the letter as an e-mail. Rachel decided to publish her friendly letter by addressing an envelope, putting her letter inside, and mailing it to her friend.

Read the final copy of Rachel's letter on Student Page 53 with the students.

Encourage students to talk with a partner about how Rachel shared her letter. Was it a good way to share writing? How else could Rachel have shared her letter?

## Using the Rubric

*Practice the Strategy Notebook* pages 40–41 provide a rubric for assessing Rachel's final friendly letter. Encourage students to work with a partner to evaluate Rachel's letter by using this rubric. After students have completed this activity, you may wish to have them share the results in a large-group activity.

**Social Studies**
# Your Own Writing
## NARRATIVE

Use what you learned in this unit to write your own personal narrative, friendly letter, or both! Try these ideas.
- Use **Your Own Writing** pages in the *Practice the Strategy Notebook*.
- Pick a topic below, and write something new.
- Choose another idea of your own.

Follow the steps in the writing process. Use the Personal Narrative Rubric on pages 22–23 in the *Practice the Strategy Notebook* or the Friendly Letter Rubric on pages 40–41 in the *Practice the Strategy Notebook* to check your writing.

| **Personal Narrative** | **Friendly Letter** |
| --- | --- |
| • how you celebrated your birthday<br>• what you did or saw at a holiday parade | • to a friend about how you celebrated a special family custom or tradition<br>• to a relative about your trip to a special museum or library |

portfolio

School–Home Connection

Keep a writing folder. Add **Your Own Writing** pages to your writing folder. You may want to take your writing folder home to share.

54    **Narrative Writing**

## Your Own Writing
## Narrative Writing for Social Studies

Assign either one or both genres to the students. Before they begin writing, review key information about each genre. Decide which of the following you wish students to do:
- Choose a topic on page 54 in the Student Edition.
- Complete one of the pieces they partially drafted in the Your Own Writing pages of the *Practice the Strategy Notebook*.
- Come up with a new idea.

## Portfolio/School-Home Connection

Encourage the students to keep portfolios of their writing.

### Work-in-Progress Portfolio

Remind students to review this portfolio often to revise existing pieces that have not been published. Encourage students to share pieces of their Work-in-Progress Portfolios with family members who can help in editing.

### Published Portfolio

Encourage students to choose pieces from their Published Portfolios to share with family members.

Name _____

# Friendly Letter Form

**Heading** (your street address) ➔ _____

_____

(your city, state, and Zip Code) ➔ _____

_____

(the date) ➔ _____

_____

⬅ **Greeting** (Dear Person's name,)

**Body** ➔ _____

_____

_____

_____

_____

_____

_____

_____

**Closing**
(words like Love, Your friend,) ➔ _____

**Signature**
(your name in your own writing) ➔ _____

**Purpose:** To help students learn the five parts of a friendly letter
This page may be duplicated for classroom use.

# DESCRIPTIVE

# Writing to Describe

## 1 Descriptive Paper

## 2 Compare-and-Contrast Paper

## Defining Writing That Describes

Display a large colorful object, such as a jacket or a backpack. Pass the object around so that students can touch it. Ask volunteers to describe it. Write some of their descriptive words on the board. Discuss which of the five senses they used to describe the object.

Read and discuss Student Page 55 with the students. Explain that the next two chapters will be about writing that describes. Tell students that a good written description helps a reader picture how a person, place, or object looks. It can also help the reader imagine how something sounds, tastes, feels, or smells.

## Books to Share With Students

For excellent examples of descriptive writing, you may wish to share these books with your students:

- *Blueberries for Sal* by Robert McCloskey
- *A House for Hermit Crab* by Eric Carle
- *Maggie and Millie and Molly and May* by e.e. cummings
- *Hello Ocean* by Pam Muñoz Ryan
- *The Listening Walk* by Paul Showers

You may also wish to use some of the titles from Zaner-Bloser Literacy.

# Tips for the Writing Classroom

by Barry Sneed, *Master Teacher*

## Involving Families

Getting your students to engage in learning can be challenging, but because they are in your care for several hours a day, time is on your side. Involving students' families—folks who often have hectic careers and schedules of their own—can be an even greater task. Many educators are unsure about how much to involve families in the classroom. However, I have always been a strong advocate of involving parents in the classroom in the early grades. One teacher for 20 to 30 six- or seven-year-olds just isn't enough to meet each student's reading and writing needs. If you can get interested, responsible parents/adults to volunteer their time, I think it is wise to accept their offer!

There are several things to consider when involving parents in your classroom. First, you, as the teacher, must be comfortable with having the other adult there. If that person's style does not fit comfortably with your own personality and

---

## Descriptive Paper

### Writing Strategies

### Prewriting

**Gather Ideas**
Choose a subject to describe. Make a list to tell what I know about it.

**Organize**
Use my list to make a five senses chart.

### Drafting

**Write**
Use my five senses chart. Write sentences to describe the subject of my paper.

### Revising

**Add (Elaborate)**
Add describing words to make my paper more interesting.

**Take Out (Clarify)**
Take out sentences that don't tell about the subject of my paper.

### Editing

**Proofread**
Make sure I start each sentence with a capital letter and end it with correct punctuation.

### Publishing

**Share**
Post my descriptive paper on our class bulletin board. Add a labeled drawing of my subject.

**Note:** A blackline master of the writing process flow chart appears on page T106. You may wish to copy and distribute it to your students.

---

### MODELED WRITING

**Descriptive Writing Mini-Lesson:** You may wish to present the following mini-lesson before the students read the model on Student Page 57. Write the following on the board, chart paper, or an overhead transparency:

> My baby brother, Sam, is very small. He has tiny hands and feet. He has a big head and pink cheeks. He sometimes makes cooing sounds. At other times, he yells!

Ask the students what the sentences on the board tell them. [Possible response: They describe how Sam looks and sounds.] Explain that this kind of writing describes. It helps readers imagine how something looks, sounds, feels, tastes, and smells. Tell students they will be learning more about descriptive writing as they read the chapter in the Student Edition. They will see a model of this kind of writing and learn and practice some strategies for writing their own descriptive paper. Write the title "My Baby Brother" above the sentences. Ask the students what words they could add that would help the reader see or hear the baby. [Possible response: Add the words *with curly brown hair* after *big head*.] Make any reasonable changes that add describing words. Explain to students that when they write a descriptive paper, they will also learn how to add more describing words.

teaching style, the situation will not work. Base your use of volunteers on how well they fit into your schedule, your style of teaching, and your students' needs.

Try to make use of any sincerely interested person in a way that matches the volunteer's skills to a particular need of your students. A parent who is not skilled at assisting students in writing may be a great listener who is capable of sitting with students and hearing them read. The most important thing is to remember that you are ultimately responsible for the learning and well-being of the children in your care, so plan your volunteers' duties accordingly. Here are some tips for involving parents, families, and even extended families in your students' reading and writing activities:

**V.I.R.'s (Very Important Readers)** Extend an open invitation to parents to read a favorite children's book (of their choice) to the class any time throughout the year. This takes only five to ten minutes, and parents and other adult family members love to come in and read to their child's class. Arrange ahead, so you know when to expect the **V.I.R.** Award the reader a **V.I.R. Certificate** when he or she is done!

**Parent Volunteers for Writing Workshop** When operating the Writing Workshop portion of the day (see Unit 2, Ch. 2), use a parent volunteer to move around the room to assist students with their writing while you hold conferences with individual students.

## Time Management for This Chapter*

| Session | | Session | | Session | |
|---|---|---|---|---|---|
| **1** | Introduce writing that describes. Read Student Page 56. Introduce Jessica. Read the model on Student Page 57. Discuss the rubric on Student Pages 58–59. | **6** | Assign *Practice the Strategy Notebook* pages 46–49. | **11** | Read **REVISING: Take Out** (Clarify) (Student Pages 72–73). |
| **2** | Read Student Pages 60–63. Discuss Jessica's assessment of the model descriptive paper. Discuss the information about Jessica on Student Page 63. | **7** | Read **DRAFTING: Write** (Student Pages 68–69). | **12** | Assign *Practice the Strategy Notebook* page 55. |
| **3** | Read **PREWRITING: Gather Ideas** (Student Pages 64–65). | **8** | Assign *Practice the Strategy Notebook* pages 50–53. | **13** | Read **EDITING: Proofread** (Student Pages 74–75). |
| **4** | Assign *Practice the Strategy Notebook* pages 42–45. | **9** | Read **REVISING: Add** (Elaborate) (Student Pages 70–71). | **14** | Assign *Practice the Strategy Notebook* pages 56–57. |
| **5** | Read **PREWRITING: Organize** (Student Pages 66–67). | **10** | Assign *Practice the Strategy Notebook* page 54. | **15** | Read **PUBLISHING: Share** (Student Pages 76–77). Assign *Practice the Strategy Notebook* pages 58–59. |

* To complete the chapter in fewer sessions, assign *Practice the Strategy Notebook* pages on the same day each targeted skill is introduced.

**WRITER'S HANDBOOK**

Remind students that they can refer to the Writer's Handbook in the back of the Student Edition for more information.

**STRATEGIES for Writers Sing-Along CD**

You may wish to use the *Strategies for Writers Sing-Along* CD throughout the chapter. See the Appendix in the back of this Teacher Edition for more information.

Writing a
# Descriptive Paper

Hi, my name is Jessica. I live in Ohio. I'm going to help you describe something. When we describe, we use our five senses. We tell about what we see, hear, touch, taste, and smell. We can describe a person, a place, or a thing. This kind of writing is called a **descriptive paper**.

First, read this descriptive paper. It's a good model.

Wrinkles
by Andy Washington

Wrinkles is a puppy. He is a special kind of dog called a Shar-Pei. Wrinkles is funny to look at because he has so much skin! It makes flaps and folds all over his body. He has a big face but tiny ears. His tail sticks up. It curls like a ribbon. He has a light brown coat with short, straight hair. When I pet him, his fur feels like a toothbrush. Wrinkles smells sweet right after his shampoo, but his bark sounds sharp!

56    Descriptive Writing • Descriptive Paper

Descriptive Writing • Descriptive Paper    57

# Introduce the Genre:
## Descriptive Paper

*(Student Pages 56–57)*

Read Student Page 56 with the students. Explain that Jessica is going to show them how to write a paper that describes something. Tell them that they will read Jessica's work as a class. They will have a chance to talk about it with a partner and with the whole class. Then they will practice using the same strategies to write their own descriptive paper. Ask the students to think of things they can see, hear, taste, touch, or smell. [Possible answers: a flower, a pizza, a bicycle, a pet]

# Read the Model:
## Descriptive Paper

Read Jessica's words on Student Page 57 with the students. Then read the model descriptive paper on Student Page 57. **Note:** *Shar-Pei* is pronounced /shär•**pay**/. Ask what makes it a good example of a descriptive paper. [Possible responses: It is about just one thing, a puppy. It helps the reader see, feel (touch), smell, and hear the puppy.] As you read the model with the students, point out that the model contains words that students may not know. You may wish to add these words to your Word Wall and encourage students to refer to the Word Wall as they proofread their own papers for spelling.

# Meeting Students' Needs:
## Second-Language Learners

Help students with the name *Wrinkles*. Explain that the letter *w* is silent. Help students understand what wrinkles are. Be sure that they make the connection between the puppy's name and the illustration in their book. As students read the model, encourage them to link details they read, such as "tiny ears," with the details they see.

## Students Who Need Extra Help

Have students predict what a writer might want to tell about a puppy. List some of the details that students name. Then have students read the model paper, looking for details that match those listed. Finally, discuss with students which details tell things for the reader to see, which tell things for the reader to feel (touch), which tell things for the reader to smell, and which tell things for the reader to hear.

## Gifted Students

Encourage students to identify other kinds of details that the writer might have included in the paper. For example, the writer might have mentioned the dog's eyes, teeth, legs, or paws.

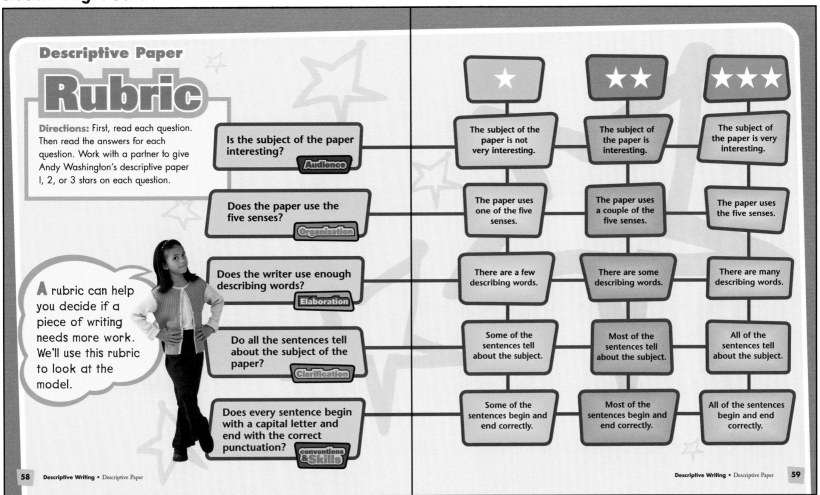

## Using a Rubric

Use the text on Student Pages 60–62 to model the use of a rubric for evaluating a piece of writing. For more information on using a rubric, please see page T21.

## Discuss the Descriptive Paper Rubric

*(Student Pages 58–59)*

Read the questions on Student Page 58 with the students. Explain that these questions are what writers use to write a good descriptive paper. Discuss each question with the students.

**Audience: Is the subject of the paper interesting?** Readers like to read about unusual and interesting things.

**Organization: Does the paper use the five senses ?** In a description, the writer wants the reader to understand how something looks, sounds, tastes, feels, or smells.

**Elaboration: Does the writer use enough describing words?** If there are not enough describing words, the reader might not get a clear picture of how something looks, sounds, smells, feels, or tastes.

**Clarification: Do all the sentences tell about the subject?** If the writing jumps around or if the writer describes many different subjects instead of just one, the reader can get confused.

**Conventions & Skills: Does every sentence begin with a capital letter and end with the correct punctuation?** Capital letters and end punctuation help readers understand where new sentences begin and end. The correct end punctuation lets readers know whether the writer is telling something, asking a question, or expressing strong feelings.

Have students evaluate the model descriptive paper with a partner, using the Descriptive Paper Rubric on Student Pages 58–59. Ask partners to share their evaluations with the whole group.

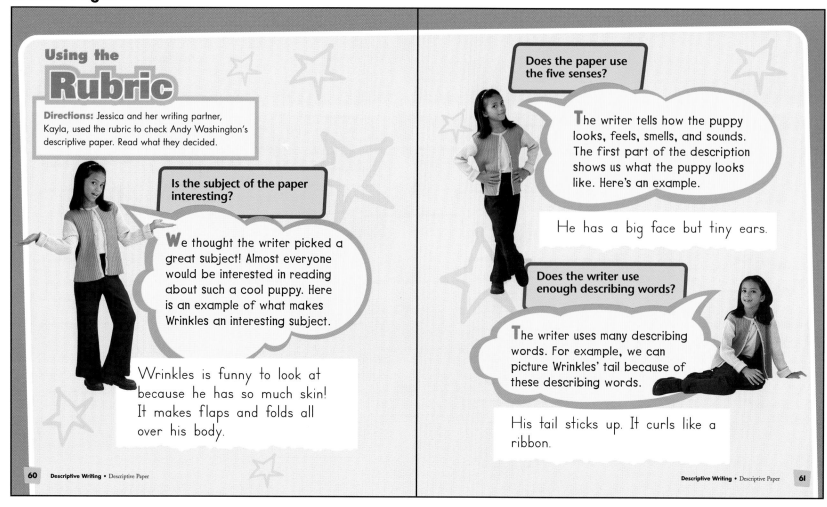

## Using the Rubric to Study the Model

*(Student Pages 60–62)*

Explain to students that Jessica and her writing partner are going to use the questions on the rubric to look at the descriptive paper on Student Page 57. Read Jessica's words on Student Page 60. Ask the students whether they agree that an unusual puppy is a good subject for a descriptive paper. Read the sentences from the model paper aloud. Ask the students whether they think that readers will be interested in the puppy.

Read Student Page 61 with the students. Did the paper help them to picture Wrinkles? Which senses besides sight did the writer use to describe Wrinkles? [Response: touch (feel), smell, sound (hearing)] Point out that describing words help the writer paint a picture for the reader. Read Student Page 62 with the students. Ask students if they agree with Jessica that all the sentences tell about the subject, the Shar-Pei puppy. Then remind students that writing sentences correctly helps readers to follow the writer's thoughts.

## Differentiating Rubrics for Assignments

by Lee Bromberger, *Assessment Specialist*

Rubrics can be easily designed and adapted for many classroom assignments. Below are some guidelines for developing and/or adapting rubrics.

**Determine the objective(s) of the writing assignment.** If the class has recently practiced using time-order signal words, "time-order signal words" could then become a focus of the assignment rubric.

**Tailor the rubric to specific writing.** If students are writing a narrative, design rubrics that incorporate narrative elements throughout the rubric. Depending on the grade level, narrative rubrics might evaluate plot, character development, inclusion of setting, dialogue, etc. A rubric tailored to descriptive writing might focus on the writer's use of descriptive words, sensory details, etc.

**Borrow successful rubrics from colleagues, applying changes that meet your objectives.** Why reinvent the wheel? Sometimes a well-prepared existing rubric can be the appropriate assessment tool, with perhaps one or two changes.

**Comb your textbook's teacher resource materials.** Many teacher editions include rubrics that correlate with textbook writing assignments. Like those rubrics you may borrow from your colleagues, these rubrics may be directly applicable as they exist or easily modified to meet your objectives.

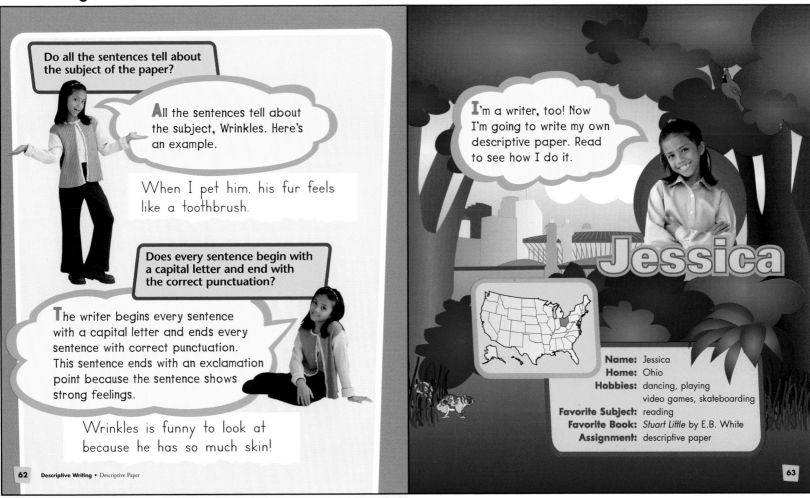

## Working With a Partner Mini-lesson:
### Take Turns

Help students understand how to work with a partner effectively by giving them some basic tips. You may wish to post tips on chart paper in a visible spot in the classroom.

Remind students that they should **take turns** with their partner. Each writer needs time to read and talk about his or her writing. Be sure that the time is not spent on only one person. You may wish to give students a copy of the Working With a Partner Sheet on page T166.

**Model the Tip** Model taking turns for the students by having a "pretend partner conference" with a student volunteer. Ask the student to read his or her paper first. Next, take your turn reading your paper to your "partner." Explain to the students that taking turns gives both partners a chance to talk, listen, and ask questions.

## Jessica:
### Writer of a Descriptive Paper

*(Student Page 63)*

Read the information about Jessica to learn more about her. Be sure students understand that Jessica will write her own descriptive paper in this chapter. Review the information given about her. Discuss what Jessica might write about in her descriptive paper based on her interests.

Point out that Jessica will go through the steps in the writing process (Prewriting, Drafting, Revising, Editing, and Publishing). At each stage, Jessica will use a good writing strategy and explain how she used it. Students should watch for key words, including **Gather, Organize, Write, Add (Elaborate), Take Out (Clarify), Proofread,** and **Share,** to follow the strategies Jessica uses as she goes through the writing process.

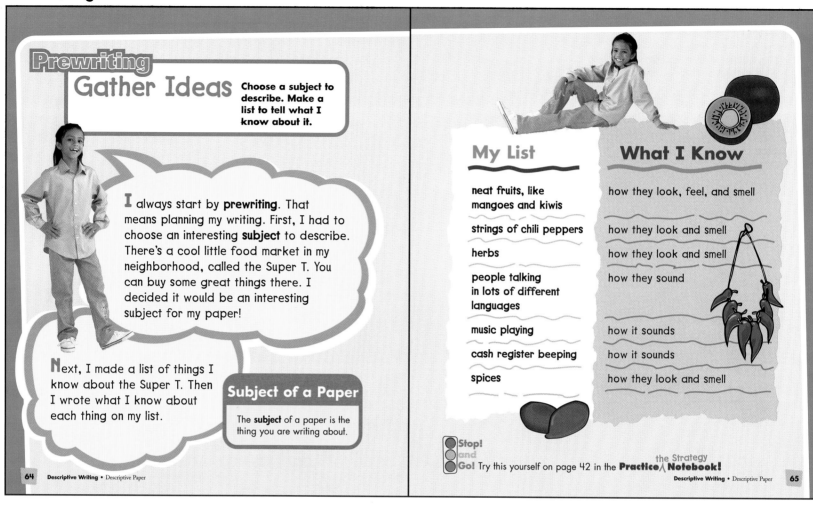

## My List | What I Know

| My List | What I Know |
|---|---|
| neat fruits, like mangoes and kiwis | how they look, feel, and smell |
| strings of chili peppers | how they look and smell |
| herbs | how they look and smell |
| people talking in lots of different languages | how they sound |
| music playing | how it sounds |
| cash register beeping | how it sounds |
| spices | how they look and smell |

Stop! and Go! Try this yourself on page 42 in the **Practice the Strategy Notebook!**

---

## Prewriting  Gather Ideas

**Strategy: Choose a subject to describe. Make a list to tell what I know about it.**

*(Student Pages 64–65)*

Read Jessica's words on Student Page 64 with the students. Explain that in this section Jessica tells how she went about writing her descriptive paper. She starts by explaining how she chose her subject. Read aloud the definition of the term *subject* on this page and discuss it with the students. Ask the students how Jessica got ideas for what to say about her subject. [**Possible response: She thought of the subject, and then she made a list of things she knew about it.**]

Point out Jessica's list of things in the Super T on Student Page 65. Discuss which of the five senses she uses. Ask the students if they think Jessica's list will make a good starting place for writing a descriptive paper.

### Practice the Strategy Notebook!

*Practice the Strategy Notebook* pages 42–43 give students a chance to decide whether certain topics would lend themselves to good descriptive writing. After students have completed this activity, you may wish to have them share their responses.

### Practice the Strategy Notebook!

*Practice the Strategy Notebook* pages 44–45 provide an opportunity for students to list and explore possible topics for their own descriptive paper, to choose a topic, and to list details about it using their senses. You may wish to assign these pages now or after students have completed this chapter in the Student Edition. You may wish to save students' *Your Own Writing* pages and add them to their Work-in-Progress Portfolios.

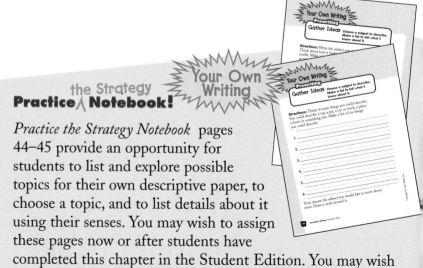

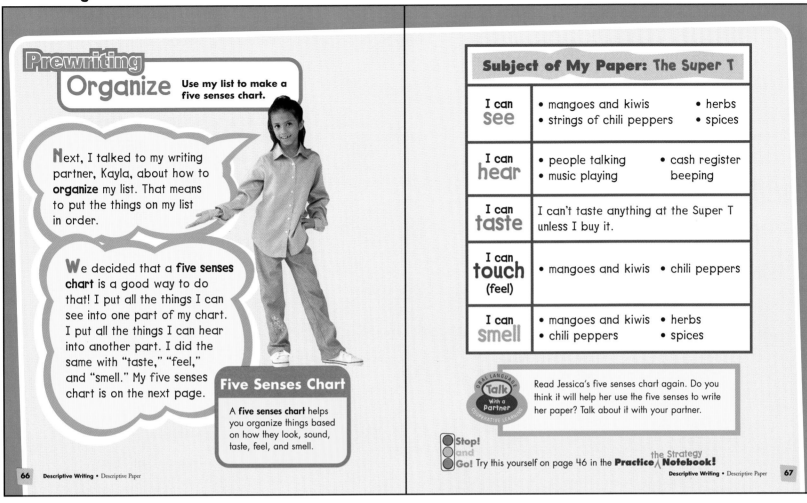

**Prewriting**
## Organize
Use my list to make a five senses chart.

Next, I talked to my writing partner, Kayla, about how to **organize** my list. That means to put the things on my list in order.

We decided that a **five senses chart** is a good way to do that! I put all the things I can see into one part of my chart. I put all the things I can hear into another part. I did the same with "taste," "feel," and "smell." My five senses chart is on the next page.

### Five Senses Chart
A **five senses chart** helps you organize things based on how they look, sound, taste, feel, and smell.

**Subject of My Paper: The Super T**

| I can **see** | • mangoes and kiwis | • herbs |
| | • strings of chili peppers | • spices |
| I can **hear** | • people talking | • cash register |
| | • music playing | beeping |
| I can **taste** | I can't taste anything at the Super T unless I buy it. | |
| I can **touch** (feel) | • mangoes and kiwis | • chili peppers |
| I can **smell** | • mangoes and kiwis | • herbs |
| | • chili peppers | • spices |

**Talk With a Partner** ORAL LANGUAGE COOPERATIVE LEARNING

Read Jessica's five senses chart again. Do you think it will help her use the five senses to write her paper? Talk about it with your partner.

**Stop! and Go!** Try this yourself on page 46 in the **Practice the Strategy Notebook!**

66 Descriptive Writing • Descriptive Paper

Descriptive Writing • Descriptive Paper 67

---

**Prewriting** ## Organize

**Strategy: Use my list to make a five senses chart.**

*(Student Pages 66–67)*

Read aloud the definition of a *five senses chart* on Student Page 66 and discuss it with the students. Then read Jessica's words with them. Explain that before Jessica starts writing, she needs to organize her information. Discuss with students why it is a good idea to talk to a writing partner at this stage. [Possible responses: A writing partner can help you find more things to describe about the person, place, or thing. A writing partner can let you know if you need to use more of the five senses.] Explain that a five senses chart is a good way to organize the details for a descriptive paper.

**Talk With a Partner** ORAL LANGUAGE COOPERATIVE LEARNING

Encourage the students to discuss Jessica's five senses chart with their partner. Ask the students if they think Jessica's five senses chart organizes her information well. You may wish to discuss the partners' findings as a large-group activity, as well.

**Note:** A five senses chart transparency is provided in the *Strategies for Writers Transparencies.*

**Practice the Strategy Notebook!**

*Practice the Strategy Notebook* pages 46–47 provide additional practice in using a five senses chart to organize the ideas for a descriptive paper. After students have completed this activity, you may wish to have them share their five senses charts with a writing partner.

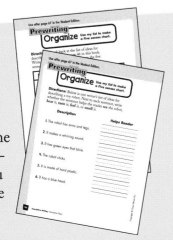

**Practice the Strategy Notebook!** Your Own Writing

*Practice the Strategy Notebook* pages 48–49 provide an opportunity for students to create a five senses chart for their own descriptive paper. You may wish to assign these pages now or after students have completed this chapter in the Student Edition.

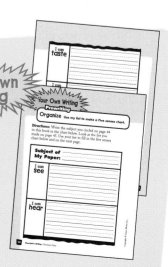

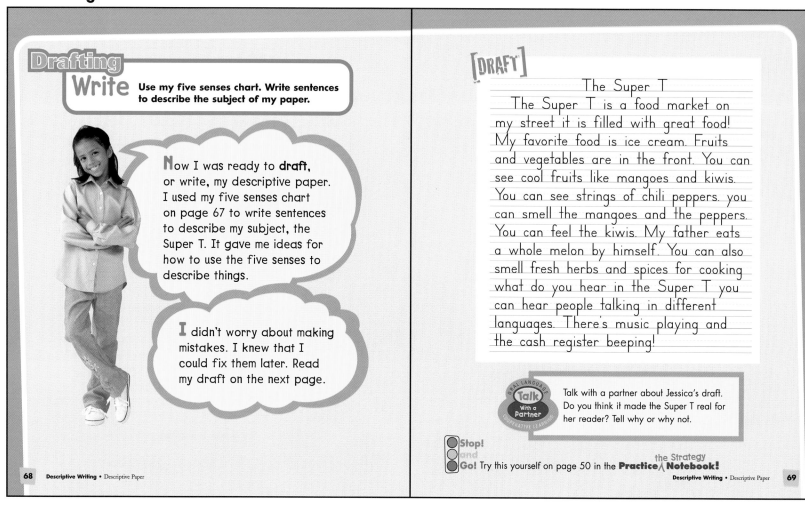

## Drafting Write

Use my five senses chart. Write sentences to describe the subject of my paper.

**N**ow I was ready to **draft**, or write, my descriptive paper. I used my five senses chart on page 67 to write sentences to describe my subject, the Super T. It gave me ideas for how to use the five senses to describe things.

**I** didn't worry about making mistakes. I knew that I could fix them later. Read my draft on the next page.

68    Descriptive Writing • Descriptive Paper

[DRAFT]

The Super T

The Super T is a food market on my street it is filled with great food! My favorite food is ice cream. Fruits and vegetables are in the front. You can see cool fruits like mangoes and kiwis. You can see strings of chili peppers. you can smell the mangoes and the peppers. You can feel the kiwis. My father eats a whole melon by himself. You can also smell fresh herbs and spices for cooking what do you hear in the Super T you can hear people talking in different languages. There's music playing and the cash register beeping!

**Talk With a Partner** ORAL LANGUAGE COOPERATIVE LEARNING

Talk with a partner about Jessica's draft. Do you think it made the Super T real for her reader? Tell why or why not.

**Stop! and Go!** Try this yourself on page 50 in the **Practice the Strategy Notebook!**

Descriptive Writing • Descriptive Paper    69

---

## Drafting Write

**Strategy:** Use my five senses chart. Write sentences to describe the subject of my paper.

*(Student Pages 68–69)*

Review the term *draft*. Remind students that a draft is an early form of a paper. It may have mistakes in it because the writer is concentrating on getting ideas down on paper. Also remind students that a draft is just one step in the writing process. There will be more steps later. Remind students that Jessica used her five senses chart to write sentences for her draft. Read Jessica's draft on Student Page 69 with the students.

**Talk With a Partner** ORAL LANGUAGE COOPERATIVE LEARNING

Encourage partners to discuss the question at the bottom of Student Page 69. Ask them to decide whether Jessica does or does not help her readers "get to know" the Super T. If students think Jessica is successful, ask them what details she uses to accomplish this. [Possible responses: Jessica names many items that can be seen in the Super T. She tells how some things feel and smell. She also tells what she hears.]

### Practice the Strategy Notebook!

*Practice the Strategy Notebook* page 50 provides practice in writing sentences by using the five senses chart students filled in on page 47. After students have completed this activity, you may wish to have them read their sentences to a partner.

### Practice the Strategy Notebook!

*Practice the Strategy Notebook* pages 51–53 provide practice for students in writing a draft of their own descriptive paper by using the notes in the five senses chart they created on pages 48–49. After students have completed this activity, you may wish to have them read their drafts to a partner or share their drafts in a large-group activity. You may wish to assign these pages now or after students have completed this chapter in the Student Edition.

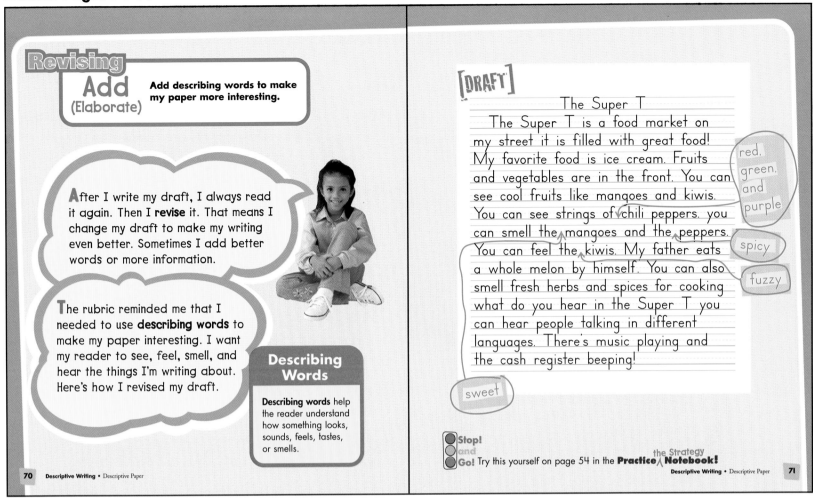

## Revising Add (Elaborate)

**Strategy: Add describing words to make my paper more interesting.**

*(Student Pages 70–71)*

Read aloud the definition of *describing word*s on Student Page 70 and discuss it with the students. Then read Jessica's words with them. Review the meaning of the term *revise*. Explain that one kind of revising is adding information to make writing more complete. In descriptive writing, writers can add describing words.

**Note:** *Strategies for Writers* employs the term **Elaborate** in grades 3–8. You may wish to explain to students that *elaborate* means "to add."

Read Jessica's revised draft on Student Page 71 with the students. Ask students how Jessica's revisions have made her paper even better. [Possible response: The new describing words make it easier for the reader to imagine how things look and feel.]

Encourage students to talk with a partner about Jessica's revisions. Did the changes make her description better? What other describing words could Jessica have added?

## Tips for Successful Conferencing:
### Making Conferencing Comfortable

Both you and the students might feel more comfortable if you hold conferences so that you and the student are at eye level. If you are doing a brief conference, you may want to kneel. If you are doing a longer conference, you may want to sit in a child-size chair.

Both you and the students might find it helpful for you to paraphrase what the student is saying. You might say something like "Are you saying that . . ?" or "Do you mean that . . ?"

Sometimes questions like "How are you doing?" or "What idea are you working on?" can open up more areas for discussion and revision.

### Practice the Strategy Notebook!

*Practice the Strategy Notebook* page 54 provides additional practice in revising a draft by adding describing words. After students have completed this activity, remind them to use this strategy to revise their own descriptive papers.

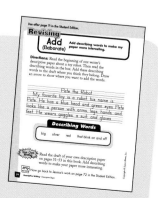

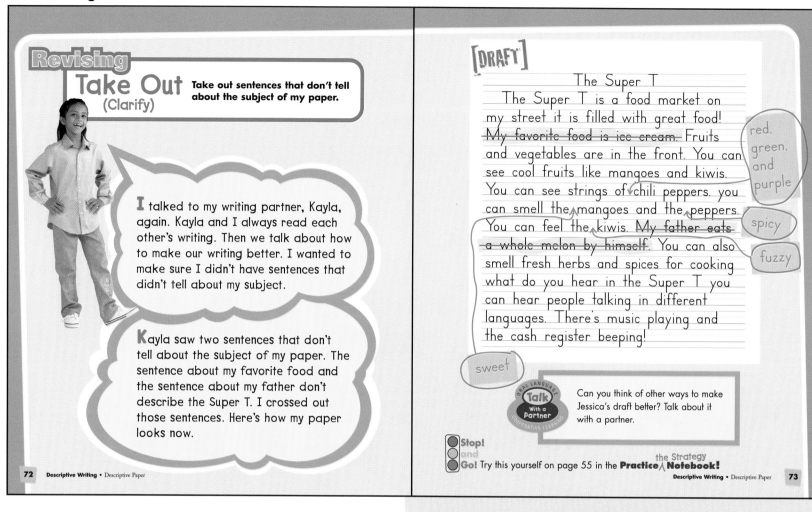

## Revising Take Out (Clarify)

**Strategy: Take out sentences that don't tell about the subject of my paper.**

*(Student Pages 72–73)*

Read Jessica's words on Student Page 72 with the students. Explain that another way to revise is to take out sentences that don't tell about the subject of the paper. Read Jessica's revised draft with the students. Point out that Jessica took out the sentence "My favorite food is ice cream" because it doesn't tell about the subject of the paper. Ask students why. [Possible response: It doesn't help tell how the Super T looks, sounds, tastes, feels, or smells.] Ask students which other sentence Jessica crossed out and why. [Possible response: "My father eats a whole melon by himself." The subject of the paper is the Super T, not Jessica's father and what he does.]

**Note:** *Strategies for Writers* employs the term **Clarify** in grades 3–8. You may wish to explain to students that *clarify* means "to make clear," usually by taking out what's unnecessary.

## Spelling Strategies: Relate the Word to a Word You Know

Before students begin the Editing portion of the chapter, you may wish to remind them that checking spelling is an important part of editing their writing. Encourage students to use several strategies to figure out the spellings of new words and words of which they are unsure.

One strategy is to **relate the word to a word you know**. For example, the word *cooking* contains the familiar word *cook* plus the familiar ending *-ing*. Additionally, some students may know the word *looking*.

### the Strategy Practice Notebook!

*Practice the Strategy Notebook* page 55 provides additional practice in revising a description by taking out sentences that don't help tell about the subject. After students have completed this activity, remind them to use this strategy to revise their own descriptive papers.

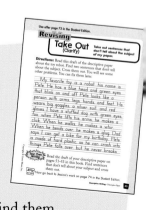

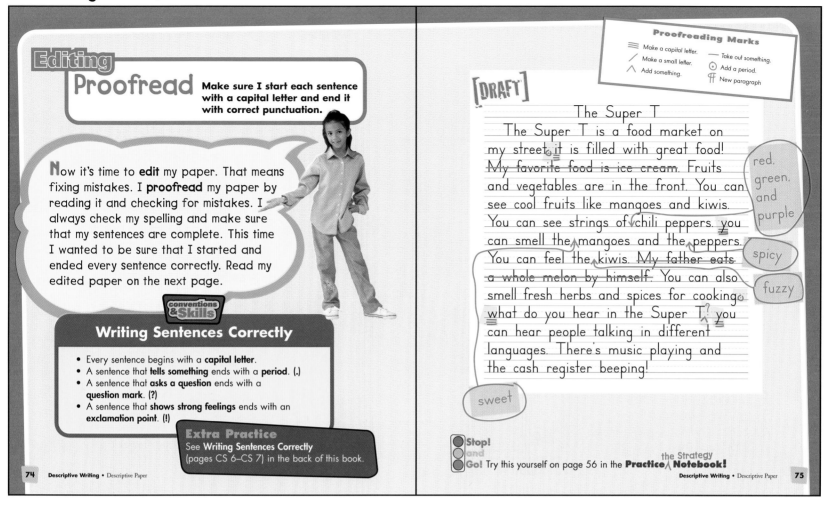

## Editing Proofread

**Strategy:** **Make sure I start each sentence with a capital letter and end it with correct punctuation.**

*(Student Pages 74–75)*

Remind students that editing is different from revising. When writers revise, they add information or take it out. When writers edit, they fix grammar and spelling mistakes. Remind students that to *proofread* means to read their paper while looking for mistakes.

Read Jessica's words on Student Page 74 to the students. Remind students that Jessica always checks her spelling and makes sure her sentences are complete. Tell students that Jessica is now going to make sure that every sentence starts with a capital letter and ends with a period, question mark, or exclamation point. Remind students that using a pencil that writes in a different color can help writers see their changes better. (**Note:** You may wish to give students their own colored pencils to edit their writing.) Read the rules for writing sentences correctly at the bottom of Student Page 74 with the students.

Review the proofreading symbols chart on Student Page 75 with the students. Read Jessica's edited draft with the students. Ask them if Jessica made all the necessary corrections. You may wish to use the corresponding Writing Model for Proofreading Practice Transparency.

## Extra Practice: Conventions & Skills

### Student Edition

If your students need more practice in writing sentences correctly, you may wish to assign Student Pages CS 6–CS 7.

### Conventions & Skills Practice

For more targeted practice related to this skill, see these lessons in the optional *Conventions & Skills Practice Book*:

Lesson 6: Sentences That Tell

Lesson 7: Sentences That Ask

Lesson 8: Telling or Asking Sentences

Lesson 10: Sentences That Show Strong Feelings

### Practice the Strategy Notebook!

*Practice the Strategy Notebook* pages 56–57 provide additional practice in editing a draft by correcting errors in capitalization and end punctuation. After students have completed this activity, remind them to use this strategy to edit their own descriptive papers.

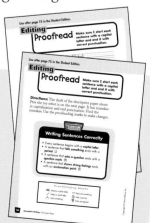

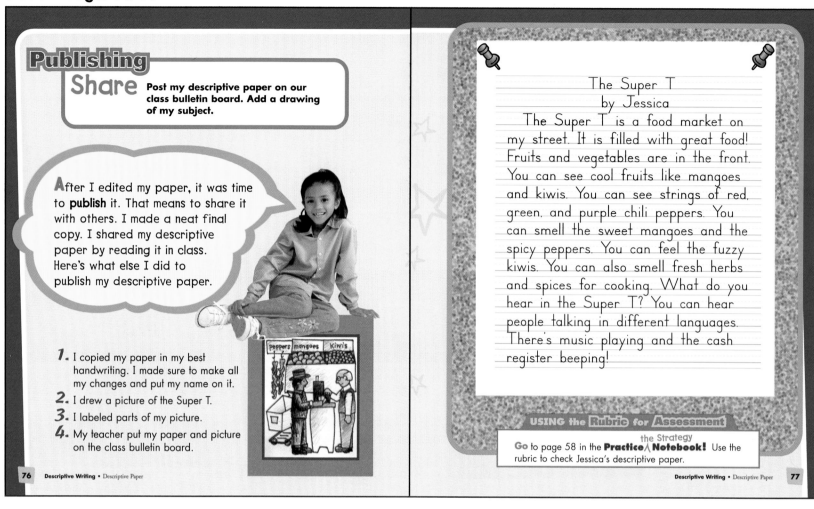

## Publishing Share

**Strategy: Post my descriptive paper on our class bulletin board. Add a drawing of my subject.**

*(Student Pages 76–77)*

Read Jessica's words to the students. Explain that publishing is the process of finishing a piece of writing to share it with others. Once writers are finished revising and editing their writing, they may publish it. They make a final copy of their writing, including all the changes they made.

Remind students that there are many ways to share published writing. Jessica decided to publish her descriptive paper by posting it on the class bulletin board and adding a labeled drawing of her subject. Tell students that there are other ways of publishing a descriptive paper. Other publishing options include putting together a class album of descriptive papers with pictures, creating a display of descriptive papers in the classroom, and compiling a class book of descriptive papers to share on "Author Day." Read the final copy of Jessica's paper on Student Page 77 with the students.

Encourage students to talk with a partner about how Jessica shared her descriptive paper. Was it a good way to share writing? How else could Jessica have shared her description?

## Using a Rubric

*Practice the Strategy Notebook* pages 58–59 provide a rubric to use for assessing Jessica's final descriptive paper. Encourage students to work with a partner to evaluate Jessica's descriptive paper by using this rubric. After students have completed this activity, you may wish to have them share the results in a large-group activity.

Dear Family,

In *Strategies for Writers*, your child is learning and practicing the writing process. This process is very important in helping people establish good writing skills and will help your child to develop communication skills that he or she will use throughout life.

The writing process is made up of five basic steps, which build on each other to help the writer produce a finished product—a piece of written work. The five steps are Prewriting, Drafting, Revising, Editing, and Publishing.

The first step is Prewriting. This is where writers Gather and Organize information. When writers Gather, they may do many things. They decide on a topic, think about their readers, and think about what they want to say. They write lists, jot notes, and do interviews. When writers Organize, they put the information they have gathered into a form that will help them make sense of it.

The second step in the writing process is Drafting. Once a writer has gathered and organized information, he or she writes a version of a document—a draft. It will be messy, and it may be full of mistakes, but that's the way it should be. The draft will go through many changes before it becomes the final copy. The important thing is for the writer to get his or her ideas down on paper.

The next step is Revising. This is where the draft gets changed as the writer works to make the writing even better. The Revising step is made up of two smaller steps— Add (Elaborate) and Take Out (Clarify). When writers elaborate, they add words or sentences that make the writing more interesting. When writers clarify, they take out words or sentences that make the writing confusing or hard to read.

The fourth step is Editing. All those mistakes in grammar, spelling, and punctuation get ironed out here. When they edit, writers proofread their work, find mistakes, and correct them. Once the fourth step is done, the draft is ready for the final step.

The final step is Publishing. The final copy of the writing can be published in many ways. A writer may choose to write a neat copy, add an illustration, and turn it in. A writer may publish by posting the final copy on a bulletin board or a Web site. The method of publication depends on what the writing is designed to do.

As you can see, writing is a process.

You may wish to copy the letter above and send it home with your students.

# Tips for the Writing Classroom

by Barry Sneed, *Master Teacher*

## Super Readers & Writing Workshop

Super Readers and Writing Workshop may be implemented in the classroom in late September or early October. Depending on your students' skills, this program can play a significant role in the development of reading and writing strategies. My students love the activities involved, and with planning and organization, you will love them, too!

The **Super Reader Program** involves having each child choose and read a book to a small group of classmates (three to four others) on the same day each week. (You can assign a day to each child.) Advise parents, as much as possible, to assist their child in choosing a book each week. The books may come from home, the public library, or may even be borrowed from the classroom, but the responsibility for choosing, preparing, and getting the book to class on the assigned day lies with the parent(s) and child. I remind students the day before they are to read, but that's a little too late if they haven't already prepared a book for that day. Four to five

---

## Compare-and-Contrast Paper

### Writing Strategies

**Prewriting**

**Gather Ideas**
Choose two things to compare and contrast. Make lists to tell what I know about each thing.

**Organize**
Use my lists to make a Venn diagram.

**Drafting**

**Write**
Use my Venn diagram. Write about how the two things are alike. Write about how they are different.

**Publishing**

**Share**
Make a class book with labeled pictures.

**Revising**

**Add (Elaborate)**
Add describing words to make my paper more interesting.

**Take Out (Clarify)**
Take out sentences that don't help tell how the two things are alike or different.

**Editing**

**Proofread**
Make sure I have written all contractions correctly.

**Note:** You may wish to copy and give students the Writing Process Flow Chart blackline master on page T106.

---

## MODELED WRITING

**Compare-and-Contrast Writing Mini-Lesson:** You may wish to present this mini-lesson before the students read the model on Student Page 79. Write the following on the board, chart paper, or an overhead transparency:

> Apples and bananas are both fruits. Both have peels. Both taste great and are good for you. Milk is good for you, too. Bananas are yellow. Apples can be red, yellow, or green. Apples are juicy. Bananas aren't juicy.

Ask the students what the sentences tell them. [Possible response: They tell how an apple and a banana are alike and different.] Explain that this kind of writing compares and contrasts two things.

Tell students they will be learning more about how to compare and contrast two things in this chapter in the Student Edition. They will see a model of this kind of writing and learn and practice some strategies for writing their own compare-and-contrast paper.

Write the title "Apples and Bananas" above the sentences. Ask the students if any sentences don't help tell how an apple and a banana are alike or different. [Response: Yes, the fourth sentence isn't about apples and bananas.] Cross out the sentence. Explain to students that when they write their own compare-and-contrast paper, they will also cross out ideas that don't belong.

students should be assigned to each day of the week. (**Note:** Once assigned, these days should not change for the rest of the school year.) Every day, the Super Readers for that day sit in chairs around the room and read for seven to ten minutes to their small group. The groups meet simultaneously. While the students read, the teacher circulates and completes a checklist on each child's presentation. A copy of the checklist should be sent home each week on that day.

After Super Readers, move into **Writing Workshop** for 20 to 30 minutes. During this time the teacher meets individually for four to six minutes with each of the Super Readers

for that day. The student and teacher review the student's various writings from the past week and select one piece to edit, which will then be sent home with a Writing Conference Sheet summarizing the meeting. Copy this piece (or choose another) to place into the student's weekly writing file, thus creating a portfolio of the child's writing progress throughout the year. If possible, it is helpful to have another adult (parent or volunteer) circulate and help the students with their writing, spelling, and other tasks as they continue to work on their writing.

## Time Management for This Chapter*

| Session | | Session | | Session | |
|---|---|---|---|---|---|
| **1** | Read Student Page 78. Introduce Calvin. Read the model on Student Page 79. Discuss the rubric on Student Pages 80–81. | **6** | Assign *Practice the Strategy Notebook* pages 64–67. | **11** | Read **REVISING: Take Out (Clarify)** (Student Pages 94–95). |
| **2** | Read Student Pages 82–85. Discuss Calvin's assessment of the model paper. Discuss the information about Calvin on Student Page 85. | **7** | Read **DRAFTING: Write** (Student Pages 90–91). | **12** | Assign *Practice the Strategy Notebook* page 73. |
| **3** | Read **PREWRITING: Gather Ideas** (Student Pages 86–87). | **8** | Assign *Practice the Strategy Notebook* pages 68–71. | **13** | Read **EDITING: Proofread** (Student Pages 96–97). |
| **4** | Assign *Practice the Strategy Notebook* pages 60–63. | **9** | Read **REVISING: Add (Elaborate)** (Student Pages 92–93). | **14** | Assign *Practice the Strategy Notebook* pages 74–75. |
| **5** | Read **PREWRITING: Organize** (Student Pages 88–89). | **10** | Assign *Practice the Strategy Notebook* page 72. | **15** | Read **PUBLISHING: Share** (Student Pages 98–99). |

* To complete the chapter in fewer sessions, assign *Practice the Strategy Notebook* pages on the same day the targeted skill is introduced.

 **STRATEGIES for Writers Sing-Along CD**

You may wish to use the *Strategies for Writers Sing-Along* CD throughout the chapter. See the Appendix in the back of this Teacher Edition for more information.

**WRITER'S HANDBOOK**

Remind students that they can refer to the Writer's Handbook in the back of the Student Edition for more information.

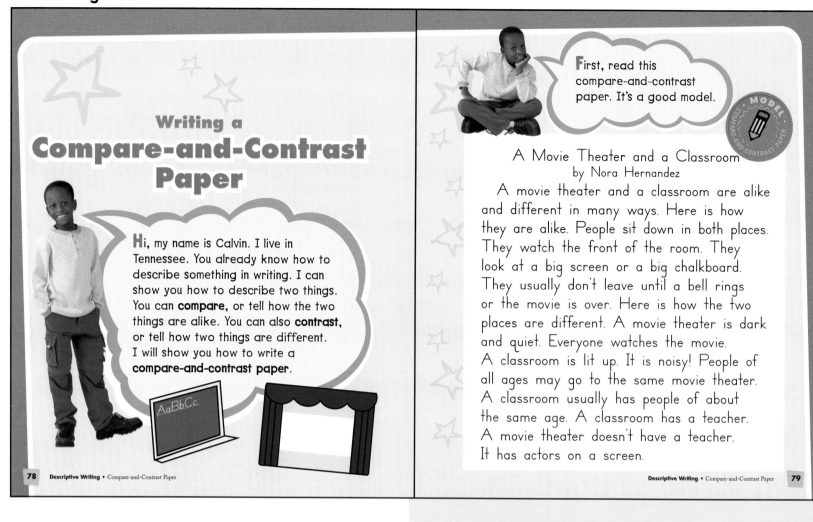

### Writing a
# Compare-and-Contrast Paper

Hi, my name is Calvin. I live in Tennessee. You already know how to describe something in writing. I can show you how to describe two things. You can **compare,** or tell how the two things are alike. You can also **contrast,** or tell how two things are different. I will show you how to write a **compare-and-contrast paper.**

First, read this compare-and-contrast paper. It's a good model.

A Movie Theater and a Classroom
by Nora Hernandez

A movie theater and a classroom are alike and different in many ways. Here is how they are alike. People sit down in both places. They watch the front of the room. They look at a big screen or a big chalkboard. They usually don't leave until a bell rings or the movie is over. Here is how the two places are different. A movie theater is dark and quiet. Everyone watches the movie. A classroom is lit up. It is noisy! People of all ages may go to the same movie theater. A classroom usually has people of about the same age. A classroom has a teacher. A movie theater doesn't have a teacher. It has actors on a screen.

**78** Descriptive Writing • Compare-and-Contrast Paper

Descriptive Writing • Compare-and-Contrast Paper **79**

## Introduce the Genre:
### Compare-and-Contrast Paper

*(Student Pages 78–79)*

Read Calvin's words on Student Page 78 with the students. Tell them that he is going to show them how to write a paper that tells how two things, or subjects, are alike and different. Tell them that they will read Calvin's work as a class. They will have a chance to talk about it with a partner and with the whole class. Then they will practice using the same strategies to write their own compare-and-contrast paper. Ask the students to think of things that are both alike and different. [Possible responses: dogs and cats, trees and flowers, a backpack and a suitcase, peanut butter and jelly]

## Read the Model:
### Compare-and-Contrast Paper

Read Calvin's words on Student Page 79 with the students. Then read the model. Ask what makes it a good example of a compare-and-contrast paper. [Possible responses: It names the two things it will describe. It tells how they are alike and how they are different.]

The model may contain words that students do not know. You may wish to add these words to your Word Wall and encourage students to refer to the Word Wall as they proofread their own papers for spelling.

## Meeting Students' Needs:
### Second-Language Learners

Students for whom English is not a first language can benefit from using two concrete objects, such as a pen and a pencil, to practice comparing and contrasting in their own language first. This will help them understand the process by providing a comfortable practice run. Second-language learners might also use a pen and a pencil, or another topic involving concrete objects, when they select their own two subjects to compare and contrast.

### Students Who Need Extra Help

Remind students that they will not have to write a compare-and-contrast paper all at once. They will use the steps of the writing process to do so. Review the steps of the writing process, and then explain, by way of previewing, what students will be doing at each step in order to write their paper.

### Gifted Students

Put gifted students to work as helpers or writing partners for students who need extra help or for second-language learners. They can help with ideas for writing, vocabulary, and spelling, as well as with specific steps in the writing process.

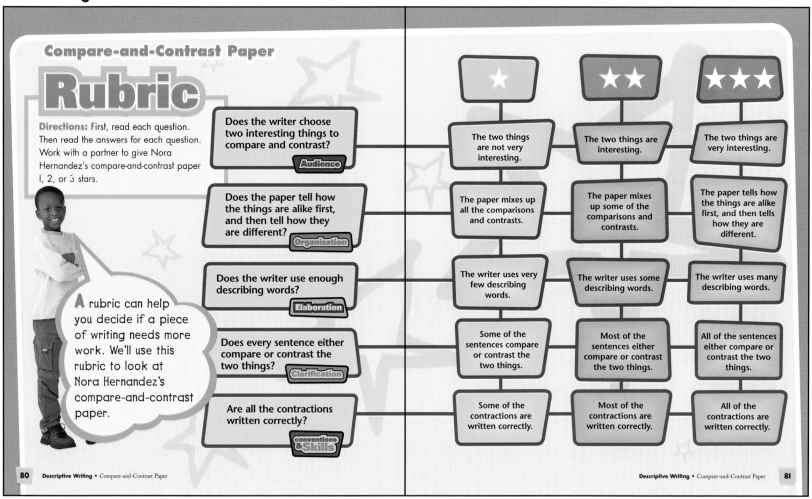

Compare-and-Contrast Paper

# Rubric

**Directions:** First, read each question. Then read the answers for each question. Work with a partner to give Nora Hernandez's compare-and-contrast paper 1, 2, or 3 stars.

A rubric can help you decide if a piece of writing needs more work. We'll use this rubric to look at Nora Hernandez's compare-and-contrast paper.

| Question | ★ | ★★ | ★★★ |
|---|---|---|---|
| Does the writer choose two interesting things to compare and contrast? **Audience** | The two things are not very interesting. | The two things are interesting. | The two things are very interesting. |
| Does the paper tell how the things are alike first, and then tell how they are different? **Organization** | The paper mixes up all the comparisons and contrasts. | The paper mixes up some of the comparisons and contrasts. | The paper tells how the things are alike first, and then tells how they are different. |
| Does the writer use enough describing words? **Elaboration** | The writer uses very few describing words. | The writer uses some describing words. | The writer uses many describing words. |
| Does every sentence either compare or contrast the two things? **Clarification** | Some of the sentences compare or contrast the two things. | Most of the sentences either compare or contrast the two things. | All of the sentences either compare or contrast the two things. |
| Are all the contractions written correctly? **Conventions & Skills** | Some of the contractions are written correctly. | Most of the contractions are written correctly. | All of the contractions are written correctly. |

80  Descriptive Writing • Compare-and-Contrast Paper

Descriptive Writing • Compare-and-Contrast Paper  81

# Using a Rubric

Use the text on Student Pages 82–84 to model the use of a rubric for evaluating a piece of writing. For more information on using a rubric, please see page T21.

## Discuss the Compare-and-Contrast Paper Rubric

*(Student Pages 80–81)*

Read the questions on Student Page 80 with the students. Explain that writers use these questions to write a good compare-and-contrast paper. Discuss each question with the students.

**Audience: Does the writer choose two interesting things to compare and contrast?** The audience will enjoy reading a paper about subjects that are interesting.

**Organization: Does the paper tell how the things are alike first, and then tell how they are different?** By discussing what is alike first and then discussing what is different, writers make their papers easier to read and to follow.

**Elaboration: Does the writer use enough describing words?** Describing words help explain how things are alike and different. They paint "word pictures" and bring the writing to life.

**Clarification: Does every sentence either compare or contrast the two things?** The paper should not contain sentences that do not tell how the two things are alike and different.

**Conventions & Skills: Are all the contractions written correctly?** Correct contractions make the writing clear and easy to understand.

Have students evaluate the model compare-and-contrast paper with a partner, using the compare-and-contrast paper rubric on Student Pages 80–81. Ask partners to share their evaluations with the whole group.

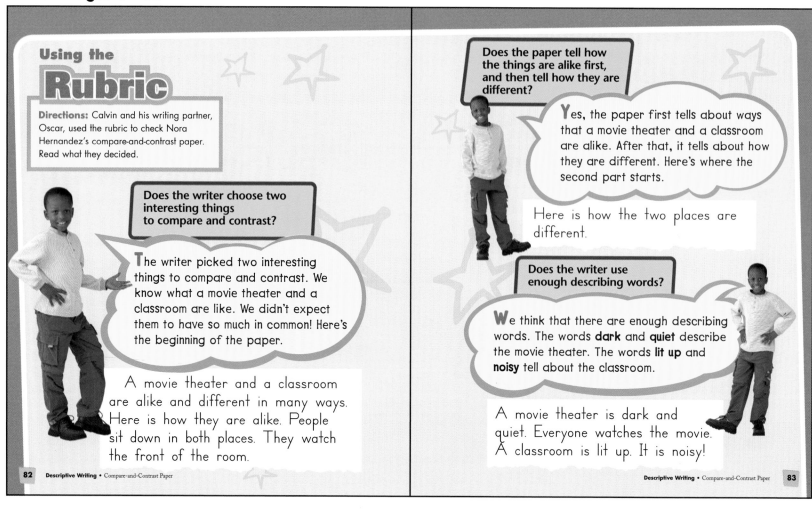

## Using the Rubric to Study the Model

*(Student Pages 82–84)*

Explain to students that now Calvin is going to use the questions on the rubric to evaluate the compare-and-contrast paper on Student Page 79.

Read the question in the box on Student Page 82, and then read Calvin's words. Ask the students whether they agree that the writer picked two interesting things to compare and contrast. Ask the students whether they agree with Calvin that these two subjects have so much in common.

Read Student Page 83 with the students. Does the paper first tell how the things are alike and then tell how they are different? Read the questions in the box and then read Calvin's responses. Do the students agree that there are enough describing words? Which senses do the describing words use? [Response: sight, sound]

Read Student Page 84 with the students. Ask students if they agree with Calvin that all the sentences tell about the two subjects, the movie theater and the classroom. Remind students that writing contractions correctly makes it easier for readers to understand their writing.

## Suggestions for Evaluating the Effectiveness of a Rubric

by Lee Bromberger, *Assessment Specialist*

Sometimes the best-designed rubric has shortcomings, which don't become obvious until it is used with an assignment. Since rubrics can be easily changed, teachers should be ready to revise them. The best time to do so, with minimum effort, is immediately after a rubric's application to an assignment.

Keep notes regarding the rubric's strengths and weaknesses. These notes could simply be placed under two columns— labeled "What Worked" and "What Failed"—on one sheet of paper. A brief note is often all that is needed. Once you have completed grading the assignment, the process of reflecting on the rubric can begin.

Consider sharing your perceptions about rubrics with colleagues, particularly if one team uses a rubric previously applied by another teacher.

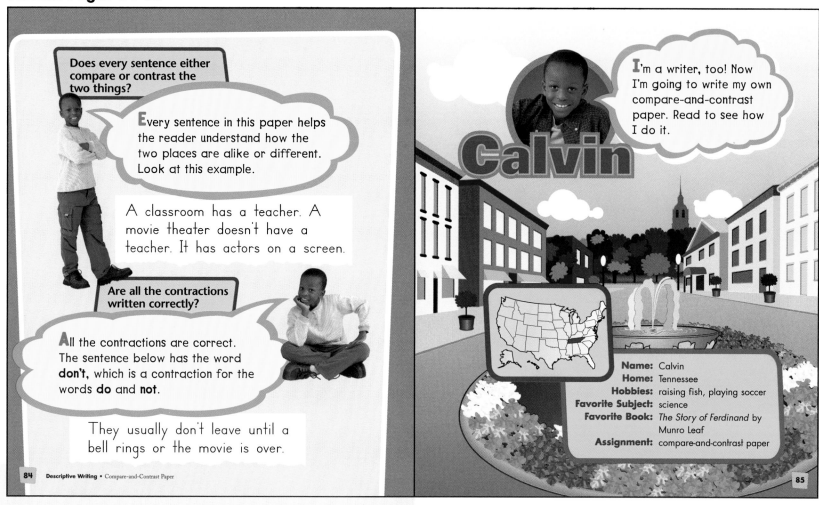

# Working With a Partner Mini-Lesson:
## Be Positive

Help students understand how to work with a partner effectively by giving them some basic tips. You may wish to post these tips on chart paper and place them in a visible place in the classroom.

Tell students that when they are working with a partner, their job is to help their partner. Encourage them to begin with a comment about something they liked in their partner's writing. Give examples, such as "This is a good topic" and "Your first sentence is just right!" Tell them to make helpful suggestions. You may wish to give students a copy of the Working With a Partner Checklist on page T166.

**Model the Tip**  Model working with a partner with a student volunteer. Bring a short piece of your own writing to use during modeling. Be sure your writing has a few problems which are easily identifiable by your students. Read your writing to your volunteer "partner." Ask your "partner" to offer one or two comments about something he or she liked about the writing. Then, ask the "partner" to identify one problem with your writing and offer a helpful suggestion for correcting it.

# Calvin:
## Writer of a Compare-and-Contrast Paper

*(Student Page 85)*

Read the information about Calvin to learn more about him. Be sure students understand that Calvin will write his own compare-and-contrast paper in this chapter. Review the information about him. Discuss what Calvin might write about in his compare-and-contrast paper based on his interests.

Point out that Calvin will go through the steps in the writing process (prewriting, drafting, revising, editing, and publishing). At each stage, he will use a good writing strategy and explain how he used it. Students should watch for key words, including **Gather, Organize, Write, Add (Elaborate), Take Out (Clarify), Proofread,** and **Share,** to follow the strategies Calvin uses as he goes through the writing process.

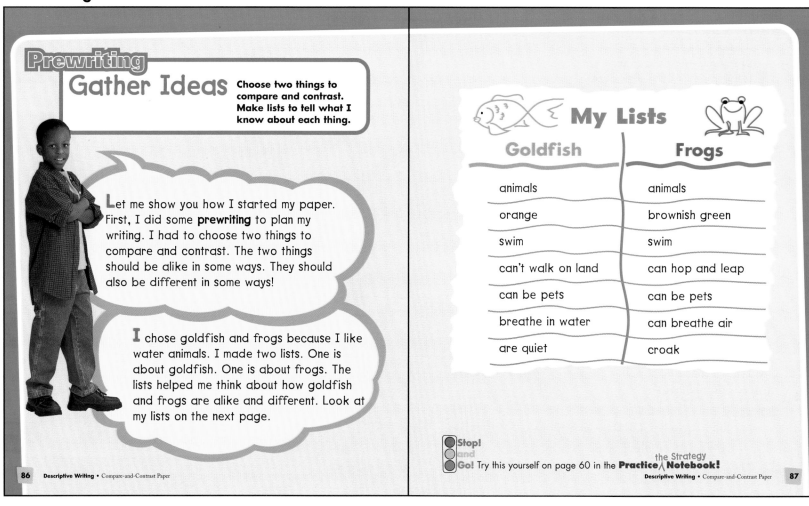

**Prewriting** Gather Ideas

Strategy: **Choose two things to compare and contrast. Make lists to tell what I know about each thing.**

*(Student Pages 86–87)*

Read Calvin's words on Student Page 86 aloud. Explain that in this section Calvin tells how he went about writing his compare-and-contrast paper. He starts by explaining how he chose his subjects and how he came up with his first ideas. Ask the students to retell what Calvin did. [Possible responses: He thought of two good things to compare and contrast. He knows about those things. He made a list about each thing.]

Point out Calvin's two lists on Student Page 87. Ask students why it is a good idea to start out with lists like these. [Possible responses: If you cannot make a list of ideas, you may not know enough about your subjects. The lists will give you ideas to write about.]

the Strategy
**Practice Notebook!**

*Practice the Strategy Notebook* pages 60–61 provide additional practice in listing ideas for another compare-and-contrast paper. After students have completed this activity, you may wish to have them share their responses.

the Strategy
**Practice Notebook!**

*Practice the Strategy Notebook* pages 62–63 provide an opportunity for students to list ideas for their own compare-and-contrast paper. You may wish to assign these pages now or after students have completed this chapter in the Student Edition.

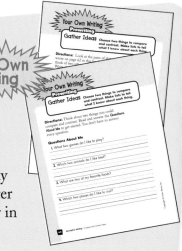

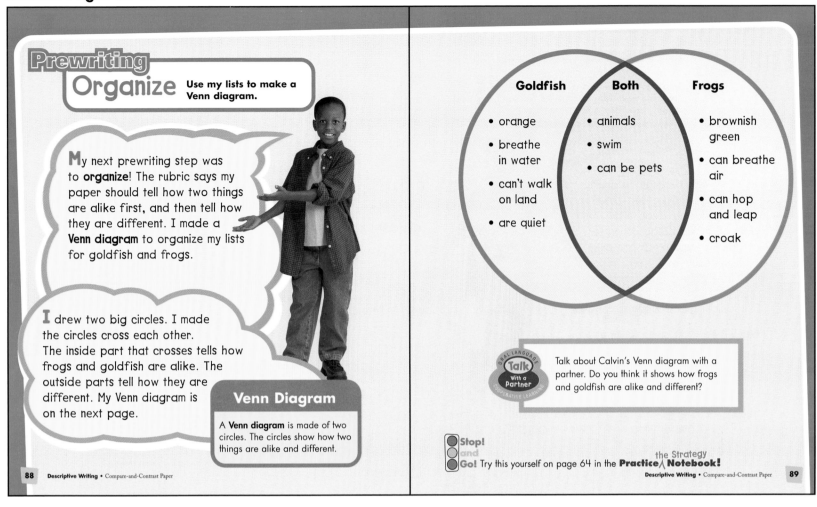

## Prewriting
### Organize — Use my lists to make a Venn diagram.

My next prewriting step was to **organize**! The rubric says my paper should tell how two things are alike first, and then tell how they are different. I made a **Venn diagram** to organize my lists for goldfish and frogs.

I drew two big circles. I made the circles cross each other. The inside part that crosses tells how frogs and goldfish are alike. The outside parts tell how they are different. My Venn diagram is on the next page.

**Venn Diagram**

A **Venn diagram** is made of two circles. The circles show how two things are alike and different.

**Goldfish**
- orange
- breathe in water
- can't walk on land
- are quiet

**Both**
- animals
- swim
- can be pets

**Frogs**
- brownish green
- can breathe air
- can hop and leap
- croak

Talk about Calvin's Venn diagram with a partner. Do you think it shows how frogs and goldfish are alike and different?

**Stop! and Go!** Try this yourself on page 64 in the **Practice Notebook!**

88  Descriptive Writing • Compare-and-Contrast Paper

Descriptive Writing • Compare-and-Contrast Paper  89

---

## Prewriting  Organize

**Strategy: Use my lists to make a Venn diagram.**

*(Student Pages 88–89)*

Read Calvin's words with the students. Discuss the definition of the Venn diagram on Student Page 88. Then read Calvin's words with the students. Explain that before he starts writing, Calvin needs to organize his information. Direct students' attention to Calvin's Venn diagram on Student Page 89. Explain that a Venn diagram is a good way to organize a compare-and-contrast paper because it lists things about each subject in a different circle, but it also shows how the subjects are alike.

**Talk With a Partner**

Encourage the students to discuss Calvin's Venn diagram with their partners. Ask the students if it seems complete. Are the ideas in the right places? You may wish to discuss the partners' findings as a large-group activity, as well.

**Note:** A Venn diagram transparency is provided in the *Strategies for Writers Transparencies*.

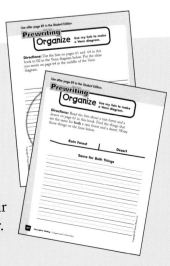

### the Strategy Practice Notebook!

*Practice the Strategy Notebook* pages 64–65 provide additional practice in using a Venn diagram to organize a compare-and-contrast paper. After students have completed this activity, you may wish to have them share their Venn diagrams with a writing partner.

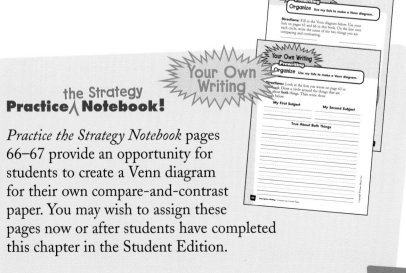

### the Strategy Practice Notebook!

*Practice the Strategy Notebook* pages 66–67 provide an opportunity for students to create a Venn diagram for their own compare-and-contrast paper. You may wish to assign these pages now or after students have completed this chapter in the Student Edition.

**Descriptive Writing** • Compare-and-Contrast Paper

Have writing partners discuss Calvin's first sentence. Does it tell the two things (subjects) he will write about? Does the draft tell how the two subjects are alike and how they are different?

# Drafting Write

**Strategy: Use my Venn diagram. Write about how the two things are alike. Write about how they are different.**

*(Student Pages 90–91)*

Review the term *draft* with students. Remind them that a draft is an early form of a paper. In a draft, writers don't worry too much about mistakes. The important thing is to get ideas down on paper. Writers know that they will have a chance to go back and fix mistakes later. Read Calvin's words and draft with the students.

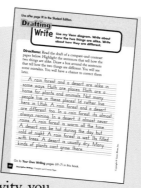

### the Strategy
## Practice ∧ Notebook!

*Practice the Strategy Notebook* page 68 provides practice in finding sentences that compare two subjects and sentences that contrast two subjects. After students have completed this activity, you may wish to have them share their findings with a partner or in a large-group activity.

### the Strategy
## Practice ∧ Notebook!

*Practice the Strategy Notebook* pages 69–71 provide practice for students in writing their own compare-and-contrast paper using the Venn diagram they created on page 67. After students have completed this activity, you may wish to have them read their drafts to a partner or share their drafts in a large-group activity. You may wish to assign these pages now or after students have completed this chapter in the Student Edition.

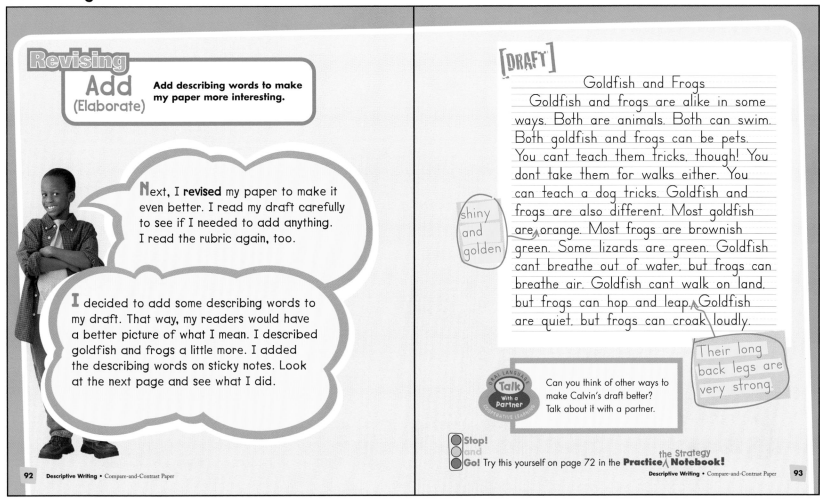

# Revising Add (Elaborate)

**Strategy:** Add describing words to make my paper more interesting.

*(Student Pages 92–93)*

Review the term *revise* with students. Explain that when writers revise their work, they change what they say or how they say it. Explain that one way to revise is to add describing words. **Note:** *Strategies for Writers* employs the term **Elaborate** in grades 3–8. You may wish to explain to students that *elaborate* means "to add."

Read Calvin's revised draft on Student Page 93 with the students. Ask how Calvin's revisions have made his paper better. [Possible responses: The reader learns more about goldfish. The reader finds out more about frogs' back legs.]

### Practice the Strategy Notebook!

*Practice the Strategy Notebook* page 72 provides more practice in revising a draft by adding describing words. After students have completed this activity, remind them to use this strategy to revise their own compare-and-contrast paper.

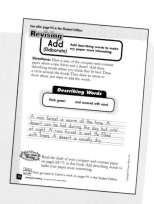

Encourage students to talk with a partner about Calvin's revisions. Did the changes make the paper better? What other describing words could Calvin have added?

## Tips for Successful Conferencing:
### Keeping a Conferencing Log

A conferencing log is a great tool for helping you organize the information gleaned from conferences. Keep the log simple and easy for you to interpret. For example, the following are symbols you may wish to use when assessing students' progress in a conferencing log.

✔    Things are going well.

✔+    Things are going great!

✔–    Things could be going better.

–    Things are not going well.

?    It is unclear to me how things are going.

A    The student was absent.

As you conference with your students, jot down a few notes to help you remember your observations for the next conference. You may wish to duplicate the Conferencing Log on page T76 to help you keep records of conferences with your students.

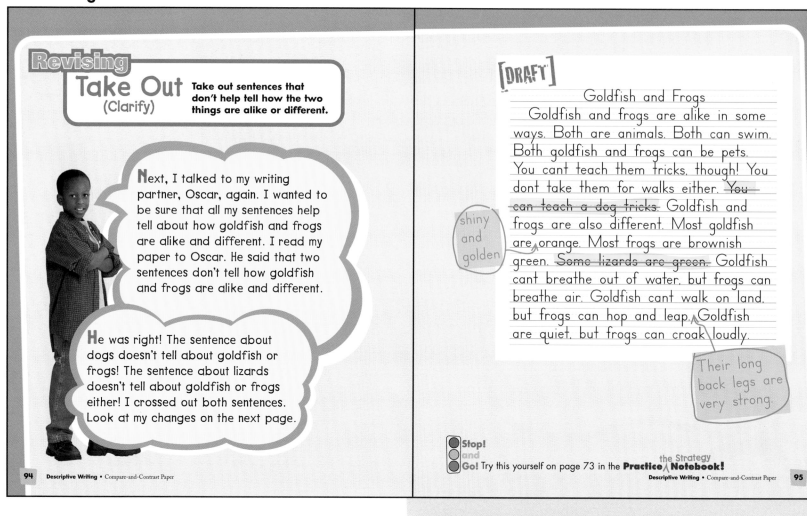

## Revising Take Out (Clarify)

**Strategy: Take out sentences that don't help tell how the two things are alike or different.**

*(Student Pages 94–95)*

Read Calvin's words on Student Page 94 with the students. Explain that another kind of revising is taking out sentences that don't tell about the subjects. Read Calvin's revised draft on Student Page 95 with the students. Point out that Calvin took out the sentence "You can teach a dog tricks" because it doesn't help tell how goldfish and frogs are alike and different. Ask students why. [**Response: It doesn't tell about goldfish or frogs.**] Repeat with "Some lizards are green."

**Note:** *Strategies for Writers* employs the term **Clarify** in grades 3–8. You may wish to explain to students that *clarify* means "to make clear," usually by taking out what's unnecessary.

## Spelling Strategies:
### Check the Dictionary

Before students begin the Editing portion of the chapter, you may wish to remind them that checking spelling is an important part of editing their writing. Encourage students to use several strategies to figure out the spellings of new words and words of which they are unsure. One strategy is to **check the dictionary**. Review how to use the dictionary to check spelling.

### the Strategy
### Practice the Notebook!

*Practice the Strategy Notebook* page 73 provides additional practice in revising a draft by taking out ideas that stray from the topic. After students have completed this activity, remind them to use this strategy to revise their own compare-and-contrast paper.

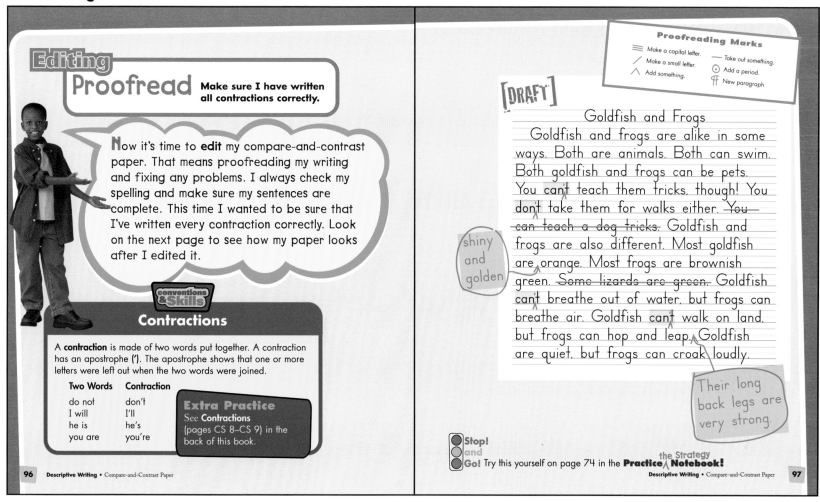

# Editing Proofread

**Strategy: Make sure I have written all contractions correctly.**

*(Student Pages 96–97)*

Remind students that editing is different from revising. When writers revise, they add missing information and they take out unnecessary information. When writers edit, they fix grammar and spelling mistakes. Remind students that to *proofread* means to read their writing while looking for mistakes.

Read Calvin's words on Student Page 96 to the students. Remind students that Calvin always checks his spelling and makes sure his sentences are complete. Tell students that Calvin is now going to fix any mistakes he made in writing contractions. Remind students that using a different color pencil to correct mistakes helps writers see their changes more easily. (**Note:** You may wish to give students colored pencils to edit their writing.) Read the explanation and examples of contractions at the bottom of Student Page 96 with the students.

Point out the proofreading symbols chart on Student Page 97 to the students. Explain that these symbols help writers remember what kind of corrections they made, so they can include those corrections when they write their final copy. Read Calvin's edited draft with the students. Ask them if Calvin made all the necessary corrections. You may wish to use the corresponding Writing Model for Proofreading Practice Transparency.

## Extra Practice: Conventions & Skills Student Edition

If your students need more practice in writing contractions correctly, you may wish to assign Student Pages CS 8–CS 9.

## Conventions & Skills Practice

For more targeted practice related to this skill, see this lesson in the optional *Conventions & Skills Practice Book*:

Lesson 46: Contractions

## Practice the Strategy Notebook!

*Practice the Strategy Notebook* pages 74–75 provide additional practice in editing a draft by correcting errors in contractions. After students have completed this activity, remind them to use this strategy to edit their own compare-and-contrast paper.

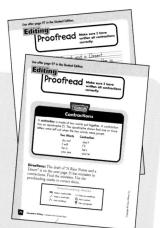

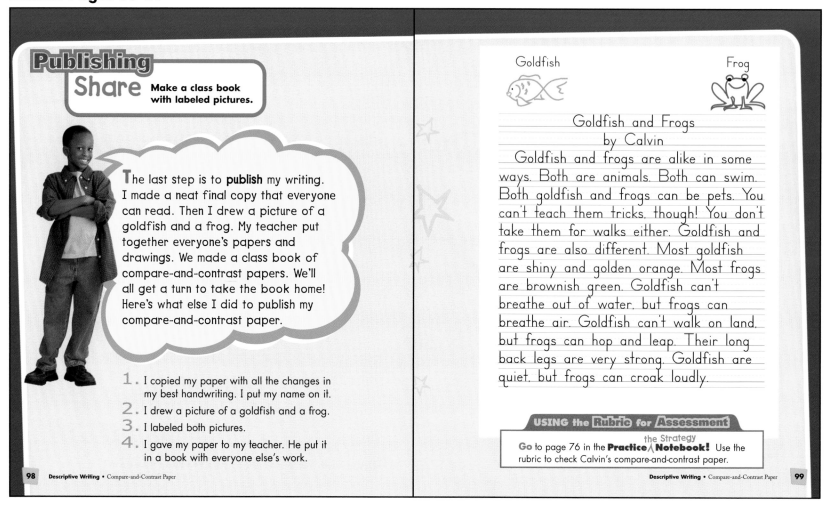

## Publishing Share

**Strategy: Make a class book with labeled pictures.**

*(Student Pages 98–99)*

Read Calvin's words on Student Page 98 to the students. Explain that publishing is the process of finishing a piece of writing to share it with others. Once writers revise and edit their writing, they may publish it. They make a final copy of their writing, being sure to include all their changes.

Remind students that there are many ways to share published writing. Calvin drew pictures of his two subjects and labeled them. His teacher put together everyone's compare-and-contrast paper and drawings in a class book. Tell the students that Calvin might have published his paper in other ways, as well. Other publishing strategies for a compare-and-contrast paper include posting the paper on a class bulletin board, posting the paper on the school's Web site, and using everyone's papers to create a class magazine. Read the final copy of Calvin's paper on Student Page 99 with the students.

Encourage students to talk with a partner about how Calvin shared his compare-and-contrast paper. Was it a good way to share writing? How else could Calvin have shared his description?

## Using a Rubric

*Practice the Strategy Notebook* pages 76–77 provide a rubric to use for assessing Calvin's final compare-and-contrast paper. Encourage students to work with a partner to evaluate Calvin's paper by using this rubric. After students have completed this activity, you may wish to have them share the results in a large-group activity.

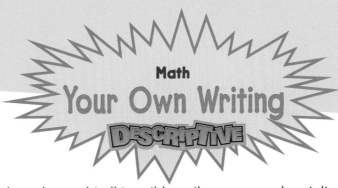

**Math**
## Your Own Writing
### DESCRIPTIVE

Use what you learned in this unit to write your own descriptive paper, compare-and-contrast paper, or both! Choose one or more of these ideas.

- Use **Your Own Writing** pages in the *Practice the Strategy Notebook*.
- Pick a topic below, and write something new.
- Choose another idea of your own.

Follow the steps in the writing process. Use the Descriptive Paper Rubric on pages 58–59 in the *Practice the Strategy Notebook* or the Compare-and-Contrast Paper Rubric on pages 76–77 in the *Practice the Strategy Notebook* to check your writing.

| Descriptive Paper | Compare-and-Contrast Paper |
|---|---|
| • an alarm clock | • a penny and a quarter |
| • a lunch-size bag of your favorite snack (count the items, too) | • a square and a triangle |
| • an orange | • a ruler and a yardstick |
| • a yo-yo | • a bar graph and a pie chart |

portfolio  School–Home Connection

Keep a writing folder. Add **Your Own Writing** pages to your writing folder. You may want to take your writing folder home to share.

**100** Descriptive Writing

## Your Own Writing
### Descriptive Writing for Math

Assign either one or both kinds of descriptive writing to the students. Before they begin writing, review key information about each kind. Decide which of the following you wish students to do:

- Choose a topic on this page in the Student Edition.
- Complete one of the Your Own Writing pieces in the *Practice the Strategy Notebook*.
- Come up with a new idea.

## Portfolio/School-Home Connection

Encourage the students to keep a portfolio of their writing. You may also wish to copy and distribute the School-Home Letter included in this unit.

### Work-in-Progress Portfolio

Remind students to review this portfolio often to revise existing pieces that have not been published. Encourage students to share pieces of their Work-in-Progress Portfolio with family members who can help in editing.

### Published Portfolio

Encourage students to choose pieces from their Published Portfolio to share with family members.

# Conferencing Log

Project

| Student's Name | Gather Ideas and Organize Date(s) | Write Date(s) | Revise Date(s) | Edit Date(s) | Publish Date(s) |
|---|---|---|---|---|---|
| | | | | | |
| | | | | | |
| | | | | | |
| | | | | | |
| | | | | | |
| | | | | | |
| | | | | | |
| | | | | | |
| | | | | | |
| | | | | | |

You may wish to copy this Conferencing Log and use it to keep records of your students' progress.
See Tips for Successful Conferencing on page T71 for more information.

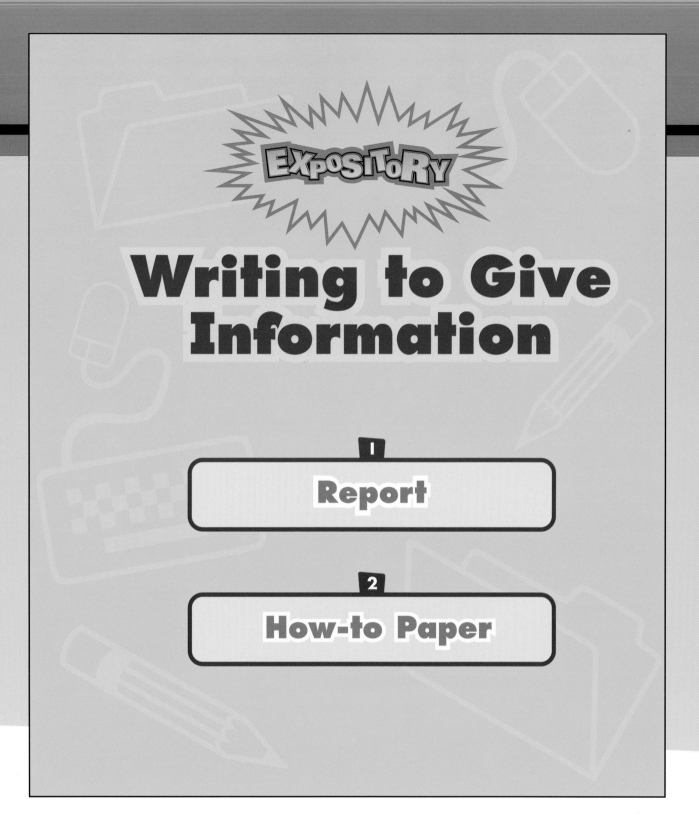

**EXPOSITORY**

# Writing to Give Information

**1** Report

**2** How-to Paper

## Defining Writing To Give Information

Ask the students which of the following are likely to give information:

- a report on bees
- a poem about clouds
- instructions for flying a kite

Explain that a report on bees and instructions for flying a kite are examples of writing that gives information.

Read Student Page 101 with the students. Tell them that the next two chapters of their book will be about writing that gives information. Explain that they will learn the steps for writing a report and a how-to paper.

## Books to Share With Students

For excellent examples of expository writing, you may wish to share these books with your students:

- *Ice Cream* by Elisha Cooper
- *Growing Up Wild: Penguins* by Sandra Markle
- *They Called Her Molly Pitcher* by Anne F. Rockwell
- *Escape North! The Story of Harriet Tubman* by Monica Kulling

You may also wish to use some of the titles from Zaner-Bloser Literacy.

## Tips for the Writing Classroom
by Barry Sneed, *Master Teacher*

### The Writing Process

Teaching children to remember the steps and terminology of the writing process in the primary grades was something I found difficult as a new teacher. It was easy to display a chart with the steps and talk about each one, but the concept never "stuck" with my students beyond the lesson at hand.

I decided two things:

1. I needed to devise a method by which students could learn the steps in a creative, developmentally appropriate way.

2. I needed to put the process to work on a regular basis, not just refer to it on a chart.

I achieved the first goal by turning the writing process into a song that children can sing and dance. Each step of the process became a verse containing lyrics and motions unique to that step. Singing the song whenever we took on a writing task made the steps of the writing process easy for

## Report
## Writing Strategies

### Prewriting

**Gather Ideas**
Write two questions I want to answer about my topic. Take notes.

**Organize**
Make a web for each of my questions.

### Drafting

**Write**
Use my webs. Write sentences to tell about my topic.

### Revising

**Add (Elaborate)**
Add facts about my topic.

**Take Out (Clarify)**
Take out sentences that don't tell about my topic.

### Editing

**Proofread**
Make sure I have written plural nouns correctly.

### Publishing

**Share**
Write my report as an article to add to our class encyclopedia.

**Note:** A blackline master of the writing process flow chart appears on page T106. You may wish to copy and distribute it to your students.

**MODELED WRITING**

**Report Writing Mini-Lesson:** You may wish to present the following mini-lesson before the students read the model on Student Page 103. Write the following on the board, chart paper, or an overhead transparency:

> Dogs are more than pets. Some dogs work. They herd animals on farms. They work as guide dogs. Some dogs help the police. Other dogs help people get better. They visit people in care centers. They help people who are sad and lonely. Cats are good only as pets.

Ask the students what the sentences on the board tell them. [Possible response: They tell what dogs can do.] Explain that this kind of writing is a report. It gives facts about a topic. Tell students they will be learning more about how to write a report as they read the chapter in the Student Edition. They will see a model of this kind of writing and learn and practice some strategies for writing their own reports. Write the title "Dogs" above the sentences.

Ask the students whether there are any sentences in the report that don't tell about dogs. [Response: Yes, the last sentence doesn't tell about dogs.] Cross out the last sentence. Explain to students that when they write their own report, they will also cross out any sentences that don't tell about their topic.

students to recall. You will find that song, "The Writing Process Hokey Pokey," on the *Strategies for Writers Sing-Along* CD. (The lyrics for "The Writing Process Hokey Pokey" and other songs on the CD appear in the Appendix in the back of this Teacher Edition.)

The second goal, putting the process to use, can be achieved in several ways. I suggest reviewing the writing process along with the simple letter-writing format early in the school year. Students can write letters to Dad and/or Mom, grandparents or relatives, elderly people in the community, and so on, using the writing process. Students can gather ideas, create drafts, revise, edit, and make final copies. Whenever it's

possible and appropriate, mail the letters to the intended recipients. This introduction to the writing process relates in a meaningful way to the students' skills and interests.

Throughout the year, engage in the writing process (and the song) when writing letters to pen pals, writing stories to publish in the room, or writing items to be displayed in the hallway. Our reason for engaging in the writing process—as opposed to jotting ideas or notes—is that the process is most helpful when creating any writing that we intend others to read. This demonstrates to students that the entire process is not necessary for such things as journal entries, lists, and notes.

## Time Management for This Chapter*

| Session | | Session | | Session | |
|---------|--|---------|--|---------|--|
| **1** | Introduce Emily and read Student Page 102. Read the model on Student Page 103. Discuss the report rubric on Student Pages 104–105. | **6** | Assign *Practice the Strategy Notebook* pages 82–85. | **11** | Read **REVISING: Take Out (Clarify)** (Student Pages 118–119). |
| **2** | Read Student Pages 106–108. Discuss Emily's assessment of the model report. Discuss the information about Emily on Student Page 109. | **7** | Read **DRAFTING: Write** (Student Pages 114–115). | **12** | Assign *Practice the Strategy Notebook* page 91. |
| **3** | Read **PREWRITING: Gather Ideas** (Student Pages 110–111). | **8** | Assign *Practice the Strategy Notebook* pages 86–89. | **13** | Read **EDITING: Proofread** (Student Pages 120–121). |
| **4** | Assign *Practice the Strategy Notebook* pages 78–81. | **9** | Read **REVISING: Add (Elaborate)** (Student Pages 116–117). | **14** | Assign *Practice the Strategy Notebook* pages 92–93. |
| **5** | Read **PREWRITING: Organize** (Student Pages 112–113). | **10** | Assign *Practice the Strategy Notebook* page 90. | **15** | Read **PUBLISHING: Share** (Student Pages 122–123). Assign *Practice the Strategy Notebook* pages 94–95. |

\* To complete the chapter in fewer sessions, assign *Practice the Strategy Notebook* pages on the same day each strategy is introduced.

## STRATEGIES for Writers Sing-Along CD

You may wish to use the *Strategies for Writers Sing-Along* CD throughout the chapter. See the Appendix in the back of this Teacher Edition for more information.

## WRITER'S HANDBOOK

Remind students that they can refer to the Writer's Handbook in the back of the Student Edition for more information.

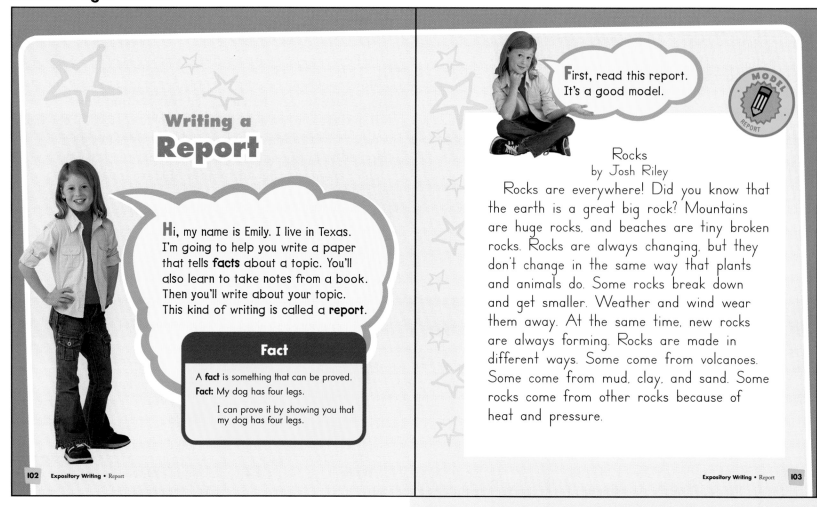

## Introduce the Genre:
### Report

*(Student Pages 102–103)*

Read Student Page 102 with the students. Go over the meaning of the term *fact*. Explain that the student guide in their books is going to show them how to write a report that explains something by using facts. Tell them that they will read Emily's work as a class. They will have a chance to talk about it with a partner and with the whole class. They will practice using the same strategies to write their own reports. Ask the students to think of topics for a report that uses facts, or true information, they could find in books. [Possible responses: bicycles, giraffes, planets, stars, flowers]

## Read the Model:
### Report

Read Emily's words on Student Page 103 with the students. Then read the model of the report. Ask what makes it a good example of a report. [Possible response: It tells many facts about rocks.] As you read the model with the students, point out that the model contains words that they may not know. You may wish to add these words to your Word Wall and encourage students to refer to the Word Wall as they proofread their own reports for spelling.

## Meeting Students' Needs:
### Second-Language Learners

Students may need help with the pronunciation or meaning of the words *huge, volcanoes,* and *pressure*. For students with a limited English vocabulary, some of the processes of change can be drawn, both by showing rock breaking down and by showing it forming.

### Students Who Need Extra Help

Read the first sentence of the report aloud to students. Ask them to name the topic of the report. Also ask them what they think they will learn in the report. Then ask students to read the report and to take at least one note on what they learn. Afterward, invite volunteers to talk about what they learned.

### Gifted Students

Gifted students may wish to come up with one or more ways to make the model report better. They might suggest a fact or idea to add. They might also suggest a way to change the wording or order of words or sentences.

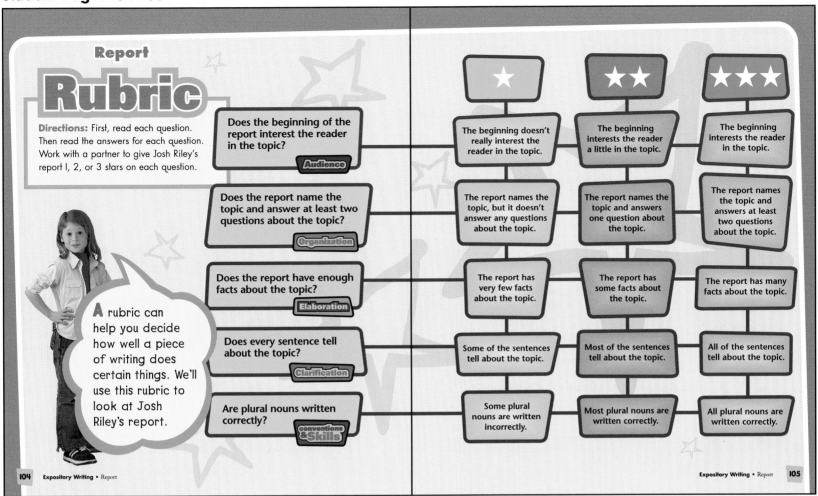

## Using a Rubric

Use the text on Student Pages 106–108 to model the use of a rubric for evaluating a piece of writing. For more information on using a rubric, please see page T21.

### Discuss the Report Writing Rubric

*(Student Pages 104–105)*

Read the questions on Student Page 104 with the students. Explain that writers use these questions to write a good report. Discuss each question with the students.

**Audience: Does the beginning of the report interest the reader in the topic?** A good first sentence will help interest readers in the topic.

**Organization: Does the report name the topic and answer at least two questions about the topic?** The reader needs to know what the topic is in order to understand the facts that explain it. Answers to questions about the topic explain the topic to the reader.

**Elaboration: Does the report have enough facts about the topic?** Facts are the most important part of a report. They present and explain the topic.

**Clarification: Does every sentence tell about the topic?** The report should not have sentences that are off the topic.

**Conventions & Skills: Are plural nouns written correctly?** Correct grammar makes writing clear and easy to follow.

Have students evaluate the model report with a partner, using the report rubric on Student Pages 104–105. Ask partners to share their evaluations with the whole group.

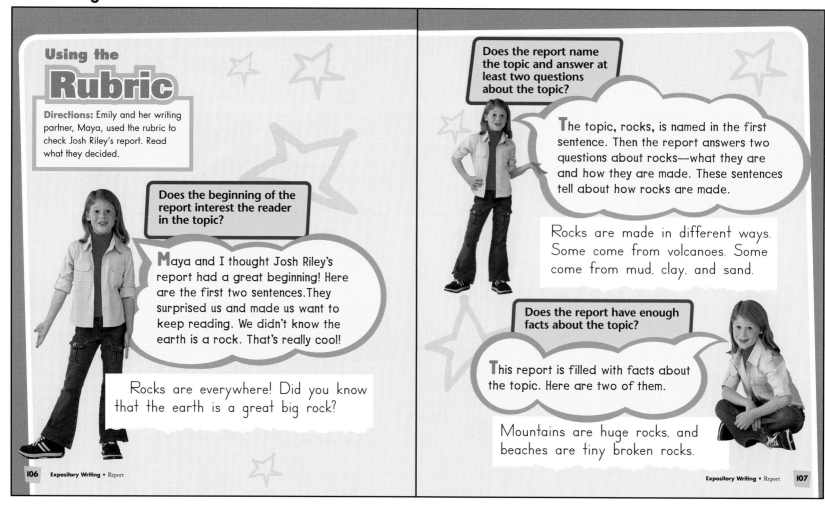

## Using the Rubric to Study the Model

*(Student Pages 106–108)*

Explain to students that now they can see how Emily is going to use the questions on the rubric to evaluate the report on Student Page 103.

Read Student Page 106 with the students. Ask the students whether they agree that the report begins in an interesting way. Read the example sentences and talk with students about how they create interest for the reader.

Read Student Page 107 with the students. Ask the students whether they agree that the report names the topic and answers two questions about the topic. Point out to students that the topic (rocks) appears in the first sentence of the report. Read the example sentences and discuss how they answer the question "How are rocks made?" Do students agree that the report has enough facts? Read the example sentences.

Finally, read Student Page 108 with the students. Ask students if they agree with Emily that all the sentences tell about the topic. Then remind students that writing plural nouns correctly makes it easier for readers to understand the report.

## When and How to Share Rubric Information With Parents

by Lee Bromberger, *Assessment Specialist*

While you have many opportunities to introduce, explain, illustrate, and apply rubrics with your students, opportunities to share rubrics with parents may not be as plentiful. Therefore, you will want to develop some ways to communicate the role rubrics play in developing and evaluating student writing. Opportunities to share rubric information with parents include the following:

**Beginning of the Year/Introductory Materials** Copies of class rubrics in the class materials sent home allow parents to review rubric standards at their leisure. You may wish to attach a brief summary of the rubric's usefulness, as well as a description as to how the rubric will be used in class.

**Open House** The open house forum allows teachers the opportunity to highlight various rubrics. One practical method to direct attention to a rubric would be to display an enlarged rubric on a classroom wall.

**Parent-Teacher Conference** The rubric can function as an effective tool during the parent-teacher conference when teachers review a writing sample with the parent(s), explaining how the rubric provides an accurate picture of the assignment's strengths and/or weaknesses.

## Working With a Partner Mini-lesson:
### Ask Questions

Help students understand how to work with a partner effectively by giving them some basic tips. You may wish to write the tips on chart paper and display them where students can readily see them.

Explain to the students that they can help each other by **asking questions** like these:

- What are you trying to say here?
- Do you think you need to tell more about this?
- Does this sound right to you?

Tell students that they don't always have to get an answer to a question. The writer might need time to think about the question before making any changes. You may wish to give students a copy of the Working With a Partner Checklist on page T166.

**Model the Tip** You may wish to model asking questions by acting out a conference with a student volunteer or a parent volunteer. Read your paper aloud. Have the volunteer "partner" ask two of the questions above. Answer one question and say that you'll think about the other. Remind the students that it's important to listen carefully when their partner asks questions and to think about the answers.

## Emily:
### Writer of a Report

*(Student Page 109)*

Read the information about Emily to learn more about her. Be sure students understand that Emily will write her own report in this chapter. Review the information given about her. Discuss what Emily might write about in her report based on her interests and hobbies.

Point out that Emily will go through the steps in the writing process (Prewriting, Drafting, Revising, Editing, and Publishing). At each stage, she will use a good writing strategy and explain how she used it. Students should watch for key words, including **Gather, Organize, Write, Add (Elaborate), Take Out (Clarify), Proofread,** and **Share,** to follow the strategies Emily uses as she goes through the writing process.

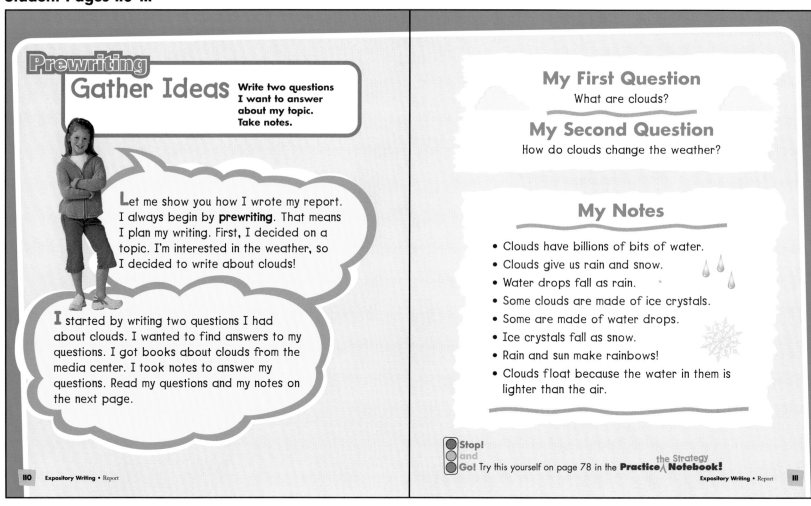

## Prewriting Gather Ideas

**Strategy: Write two questions I want to answer about my topic. Take notes.**

*(Student Pages 110–111)*

Read Emily's words on Student Page 110 aloud. Explain to the students that in this section Emily tells how she went about writing her report. She starts by explaining how she chose her topic and how she got started on her prewriting. Ask the students to retell what Emily did. [**Possible responses: She thought of a topic that she was interested in. Then she wrote two questions about it. Then she got a book about the topic, so she could take notes to answer her own questions.**]

Point out Emily's two questions and her notes on Student Page 111. Ask students why it is a good idea to start out with questions and notes. [**Possible responses: The questions help you get started and tell you what to look for. The notes help you start writing down facts about your topic.**]

### the Strategy
### Practice Notebook!

*Practice the Strategy Notebook* pages 78–79 provide practice in choosing a topic for a report and identifying notes that answer one writer's questions about a topic. After students have completed this activity, you may wish to have them share their responses.

### the Strategy
### Practice Notebook!    Your Own Writing

*Practice the Strategy Notebook* pages 80–81 provide an opportunity for students to choose a topic, write questions, and take notes for their own report. You may wish to assign these pages now or after students have completed this chapter in the Student Edition. You may wish to save students' *Your Own Writing* pages and add them to their Work-in-Progress Portfolios.

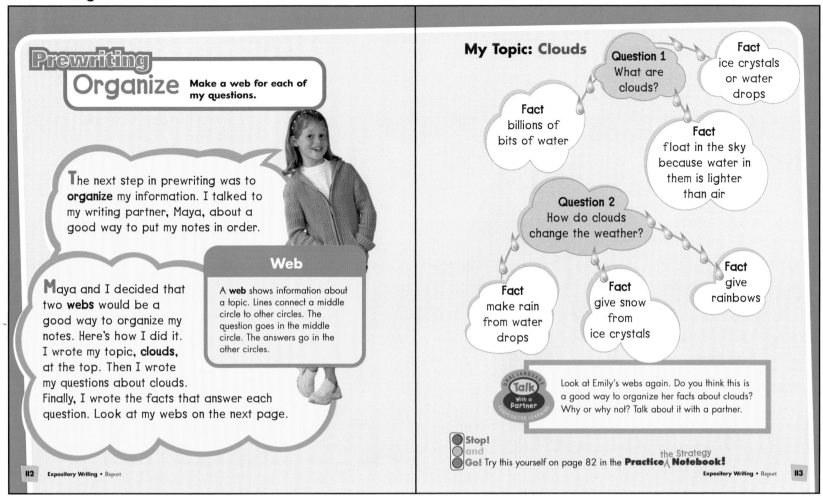

## Prewriting Organize — Make a web for each of my questions.

The next step in prewriting was to **organize** my information. I talked to my writing partner, Maya, about a good way to put my notes in order.

**Maya** and I decided that two **webs** would be a good way to organize my notes. Here's how I did it. I wrote my topic, **clouds,** at the top. Then I wrote my questions about clouds. Finally, I wrote the facts that answer each question. Look at my webs on the next page.

**Web**

A **web** shows information about a topic. Lines connect a middle circle to other circles. The question goes in the middle circle. The answers go in the other circles.

**My Topic: Clouds**

**Question 1** What are clouds?

**Fact** ice crystals or water drops

**Fact** billions of bits of water

**Fact** float in the sky because water in them is lighter than air

**Question 2** How do clouds change the weather?

**Fact** make rain from water drops

**Fact** give snow from ice crystals

**Fact** give rainbows

**Talk With a Partner** ORAL LANGUAGE • COOPERATIVE LEARNING

Look at Emily's webs again. Do you think this is a good way to organize her facts about clouds? Why or why not? Talk about it with a partner.

**Stop! and Go!** Try this yourself on page 82 in the **Practice the Strategy Notebook!**

Expository Writing • Report  112

Expository Writing • Report  113

---

## Prewriting Organize

**Strategy: Make a web for each of my questions.**

*(Student Pages 112–113)*

Read aloud the definition of the term *web* on Student Page 112 and discuss it with the students. Then read Emily's words with the students. Explain that before Emily begins her draft, she needs to organize her information. She does this by making a web for each of her questions. Also discuss with students why it's a good idea to talk to a writing partner. [Possible responses: A writing partner can give you new ideas for writing. A writing partner can help you put your ideas into a web.]

Direct students' attention to Emily's webs on Student Page 113. Explain that a web is a good way to organize information for a report because the web makes everything clear: the topic, the questions, and the facts that are answers to the questions.

**Talk With a Partner** ORAL LANGUAGE • COOPERATIVE LEARNING

Encourage the students to discuss Emily's webs with their partners. Ask the students if Emily's webs seem complete. You may wish to discuss the partners' findings as a large-group activity, as well.

**Note:** A web transparency is provided in the *Strategies for Writers Transparencies.*

### Practice the Strategy Notebook!

*Practice the Strategy Notebook* pages 82–83 provide additional practice in understanding how webs can be used to organize ideas for a report. After students have completed this activity, you may wish to have writing partners share their webs with each other or in a large-group activity.

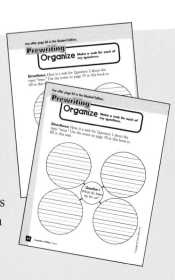

### Practice the Strategy Notebook! Your Own Writing

*Practice the Strategy Notebook* pages 84–85 provide an opportunity for students to create webs for their own report. You may wish to assign these pages now or after students have completed this chapter in the Student Edition.

**Expository Writing • Report**

**Drafting**
**Write** Use my webs. Write sentences to tell about my topic.

Now I was ready to **draft**, or write, my report. My webs helped me organize my ideas and write my draft. I used my webs to write sentences to tell about my topic. First, I wrote sentences that answered my first question. Then, I wrote sentences that answered my second question.

I didn't worry too much about making mistakes this time. I can fix them later. Read my draft on the next page.

[DRAFT]

Clouds

Clouds are made of billion of tiny water drop's. Clouds can also be made of ice crystal. The water drop's or the ice crystal make a mist. We see that mist as clouds. You can hear thunder before a storm. The drop's and crystal float because they are lighter than air. Clouds give us rain and snow. Snow is great if you like to go sledding! Both rain and snow start out as ice crystal. Some ice crystal fall as snow. Other ice crystal become water drops. They fall as rain. Clouds also give us rainbowes.

**Talk With a Partner** ORAL LANGUAGE COOPERATIVE LEARNING

Talk about Emily's draft with a partner. Do you think her sentences answer her questions about the topic? Tell why or why not.

**Stop! and Go!** Try this yourself on page 86 in the **Practice the Strategy Notebook!**

114 Expository Writing • Report

115 Expository Writing • Report

---

**Drafting** Write

**Strategy: Use my webs. Write sentences to tell about my topic.**

*(Student Pages 114–115)*

Review the term *draft* with students. Remind them that a draft is a first try at writing the whole paper. In a draft, writers don't worry too much about mistakes. The important thing is to get ideas down on paper. Writers know they will have a chance to go back and fix any problems later. Read Emily's draft on Student Page 115 with the students.

After reading the draft, read Emily's words on Student Page 114. Be sure students understand that it's important to name the topic right at the beginning of the report. Ask the students their opinions about how Emily began her report. Did she tell the topic at the beginning? Did she answer her two questions about her topic?

**Talk With a Partner** ORAL LANGUAGE COOPERATIVE LEARNING

Encourage the students to discuss Emily's draft. Ask the partners to decide whether they think Emily answered the questions about her topic.

**the Strategy Practice Notebook!**

*Practice the Strategy Notebook* pages 86–87 provide students with an opportunity to use the webs they filled in on pages 82–83 to write sentences for a draft of a report about trees. After students have completed this activity, you may wish to have them read their sentences with a partner or share their sentences in a large-group activity.

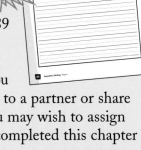

**the Strategy Practice Notebook!** Your Own Writing

*Practice the Strategy Notebook* pages 88–89 provide an opportunity for students to write a draft of their own report. After students have completed this activity, you may wish to have them read their drafts to a partner or share their drafts in a large-group activity. You may wish to assign these pages now or after students have completed this chapter in the Student Edition.

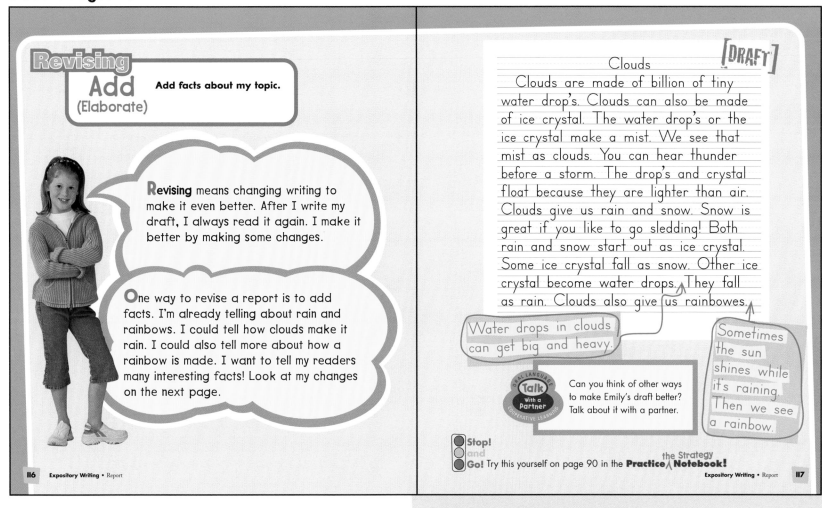

**Revising Add (Elaborate)**

Add facts about my topic.

**R**evising means changing writing to make it even better. After I write my draft, I always read it again. I make it better by making some changes.

**O**ne way to revise a report is to add facts. I'm already telling about rain and rainbows. I could tell how clouds make it rain. I could also tell more about how a rainbow is made. I want to tell my readers many interesting facts! Look at my changes on the next page.

---

[DRAFT]

Clouds

Clouds are made of billion of tiny water drop's. Clouds can also be made of ice crystal. The water drop's or the ice crystal make a mist. We see that mist as clouds. You can hear thunder before a storm. The drop's and crystal float because they are lighter than air. Clouds give us rain and snow. Snow is great if you like to go sledding! Both rain and snow start out as ice crystal. Some ice crystal fall as snow. Other ice crystal become water drops. They fall as rain. Clouds also give us rainbowes.

Water drops in clouds can get big and heavy.

Sometimes the sun shines while it's raining. Then we see a rainbow.

**Talk** With a Partner — Can you think of other ways to make Emily's draft better? Talk about it with a partner.

🔴🟡🟢 **Stop! and Go!** Try this yourself on page 90 in the **Practice the Strategy Notebook!**

---

# Revising Add (Elaborate)

**Strategy: Add facts about my topic.**

*(Student Pages 116–117)*

Remind the students of the definition of the term *fact*. Then read Emily's words on Student Page 116 with the students. Remind students why a writing partner is a good idea. Review the term *revise* with students. Explain that when writers revise their work, they change what they say or how they say it. Explain that one way to revise a report is to add more facts about the topic.

**Note:** *Strategies for Writers* employs the term **Elaborate** in grades 3–8. You may wish to explain to students that *elaborate* means "to add."

Read Emily's revised draft on Student Page 117 with the students. Ask students how Emily's revisions have made her report better. [**Possible response: The new facts make the report better because they explain why rain falls from clouds and how clouds help make rainbows.**]

**Talk** With a Partner — Encourage students to talk with a partner about Emily's revisions. Did the changes make her report better? What other facts could Emily have added?

---

## Spelling Strategies:
### Ask a Friend

Before students begin the Editing portion of the chapter, you may wish to remind them that checking spelling is an important part of editing their writing. Encourage students to use several strategies to figure out the spelling of new words and words about which they are unsure. One strategy is to **ask a friend**. Students can benefit from giving and receiving help as they work cooperatively. Remind the students that they can also work with other students to figure out the spelling of unfamiliar words by sounding them out, looking on the Word Wall, or using another spelling strategy.

**Practice the Strategy Notebook!**

*Practice the Strategy Notebook* page 90 provides more practice in revising a draft by adding facts. After students have completed this activity, remind them to use this strategy to revise their own report.

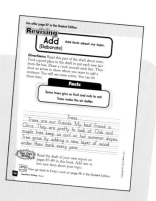

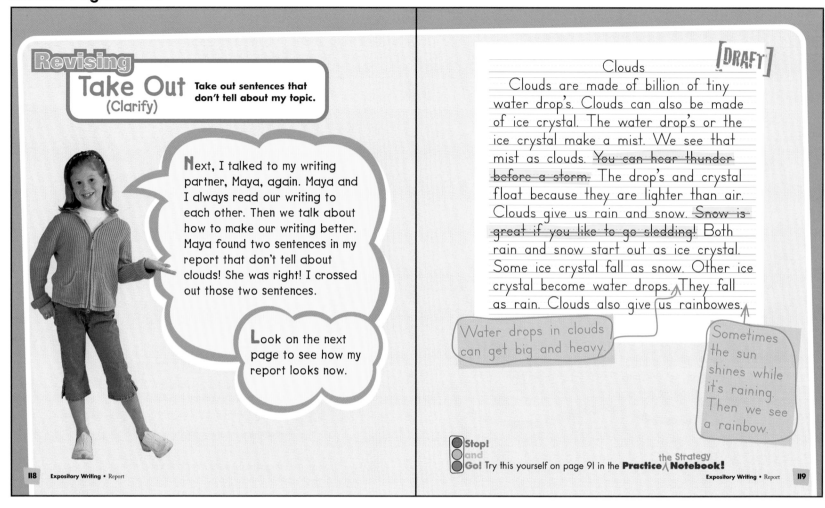

## Revising Take Out (Clarify)

**Strategy: Take out sentences that don't tell about my topic.**

*(Student Pages 118–119)*

Read Emily's words on Student Page 118 with the students. Explain that another kind of revising is taking out sentences that don't tell about the topic. Read Emily's revised draft on Student Page 119 with the students. Point out that Emily took out the sentence "You can hear thunder before a storm." Ask students why. **[Response: The sentence doesn't tell about clouds.]** Ask students which other sentence Emily crossed out. **[Response: "Snow is great if you like to go sledding!"]** Again ask students why. **[Response: This sentence doesn't tell about clouds either.] Note:** *Strategies for Writers* employs the term **Clarify** in grades 3–8. You may wish to explain to students that *clarify* means "to make clear," usually by taking out what's unnecessary.

## Tips for Successful Conferencing: Taking Notes

Second graders may not have taken notes before. Note taking is a skill you might help students with while conferencing. Ask students to show you both their notes and the book they used. Then, make comments like the following, depending on the quality of the student's work.

• These are excellent notes! I see you found facts that answer your questions. You also did not copy the author's exact words. That's great.

• You've made a great start. These are good facts for your report. Now, put the notes in your own words.

• It's hard to take notes, isn't it? Let me show you how I would take notes on these pages. (Model the process of taking notes. Next, give the student an opportunity to take a note, and congratulate him or her on any good note-taking strategies used.)

### the Strategy Practice Notebook!

*Practice the Strategy Notebook* page 91 provides additional practice in revising a draft by taking out sentences that don't tell about the topic. After students have completed this activity, remind them to use this strategy to revise their own report.

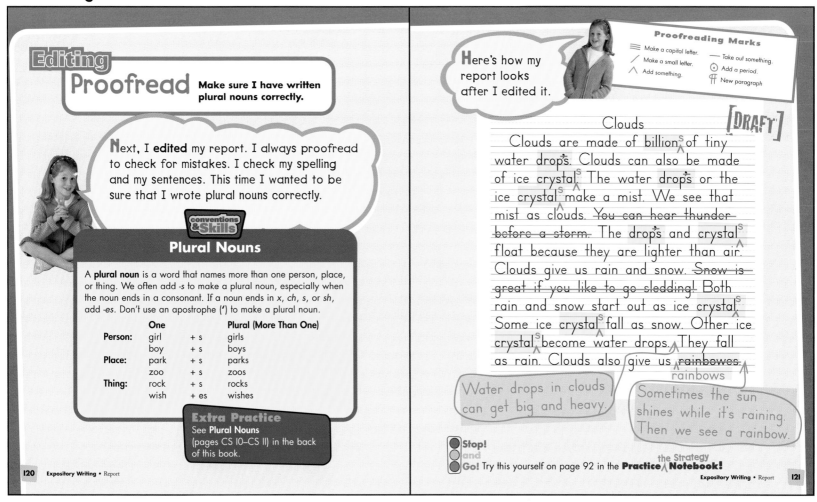

# Editing Proofread

**Strategy: Make sure I have written plural nouns correctly.**

*(Student Pages 120–121)*

Remind students that when writers edit, they fix any problems in spelling, capitalization, punctuation, and grammar. Remind students that to *proofread* means to read their writing while looking for mistakes.

Read Emily's words on Student Page 120 with the students. Remind students that Emily always checks her spelling and makes sure her sentences are complete. Tell students that Emily is now going to fix any mistakes in plural nouns. Remind students that using a pencil that writes in a different color to correct mistakes helps writers see their corrections more easily so that they can be sure to include them when they write their final copy. (**Note:** You may wish to give students their own colored pencils to edit their writing.) Read the explanation and examples of plural nouns at the bottom of Student Page 120 with the students.

Point out the proofreading marks chart on Student Page 121 to the students. Explain that these symbols help writers remember what kinds of corrections they made so they can include those corrections when they write their final copy. You may wish to give students a copy of the Proofreading Marks black line master on page T136. Read Emily's edited draft

with the students. Ask them if Emily made all the necessary corrections. You may wish to use the corresponding Writing Model for Proofreading Practice Transparency.

## Extra Practice: Conventions & Skills

### Student Edition

If your students need more practice writing regular plural nouns, you may wish to assign Student Pages CS 10–CS 11.

## Conventions & Skills Practice

For more targeted practice related to this skill, see these lessons in the optional *Conventions & Skills Practice Book*:

Lesson 11: Nouns

Lesson 14: Singular and Plural Nouns

### the Strategy
### Practice ∧ Notebook!

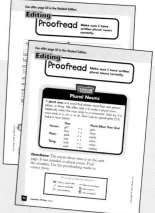

*Practice the Strategy Notebook* pages 92–93 provide additional practice in editing a draft by correcting errors in regular plural nouns. After students have completed this activity, remind them to use this strategy to edit their own report.

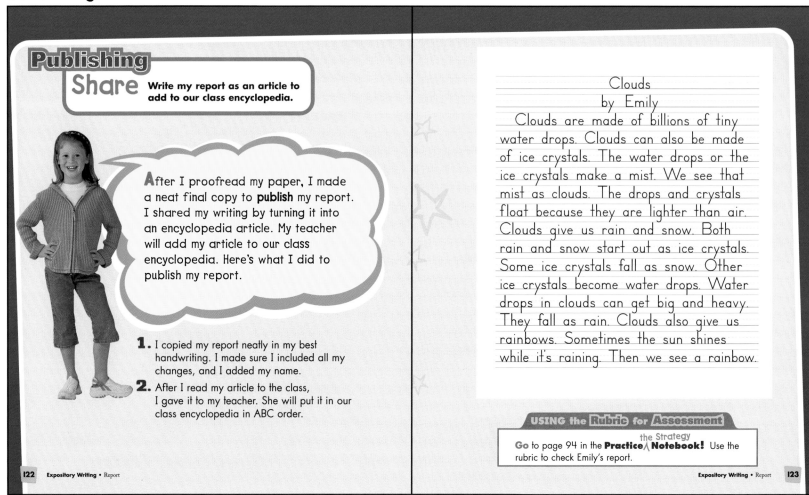

**Publishing** **Share**

**Strategy: Write my report as an article to add to our class encyclopedia.**

*(Student Pages 122–123)*

Read Emily's words on Student Page 122 to the students. Explain that publishing is the process of finishing a piece of writing to share it with others. Once writers are finished revising and editing their writing, they may publish it. They make a final copy of their writing, being sure to include all their changes.

Remind students that there are many ways to share published writing. Emily turned her report into an article to add to a class encyclopedia. Ask the students why that might be a good idea. [Possible response: An encyclopedia could be very useful to the class. Students could use it to look up facts on many different topics.] Tell the students that there are other ways Emily could have published her report. Other publishing options include posting the report on the school's Web site, submitting the report to a children's magazine, or posting the report in the hallway as part of a class display.

Read the final copy of Emily's report on Student Page 123 with the students.

Encourage students to talk with a partner about how Emily shared her report. Was it a good way to share writing? How else could Emily have shared her report?

## Using a Rubric

*Practice the Strategy Notebook* pages 94–95 provide a rubric for assessing Emily's final report. Encourage students to work with a partner to evaluate Emily's report by using this rubric. After students have completed this activity, you may wish to have them share the results in a large-group activity.

## School–Home Connection

Dear Family,

In this program, your child will be learning and practicing five types of writing—Expository, Narrative, Descriptive, Persuasive, and Writing for a Test.

Expository writing is writing that explains or informs. It can be a report, a set of directions, or an essay. It can't be a fictional story or a persuasive letter. Your child will be learning and practicing two examples of expository writing—a report and a how-to paper.

Narrative writing is writing that tells a story. It can be an adventure story, a mystery, or a personal story. It can't be a set of instructions or a research report. Your child will be learning and practicing four examples of narrative writing—a personal narrative, a friendly letter, rewriting a Once Upon a Time Story, and rewriting a fable.

Descriptive writing paints pictures with words. It is meant to help the reader "see" what the writer is writing about. Descriptive writing can describe a person, place, event, or thing. Your child will be learning and practicing two examples of descriptive writing—a descriptive paper and a compare-and-contrast paper.

Persuasive writing is meant to convince the reader to agree with a writer's opinion. Sometimes, persuasive writing even calls for action on the reader's part. Persuasive writing includes advertising, letters to the editor, and some speeches. Persuasive writing is not meant to tell a story or entertain. Your child will be learning and practicing two examples of persuasive writing—a persuasive paper and a persuasive speech.

Writing to take a test is different from any other kind of writing. To write for a test, a writer needs a specific set of skills. Your child will be learning to work with the writing prompt and other skills to prepare him or her for writing for a test.

You may wish to copy the letter above and send it home with your students.

 **for the Writing Classroom**

by Barry Sneed, *Master Teacher*

## The *Real* Word

If our goal as educators is to produce engaging, meaningful lessons for students, then we must apply this goal toward making writing engaging and meaningful, as well. We need to instill in students the belief that writing is a way to communicate their thoughts to others, as well as a useful tool to organize and simplify their own learning. Below are two ideas for writing activities in the classroom that bring writing to life and give writing purpose in the day-to-day lives of your students.

**Pen Pals (Writing Buddies)** Having students write real letters to real pen pals is a great way to get young children excited about writing. This activity need not take money or the help of a large organization. It can be as simple as pairing up with another classroom in your own building or, better yet, a classroom in a neighboring district. Since most teachers know teachers in other districts, it is usually easy to set up

## How-to Paper

### Writing Strategies

**Publishing**

**Share**
Post my how-to paper on our school's Web site.

**Prewriting**

**Gather Ideas**
Think about what I know how to do. Pick something to write about.

**Organize**
Decide on the steps. Use an order chain to put the steps in the right order.

**Drafting**

**Write**
Use my order chain. Write sentences that tell the steps in correct order.

**Editing**

**Proofread**
Make sure I have used periods, question marks, and exclamation points correctly.

**Revising**

**Add (Elaborate)**
Add missing information so the reader can follow the steps.

**Take Out (Clarify)**
Take out anything that doesn't fit.

**Note:** A blackline master of the writing process flow chart appears on page T106. You may wish to copy and distribute it to your students.

**MODELED WRITING**

**"How-to Paper" Mini-Lesson:** You may wish to present the following mini-lesson before the students read the model on Student Page 125. Write the following sentences on the board, chart paper, or an overhead transparency:

> Put an egg in a pan with some water. Read a good book. Put the pan on the stove. Boil the egg in the water. Wait five minutes. Cool the egg in cold water.

Ask the students what the sentences on the board tell them. [Possible response: They are steps for making a boiled egg.] Explain that this is an example of a **how-to paper**. It tells the reader how to do something by following the steps from beginning to end.

Tell students they will be learning about writing a how-to paper as they read the chapter in the Student Edition. Write the title "How to Make a Boiled Egg" above the sentences.

Ask the students whether they think any of the sentences on the board don't fit. [Response: Yes, sentence #2 doesn't tell about making a boiled egg.] Cross out sentence #2. Explain that when they write how-to papers, students will be learning how to take out things that don't fit.

a pen pal situation between classrooms. Once the process of letter writing is established, the classes can exchange writings, drawings, a classroom video, and even students' pictures (with parental permission). The end of the school year may even provide an opportunity for the two classes to meet in person in the form of a "meet your pen pal party."

**Note-Taking Journals** Several times throughout the year, I have students gather up front by the board with their "lap desks" (these can be clipboards, individual chalkboards, etc.) and their note-taking journals. Students use these journals to take notes when I'm introducing a new unit, or to take notes on a given topic, e.g., animals. Later, we use the notes to review information from the unit of study. I model the note-taking method on the board and include little pictures that students can use in case they have difficulty rereading their notes later. The purpose of this activity is to demonstrate to students how to take and use notes for the real purpose of learning. Students love to do this, as I tell them that they are learning things that "college" students learn! Kids love to play grown-up, and this activity also helps them take pride in and ownership of their notebooks. They love taking their note-taking journals home to share their learning with their families, as well!

## Time Management for This Chapter*

| Session | | Session | | Session | |
|---|---|---|---|---|---|
| **1** | Read Student Page 124. Introduce Tai. Read the model on Student Page 125. Discuss the "how-to" writing rubric on Student Pages 126–127. | **6** | Assign *Practice the Strategy Notebook* pages 100–103. | **11** | Read **REVISING: Take Out (Clarify)** (Student Pages 140–141). |
| **2** | Read Student Pages 128–131. Discuss Tai's assessment of the paper. Discuss the information about Tai on page 131. | **7** | Read **DRAFTING: Write** (Student Pages 136–137). | **12** | Assign *Practice the Strategy Notebook* page 109. |
| **3** | Read **PREWRITING: Gather Ideas** (Student Pages 132-–133). | **8** | Assign *Practice the Strategy Notebook* pages 104–107. | **13** | Read **EDITING: Proofread** (Student Pages 142–143). |
| **4** | Assign *Practice the Strategy Notebook* pages 96–99. | **9** | Read **REVISING: Add (Elaborate)** (Student Pages 138–139). | **14** | Assign *Practice the Strategy Notebook* pages 110–111. |
| **5** | Read **PREWRITING: Organize** (Student Pages 134–135). | **10** | Assign *Practice the Strategy Notebook* page 108. | **15** | Read **PUBLISHING: Share** (Student Pages 144–145). Assign *Practice the Strategy Notebook* pages 112–113. |

\* To complete the chapter in fewer sessions, assign *Practice the Strategy Notebook* pages on the same day the targeted strategy is introduced.

**STRATEGIES for Writers Sing-Along CD**

You may wish to use the *Strategies for Writers Sing-Along* CD throughout the chapter. See the Appendix in the back of this Teacher Edition for more information.

### WRITER'S HANDBOOK

Remind students that they can refer to the Writer's Handbook in the back of the Student Edition for more information.

**Writing a How-to Paper**

Hi, my name is Tai. I live in Massachusetts. I'm going to help you write how to do something. You know how to do lots of things. I will help you share what you know with a reader. This kind of writing is called a **how-to paper**.

124  Expository Writing • How-to Paper

First, read this how-to paper. It's a good model.

How to Make a Piñata
by Leo Graber

Any party can be great if you have a piñata. I'll tell you how you can make one. Get a balloon and a newspaper. You will also need flour, water, paint, and scissors. First, blow up the balloon and tie it. Then, cut the newspaper into small strips. Now, mix the flour and water to make glue. Dip the paper strips in the glue and cover the balloon with them. Put two layers of newspaper on the balloon. Let the piñata dry. You can paint the piñata after it's dry. Cut a flap in the bottom. Take out the balloon. Finally, fill your piñata with candy and tape the flap closed. Now you're ready for a party!

Expository Writing • How-to Paper  125

# Introduce the Genre:
## How-to Paper

*(Student Pages 124–125)*

Read Tai's words with the students. Explain to them that he is going to show them how to write a paper that explains how to do something. Tell them that they will read Tai's work as a class. They will have a chance to talk about it with a partner. They will practice using the same strategies to write their own how-to papers.

# Read the Model:
## How-to Paper

Read Tai's words and the model of a how-to paper on Student Page 125 with the students. Ask what makes it a good example of a how-to paper. [Possible responses: It lists the steps in order. The steps are easy to understand.] As you read the model with the students, point out that the model contains words that students may not know. Work with the students to choose and add high-frequency words from the model to your room's Word Wall, if you currently use one.

# Meeting Students' Needs:
## Second-Language Learners

Pair second-language learners with English-speaking students. Explain that they will take turns explaining to each other how to do something. Tell the partners to use their first languages and pictures, symbols, hand gestures, or other tools to help. You may wish to call on volunteers to model explaining something to the entire class with the help of such aids.

## Students Who Need Extra Help

Students may benefit from having things explained to them in a variety of ways. Help these students by stating directions verbally, writing directions on a piece of paper or the board, or using symbols in place of some words. For kinesthetic learners, ask them to help you put together the instructions for the entire class by drawing pictures or doing some of the writing.

## Gifted Students

Challenge students who are exceeding your expectations by encouraging them to expand on their writing. For example, students may want to go beyond simply explaining a process to comparing two similar processes or contrasting two processes that are different from each other.

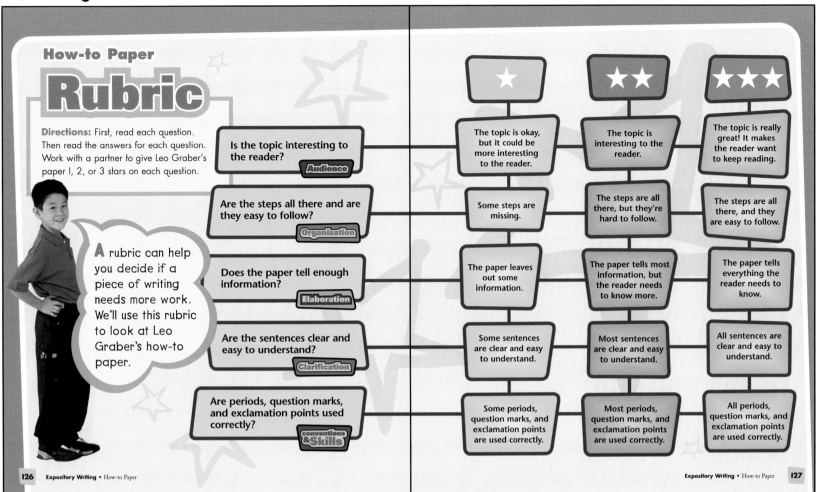

## Using a Rubric

*(Student Pages 126–127)*

Use the text on Student Pages 128–130 to model the use of a rubric for evaluating a piece of writing. For more information on using a rubric, please see page T21.

## Discuss the How-to Writing Rubric

*(Student Pages 126–127)*

Read the questions on Student Page 126 with the students. Explain that these questions are what writers use to write good how-to papers. Discuss each question with the students.

**Audience: Is the topic interesting to the reader?** The audience will want to read about how to do something that interests them.

**Organization: Are the steps all there and are they easy to follow?** It's important to give all the steps and make them easy to follow, so readers can understand them. If steps are left out or unclear, readers will become confused.

**Elaboration: Does the paper tell enough information?** If information is not all there, readers will not fully understand how to do what the paper is trying to explain.

**Clarification: Are the sentences clear and easy to understand?** If readers can't understand the writing because sentences are unclear or don't make sense, they won't learn anything from it.

**Conventions & Skills: Are periods, question marks, and exclamation points used correctly?** Correct end punctuation makes writing clear and easy to follow.

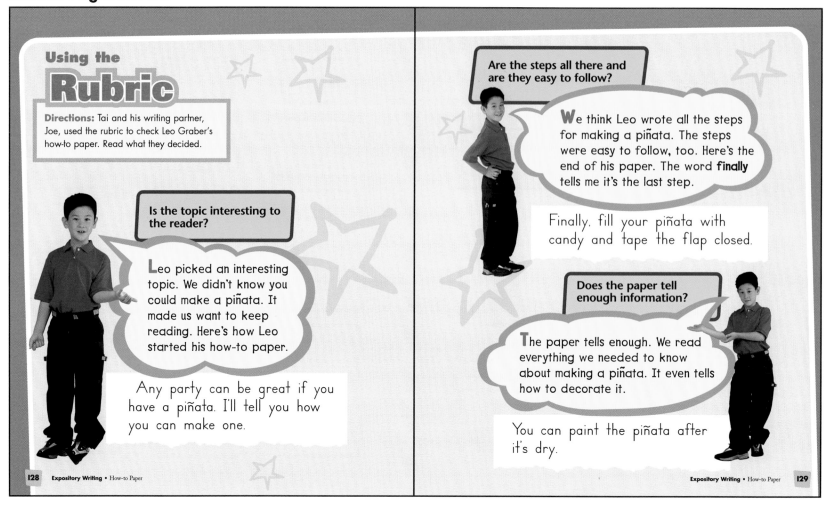

## Using the Rubric to Study the Model

*(Student Pages 128–130)*

Read Tai's words on Student Page 128. Ask the students whether they agree that "how to make a piñata" is an interesting topic. Ask the students whether they agree that it makes the reader want to keep reading. Read Student Page 129 with the students. Did the paper tell them all they needed to know to be able to make a piñata? Were they able to follow the steps? Point out to students the word *finally* in the model. Explain that this is a time-order word. Time-order words show the reader when things happen in the paper.

Read Student Page 130 with the students. Remind students that correct end punctuation makes it easier for the readers to understand their writing. Did the writer use correct end punctuation in his how-to paper? Explain that now Tai is going to write his own how-to paper. Tell students that Tai is going to show them good writing strategies for writing a how-to paper.

## Raising Rubric Awareness Outside the Classroom

by Lee Bromberger, *Assessment Specialist*

As teachers work hard to incorporate rubrics into their classroom routine, they must also recognize the need to continue to promote their rubric assessments outside the classroom.

When a new rubric is developed, teachers should consider forwarding a copy of it to the students' homes. (In *Strategies for Writers*, the rubric for each chapter is found in the *Practice the Strategy Notebook*.) Teachers may also wish to include an explanatory letter with the rubric. As the expectations for student work increase, teachers may also wish to include an explanation of these changes, as well as the role (if appropriate) students played in developing the new rubric.

Another effective technique teachers can use to raise rubric awareness outside of the classroom is to appear before a parent-teacher organization meeting. One or more teachers could present rubrics to parents and perhaps even demonstrate using a rubric to evaluate a piece of writing.

## Working With a Partner Mini-Lesson:
### Write on Your Own Paper

Help students understand how to work with a partner effectively by giving them some basic tips. You may wish to display the tips on chart paper in a visible spot in the classroom.

Tell students that when they are working with a partner, they should **write on their own papers**. Explain that partners should give each other good ideas for making their writing better, but they should not write on each other's paper. This allows students to retain control of their writing while benefiting from peer input.

**Model the Tip** You may wish to model this tip by working with a student volunteer to "act out" a time when partners would write on their own papers.

You may wish to give students a copy of the Working With a Partner Checklist on page T166.

## Tai:
### Writer of a How-to Paper

*(Student Page 131)*

Read the information about Tai to learn more about him. Be sure students understand that Tai will write his own how-to paper in this chapter. Review the information about him. Discuss what Tai might write about in his how-to paper based on his interests.

Point out that Tai will go through the steps in the writing process (Prewriting, Drafting, Revising, Editing, and Publishing). At each stage, Tai will use a good writing strategy and explain how he used it. Students should watch for key words, including **Gather, Organize, Write, Add (Elaborate), Take Out (Clarify), Proofread,** and **Share,** to follow the strategies Tai uses as he goes through the writing process.

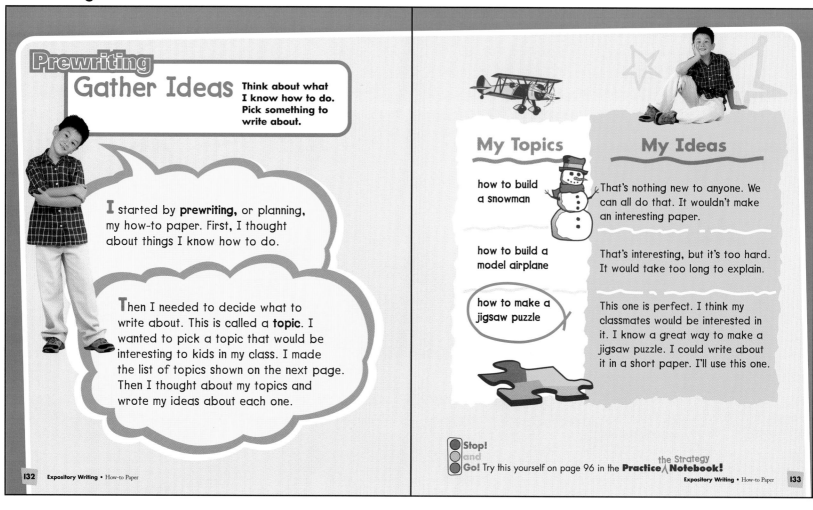

---

# Prewriting  Gather Ideas

**Strategy:** Think about what I know how to do. Pick something to write about.

*(Student Pages 132-133)*

Read Tai's words aloud. Explain to the students that in this section Tai is explaining how he went about writing his how-to paper. He starts by explaining how he chose his topic. Ask the students how Tai decided on his topic. [**Possible responses: It had to be something he knew how to do. He wanted to write about something his classmates would like.**]

Point out Tai's list of possible topics on Student Page 133. Discuss Tai's reasons for not choosing any of the topics other than how to make a jigsaw puzzle. Ask the students if they agree with his decision.

## the Strategy
## Practice ∧ Notebook!

*Practice the Strategy Notebook* pages 96–97 provide practice in selecting a topic for a how-to paper. After students have completed this activity, you may wish to have them share their responses.

## the Strategy
## Practice ∧ Notebook!

*Practice the Strategy Notebook* pages 98–99 provide practice in selecting a topic for students' own how-to papers. *Your Own Writing* pages should be used as time and students' abilities permit. You may wish to assign these pages now or after students have completed this chapter in the Student Edition. You may wish to save students' *Your Own Writing* pages and add them to their Work-in-Progress Portfolios.

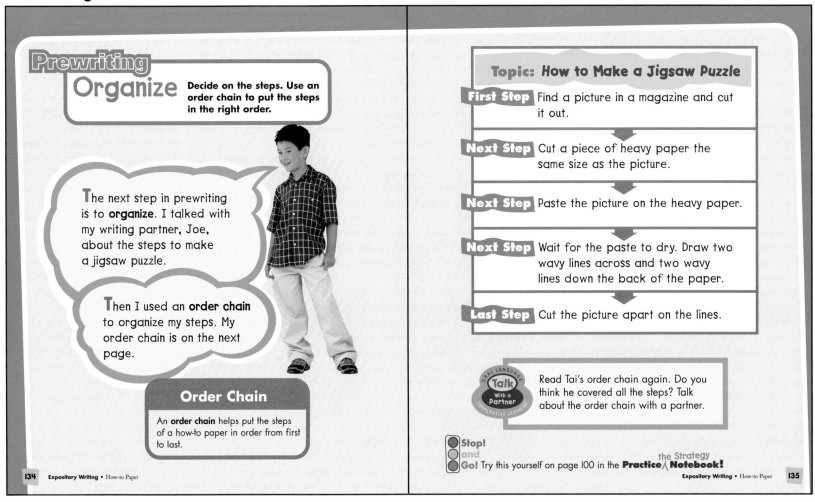

# Prewriting Organize

**Strategy: Decide on the steps. Use an order chain to put the steps in the right order.**

*(Student Pages 134–135)*

Read Tai's words with the students. Explain that before he starts writing, Tai needs to organize his information. He has to decide the order of the steps in his paper. Discuss with students why it's a good idea to talk to a writing partner. [Possible responses: a writing partner can give you new ideas for writing; a writing partner might notice something you didn't see.]

Direct students' attention to Tai's order chain on Student Page 135. Explain that an order chain is a good way to organize the steps in a how-to paper because it lists the steps in order from first to last. It also allows the writer to see if any steps are missing or out of order.

Encourage the students to discuss Tai's order chain with their partners. Are the steps in order? Do the steps seem clear and easy to understand? You may also wish to discuss this with the whole class.

**Note:** An order chain transparency is provided in the *Strategies for Writers Transparencies.*

### the Strategy
## Practice the Notebook!

*Practice the Strategy Notebook* pages 100–101 provide practice in using an order chain to organize the steps for a how-to paper. After students have completed this activity, you may wish to have them share their order chains with a writing partner.

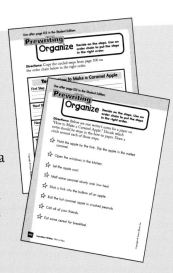

### the Strategy
## Practice the Notebook!

*Practice the Strategy Notebook* pages 102–103 provide an opportunity for students to create an order chain for their own how-to papers.

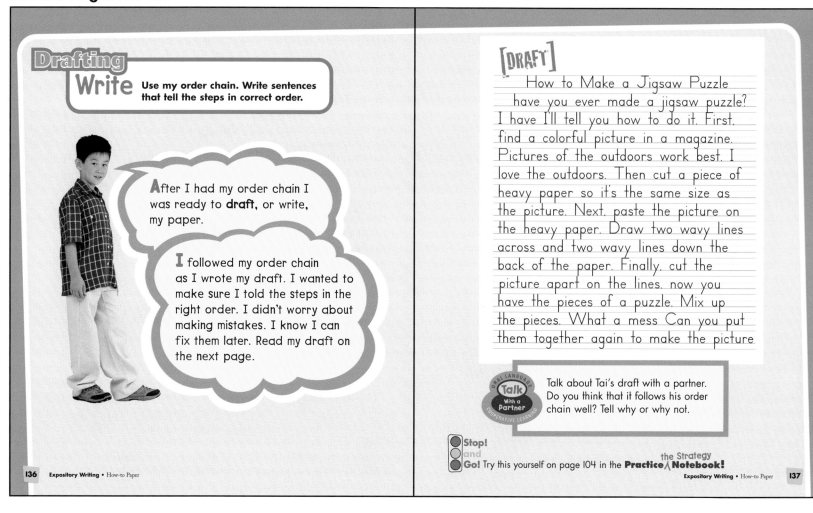

Encourage the students to discuss Tai's draft with a partner. Ask the partners to decide what they think of his draft.

# Drafting Write

**Strategy: Use my order chain. Write sentences that tell the steps in correct order.**

*(Student Pages 136–137)*

Discuss the term *draft* with students. Explain that a draft is an early form of a paper. In a draft, writers don't worry too much about mistakes. The important thing is to get ideas down on paper. Writers know that they will have a chance to go back and fix mistakes later. Read Tai's draft with the students.

## Practice the Strategy Notebook!

*Practice the Strategy Notebook* page 104 provides practice in using the order chain they filled in on page 101 to write sentences for a draft. After students have completed this activity, you may wish to have them read their drafts to a partner.

## Practice the Strategy Notebook!

*Practice the Strategy Notebook* pages 105–107 provide practice in writing a draft of their own how-to paper by following the steps in the order chain they created on pages 102–103. After students have completed this activity, you may wish to have them read their drafts to a partner or share their drafts in a large-group activity.

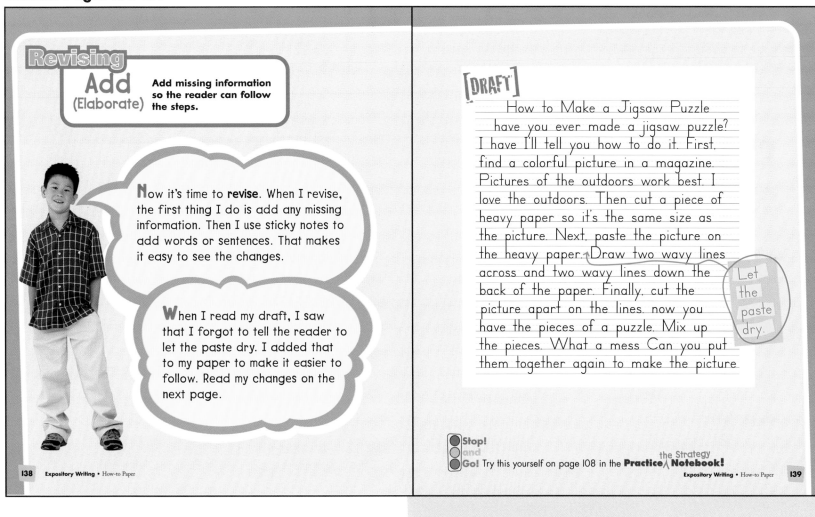

## Revising Add (Elaborate)

**Strategy: Add missing information so the reader can follow the steps.**

*(Student Pages 138–139)*

Read Tai's words with the students. Remind students why a writing partner is a good idea. Explain the term *revise* to students. Tell them that it means "to change." When writers revise their work, they change what they say or how they say it.

Explain that one kind of revising is adding information that's missing. **Note:** *Strategies for Writers* employs the term **Elaborate** in grades 3–8. You may wish to explain to students that *elaborate* means "to add."

Read Tai's revised draft on Student Page 139 with the students. Ask students how his revisions have made his paper even better. [Possible response: Adding information about letting the paste dry makes the paper more complete.]

Encourage students to talk about Tai's revision with a partner. Did the change make his paper better? What other change could Tai have made?

## Spelling Strategies:
### Look on the Word Wall

Before students begin the Editing portion of the chapter, you may wish to remind them that checking spelling is an important part of editing their writing. Encourage students to use several strategies to figure out the spellings of new words and words of which they are unsure. One strategy is to **look on the Word Wall**. Many of the words students are unsure of may already be there.

the Strategy
**Practice⋀Notebook!**

*Practice the Strategy Notebook* page 108 provides additional practice in revising a draft by adding missing information. After students have completed this activity, remind them to use this strategy to revise their own how-to papers.

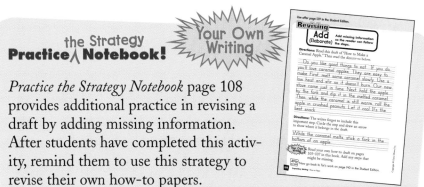

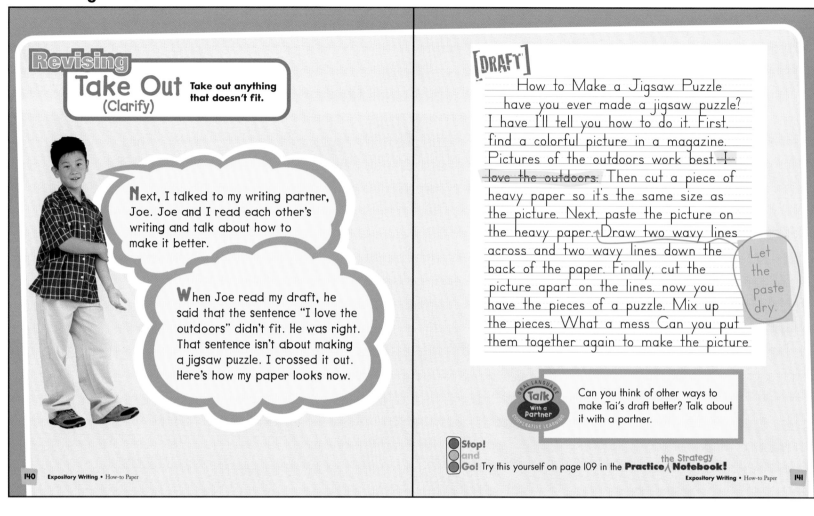

**Stop!** **and** **Go!** Try this yourself on page 109 in the **Practice Λ Notebook!** the Strategy

---

## Revising Take Out (Clarify)

**Strategy: Take out anything that doesn't fit.**

*(Student Pages 140–141)*

Read Tai's words with the students. Explain that another kind of revising is taking out information that doesn't fit. Read Tai's revised draft with the students. Point out that Tai took out the sentence "I love the outdoors" because it didn't fit. Ask students why it didn't fit. [**Response: It doesn't tell about the topic of Tai's paper—how to make a jigsaw puzzle.**] **Note:** *Strategies for Writers* employs the term **Clarify** in grades 3–8. You may wish to explain to students that *clarify* means "to make clear," usually by taking out what's unnecessary.

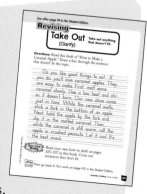

### the Strategy
**Practice Λ Notebook!**

*Practice the Strategy Notebook* page 109 provides additional practice in revising a draft by taking out information that doesn't fit. After students have completed this activity, remind them to use this strategy to revise their own how-to papers.

## Tips for Successful Conferencing:
### Asking Questions

In a conference, ask questions that probe students' understanding of the writing process and the product. At the revising stage, you might ask the following:

- **What did you write about?** If the subjects don't sound like a good choice, try to find out what the student needs to learn about subjects for a compare-and-contrast paper and guide the student accordingly.

- **How did you say these two things are alike?** If the student is not able to name several ways, guide the student to discover an additional likeness or two.

- **How did you say these two things are different?** If the student is not able to name several ways, guide the student to discover an additional difference or two.

- **What describing words can you add?** Encourage the student to make the addition(s) he or she names or ask questions to help the student think of additional words if he or she cannot think of any alone.

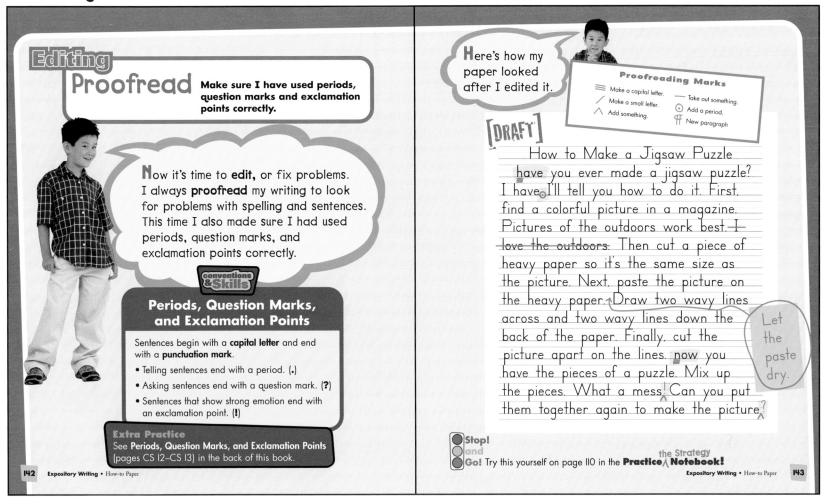

## Editing Proofread

**Strategy: Make sure I have used periods, question marks, and exclamation points correctly.**

*(Student Pages 142–143)*

Remind students that editing is different from revising. When writers revise, they take out unnecessary information and add information that's missing. When writers edit, they fix grammar and spelling mistakes. Remind students that *proofread* means to read the paper while looking for mistakes.

Read Tai's words on Student Page 142 to the students. Remind students that Tai always checks his spelling and makes sure his sentences are complete. Tell students that Tai is now going to fix mistakes in periods, question marks, and exclamation points.

Read the rules for capitalizing and punctuating sentences at the bottom of Student Page 142 with the students.

Point out the proofreading symbols chart on Student Page 143 to the students.

Read Tai's edited draft with the students. Ask them if Tai made all the necessary corrections. Are there any mistakes left? You may wish to use the corresponding Writing Model for Proofreading Practice Transparency.

## Extra Practice: Conventions & Skills Student Edition

If your students need more practice in capitalizing and punctuating sentences, you may wish to assign Student Pages CS 12–CS 13.

## Conventions & Skills Practice

For more targeted practice related to this skill, see these lessons in the optional *Conventions & Skills Practice Book*:

Lesson 7:  Sentences That Ask
Lesson 8:  Telling or Asking Sentences
Lesson 10: Sentences That Show Strong Feelings
Lesson 42: Periods and Question Marks
Lesson 43: Periods and Exclamation Points

### Practice the Strategy Notebook!

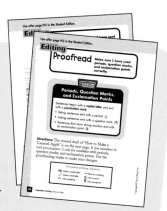

*Practice the Strategy Notebook* pages 110–111 provide additional practice in editing a draft by correcting errors in capitalizing and punctuating sentences. After students have completed this activity, remind them to use this strategy to edit their own how-to papers.

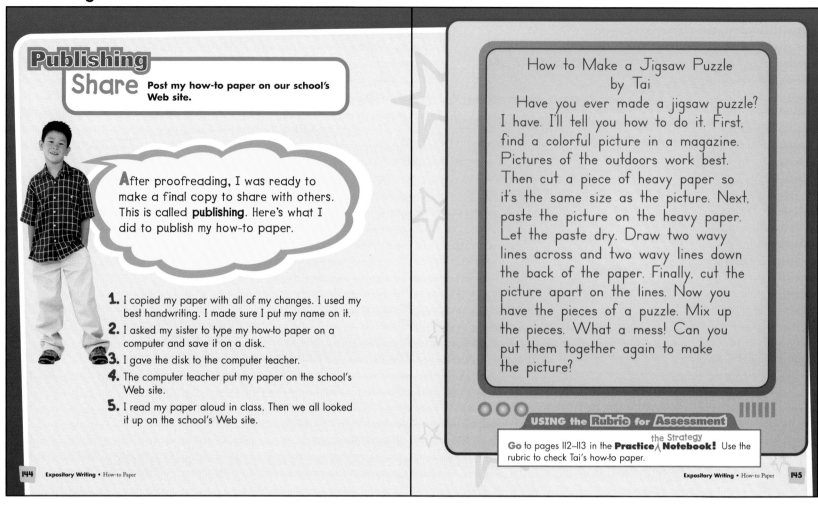

# Publishing Share

**Strategy: Post my how-to paper on our school's Web site.**

*(Student Pages 144–145)*

Read Tai's words to the students. Explain that publishing is the process of finishing a piece of writing to share it with others. Once writers are finished revising and editing their writing, they may publish it. They write a final copy of their papers, making sure they include all the changes they made.

Remind students that there are many ways to share published writing. Tai decided to publish his how-to paper on the school's Web site. Other publishing options include submitting the how-to paper to a magazine, putting together everyone's how-to papers in a class "activities book," and acting out the how-to paper in a "show and tell."

Read the final copy of Tai's paper on Student Page 145 with the students.

Encourage students to talk with a partner about how Tai shared his essay. Was it an effective way to share writing? How else could Tai have shared his writing?

## Using the Rubric

*Practice the Strategy Notebook* pages 112–113 provide a rubric for use in assessing Tai's final how-to paper. Encourage students to work with a partner to evaluate Tai's how-to paper by using this rubric. After students have completed this activity, you may wish to have them share the results in a large-group activity.

**Science**
## Your Own Writing
### EXPOSITORY

Use what you learned in this unit to write your own report, how-to paper, or both! Try these ideas.
- Use **Your Own Writing** pages in the *Practice the Strategy Notebook*.
- Pick a topic below, and write something new.
- Choose another idea of your own.

Follow the steps in the writing process. Use the Report Rubric on pages 94–95 in the *Practice the Strategy Notebook* or the How-to Paper Rubric on pages 112–113 in the *Practice the Strategy Notebook*.

| Report | How-to Paper |
|---|---|
| • an animal<br>• a planet or the moon<br>• a force of nature (tornado, lightning, or volcano)<br>• an invention | • how to make a special food<br>• how to do a job<br>• how to play a game<br>• how to grow a plant<br>• how to care for a pet |

portfolio

**School–Home Connection**

Keep a writing folder. Add **Your Own Writing** pages to your writing folder. You may want to take your writing folder home to share.

## Your Own Writing
## Narrative Writing for Science

Assign either one or both genres to the students. Before they begin writing, review key information about each genre. Decide which of the following you wish students to do:
- Choose a topic on page 146 in the Student Edition.
- Complete one of the Your Own Writing pieces in the *Practice the Strategy Notebook*.
- Come up with a new idea.

## Portfolio/School-Home Connection

Encourage the students to keep a portfolio of their writing.

## Work-in-Progress Portfolio

Remind students to review this portfolio often to revise existing pieces from their Work-in-Progress Portfolio with family members who can help in editing.

## Published Portfolio

Encourage students to choose pieces from their Published Portfolio to share with family members.

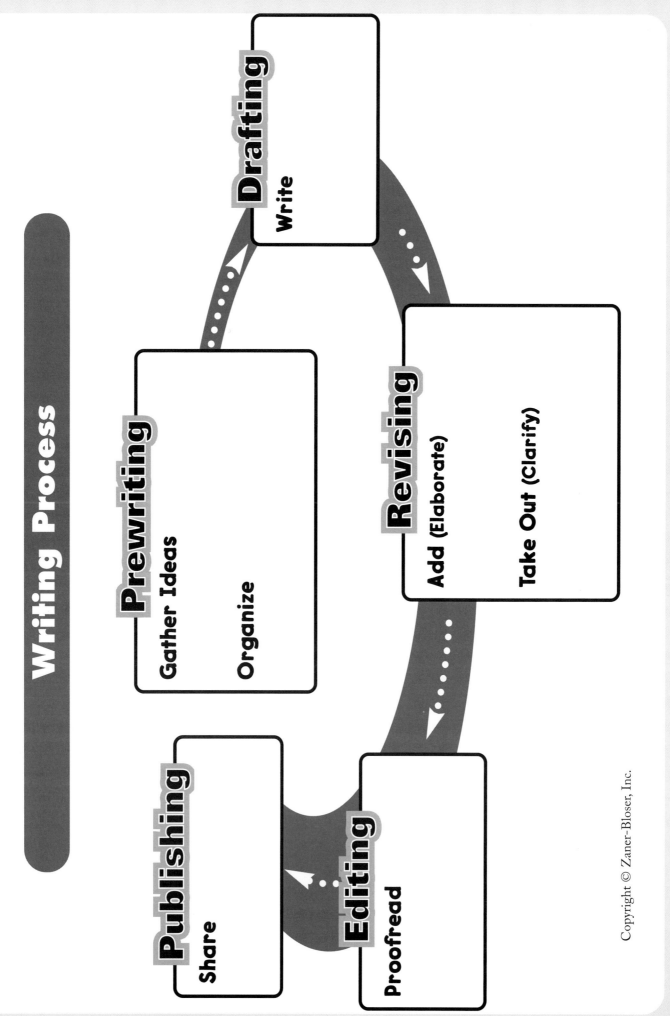

# Writing Process

**Drafting**
- Write

**Prewriting**
- Gather Ideas
- Organize

**Revising**
- Add (Elaborate)
- Take Out (Clarify)

**Publishing**
- Share

**Editing**
- Proofread

You may wish to duplicate and distribute this flow chart to your students. Tell students to jot down key words for each strategy.

# NARRATIVE

# Writing to Tell a Story About Someone Else

## 1 Once Upon a Time Story

## 2 Fable

## Defining Writing to Tell a Story About Someone Else

Read and discuss the unit opener (Student Page 147) with the students. Remind them that they have already learned to write stories about themselves (a personal narrative and a friendly letter). Explain that now they will learn to write stories about someone else. They will learn to rewrite the characters and events in famous Once Upon a Time stories and fables.

## Books to Share With Students

For excellent examples of writing in the fairy tale and fable formats, you may wish to share these books with your students.

- *Piggybook* by Anthony Browne
- *Mufaro's Beautiful Daughters* by John Steptoe
- *The Wolf Who Cried Boy* by Bob Hartman
- *Squids Will Be Squids: Fresh Morals, Beastly Fables* by Jon Scieszka

You may also wish to use some of the titles from Zaner-Bloser Literacy.

# Tips for the Writing Classroom

by Barry Sneed, *Master Teacher*

## Knock, Knock...Who's There?

As educators, we often avoid adult terms because they are too complicated for most children's background knowledge or experience. *Narrative, descriptive, expository,* and *persuasive* are examples of such words. Alone, these words are too vague, so it is a good idea to provide children with some associations for these terms.

I often use songs to form lasting associations for students with unfamiliar words and labels. One of the songs included on the *Strategies for Writers Sing-Along* CD, "Writer, Writer...You're a Star!," will help students understand the rather grown-up labels for the four writing modes. (The lyrics for "Writer, Writer...You're a Star!" can be found in the Appendix at the end of this Teacher Edition.)

Here are some other tips for introducing the four writing modes to young children:

**Narrative Writing:** Incorporate discussions of "what a narrative is" into stories you've read as your lead into narrative

## Once Upon a Time Story

### Writing Strategies

**Prewriting**

**Gather Ideas**
Decide which story to rewrite. Make notes about the story.

**Organize**
Make a story map to tell who is in the story and what happens.

**Publishing**

**Share**
Post my Once Upon a Time Story on our class bulletin board.

**Drafting**

**Write**
Use my story map. Write sentences to tell what happens at the beginning, middle, and end.

**Editing**

**Proofread**
Make sure I begin every proper noun with a capital letter.

**Revising**

**Add** (Elaborate)
Add action verbs to make the story more exciting.

**Take Out** (Clarify)
Take out sentences that don't fit the story.

**Note:** A blackline master of the writing process flow chart appears on page T106. You may wish to copy and distribute it to your students.

### MODELED WRITING

**Once Upon a Time Story Mini-Lesson:** You may wish to present the following mini-lesson before the students read the model on Student Page 149. Write the following on the board, chart paper, or an overhead transparency:

> Once upon a time, a boy called Little Green Biking Shoes rode his bike to visit Grandpa. When he reached Grandpa's house, a man was making dinner in Grandpa's kitchen. Little Green Biking Shoes rode his bike to tell his parents.

Ask the students what this story reminds them of. [Response: "Little Red Riding Hood"] Tell students that in this chapter they will learn about writing a

Once Upon a Time Story. They will see a model and practice strategies for writing their own stories. Write "Little Green Biking Shoes" above the sentences.

Ask the students what problem they see with this Once Upon a Time story. [Response: It doesn't have an end.] Ask students to come up with a possible ending. [Possible response: His parents came to Grandpa's house right away. The man in the kitchen was Little Green Biking Shoes's uncle. Then they had a party.] Explain that in this chapter, they will also learn to write a story that has a clear beginning, middle, and end.

writing. Look at books you've already read and allow the students to come up with a list of the characteristics all narratives possess (e.g., they have people or characters who are doing things, the events tell a story, etc.).

**Descriptive Writing:** Ask students to picture a scene in their heads (e.g., a dog playing). Ask students to share their scenarios aloud. Compare different pictures students generate, then write this sentence on the chalkboard: **The dog played.** Have students assist in adding descriptive words to make the sentence more vivid, e.g., **The big black and white dog played ball in the rain.** Rewrite the sentence using the new words and have students illustrate the sentence. Repeat the activity at a later time, challenging students to come up

with their own "more descriptive" sentence.

**Expository Writing:** Pick a topic (e.g., dogs). Have students generate facts about the topic as you list them on a chart. Model writing a few brief sentences about the topic. To introduce "how-to" writing, you may wish to make a peanut butter and jelly sandwich with the class, and model writing directions for making it.

**Persuasive Writing:** Role-play scenarios with students trying to persuade one another to do something. Read a book about a character trying to persuade a friend to do something. Discuss the story and introduce the word *persuade*.

## Time Management for This Chapter*

| Session | | Session | | Session | |
|---|---|---|---|---|---|
| **1** | Read Student Pages 147–148. Introduce Jaime. Read the model on Student Page 149. Discuss the rubric on Student Pages 150–151. | **6** | Assign *Practice the Strategy Notebook* pages 118–121. | **11** | Read **Revising: Take Out (Clarify)** (Student Pages 164–165). |
| **2** | Read Student Pages 152–154. Discuss Jaime's assessment of the model story. Discuss the information about Jaime on Student Page 155. | **7** | Read **Drafting: Write** (Student Pages 160–161). | **12** | Assign *Practice the Strategy Notebook* page 129. |
| **3** | Read **PREWRITING: Gather Ideas** (Student Pages 156–157). | **8** | Assign *Practice the Strategy Notebook* pages 122–127. | **13** | Read **Editing: Proofread** (Student Pages 166–167). |
| **4** | Assign *Practice the Strategy Notebook* pages 114–117. | **9** | Read **Revising: Add (Elaborate)** (Student Pages 162–163). | **14** | Assign *Practice the Strategy Notebook* pages 130–131. |
| **5** | Read **PREWRITING: Organize** (Student Pages 158–159). | **10** | Assign *Practice the Strategy Notebook* page 128. | **15** | Read **PUBLISHING: Share** (Student Pages 168–169). Assign *Practice the Strategy Notebook* pages 132–133. |

* To complete the chapter in fewer sessions, assign the *Practice the Strategy Notebook* pages on the same day the targeted skill is introduced.

**STRATEGIES for Writers Sing-Along CD**

You may wish to use the *Strategies for Writers Sing-Along* CD throughout the chapter. See the Appendix in the back of this Teacher Edition for more information.

**WRITER'S HANDBOOK**

Remind students that they can refer to the Writer's Handbook in the back of the Student Edition for more information.

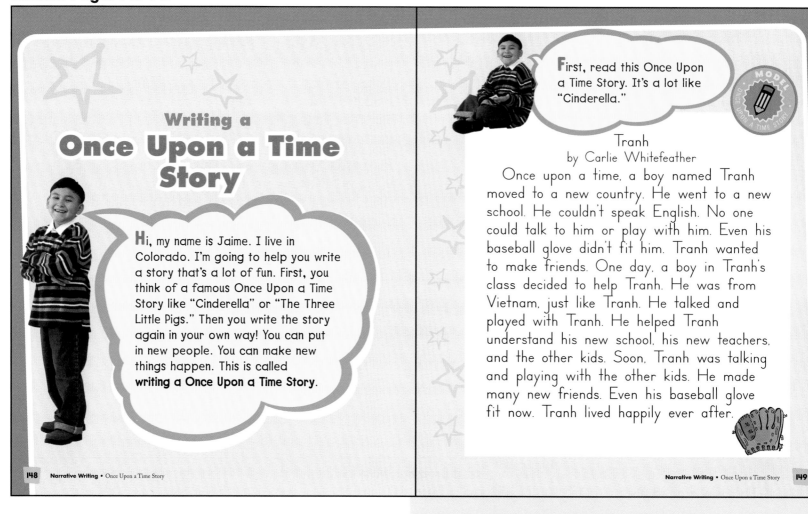

## Introduce the Genre:
### Once Upon a Time Story

*(Student Pages 148–149)*

Read Student Page 148 with the students. Explain that the student guide in their books is going to show them how to rewrite a Once Upon a Time Story. Tell them that they will read Jaime's work as a class. They will have a chance to talk about it with a partner and with the whole class. Then they will practice using the same strategies to write their own Once Upon a Time Story. Ask the students to think of Once Upon a Time Stories that they could rewrite. [Possible responses: "Cinderella," "The Three Little Pigs," "Jack and the Beanstalk"]

## Read the Model:
### Once Upon a Time Story

Read Jaime's words on Student Page 149 with the students. Then read the model of the Once Upon a Time Story. Ask how it is like "Cinderella." [Sample response: Life was very hard for both Cinderella and Tranh, but Cinderella's fairy godmother and Tranh's new friend helped them live happily ever after.] As you read the model with the students, point out that the model contains words they may not know. You may wish to add these words to your Word Wall and encourage students to refer to the Word Wall as they proofread their own stories for spelling.

## Meeting Students' Needs:
### Second-Language Learners

Some second-language learners may be unfamiliar with fairy tales that are popular in the United States. Encourage these students to choose a story from their own culture to rewrite. Also, fill in any gaps by explaining all the original stories of the models shown. When students are using this page, tell the story of Cinderella. Later, tell "The Three Little Pigs" and "The Ugly Duckling." You might want to read the stories from a book of fairy tales or to enhance your own stories by showing illustrations from books.

## Students Who Need Extra Help

Read the first paragraph of the model with students. Then ask students to tell in their own words what the first paragraph is about. Help them make the connections between the model and the Cinderella story. Repeat the process with the second and third paragraphs.

## Gifted Students

Challenge students to add more "Cinderella elements" to the story about Tranh. For example, they may add a prince or a princess, helpful mice or other animals, or something that makes Tranh's baseball glove function more like Cinderella's glass slipper.

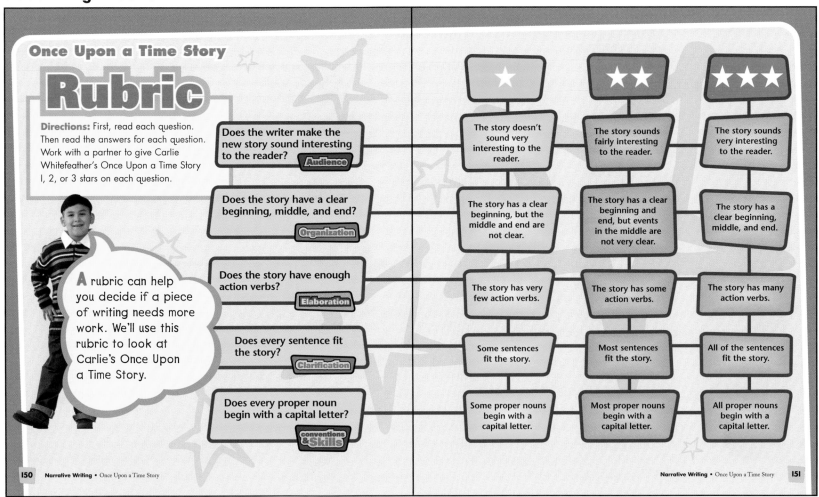

## Once Upon a Time Story

# Rubric

**Directions:** First, read each question. Then read the answers for each question. Work with a partner to give Carlie Whitefeather's Once Upon a Time Story 1, 2, or 3 stars on each question.

*A rubric can help you decide if a piece of writing needs more work. We'll use this rubric to look at Carlie's Once Upon a Time Story.*

| Question | ★ | ★★ | ★★★ |
|---|---|---|---|
| Does the writer make the new story sound interesting to the reader? **Audience** | The story doesn't sound very interesting to the reader. | The story sounds fairly interesting to the reader. | The story sounds very interesting to the reader. |
| Does the story have a clear beginning, middle, and end? **Organization** | The story has a clear beginning, but the middle and end are not clear. | The story has a clear beginning and end, but events in the middle are not very clear. | The story has a clear beginning, middle, and end. |
| Does the story have enough action verbs? **Elaboration** | The story has very few action verbs. | The story has some action verbs. | The story has many action verbs. |
| Does every sentence fit the story? **Clarification** | Some sentences fit the story. | Most sentences fit the story. | All of the sentences fit the story. |
| Does every proper noun begin with a capital letter? **Conventions & Skills** | Some proper nouns begin with a capital letter. | Most proper nouns begin with a capital letter. | All proper nouns begin with a capital letter. |

# Using a Rubric

Use the text on Student Pages 152–154 to model the use of a rubric for evaluating a piece of writing. For more information on using a rubric, please see page T21.

## Discuss the Once Upon a Time Story Rubric

*(Student Pages 150–151)*

Read Jaime's words and the questions on Student Page 150 with the students. Explain that a writer can use these questions to write a Once Upon a Time Story. Discuss each question with the students.

**Audience: Does the writer make the new story sound interesting to the reader?** The story should be interesting so that the reader will want to read it. It should be in the voice of the writer.

**Organization: Does the story have a clear beginning, middle, and end?** A Once Upon a Time Story begins by telling who is in the story and what the problem is. The middle should tell what happens, and the end should tell how the problem gets solved.

**Elaboration: Does the story have enough action verbs?** Action verbs help make the writing more interesting and exciting.

**Clarification: Does every sentence fit the story?** Every sentence should have something to do with the characters and events in the Once Upon a Time Story.

**Conventions & Skills: Does every proper noun begin with a capital letter?** Correct capitalization makes writing clear and easy to follow.

Have students evaluate the Once Upon a Time Story with a partner, using the Once Upon a Time Story Rubric on Student Pages 150–151. Ask partners to share their evaluations with the whole group.

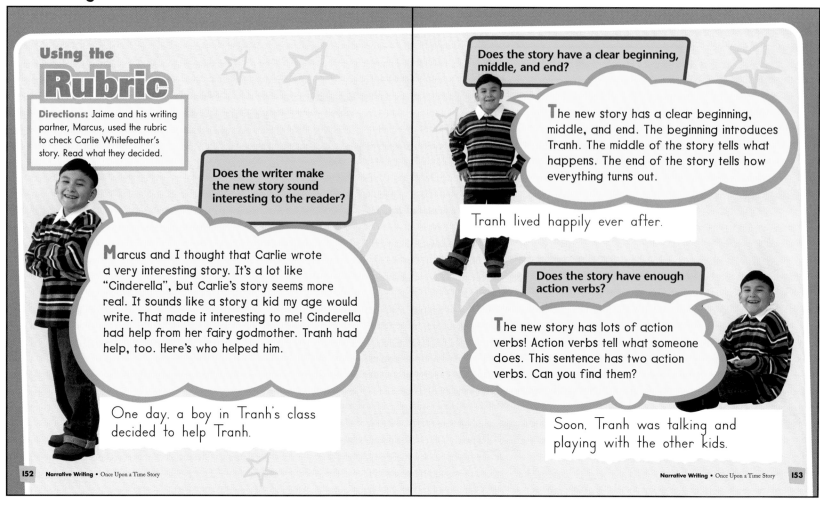

## Using the Rubric to Study the Model

*(Student Pages 152–154)*

Explain to students that now they can see how Jaime is going to use the questions on the rubric to evaluate the Once Upon a Time Story on Student Page 149. Read Student Page 152. Ask the students whether they agree that the new story is interesting. Read the example sentence. Talk with students about how making the story of Cinderella more real makes the new story interesting to read.

Read Student Page 153 with the students. Do they agree that the story has a clear beginning, middle, and end? Do students agree that the story has enough action verbs? You might want to look back at the model on Student Page 149 and point out (or have students point out) more action verbs. Read Student Page 154 with the students. Ask students if they agree with Jaime that all the sentences fit the story. Then remind students that beginning every proper noun with a capital letter makes it easier for readers to understand their writing.

## Internet Sources Related to Rubrics

The Internet provides a variety of information about understanding, developing, and using rubrics for a variety of needs in the classroom. The following Web sites may prove helpful. (**Note:** As of the date of publication, these Web sites were running and appropriate to this topic. Web sites are subject to change at any time.)

**http://www.interactiveclassroom.com** This site contains information about various forms of assessment, as well as tips for using rubrics and some rubric templates.

**http://www.odyssey.on.ca/~elaine.coxon/rubrics.htm** This site provides a multitude of rubric templates for every imaginable field of study and content area. Every content area—from traditional writing rubrics to dance, mathematics, science, physical education, and thinking skills—is represented by one or more rubrics.

**http://www.ncsu.edu/midlink/ho.html** This site offers many resources related to rubrics, including several multimedia rubrics.

**http://pegasus.cc.ucf.edu/~jmorris/rubric.htm** This site contains an extensive list of Web resources for rubrics.

## Working With a Partner Mini-Lesson:
### Think About It

Help students understand how to work with a partner effectively by giving them some basic tips. You may wish to write the tips on chart paper and display them where students can readily see them.

Explain to the students that when a writing partner thinks they should change something, they might not want to do it. Remind students that their writing partner's job is to help them improve their writing. Suggest to students that they take time to **think about** their partner's suggestions. Perhaps they will decide to make some changes but not others. Remind students again that the decision is always up to the writer. You may wish to give students a copy of the Working With a Partner Checklist on page T166.

**Model the Tip** Model this tip for the students by reading a piece of your own writing to the entire class. Invite the students to offer suggestions for changes to your writing. Listen to each suggestion and say something like, "Thank you. I'll think about making this change." Remind students that the writer needs to think about his or her writing, including making changes.

## Jaime:
### Writer of a Once Upon a Time Story

*(Student Page 155)*

Read the information about Jaime to learn more about him. Be sure students understand that in this chapter Jaime will write his own Once Upon a Time Story. Review the information given about Jaime. Discuss what he might write about based on his interests.

Point out that Jaime will go through the steps in the writing process (Prewriting, Drafting, Revising, Editing, and Publishing). At each stage, he will use a good writing strategy and explain how he used it. Students should watch for key words, including **Gather, Organize, Write, Add (Elaborate), Take Out (Clarify), Proofread,** and **Share,** to follow the strategies Jaime uses as he goes through the writing process.

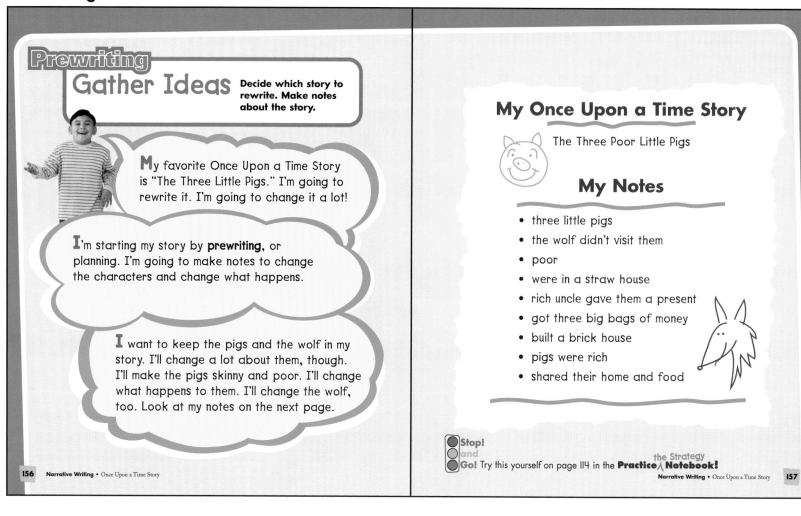

## Prewriting   Gather Ideas

**Strategy: Decide which story to rewrite. Make notes about the story.**

*(Student Pages 156–157)*

Read Jaime's words on Student Page 156 aloud. Tell the students that in this section Jaime will explain how he went about writing his own Once Upon a Time Story. He starts by telling how he chose his story and how he got started on his prewriting. Ask the students to retell what Jaime did. [Possible responses: Jaime thought of his favorite Once Upon a Time Story. Then he made notes about the way he wanted to rewrite the story.]

Read Jaime's notes on Student Page 157 with the students. Ask them why it is a good idea to start out with notes. [Possible responses: If you have a lot of ideas for notes, that's probably a good story for you to write. If you can't think of any ideas for notes, maybe you should choose a different story.]

### Practice the Strategy Notebook!

*Practice the Strategy Notebook* pages 114–115 provide ideas for topics and an exercise to help students make a concrete link between a famous story ("The Ugly Duckling") and a rewrite ("The Ugly Zebra"). After students have completed these two activities, you may wish to have them share their responses.

### Practice the Strategy Notebook!

*Practice the Strategy Notebook* pages 116–117 give students an opportunity to explore ideas for stories they could rewrite, to choose a story idea, and to make some notes about it. You may wish to assign these pages now or after students have completed this chapter in the Student Edition. You may wish to save students' *Your Own Writing* pages and add them to their Work-in-Progress Portfolios.

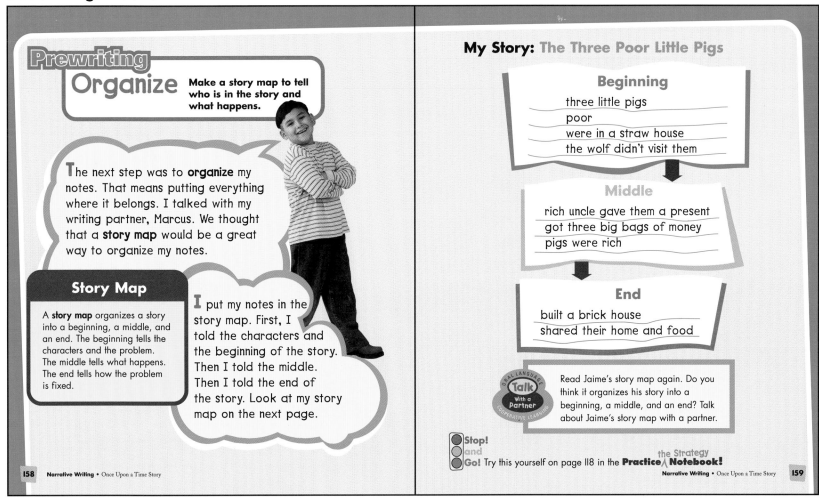

### Prewriting Organize

Make a story map to tell who is in the story and what happens.

The next step was to **organize** my notes. That means putting everything where it belongs. I talked with my writing partner, Marcus. We thought that a **story map** would be a great way to organize my notes.

**Story Map**

A **story map** organizes a story into a beginning, a middle, and an end. The beginning tells the characters and the problem. The middle tells what happens. The end tells how the problem is fixed.

I put my notes in the story map. First, I told the characters and the beginning of the story. Then I told the middle. Then I told the end of the story. Look at my story map on the next page.

**My Story:** The Three Poor Little Pigs

**Beginning**
three little pigs
poor
were in a straw house
the wolf didn't visit them

**Middle**
rich uncle gave them a present
got three big bags of money
pigs were rich

**End**
built a brick house
shared their home and food

**Talk With a Partner** — ORAL LANGUAGE / COOPERATIVE LEARNING

Read Jaime's story map again. Do you think it organizes his story into a beginning, a middle, and an end? Talk about Jaime's story map with a partner.

**Stop! and Go!** Try this yourself on page 118 in the **Practice the Strategy Notebook!**

158 — Narrative Writing • Once Upon a Time Story
159 — Narrative Writing • Once Upon a Time Story

---

### Prewriting Organize

**Strategy: Make a story map to tell who is in the story and what happens.**

*(Student Pages 158–159)*

Read aloud the definition of the term *story map* on Student Page 158 and discuss it with the students. Then read Jaime's words with them. Explain that before Jaime begins his draft, he needs to organize his ideas. He does this by making a story map. Also discuss with students why it is a good idea to talk with a writing partner. [Possible responses: A writing partner can give you new ideas for writing. A writing partner can help you put your ideas into your story map.]

Direct students' attention to Jaime's story map on Student Page 159. Point out that Jaime tells who is in the story and what the problem is at the beginning of the story. He uses the middle to tell what happens. He shows how the problem is fixed in the end.

Encourage the students to discuss Jaime's story map with their partners. Ask the students if Jaime's story map seems complete. Does it tell all the important things that happen? Is there more to add? You may wish to discuss the partners' findings as a large-group activity, as well.

**Note:** A story map transparency is provided in the *Strategies for Writers Transparencies*.

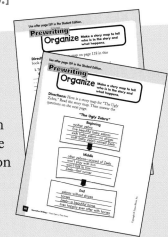

**the Strategy Practice Notebook!**

*Practice the Strategy Notebook* pages 118–119 provide additional practice in understanding how a story map can be used to organize ideas for a Once Upon a Time Story. After students have completed this activity, you may wish to have writing partners share their answers to the questions on page 119.

**the Strategy Practice Notebook!**

*Practice the Strategy Notebook* pages 120–121 provide an opportunity for students to create a story map for their own Once Upon a Time Story. You may wish to assign these pages now or after students have completed this chapter in the Student Edition.

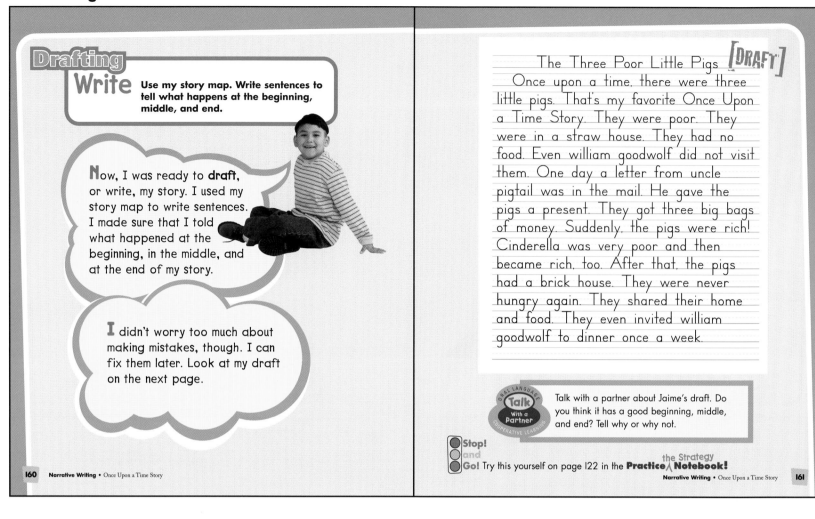

# Drafting Write

**Strategy: Use my story map. Write sentences to tell what happens at the beginning, middle, and end.**

*(Student Pages 160–161)*

Read Jaime's words on Student Page 160, and review the term *draft* with the students. Read Jaime's draft with the students. You might want to note that Jaime has a few mistakes in his draft but that he will go back to fix them later.

Be sure students understand that it is important to tell who is in the story at the beginning of the story. Ask the students whether they think Jaime's story has a beginning, middle, and end. You might want to ask students to identify which section tells the beginning, which section tells the middle, and which section tells the end of the story. [**Responses: first, second, and third sections, respectively**]

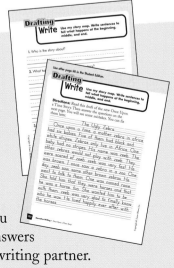

## the Strategy Practice the Notebook!

*Practice the Strategy Notebook* pages 122–123 provide students with an opportunity to read another Once Upon a Time Story draft and to answer questions about it. After students have completed this activity, you may wish to have them share their answers to the questions on page 123 with a writing partner.

## the Strategy Practice the Notebook!

*Practice the Strategy Notebook* pages 124–127 provide an opportunity for students to write a draft of their own Once Upon a Time Story by following the story map they created on pages 120–121. After students have completed this activity, you may wish to have them read their draft to a partner or share their draft in a large-group activity. You may wish to assign these pages now or after students have completed this chapter in the Student Edition.

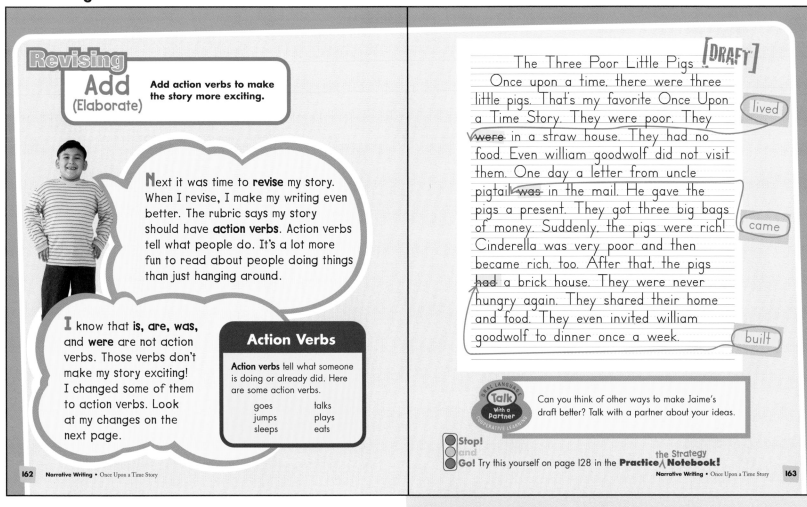

### Revising

## Add (Elaborate)

Add action verbs to make the story more exciting.

**N**ext it was time to **revise** my story. When I revise, I make my writing even better. The rubric says my story should have **action verbs**. Action verbs tell what people do. It's a lot more fun to read about people doing things than just hanging around.

**I** know that **is, are, was,** and **were** are not action verbs. Those verbs don't make my story exciting! I changed some of them to action verbs. Look at my changes on the next page.

**Action Verbs**

**Action verbs** tell what someone is doing or already did. Here are some action verbs.

| | |
|---|---|
| goes | talks |
| jumps | plays |
| sleeps | eats |

162 **Narrative Writing** • Once Upon a Time Story

[DRAFT]

The Three Poor Little Pigs
Once upon a time, there were three little pigs. That's my favorite Once Upon a Time Story. They were poor. They ~~were~~ in a straw house. They had no food. Even william goodwolf did not visit them. One day a letter from uncle pigtail ~~was~~ in the mail. He gave the pigs a present. They got three big bags of money. Suddenly, the pigs were rich! Cinderella was very poor and then became rich, too. After that, the pigs ~~had~~ a brick house. They were never hungry again. They shared their home and food. They even invited william goodwolf to dinner once a week.

*(margin notes: lived, came, built)*

**Talk With a Partner** — Can you think of other ways to make Jaime's draft better? Talk with a partner about your ideas.

**Stop! and Go!** Try this yourself on page 128 in the **Practice the Strategy Notebook!**

**Narrative Writing** • Once Upon a Time Story 163

---

### Revising

## Add (Elaborate)

**Strategy: Add action verbs to make the story more exciting.**

*(Student Pages 162–163)*

Discuss the definition of *action verbs* on Student Page 162. Then read Jaime's words with the students. Review the term *revise* with them. Explain that when writers revise their work, they rewrite what they say or how they say it. Explain that one way to revise a Once Upon a Time Story is to replace verbs that are not action verbs with action verbs. Action verbs make the writing livelier and more real for the reader.

**Note:** *Strategies for Writers* employs the term **Elaborate** in grades 3–8. You may wish to explain to students that *elaborate* means "to add."

Read Jaime's revised draft on Student Page 163 with the students. Ask students how Jaime's revisions have made his story better. [Possible responses: Action verbs make the story more interesting. They help the reader know exactly what happens.]

**Talk With a Partner** — Encourage students to talk with a partner about Jaime's revisions. What other action verbs could Jaime have added?

## Spelling Strategies:
### Ask Someone Who Spells Well

Before students begin the Editing portion of the chapter, you may wish to remind them that checking spelling is an important part of editing their writing. Encourage students to use several strategies to figure out the spellings of new words and words about which they are unsure. One strategy is to **ask someone who spells well**. Sometimes, the expert can be a writing partner or another student. Often, the expert in the classroom is the teacher.

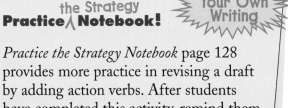

### the Strategy
**Practice the Notebook!**

*Your Own Writing*

*Practice the Strategy Notebook* page 128 provides more practice in revising a draft by adding action verbs. After students have completed this activity, remind them to use this strategy to revise their own Once Upon a Time Story.

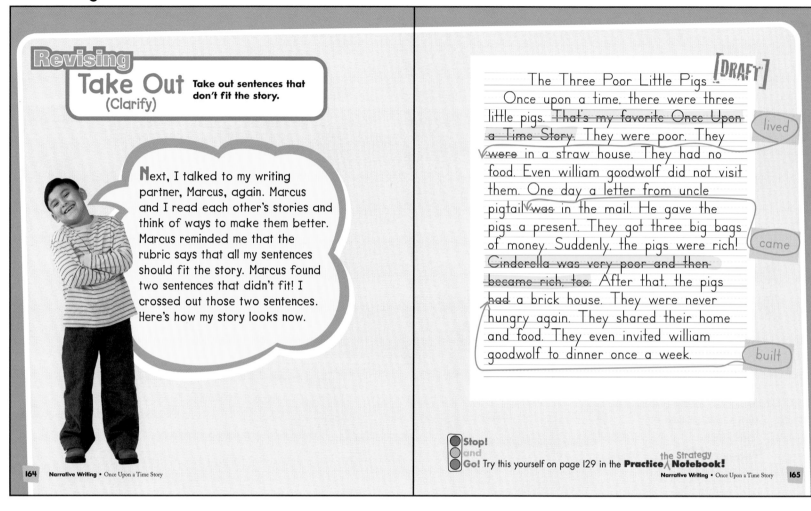

## Revising Take Out (Clarify)

**Strategy: Take out sentences that don't fit the story.**

*(Student Pages 164–165)*

Read Jaime's words on Student Page 164 with the students. Explain that another kind of revising is taking out sentences that don't fit the story or don't help to tell the story. Read Jaime's revised draft on Student Page 165 with the students. Point out that Jaime took out the sentences "That's my favorite Once Upon a Time Story" and "Cinderella was very poor and then became rich, too." Ask students why he did this. [**Possible response: They didn't have anything to do with what happens in the story.**]

**Note:** *Strategies for Writers* employs the term **Clarify** in grades 3–8. You may wish to explain to students that *clarify* means "to make clear," usually by taking out what's unnecessary.

## Tips for Successful Conferencing: Developing Story Lines

Here are some ways you can help students develop story lines:

- After a student tells you an idea, restate it. Hearing it can help the student confirm the idea, clarify it, or rewrite it.

- If you don't understand something, ask about it. You might ask, "Who is going to do that?" or "When will that happen?"

- At appropriate times, remind students of what they have learned. You might ask, "Where are you going to tell who is in the story?" or "What happens in the middle of the story?"

- Ask leading questions, such as "Then what will you write?" or "What does the character do about that?"

### Practice the Strategy Notebook!

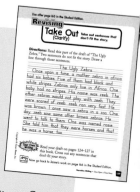

*Practice the Strategy Notebook* page 129 provides additional practice in revising a draft by taking out sentences that don't fit the story. After students have completed this activity, remind them to use this strategy to revise their own Once Upon a Time Story.

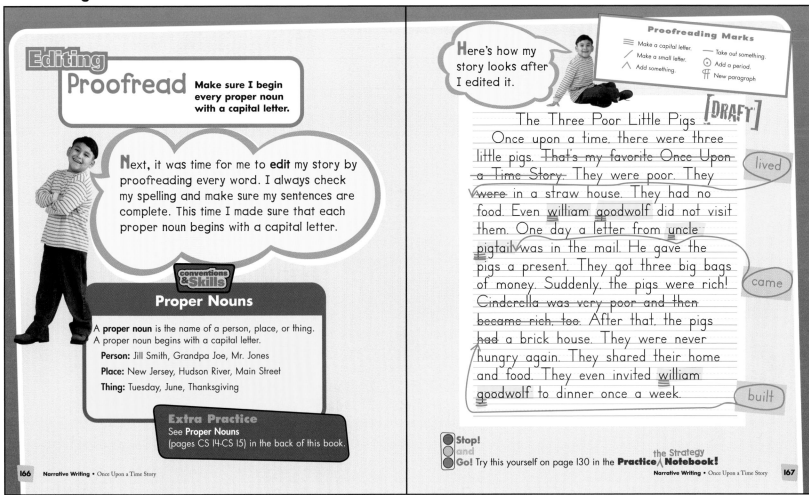

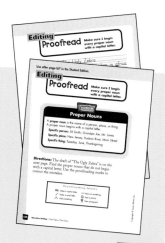

## Editing Proofread

**Strategy: Make sure I begin every proper noun with a capital letter.**

*(Student Pages 166–167)*

Remind students that when writers edit, they fix any problems in spelling, capitalization, punctuation, and grammar. Remind students that to *proofread* is to read their own writing while looking for mistakes.

Read Jaime's words on Student Page 166 with the students. Remind students that Jaime always checks his spelling and makes sure his sentences are complete. This time he is going to fix any mistakes in proper nouns. Remind students that using a different color to correct mistakes helps writers see their corrections more easily. **Note:** You may wish to give students their own colored pencils for editing. Read the explanation and examples of proper nouns at the bottom of Student Page 166.

Point out the proofreading symbols chart on Student Page 167 to the students. Explain that these symbols help writers remember the corrections they made, so they can include them in their final copy. You may wish to give students a copy of the Proofreading Marks blackline master on page T136. Read Jaime's edited draft with the students. Ask them if Jaime made all the necessary corrections. You may wish to use the corresponding Writing Model for Proofreading Practice Transparency.

## Extra Practice: Conventions & Skills

### Student Edition

If your students need more practice in beginning proper nouns with a capital letter, you may wish to assign Student Pages CS 14–CS 15.

### Conventions & Skills Practice

For more targeted practice related to this skill, see these lessons in the optional *Conventions & Skills Practice Book*:

Lesson 12: Proper Nouns

Lesson 13: Common Nouns and Proper Nouns

Lesson 44: Proper Nouns

### the Strategy Practice Notebook!

*Practice the Strategy Notebook* pages 130–131 provide additional practice in editing a draft by correcting errors in proper nouns. After students have completed this activity, remind them to use this strategy to edit their own Once Upon a Time Story.

**Narrative Writing** • Once Upon a Time Story

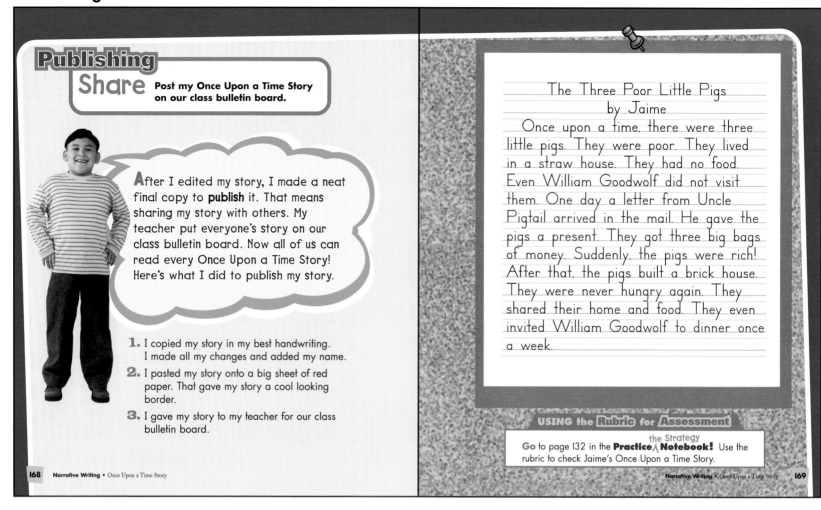

Go to page 132 in the **Practice the Strategy Notebook!** Use the rubric to check Jaime's Once Upon a Time Story.

# Publishing Share

**Strategy: Post my Once Upon a Time Story on our class bulletin board.**

*(Student Pages 168–169)*

Read Jaime's words on Student Page 168 to the students. Explain that publishing is the process of finishing a piece of writing to share it with others. Once writers have finished revising and editing their writing, they may publish it. They make a final copy, being sure to include all the changes they made when they revised and edited.

Remind students that there are many ways to share published writing. Jaime liked the idea of posting his story on the class bulletin board. Ask the students why he might have liked that. [Possible response: He is proud of his work and wants to share it.] Other publishing options include making a big book, posting the story on the school's Web site, sharing the story in an authors' circle, and illustrating the story and posting it on a class hallway display.

Read the final copy of Jaime's Once Upon a Time Story on Student Page 169 with the students.

Encourage students to talk with a partner about how Jaime shared his story. Was it a good way to share writing? How else could Jaime have shared his Once Upon a Time Story?

## Using the Rubric

*Practice the Strategy Notebook* pages 132–133 provide a rubric for assessing Jaime's final Once Upon a Time Story. Encourage students to work with a partner to evaluate Jaime's story by using this rubric. After students have completed this activity, you may wish to have them share the results in a large-group activity.

**School–Home Connection**

Dear Family,

As your child learns and practices different kinds of writing, he or she is working with a very important writing device—a graphic organizer. Graphic organizers are the charts, webs, tables, and other visual tools we use to help us make sense of information for our writing projects. This year, your child is using the following graphic organizers:

A Storyboard—plots the events in a story in the order in which they happen.

A 5 Senses Chart—organizes information that has been gathered by using sight, sound, touch, taste, and smell.

A Venn Diagram—shows how two things are alike and different.

A Web—organizes information about one topic. The topic is written in the center of the web. Details about the topic are written in the surrounding circles.

An Order Chain—shows steps or events in the order in which they happen.

A Story Map—organizes events at the beginning, middle, and end of the story.

A Spider Map—organizes information about one topic. The topic is written in the center of the "spider." Details related to the topic are written on the "legs" of the spider.

There are many kinds of graphic organizers. Your child may show a preference for one kind over another. It doesn't matter what kind he or she uses, as long as the organizer helps your child make sense of information to improve his or her writing.

You may wish to copy the letter above and send it home with your students.

 **for the Writing Classroom**

by Barry Sneed, *Master Teacher*

## Rhyme Time: Using Poetry in the Classroom

Children generally learn the concept of rhyming quite easily. In fact, they should come into second grade with this concept already in their bank of knowledge. If not, rhyming is a skill that can be introduced and mastered early in the school year. Taking advantage of this fact, it is wise to put rhyming to

good use in the writing classroom. I highly recommend using any (or all) of Shel Silverstein's three poetry books: *Where the Sidewalk Ends*, *A Light in the Attic*, and *Falling Up*. These poems (and others of your choice) are an ideal way to entertain students while capturing their attention and sparking their imagination.

Children feel "BIG" when they can mimic adult behaviors or tasks, so they love to try their hands at poetry. It's best to start out by providing lines out loud and having students fill in the missing final (rhyming) words at the end (e.g., "There

## Fable

## Writing Strategies

### Prewriting

**Gather Ideas**
Decide which fable to rewrite. Make notes about the fable.

**Organize**
Make a story map to tell who is in the fable and what happens.

### Publishing

**Share**
Draw a picture to go with my fable. Put fables together to make a class book.

### Drafting

**Write**
Use my story map. Write sentences to tell what happens at the beginning, middle, and end.

### Editing

**Proofread**
Make sure I use quotation marks correctly.

### Revising

**Add (Elaborate)**
Add describing words to make the characters more real.

**Take Out (Clarify)**
Take out sentences that make the fable confusing.

**Note:** A blackline master of the writing process flow chart appears on page T106. You may wish to copy and distribute it to your students.

**MODELED WRITING**

**Rewriting a Fable Mini-Lesson:** You may wish to present the following mini-lesson before the students read the model on Student Page 171. Write the following on the board, chart paper, or an overhead transparency:

A boy and his father were waiting for the painter to come and paint the house. The boy's father was working in the study. The father said, "Call me when the painter comes." The boy was bored. He called his father. His father came, but there was no painter. The next day, the same thing happened.

Ask the students if this story reminds them of another story. [Response: "The Boy Who Cried Wolf"] Explain that this kind of writing is a fable. Tell

students they will be learning more about what makes a fable and how to write a fable. They will see a model and learn and practice some strategies for writing their own fable. Write the title "The Boy Who Cried Painter" above the sentences.

Ask the students what's wrong with this fable. [Response: It doesn't have an ending.] Ask students to come up with an ending that's like the one in the famous fable. [Possible response: Finally, the painter came. The boy called his father. The father didn't come. The painter left.] Explain that when students write their own fable, they will also learn to write a story that has a clear beginning, middle, and end.

once was a frog who sat on a [log].”). Next, examine simple poems in writing by reproducing them on a chart or the overhead projector. After this, model creating/writing a poem with the class, allowing students to assist you in your efforts.

I find that the simple **AABB** rhyming pattern is best (and easiest) for this age group. Here's an example of a poem that follows this scheme:

> There was a green **frog**,
> sitting on a **log**.
> He was alone in the *lake*,
> 'til he met a big *snake*.

You may want to challenge some students to attempt a poem written with the **ABAB** pattern as well. Here's an example:

> There was a green **frog**,
> alone in the *lake*.
> He sat on a **log**,
> 'til he met a big *snake*.

I have my fifth grade teacher to thank for starting me on a lifetime of writing. She ignited a spark that began when she read aloud silly poems to a classroom of young minds. Eventually, she encouraged me to write my own silly poems. I can only hope to do the same for the students I encounter!

## Time Management for This Chapter*

| Session | | Session | | Session | |
|---|---|---|---|---|---|
| **1** | Introduce the student guide. Read the model on Student Page 171. Discuss the fable rubric on Student Pages 172–173. | **6** | Assign *Practice the Strategy Notebook* pages 138–141. | **11** | Read **REVISING: Take Out (Clarify)** (Student Pages 186–187). |
| **2** | Read Student Pages 174–177. Discuss Mina's assessment of the model fable. Discuss the information about Mina on Student Page 177. | **7** | Read **DRAFTING: Write** (Student Pages 182–183). | **12** | Assign *Practice the Strategy Notebook* page 147. |
| **3** | Read **PREWRITING: Gather Ideas** (Student Pages 178–179). | **8** | Assign *Practice the Strategy Notebook* pages 142–145. | **13** | Read **EDITING: Proofread** (Student Pages 188–189). |
| **4** | Assign *Practice the Strategy Notebook* pages 134–137. | **9** | Read **REVISING: Add (Elaborate)** (Student Pages 184–185). | **14** | Assign *Practice the Strategy Notebook* pages 148–149. |
| **5** | Read **PREWRITING: Organize** (Student Pages 180–181). | **10** | Assign *Practice the Strategy Notebook* page 146. | **15** | Read **PUBLISHING: Share** (Student Pages 190–191). Assign *Practice the Strategy Notebook* pages 150–151. |

*To complete the chapter in fewer sessions, assign the *Practice the Strategy Notebook* pages on the same day the targeted skill is introduced.

**STRATEGIES for Writers Sing-Along CD**

You may wish to use the *Strategies for Writers Sing-Along* CD throughout the chapter. See the Appendix in the back of this Teacher Edition for more information.

**WRITER'S HANDBOOK**

Remind students that they can refer to the Writer's Handbook in the back of the Student Edition for more information.

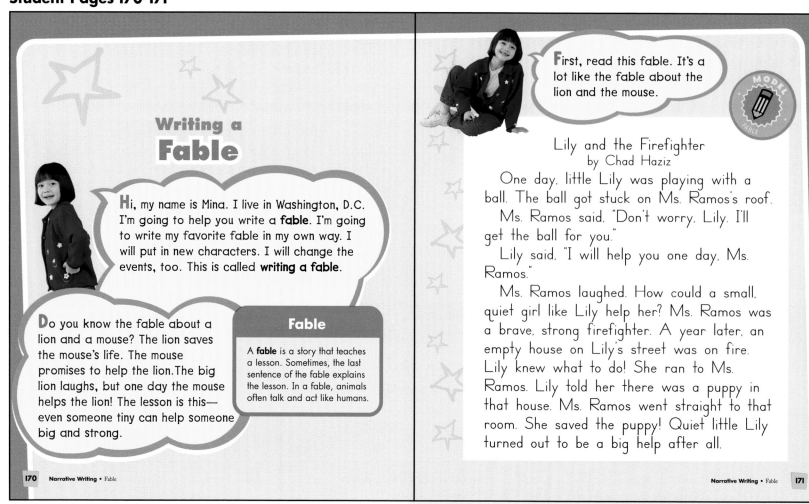

## Introduce the Genre:
### Fable

*(Student Pages 170–171)*

Read Student Page 170 with the students. Explain that the student guide in their books is going to show them how to rewrite a fable. Tell them that they will read Mina's work as a class. They will have a chance to talk about it with a partner and with the whole class. Then they will practice using the same strategies to write their own fables. Ask the students to think of fables they could rewrite. [Possible responses: "The Tortoise and the Hare," "The Grasshopper and the Ants," "The Dog and the Bone," "The Fox and the Grapes"]

## Read the Model:
### Fable

Read Mina's words on Student Page 171 with the students. Then read the model of the fable. Ask how it is like the fable "The Lion and the Mouse." [Possible responses: Lily is like the mouse. Ms. Ramos is like the lion. Little Lily helps strong Ms. Ramos the way the mouse helps the lion.] As you read the model with the students, point out that the model contains words that students may not know. You may wish to add these words to your Word Wall and encourage students to refer to the Word Wall as they proofread their own fables for spelling.

## Meeting Students' Needs:
### Second-Language Learners

Some students may be unfamiliar with the fables that others know. Encourage these students to choose fables from their own cultural background to rewrite. In addition, fill in any gaps by explaining all the original fables. When students are using this page, tell the fable about the lion and the mouse. Later, tell "The Grasshopper and the Ants" and "The Tortoise and the Hare."

### Students Who Need Extra Help

Students who need help using a story map or understanding the concept of beginning, middle, and end may get extra practice by mapping the model with a partner. Help students relate the idea of the first paragraph to the beginning of the story; the second, or middle, paragraph to the middle of the story; and the last paragraph to the end of the story.

### Gifted Students

Motivated students might enjoy doing a detailed compare-and-contrast analysis of "The Lion and the Mouse" with "Lily and the Firefighter." They might make comparisons and contrasts verbally, pictorially (by drawing a chart or a Venn diagram), or in writing.

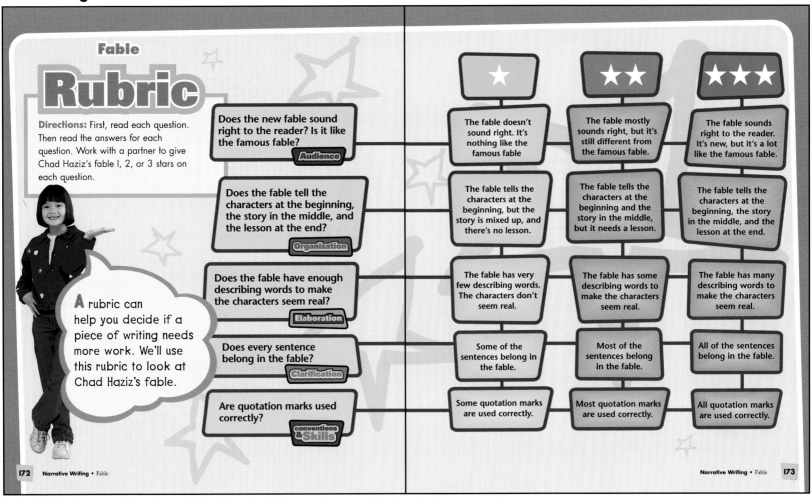

## Using a Rubric

Use the text on Student Pages 174–176 to model the use of a rubric for evaluating a piece of writing. For more information on using a rubric, please see page T21.

### Discuss the Fable Writing Rubric

*(Student Pages 172–173)*

Read Mina's words and the questions on Student Page 172 with the students. Explain that a writer can use these questions to write a good fable. Discuss each question with the students.

**Audience: Does the new fable sound right to the reader? Is it like the famous fable?** Remind students that the new fable should sound like the famous fable, but it should be in the voice of the writer.

**Organization: Does the fable tell the characters at the beginning, the story in the middle, and the lesson at the end?** Explain that the beginning of the fable should tell who is in the story and what the problem is. The middle should tell what happens. The end should bring the story to a close and state the lesson of the fable.

**Elaboration: Does the fable have enough describing words to make the characters seem real?** Describing words make each character special.

**Clarification: Does every sentence belong in the fable?** The fable should not contain sentences that are confusing or don't help tell the story.

**Conventions & Skills: Are quotation marks used correctly?** Correct grammar and punctuation make writing clear and easy to follow.

Have students evaluate the fable with a partner, using the fable writing rubric on Student Pages 172–173. Ask partners to share their evaluations with the whole group.

## Using the Rubric to Study the Model

*(Student Pages 174–176)*

Explain to students that now they can see how Mina is going to use the questions on the rubric to evaluate the fable on Student Page 171.

Read the questions in the box on Student Page 174, and then read Mina's words. Ask the students whether they agree that the fable teaches the reader a lesson. Read the example sentence. Explain the point that it makes.

Read the question in the first box on Student Page 175 with the students. Do they agree that the fable does all the things it's supposed to do at the beginning, the middle, and the end? Read the question in the second box. Do students agree that the fable uses enough describing words to make the characters more real? You might want to have the students look back at the model on Student Page 171 and point out more describing words.

Read Student Page 176 with the students. Ask students if they agree with Mina that every sentence belongs in the fable. Then remind students that using quotation marks correctly makes it easier for readers to understand their writing.

## Developing Rubrics With Student Input

by Lee Bromberger, *Assessment Specialist*

Allowing students to participate in the development of an assignment rubric yields the following bonus outcomes:

- Students must understand the objectives of the unit. Of course, students will need some guidance from the teacher to help them think about what they learned. A class discussion is a good way to help students review and remember the criteria.

- Students offer a "sounding board" for the teacher before beginning an assignment. Sometimes gathering students' perspectives will yield results that may surprise a teacher. Contributions from the students' points of view can provide a fresh perspective that can help overcome potential obstacles.

- Students take ownership of the assignment. Having contributed to the development of the rubric, students will stake their claim to the assignment, as well.

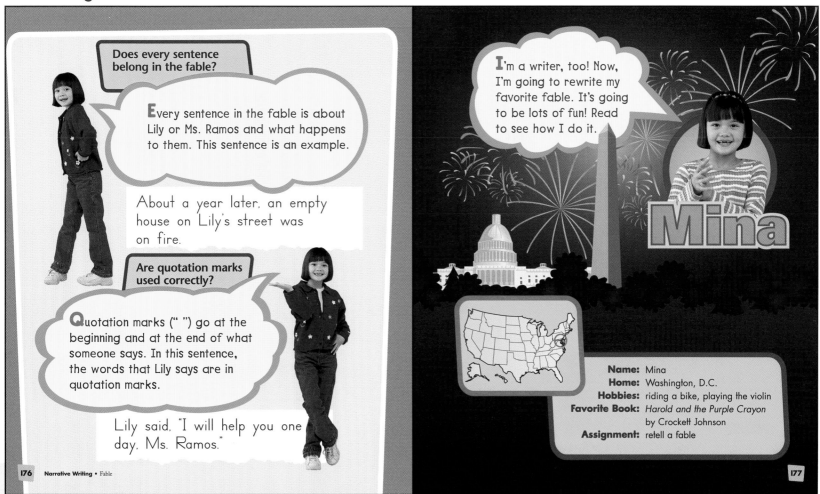

## Working With a Partner Mini-Lesson:
### Listen Without Interrupting

Help students understand how to work with a partner effectively by giving them some basic tips. You may wish to write these on chart paper and display them where students can readily see them.

Review some of the advice you have already given students for working with a partner. Explain that there is another skill that can be helpful to them. Students should **listen without interrupting** to what their partner has to say. They should let their partner finish before asking questions or disagreeing. You might want to remind students that this is a good skill for working with people on anything, not just for working with a writing partner!

**Model the Tip** Consider having two students role-play to model the skill or asking a student to respond to your writing while you model listening carefully and not saying a word until the speaker is finished. You may wish to give students a copy of the Working With a Partner Checklist on page T166.

## Mina:
### Writer of a Fable

*(Student Page 177)*

Read the information about Mina to learn more about her. Be sure students understand that Mina will write her own fable in this chapter. Review the information given about her. Discuss what Mina might write about in her fable based on her interests.

Point out that Mina will go through the steps in the writing process (Prewriting, Drafting, Revising, Editing, and Publishing). At each stage, she will use a good writing strategy and explain how she used it. Students should watch for key words, including **Gather, Organize, Write, Add (Elaborate), Take Out (Clarify), Proofread,** and **Share,** to follow the strategies Mina uses as she goes through the writing process.

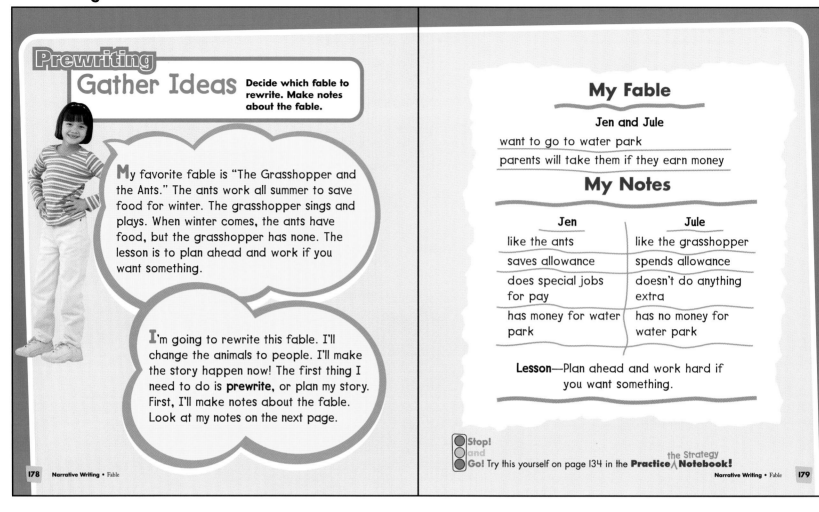

Read Mina's notes on Student Page 179 with the students. Ask them why it is a good idea to start out by writing notes. [Possible responses: Writing notes helps you decide who your characters will be and what will happen. Writing notes helps you plan.]

# Prewriting Gather Ideas

**Strategy: Decide which fable to rewrite. Make notes about the fable.**

*(Student Pages 178–179)*

Read Mina's words on Student Page 178 with the students. Tell them that in this section Mina will explain how she went about writing her fable. She starts by telling how she chose her fable and how she got started on her prewriting. Ask the students to retell what Mina did. [Possible responses: Mina thought of her own favorite fable. Then she made notes about the way she wanted to rewrite the fable.]

## Practice the Strategy Notebook!

*Practice the Strategy Notebook* pages 134–135 provide ideas for fable topics as well as an example of another writer's notes. After students have completed the activity on page 135, you may wish to have them share their responses.

## Practice the Strategy Notebook!

*Practice the Strategy Notebook* pages 136–137 provide an opportunity for students to explore more ideas for a fable they could rewrite and then to make some notes about their fable. You may wish to assign these pages now or after students have completed this chapter in the Student Edition. You may wish to save students' *Your Own Writing* pages and add them to their Work-in-Progress Portfolios.

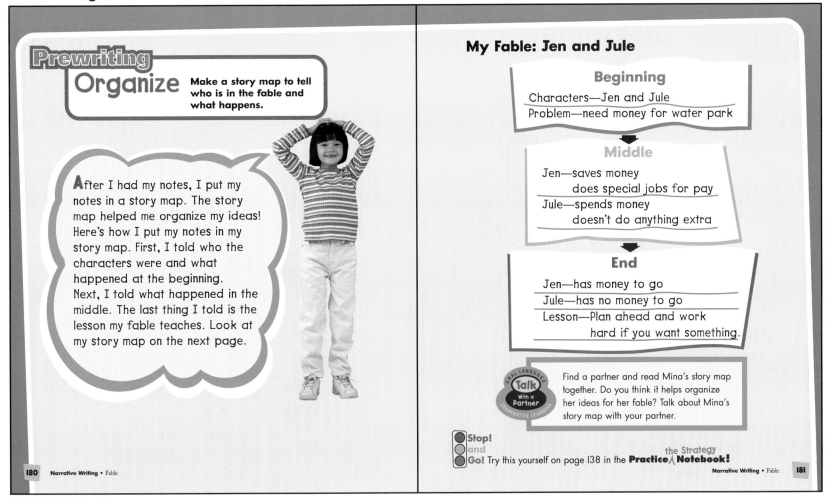

**Prewriting**

## Organize

Make a story map to tell who is in the fable and what happens.

After I had my notes, I put my notes in a story map. The story map helped me organize my ideas! Here's how I put my notes in my story map. First, I told who the characters were and what happened at the beginning. Next, I told what happened in the middle. The last thing I told is the lesson my fable teaches. Look at my story map on the next page.

### My Fable: Jen and Jule

**Beginning**
Characters—Jen and Jule
Problem—need money for water park

**Middle**
Jen—saves money
    does special jobs for pay
Jule—spends money
    doesn't do anything extra

**End**
Jen—has money to go
Jule—has no money to go
Lesson—Plan ahead and work
    hard if you want something.

**Talk With a Partner** — ORAL LANGUAGE COOPERATIVE LEARNING

Find a partner and read Mina's story map together. Do you think it helps organize her ideas for her fable? Talk about Mina's story map with your partner.

Stop! and Go! Try this yourself on page 138 in the **Practice the Strategy Notebook!**

---

**Prewriting**  Organize

**Strategy: Make a story map to tell who is in the fable and what happens.**

*(Student Pages 180–181)*

Read Mina's words on Student Page 180 with the students. Explain that before Mina begins her draft, she needs to organize her ideas. She does this by making a story map. Discuss with the students why a story map is a good choice for organizing a fable. [Possible responses: A story map helps you to put the characters, the story, and the lesson where they are supposed to go. It helps you make sure you have everything you need for a fable.]

Direct students' attention to Mina's story map on Student Page 181. Point out that Mina tells who is in the fable and what the problem is at the beginning. Mina uses the middle of the story map to show what happens. She uses the end to tell the end of the fable and the lesson. Explain that Mina will fit the lesson with the fable and write the lesson as the last sentence of her draft.

Encourage the students to discuss Mina's story map with their partners. Ask the students if Mina's story map seems complete. You may wish to discuss the partners' findings as a large-group activity, as well.

**Note:** A story map transparency is provided in the *Strategies for Writers Transparencies*.

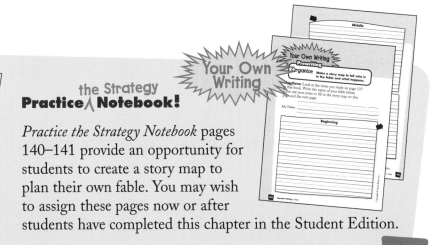

**Practice the Strategy Notebook!**

*Practice the Strategy Notebook* pages 138–139 provide additional practice in understanding how a story map can be used to organize ideas for a fable. After students have completed this activity, you may wish to have them share their answers to the questions on page 139 with a writing partner.

**Your Own Writing**
**Practice the Strategy Notebook!**

*Practice the Strategy Notebook* pages 140–141 provide an opportunity for students to create a story map to plan their own fable. You may wish to assign these pages now or after students have completed this chapter in the Student Edition.

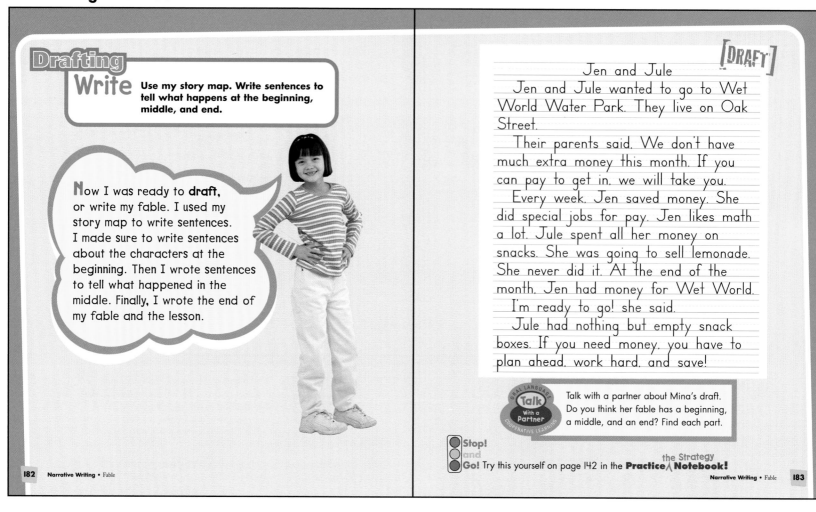

**Drafting**
## Write
Use my story map. Write sentences to tell what happens at the beginning, middle, and end.

Now I was ready to **draft**, or write my fable. I used my story map to write sentences. I made sure to write sentences about the characters at the beginning. Then I wrote sentences to tell what happened in the middle. Finally, I wrote the end of my fable and the lesson.

182    **Narrative Writing • Fable**

[DRAFT]

Jen and Jule

Jen and Jule wanted to go to Wet World Water Park. They live on Oak Street.

Their parents said, We don't have much extra money this month. If you can pay to get in, we will take you.

Every week, Jen saved money. She did special jobs for pay. Jen likes math a lot. Jule spent all her money on snacks. She was going to sell lemonade. She never did it. At the end of the month, Jen had money for Wet World. I'm ready to go! she said.

Jule had nothing but empty snack boxes. If you need money, you have to plan ahead, work hard, and save!

**Talk With a Partner** — ORAL LANGUAGE COOPERATIVE LEARNING

Talk with a partner about Mina's draft. Do you think her fable has a beginning, a middle, and an end? Find each part.

**Stop! and Go!** Try this yourself on page 142 in the **Practice Notebook!**

**Narrative Writing • Fable**    183

---

**Drafting** Write

**Strategy:** Use my story map. Write sentences to tell what happens at the beginning, middle, and end.

*(Student Pages 182–183)*

Read Mina's words on Student Page 182, and review the term *draft*. Then read Mina's draft with the students. Call on a volunteer to tell the ways in which this is a "first try" at a fable, or guide students to see that the first try at writing a whole story does not have to be perfect. Remind students that when they draft, their most important goal is to get the fable written completely, as Mina did, and not to worry about any problems they have with spelling or punctuation.

Ask the students whether Mina's fable has all three parts: a beginning, a middle, and an end. Then have students identify which paragraph tells the beginning, which paragraph tells the middle, and which paragraph tells the end.

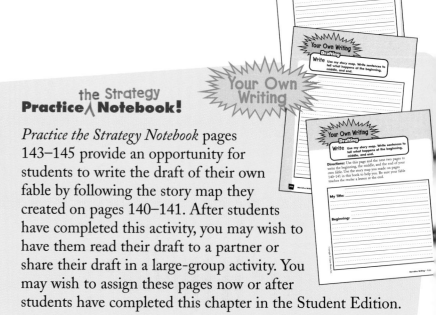

**the Strategy Practice Notebook!**

*Practice the Strategy Notebook* page 142 provides students with an opportunity to read another fable draft and to identify the beginning, middle, and end as well as the lesson of the fable. After students have completed this activity, you may wish to have them share their answers with a writing partner.

**the Strategy Practice Notebook!**

*Practice the Strategy Notebook* pages 143–145 provide an opportunity for students to write the draft of their own fable by following the story map they created on pages 140–141. After students have completed this activity, you may wish to have them read their draft to a partner or share their draft in a large-group activity. You may wish to assign these pages now or after students have completed this chapter in the Student Edition.

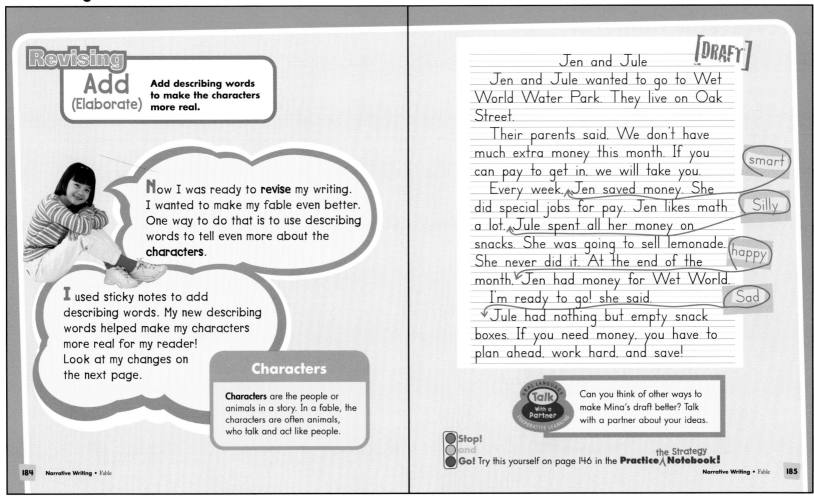

## Revising Add (Elaborate)

**Strategy: Add describing words to make the characters more real.**

*(Student Pages 184–185)*

Discuss the definition of the term *characters* on Student Page 184. Also review the term *revise*. Then read Mina's words with the students. Explain that one way to revise a fable is to add describing words to make the characters more real.

**Note:** *Strategies for Writers* employs the term **Elaborate** in grades 3–8. You may wish to explain to students that *elaborate* means "to add."

Read Mina's revised draft on Student Page 185 with the students. Ask students how Mina's revisions have made her fable even better. [Possible responses: The describing words tell more about the characters. They make the fable more interesting.]

### the Strategy Practice∧Notebook!

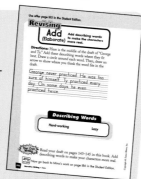

*Practice the Strategy Notebook* page 146 provides additional practice in revising a draft by adding describing words. After students have completed this activity, remind them to use this strategy to revise their own fable.

Encourage students to talk about Mina's revisions with a partner. Did her revisions make her fable better? What other changes could Mina have made?

## Tips for Successful Conferencing: Evaluating Writing Experiences

You might want to devote some conference time to having your students evaluate their own writing experiences. Your questions may help them understand their writing process better or become more aware of the writing choices they make. You might ask questions like these and continue the discussion based on the student's answers:

• How did you feel while you were writing today?
• Which of your papers do you think is your best? Why?
• Which piece of writing was easiest for you? Why?
• Which piece of writing was hardest for you? Why?
• Do you think you are a good writer? Why? (Why not?)
• What is the most important thing for you about writing?
• What do you want to learn more about to help you as a writer?

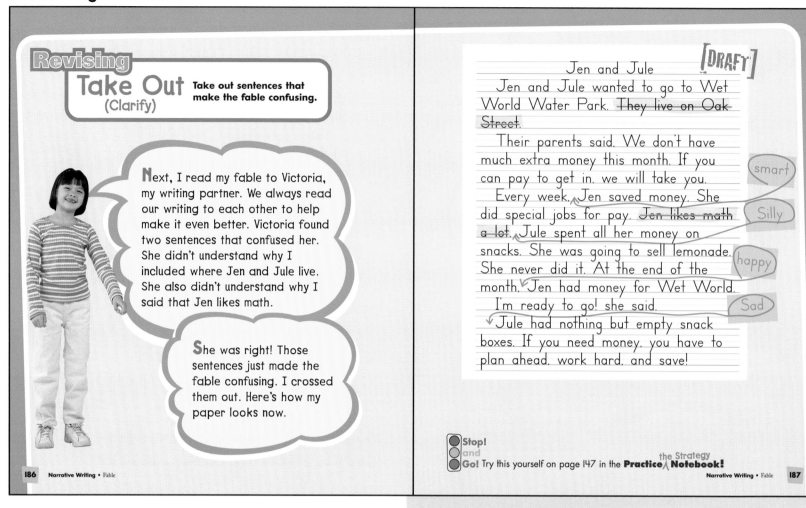

## Revising Take Out (Clarify)

**Strategy: Take out sentences that make the fable confusing.**

*(Student Pages 186–187)*

Read Mina's words on Student Page 186 with the students. Explain that another kind of revising is taking out sentences that make a story confusing. Read Mina's revised draft on Student Page 187 with the students. Point out that Mina took out the sentence "They live on Oak Street" because it doesn't help to tell the fable. Ask students why not. [**Possible response: Where Jen and Jule live has nothing to do with the story.**] Ask which other sentence Mina took out. [**Response: "Jen likes math a lot."**] Again ask students why Mina crossed out the sentence. [**Possible response: What subject(s) Jen likes has nothing to do with earning money for the water park.**]

**Note:** *Strategies for Writers* employs the term **Clarify** in grades 3–8. You may wish to explain to students that *clarify* means "to make clear," usually by taking out what's unnecessary.

## Spelling Strategies:
### Use Sentence Memory Tricks

Before students begin the Editing portion of the chapter, you may wish to remind them that checking spelling is an important part of editing their writing. Encourage students to use several strategies to figure out the spelling of new or hard words. One strategy is to **use sentence memory tricks**. Students can make up sentences like the following as mnemonic devices for remembering the spelling of words.

Using familiar words like "arm" and "ant" will help students remember less familiar words.

- My <u>arm</u> will keep you <u>warm</u>.
- The <u>ant</u> <u>wants</u> water.
- I am <u>here</u>. You are <u>there</u>.

### the Strategy Practice Notebook!

*Practice the Strategy Notebook* page 147 provides additional practice in revising a draft by taking out ideas that make the story confusing. After students have completed this activity, remind them to use this strategy to revise their own fable.

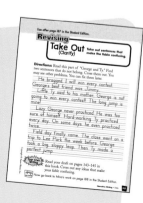

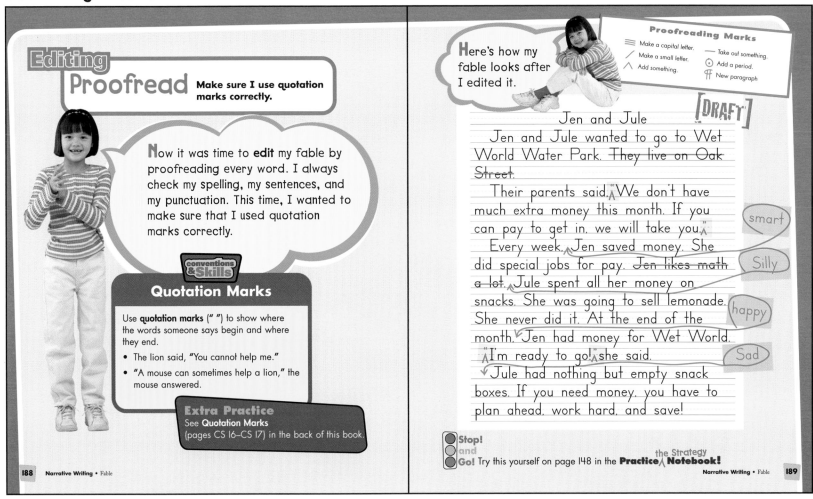

# Editing Proofread

**Strategy: Make sure I use quotation marks correctly.**

*(Student Pages 188–189)*

Remind students that when writers edit, they fix any mistakes in spelling, capitalization, punctuation, and grammar. Remind students that to *proofread* is to read their own writing while looking for mistakes.

Read Mina's words on Student Page 188 with the students. Remind students that Mina always checks her spelling and makes sure her sentences are complete. Tell students that Mina is now going to use a colored pencil to fix problems with quotation marks. Remind students that using a different color to correct mistakes helps writers see the corrections better so that they can be sure to include them when they write their final copy. **Note:** You may wish to give students their own colored pencils to edit their writing.

Read the information about quotation marks at the bottom of Student Page 188 with the students. Read the examples to emphasize which words are the direct words of the speaker.

Point out the proofreading symbols chart on Student Page 189 to the students. Explain that these symbols help writers remember what kind of corrections they made so that they can include those corrections when they write their final copy.

Read Mina's edited draft with the students. Ask them if Mina made all the necessary corrections. You may wish to use the corresponding Writing Model for Proofreading Practice Transparency.

## Extra Practice: **Conventions & Skills**

### Student Edition

If your students need more practice in using quotation marks correctly, you may wish to assign Student Pages CS 16–CS 17.

### Conventions & Skills Practice

For more targeted practice related to this skill, see this lesson in the optional *Conventions & Skills Practice Book*:

    Lesson 49: Quotation Marks

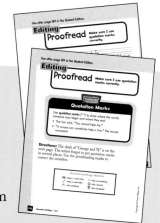

### the Strategy Practice Notebook!

*Practice the Strategy Notebook* pages 148–149 provide additional practice in editing a draft by correcting errors in the use of quotation marks. After students have completed this activity, remind them to use this strategy to edit their own fable.

**Narrative Writing • Fable**   **T133**

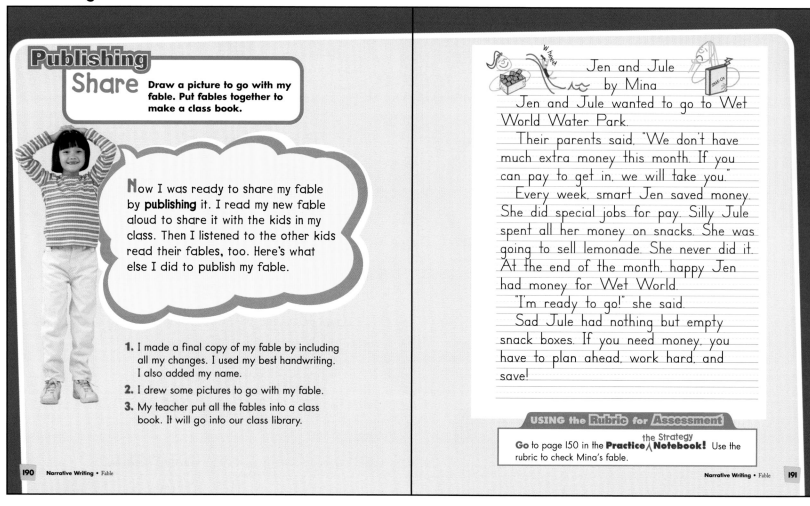

# Publishing Share

**Strategy: Draw a picture to go with my fable. Put fables together to make a class book.**

*(Student Pages 190–191)*

Read Mina's words on Student Page 190 to the students. Explain that publishing is the process of finishing a piece of writing to share it with others. Once writers have revised and edited their writing, they may publish it. They make a final copy, being sure to include all the changes they made when they revised and edited their writing.

Remind students that there are many ways to share published writing. Mina's class decided to put their fables together to make a class book that would become part of the class library. Ask the students why this is a good idea. [Possible response: If the fable is in the class library, all the other students and classroom visitors can read it.] Other publishing options include posting the fable on a class display, reading the fable aloud during "Author Day," and acting out the fable for another class.

Read the final copy of Mina's fable on Student Page 191 with the students.

Encourage students to talk with a partner about how Mina shared her fable. Was it a good way to share writing? How else could Mina have shared her fable?

## Using a Rubric

*Practice the Strategy Notebook* pages 150–151 provide a rubric for assessing the final copy of Mina's fable. Encourage students to work with a partner to evaluate Mina's fable by using this rubric. After students have completed this activity, you may wish to have them share the results in a large-group activity.

**Responding to Literature**
## Your Own Writing
NARRATIVE

Use what you learned in this unit to retell your own once upon a time story, fable, or both! Try these ideas.
- Use **Your Own Writing** pages in the *Practice the Strategy Notebook*.
- Pick a topic below, and write something new.
- Choose another idea of your own.

Follow the steps in the writing process. Use the Once Upon a Time Story Rubric on pages 132–133 in the *Practice the Strategy Notebook* or the Fable Rubric on pages 172–173 in the *Practice the Strategy Notebook* to check your writing.

| Once Upon a Time Story | Fable |
|---|---|
| • "The Elves and the Shoemaker"<br>• "Three Billy Goats Gruff"<br>• "Rumpelstiltskin"<br>• "Stone Soup" | • "The Tortoise and the Hare"<br>• "Fox and the Crow"<br>• "The City Mouse and the Country Mouse"<br>• "The North Wind and the Sun" |

portfolio  School-Home Connection

Keep a writing folder. Add **Your Own Writing** pages to your writing folder. You may want to take your writing folder home to share.

## Your Own Writing
## Narrative Writing for Responding to Literature

Assign either one or both kinds of narrative writing to the students. Before they begin writing, review key information about each kind. Decide which of the following you wish students to do:

- Choose a topic on this page in the Student Edition.
- Complete one of the Your Own Writing pieces in the *Practice the Strategy Notebook*.
- Come up with a new idea.

## Portfolio/School-Home Connection

Encourage the students to keep a portfolio of their writing.

### Work-in-Progress Portfolio

Remind students to review this portfolio often to revise existing pieces that have not been published. Encourage students to share pieces of their Work-in-Progress Portfolios with family members who can help in editing.

### Published Portfolio

Encourage students to choose pieces from their Published Portfolios to share with family members.

# Proofreading Marks

≡    Make a capital letter.

/    Make a small letter.

∧    Add something.

—    Take out something.

⊙    Add a period.

¶    New paragraph

You may wish to copy this chart and distribute it to your students.

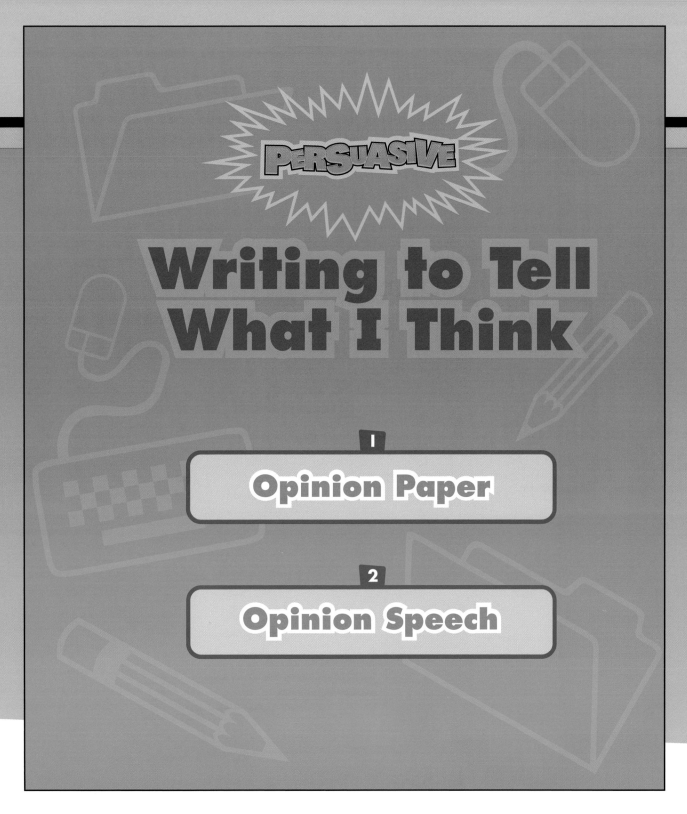

**PERSUASIVE**

# Writing to Tell What I Think

**1 Opinion Paper**

**2 Opinion Speech**

## Defining Writing to Tell What I Think

Ask the students to name a favorite book or television show. Then ask why they like it. List their reasons on the board. Explain that some writing tells reasons for liking something.

Then ask for some opinions about what should be changed on television. List the reasons for the opinions on the board. Explain that some writing tells reasons for thinking something. Both kinds of writing give an opinion.

Read and discuss Student Page 193 with the students. Tell students that in this unit they will be writing about what they think. First, they will write an opinion paper. Then they will write an opinion speech.

## Books to Share With Students

For excellent examples of children's books that use persuasive writing, you may wish to share these books with your students.

- *Miss Rumphius* by Barbara Cooney
- *Animals Should Definitely <u>Not</u> Wear Clothing* by Judi Barrett
- *Should There Be Zoos: A Persuasive Text* by Tony Stead

You may also wish to use some of the titles from Zaner-Bloser Literacy.

## for the Writing Classroom

by Barry Sneed, *Master Teacher*

### Writing Conventions

Teaching writing conventions to young children is one thing, but instilling students' use of those conventions as part of their natural writing efforts is another. Such noble endeavors on our part as educators require repetition, practice, and patience. For a few children, learning to use proper conven-

tions and editing their work for correctness will be easy, but for most it will take constant reminding, a lot of practice, the use of a checklist/rubric, peer and teacher support, and maybe even a song to help out!

With that in mind, I recommend using "The Writing Process Hokey Pokey" and "Oh, Dear! What Can the Matter Be?" to instill in students the key concepts you want them to use. Both songs are on the *Strategies for Writers Sing-Along* CD. (The lyrics for the songs appear in the Appendix at the end of this Teacher Edition.)

## Opinion Paper
### Writing Strategies

### Prewriting

**Gather Ideas**
Think about foods I like. Pick one to write about.

**Organize**
Make a spider map to organize my reasons.

### Drafting

**Write**
Use my spider map. Write one paragraph about each spider leg.

### Publishing

**Share**
Post my paper on a "Class Opinions" bulletin board.

### Revising

**Add (Elaborate)**
Add details to explain my reasons.

**Take Out (Clarify)**
Take out sentences that don't help explain my opinion.

### Editing

**Proofread**
Make sure every sentence has a subject and a predicate.

**Note:** A blackline master of the writing process flow chart appears on page T106. You may wish to copy and distribute it to your students.

### MODELED WRITING

**Opinion Paper Writing Mini-Lesson:** You may wish to present the following mini-lesson before the students read the model on Student Page 195. Write the following on the board, chart paper, or an overhead transparency:

> Peanut butter on toast is the best snack. It is good for you. It gives you energy. It is easy to make. This snack is also easy to share. Tammy likes cereal for a snack.

Ask the students what the sentences on the board tell them. [Possible response: They tell why peanut butter on toast is the best snack.] Explain that this kind of writing is called an opinion paper. Tell

students they will be learning more about how to write an opinion paper in this chapter in the Student Edition. They will see a model of this kind of writing and learn and practice some strategies for writing their own opinion paper. Write the title "The Best Snack" above the sentences.

Ask the students whether they can find any problem in the writing. [Response: Yes, the last sentence does not belong there.] Cross out the last sentence. Explain that when they write their own opinion paper, they will also learn how to revise by crossing out sentences that don't help explain the opinion.

You can use these songs in a variety of ways:

- You can teach one verse at a time (as a specific writing convention is introduced).
- You can teach the whole song when you are ready for students to begin self-monitoring their work.
- You can use the song to help students support each other's efforts using peer editing.

The main skills to focus on with second grade writers include capitalizing the first letter of the first word in a sentence, capitalizing the word *I*, including end punctuation (primarily periods and question marks), maintaining spacing between words, using correct spelling in final copies, determining whether the writing makes sense, and using commas between items in a series.

This is a large body of knowledge, so don't get discouraged if students don't master it all quickly, even though they probably encountered most of these conventions in the first grade. Remember, research shows that for children to become familiar with a word or concept, they must encounter it a minimum of 50 times, so you will have to provide plenty of opportunities for children to encounter and use the writing conventions you teach.

## Time Management for This Chapter*

| Session | | Session | | Session | |
|---|---|---|---|---|---|
| **1** | Read Student Pages 193–194. Introduce Nicole. Read the model on Student Page 195. Discuss the rubric on Student Pages 196–197. | **6** | Assign *Practice the Strategy Notebook* pages 156–159. | **11** | Read **REVISING: Take Out (Clarify)** (Student Pages 210–211). |
| **2** | Read Student Pages 198–201. Discuss Nicole's assessment of the model opinion paper. Discuss the information about Nicole on Student Page 201. | **7** | Read **DRAFTING: Write** (Student Pages 206–207). | **12** | Assign *Practice the Strategy Notebook* page 165. |
| **3** | Read **PREWRITING: Gather Ideas** (Student Pages 202–203). | **8** | Assign *Practice the Strategy Notebook* pages 160–163. | **13** | Read **EDITING: Proofread** (Student Pages 212–213). |
| **4** | Assign *Practice the Strategy Notebook* pages 152–155. | **9** | Read **REVISING: Add (Elaborate)** (Student Pages 208–209). | **14** | Assign *Practice the Strategy Notebook* pages 166–167. |
| **5** | Read **PREWRITING: Organize** (Student Pages 204–205). | **10** | Assign *Practice the Strategy Notebook* page 164. | **15** | Read **PUBLISHING: Share** (Student Pages 214–215). Assign *Practice the Strategy Notebook* pages 168–169. |

*To complete the chapter in fewer sessions, assign the *Practice the Strategy Notebook* pages on the same day the targeted skill is introduced.

## STRATEGIES for Writers Sing-Along CD

You may wish to use the *Strategies for Writers Sing-Along* CD throughout the chapter. See the Appendix in the back of this Teacher Edition for more information.

### WRITER'S HANDBOOK

Remind students that they can refer to the Writer's Handbook in the back of the Student Edition for more information.

# Introduce the Genre:
## Opinion Paper

*(Student Pages 194–195)*

Read Student Page 194 with the students. Explain that the student guide in their books is going to show them how to write an opinion paper. Tell them that they will read Nicole's work as a class. They will have a chance to talk about it with a partner and with the whole class. Then they will practice using the same strategies to write their own opinion papers. Ask the students to think of some favorite foods. [**Possible responses: pizza, hamburgers, popcorn**]

# Read the Model:
## Opinion Paper

Read Nicole's words on Student Page 195 with the students. Then read the model of the opinion paper. Ask what makes it a good example of an opinion paper. [**Possible responses: It tells what someone thinks. It gives reasons.**]

As you read the model with the students, point out that the model contains words that students may not know. You may wish to add these words to your Word Wall and encourage students to refer to the Word Wall as they proofread their own opinion papers for spelling.

# Meeting Students' Needs:
## Second-Language Learners

Introduce the model paper by reading and pointing out the opinion in the first sentence. Tell students that the rest of the paper will give reasons for the opinion. Have students work in pairs to coach each other as they read the paper aloud. If appropriate, assign a fluent English-speaking student to each pair to help them.

## Students Who Need Extra Help

Suggest that students preview the paper by reading the title and the first sentence and then predicting what reasons the writer might give to support the opinion. Ask the students to look for three main reasons as they read. Afterward, invite volunteers to list the writer's three reasons.

## Gifted Students

Explain that an example is something that helps explain a reason. Then challenge students to add one or more good examples to the reasons in the model opinion paper.

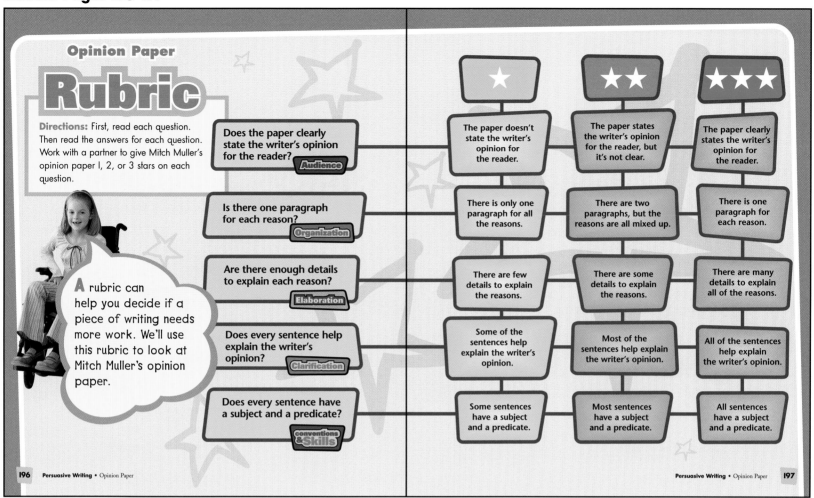

# Using a Rubric

Use the text on Student Pages 198–200 to model the use of a rubric for evaluating a piece of writing. For more information on using a rubric, please see page T21.

## Discuss the Opinion Paper Rubric

*(Student Pages 196–197)*

Read Nicole's words and the questions on Student Page 196 with the students. Explain that a writer can use these questions to write a good opinion paper. Discuss each question with the students.

**Audience: Does the paper clearly state the writer's opinion for the reader?** The opinion should be stated clearly for the reader.

**Organization: Is there one paragraph for each reason?** The opinion should be supported by reasons. Each reason should be stated in a separate paragraph.

**Elaboration: Are there enough details to explain each reason?** Details help explain the reasons and make it easier to understand the opinion.

**Clarification: Does every sentence help explain the writer's opinion?** The writing should stick to the point. The paper should not contain sentences that don't help explain the opinion.

**Conventions & Skills: Does every sentence have a subject and a predicate?** Correct grammar makes writing clear and easy to follow.

Have students evaluate the model opinion paper with a partner, using the opinion paper rubric on Student Pages 196–197. Ask partners to share their evaluations with the whole group.

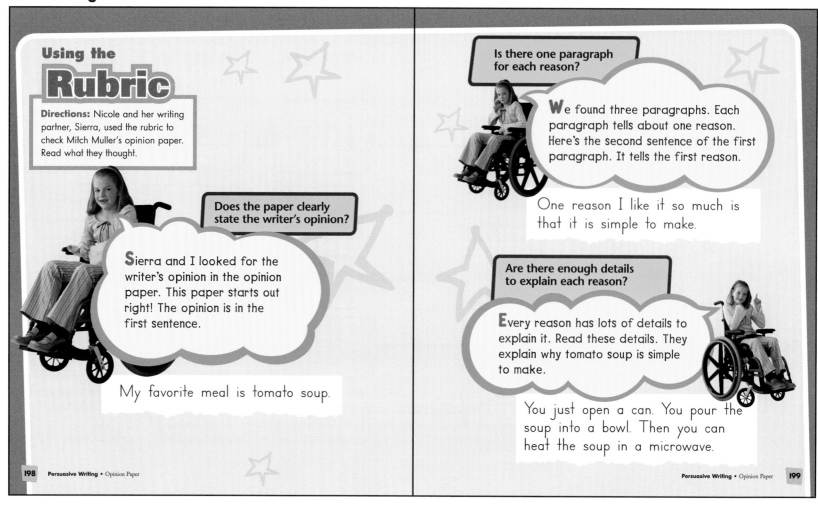

## Using the Rubric to Study the Model

*(Student Pages 198–200)*

Explain to students that now they can see how Nicole is going to use the questions on the rubric to evaluate the opinion paper on Student Page 195.

Read the question in the box on Student Page 198, and then read Nicole's words. Ask the students whether they agree that the paper begins with an opinion. Read the example sentence.

Read the question in the first box on Student Page 199 with the students. You might want to return to the model on Student Page 195 after reading Nicole's words and the example sentence. Do students agree that the opinion paper has one paragraph for each reason? Read the question in the second box. Again, you might want to return to the model on Student Page 195 after reading Nicole's words and the example sentences. Do details explain each of the reasons?

Read Student Page 200 with the students. Remind them that an opinion paper should not include any sentences that don't help explain the opinion. Remind them also that having a subject and a predicate in every sentence makes it easier for readers to understand the writing.

## Incorporating Rubrics Into the Classroom

by Lee Bromberger, *Assessment Specialist*

Beyond getting student input and teaching students how rubrics will be used with assignments, teachers can introduce other ways to make rubrics a consistent part of the classroom routine. The following are some suggestions:

- Provide each student with a copy of the rubric with each new assignment.
- Practice using rubrics with students to evaluate actual student writings. (It's helpful to use papers from previous classes. Always keep the writer's name a secret.)
- Ask for student input when developing a new rubric.
- If a rubric is used for several assignments, enlarge the rubric and post it in the classroom as a visual reminder.
- Place student writings and rubrics into a writing folder for each student. Review the strengths and weaknesses of previous writings when conferencing with students.

As teachers incorporate these and other measures, students will become more comfortable with rubrics, which in time can lead to better writing, less time needed to assess student writing, and an acceptance of rubrics as part of the class curriculum.

**Does every sentence help explain the writer's opinion?**

Every sentence helps explain why tomato soup is the writer's favorite meal. Read these sentences.

You can eat it with crackers or toast. It tastes great with most sandwiches.

**Does every sentence have a subject and a predicate?**

The subject of a sentence tells who or what does something. The predicate tells what the subject does or is. All the sentences in this opinion paper have a subject and a predicate. Can you find the subject and the predicate in this sentence?

Tomato soup warms up your insides, too.

200    Persuasive Writing • Opinion Paper

I'm a writer, too! Now I'm going to write my own opinion paper. Read to see how I do it.

Nicole

**Name:** Nicole
**Home:** Utah
**Hobbies:** playing the flute, collecting baseball cards
**Favorite Book:** *Strega Nona* by Tomie de Paola
**Favorite Foods:** apple pie, mashed potatoes, lasagna
**Assignment:** opinion paper

201

# Working With a Partner Mini-Lesson:
## Write It Down

Help students understand how to work with a partner effectively by giving them some basic tips. You may wish to write these on chart paper and display them where students can readily see them.

Before students meet with their writing partners on opinion writing for the first time, offer a new strategy for working effectively with a partner: **Write it down.** Explain to the students that they should jot down notes as their partners make suggestions. That way, they can be sure to remember the ideas when it is time to develop their prewriting or do other tasks. Remind students to give their partners plenty of time to write their notes as they are working together. You may wish to give students a copy of the Working With a Partner Checklist on page T166.

**Model the Tip** You may wish to model this tip by acting out a conference with a volunteer "partner." Read a piece of your own writing to your partner. Listen carefully as your partner gives suggestions and take notes as he or she is talking. After the conference, read your notes to the students. Explain that you will read these notes again and decide which suggestions you are going to use to improve your writing.

# Nicole:
## Writer of an Opinion Paper

*(Student Page 201)*

Read the information about Nicole to learn more about her. Be sure students understand that Nicole will write her own opinion paper in this chapter. Review the information given about her. Discuss what Nicole might write about in her opinion paper, based on her favorite foods.

Point out that Nicole will go through the steps in the writing process (Prewriting, Drafting, Revising, Editing, and Publishing). At each stage, she will use a good writing strategy and explain how she used it. Students should watch for key words, including **Gather, Organize, Write, Add (Elaborate), Take Out (Clarify), Proofread,** and **Share,** to follow the strategies Nicole uses as she goes through the writing process.

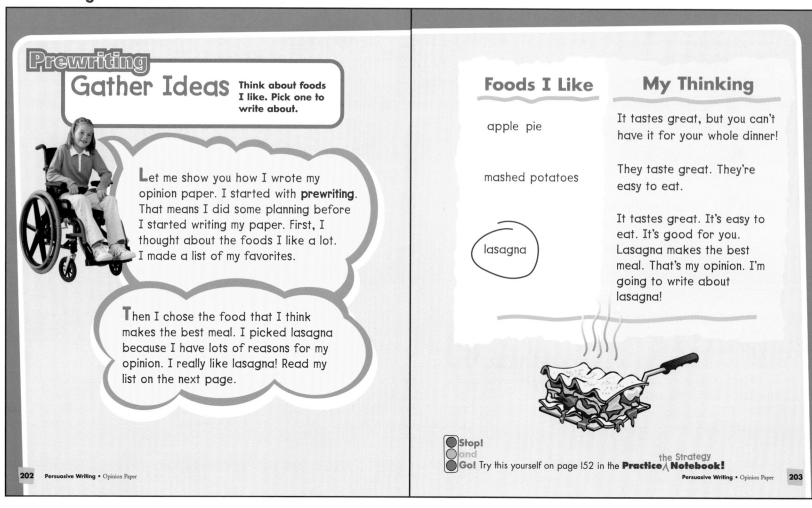

### Prewriting
## Gather Ideas
Think about foods I like. Pick one to write about.

Let me show you how I wrote my opinion paper. I started with **prewriting**. That means I did some planning before I started writing my paper. First, I thought about the foods I like a lot. I made a list of my favorites.

Then I chose the food that I think makes the best meal. I picked lasagna because I have lots of reasons for my opinion. I really like lasagna! Read my list on the next page.

| Foods I Like | My Thinking |
|---|---|
| apple pie | It tastes great, but you can't have it for your whole dinner! |
| mashed potatoes | They taste great. They're easy to eat. |
| (lasagna) | It tastes great. It's easy to eat. It's good for you. Lasagna makes the best meal. That's my opinion. I'm going to write about lasagna! |

**Stop! and Go!** Try this yourself on page 152 in the **Practice the Strategy Notebook!**

---

### Prewriting Gather Ideas

**Strategy: Think about foods I like. Pick one to write about.**

*(Student Pages 202–203)*

Read Nicole's words on Student Page 202 with the students. Tell the students that in this section Nicole will explain how she went about writing her opinion paper. She starts by telling how she chose her topic and how she got started on her prewriting. Ask the students to retell what Nicole did. [Possible response: Nicole thought about foods she likes. Then she made a list of her favorite foods.]

Point out Nicole's list and thoughts on Student Page 203. Ask students why it is a good idea to start out this way. [Possible response: It helps you decide on the best topic.]

### the Strategy Practice Notebook!

*Practice the Strategy Notebook* page 152 helps students identify a good topic for an opinion paper. Page 153 helps students differentiate an opinion from other statements. After students have completed these two activities, you may wish to have students share their responses.

### the Strategy Practice Notebook!

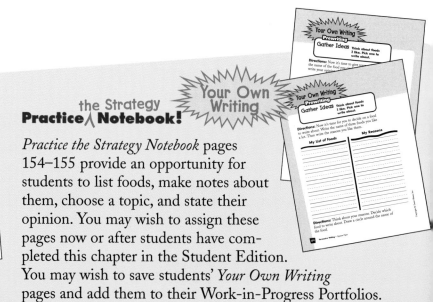

*Practice the Strategy Notebook* pages 154–155 provide an opportunity for students to list foods, make notes about them, choose a topic, and state their opinion. You may wish to assign these pages now or after students have completed this chapter in the Student Edition. You may wish to save students' *Your Own Writing* pages and add them to their Work-in-Progress Portfolios.

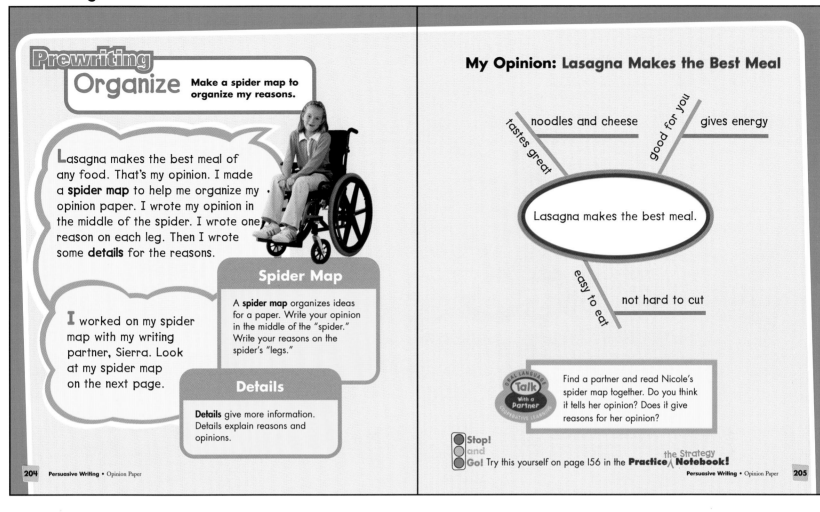

**Prewriting**
## Organize
Make a spider map to organize my reasons.

Lasagna makes the best meal of any food. That's my opinion. I made a **spider map** to help me organize my opinion paper. I wrote my opinion in the middle of the spider. I wrote one reason on each leg. Then I wrote some **details** for the reasons.

I worked on my spider map with my writing partner, Sierra. Look at my spider map on the next page.

### Spider Map
A **spider map** organizes ideas for a paper. Write your opinion in the middle of the "spider." Write your reasons on the spider's "legs."

### Details
**Details** give more information. Details explain reasons and opinions.

**204** Persuasive Writing • Opinion Paper

**My Opinion: Lasagna Makes the Best Meal**

noodles and cheese    good for you    gives energy

tastes great

Lasagna makes the best meal.

easy to eat    not hard to cut

**Talk** With a Partner — Find a partner and read Nicole's spider map together. Do you think it tells her opinion? Does it give reasons for her opinion?

Stop! and Go! Try this yourself on page 156 in the **Practice the Strategy Notebook!**

Persuasive Writing • Opinion Paper **205**

---

**Prewriting** ## Organize

**Strategy: Make a spider map to organize my reasons.**

*(Student Pages 204–205)*

Read aloud the definition of *spider map* on Student Page 204, and discuss it with the students. Do the same with the term *details*. Then read Nicole's words with the students. Explain that before Nicole begins her draft, she needs to organize her ideas. She does this by making a spider map. Discuss with students why it is a good idea to talk to a writing partner. [Possible response: A writing partner can help you think of new ideas for your spider map.]

Direct students' attention to Nicole's spider map on Student Page 205. Have students notice where Nicole writes her opinion. Point out where Nicole writes her reasons and details.

Encourage the students to discuss Nicole's spider map with their partners. Ask the students if Nicole's spider map seems complete. You may wish to discuss the partners' findings as a large-group activity, as well.

**Note:** A spider map transparency is provided in the *Strategies for Writers Transparencies*.

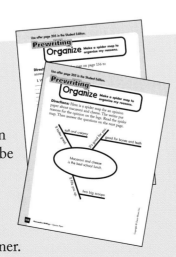

the Strategy
**Practice Notebook!**

*Practice the Strategy Notebook* pages 156–157 provide additional practice in understanding how a spider map can be used to organize ideas for an opinion paper. After students have completed this activity, you may wish to have them share their answers to the questions on page 157 with a writing partner.

the Strategy
**Practice Notebook!**

*Practice the Strategy Notebook* pages 158–159 provide an opportunity for students to plan and complete a spider map for their own opinion papers. You may wish to assign these pages now or after students have completed this chapter in the Student Edition.

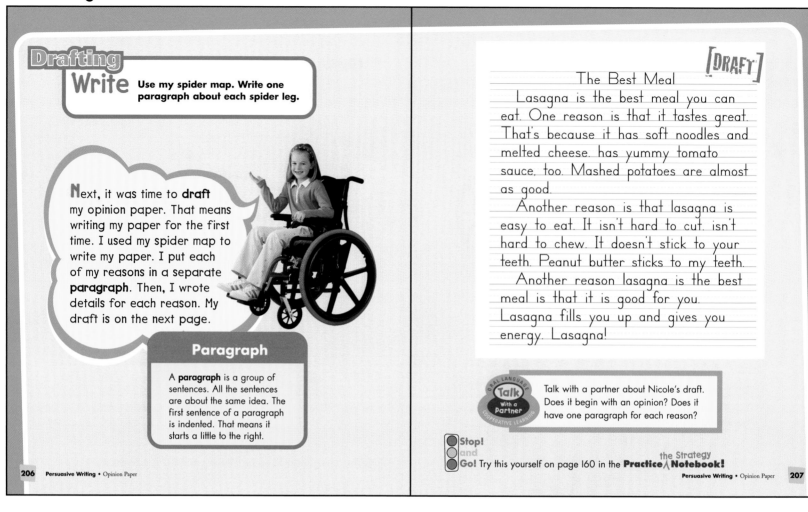

### Drafting Write

**Strategy: Use my spider map. Write one paragraph about each spider leg.**

*(Student Pages 206–207)*

Read aloud the definition of the term *paragraph* on Student Page 206, and discuss it with the students. Then read Nicole's words with them. Remind students of the definition of the term *draft*. Read Nicole's draft with the students. Note that Nicole's draft has a few mistakes that she will need to fix later, but that it's a fine start for now. Be sure students understand that it is important to write the opinion at the beginning of

the paper. Ask the students whether Nicole's paper has three different reasons in three different paragraphs. Have students identify the first paragraph and the first reason, the second paragraph and the second reason, and the third paragraph and the third reason.

 Encourage the students to discuss Nicole's draft. Ask the partners to decide whether Nicole wrote a clear paragraph for each reason.

### the Strategy Practice∧Notebook!

*Practice the Strategy Notebook* page 160 provides students with an opportunity to read an opinion paper draft and to analyze its structure. After students have completed this activity, you may wish to have them share their answers with a writing partner.

### the Strategy Practice∧Notebook!

*Practice the Strategy Notebook* pages 161–163 provide an opportunity for students to write the draft of their own opinion paper by following the spider map they filled out on page 159. After students have completed this activity, you may wish to have them read their draft to a partner or share their draft in a large-group activity. You may wish to assign these pages now or after students have completed this chapter in the Student Edition.

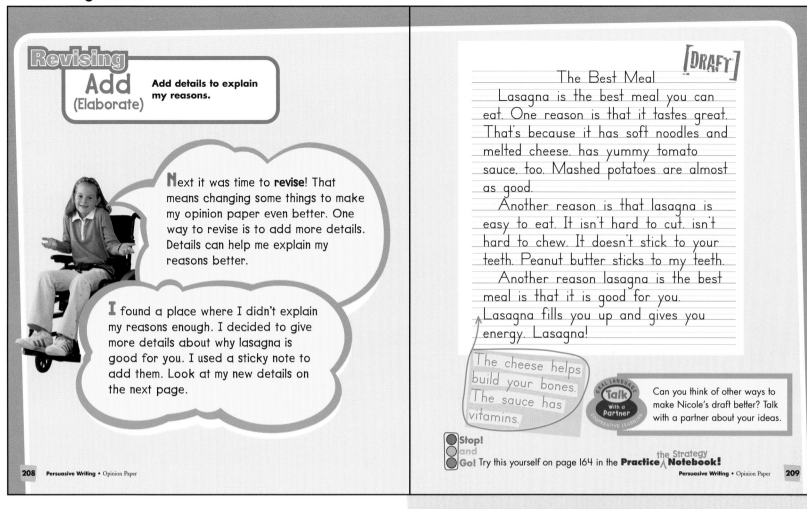

## Revising Add (Elaborate)

**Strategy: Add details to explain my reasons.**

*(Student Pages 208–209)*

Read Nicole's words on Student Page 208 with the students. Review the meaning of the term *revise*. Explain that when writers revise their work, they change what they say or how they say it. Explain that one way to revise an opinion paper is to add more details that explain the reasons for the writer's opinions.

Read Nicole's revised draft on Student Page 209 with the students. Ask students how Nicole's revisions have made her paper better. [Possible responses: The details tell more about why lasagna is good for you. The details make the paper more interesting.]

**Note:** *Strategies for Writers* employs the term **Elaborate** in grades 3–8. You may wish to explain to students that *elaborate* means "to add."

Encourage students to talk about Nicole's revisions with a partner. Did her changes make her opinion paper better? What other changes could Nicole have made?

## Spelling Strategies:
### Use Picture Memory Tricks

Before students begin the Editing portion of the chapter, you may wish to remind them that checking spelling is an important part of editing their writing. Encourage students to use several strategies to figure out the spellings of new words and hard words. One strategy is to **use picture memory tricks**. Students can make up pictures and sentences like the following as mnemonic devices:

• They can draw a hat over the word *hat* in the words *what* and *that*. What hat? That hat! They can write the e's in *eye* to look like eyes.
• They can draw an owl over the word *owl* in *bowl*.

### Practice the Strategy Notebook!

*Practice the Strategy Notebook* page 164 provides additional practice in revising a draft by adding examples to explain reasons. After students have completed this activity, remind them to use this strategy to revise their own opinion paper.

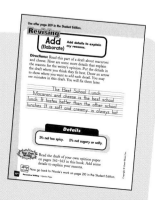

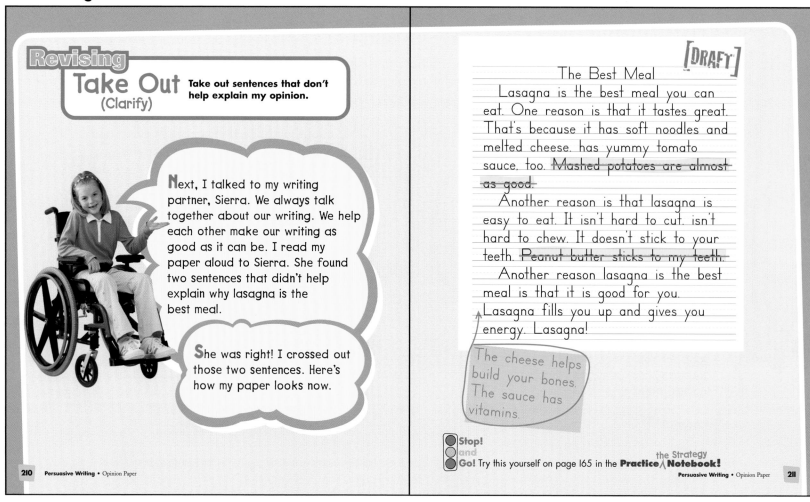

## Revising Take Out (Clarify)

**Strategy: Take out sentences that don't help explain my opinion.**

*(Student Pages 210–211)*

Read Nicole's words with the students. Explain that another kind of revising is taking out sentences that don't help explain the writer's opinion. Read Nicole's revised draft with the students. Point out that Nicole took out the sentence "Mashed potatoes are almost as good." Ask students why. [**Possible response: Mashed potatoes don't have anything to do with lasagna.**] Ask which other sentence Nicole crossed out. [**Response: "Peanut butter sticks to my teeth."**] Again ask students why Nicole crossed out the sentence. [**Possible response: It is about peanut butter, not lasagna.**]

**Note:** *Strategies for Writers* employs the term **Clarify** in grades 3–8. You may wish to explain to students that *clarify* means "to make clear," usually by taking out what's unnecessary.

## Tips for Successful Conferencing: More Reminders

As the school year progresses, conference time most likely will become more and more productive. Still, you may find some of these reminders useful:

- Enjoy yourself. A conference is yet another opportunity to take pleasure in talking with and getting to know the students.

- From time to time, forget any agenda you might have come into the conference with. Instead, just listen to the students and learn what you can from them.

- Focus on what students are doing well, rather than correcting problems.

- Continue to keep good records that will remind you of what you have learned about each writer.

### the Strategy Practice∧Notebook!

*Practice the Strategy Notebook* page 165 provides additional practice in revising a draft by taking out sentences that don't help explain an opinion. After students have completed this activity, remind them to use this strategy to revise their own opinion paper.

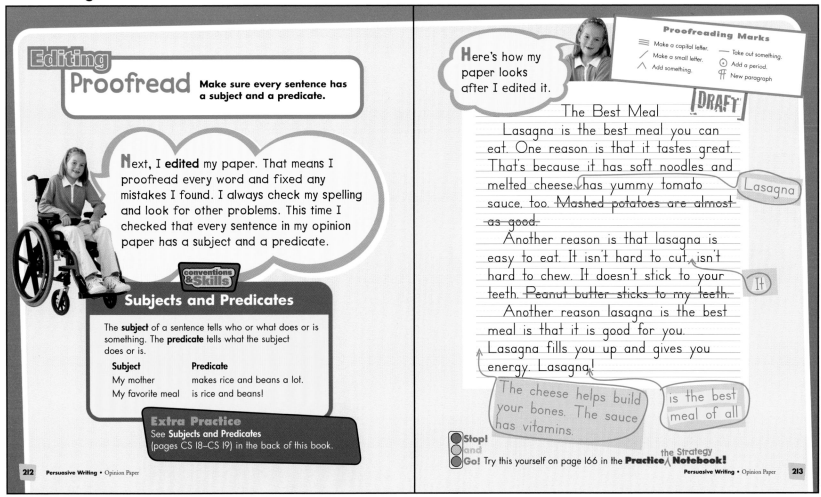

# Editing Proofread

*(Student Pages 212–213)*

**Strategy: Make sure every sentence has a subject and a predicate.**

Remind students that when writers edit, they fix any problems in spelling, capitalization, punctuation, and grammar. Remind students that *proofreading* means reading their own writing to find and fix these kinds of problems.

Read Nicole's words on Student Page 212 to the students. Remind students that Nicole always checks her spelling and punctuation. Tell students that Nicole is now going to add missing subjects or predicates. Remind students that using a pencil that writes in a different color helps writers see their revisions better. **Note:** You may wish to give students their own colored pencils to edit their writing.

Read the explanation and examples of subjects and predicates at the bottom of Student Page 212 with the students. Point out the proofreading symbols chart on Student Page 213 to the students. Explain that these symbols help writers remember what kinds of corrections they made. You may wish to give students a copy of the Proofreading Marks blackline master on page T136.

Read Nicole's edited draft with the students. Ask them if Nicole made all the necessary corrections. You may wish to use the corresponding Writing Model for Proofreading Practice Transparency.

## Extra Practice: Conventions & Skills

### Student Edition

If your students need more practice in writing complete sentences, you may wish to assign Student Pages CS 18–CS 19.

### Conventions & Skills Practice

For more targeted practice related to this skill, see these lessons in the optional *Conventions & Skills Practice Book*:

Lesson 2: Complete Subject and Complete Predicate
Lesson 3: Simple Subject
Lesson 4: Simple Predicate
Lesson 5: Sentence Fragments

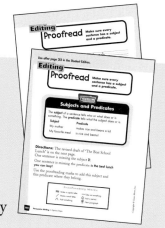

### the Strategy Practice∧Notebook!

*Practice the Strategy Notebook* pages 166–167 provide additional practice in editing a draft by correcting fragments that lack either a subject or a predicate. After students have completed this activity, remind them to use this strategy to edit their own opinion paper.

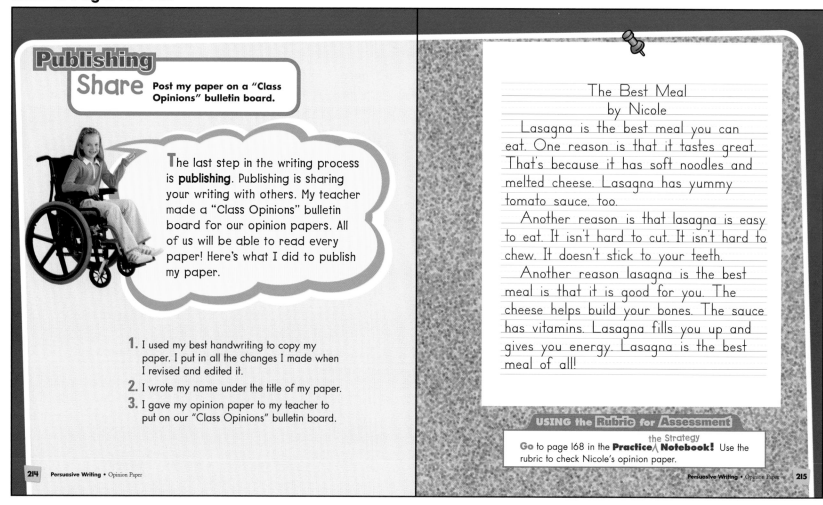

## Publishing Share

**Strategy: Post my paper on a "Class Opinions" bulletin board.**

*(Student Pages 214–215)*

Read Nicole's words to the students. Explain that *publishing* is sharing a finished piece of writing with others. Once writers are finished revising and editing their writing, they may publish it. They make a final copy of their writing, being sure they include all the changes they made.

Remind students that there are many ways to share published writing. Nicole wants to post her paper on the "Class Opinions" bulletin board. Ask the students why it's a good idea to do this. [Possible response: All the students can read one another's opinions.]

Other publishing options include posting the paper on the school's Web site or submitting the paper to a school newspaper or magazine.

Read the final copy of Nicole's paper on Student Page 215 with the students.

Encourage students to talk with a partner about how Nicole shared her paper. Was it a good way to share writing? How else could Nicole have shared her writing?

## Using a Rubric

*Practice the Strategy Notebook* pages 168–169 provide a rubric for assessing Nicole's final opinion paper. Encourage students to work with a partner to evaluate Nicole's opinion paper by using this rubric. After students have completed this activity, you may wish to have them share the results in a large-group activity.

## School–Home Connection

Dear Family,

Our class is learning and practicing many different kinds of writing. Writing is an opportunity for people to express their thoughts and feelings, as well as a chance to communicate information to others. Encourage your child to think of himself or herself as a writer. Every piece of written material your child produces brings him or her one step closer to being a good communicator and a person who thinks creatively. Your support and encouragement mean a great deal.

Encourage and celebrate your child's writing. Here are some ideas:

Create a quiet place for your child to write. Set aside a small space where your child can daydream, take notes, doodle, whatever. It doesn't have to be anything fancy—just a spot where your child can go that's just for writing.

Participate in your child's writing efforts. Offer to be interviewed for a writing assignment. Your memories or experiences may prove valuable to your young writer.

Post your child's writing in a special place at home. A refrigerator door is a great place to display your child's published works. Another idea is a simple bulletin board.

Encourage your child to read. Try your public library for a great selection of books on any topic your child is interested in. People who love to read often become people who love to write.

Encourage your child to do a daily writing activity, such as writing in a diary or keeping a journal. This kind of writing is especially helpful as an outlet for thoughts and feelings.

Help your child to develop real-life application skills by encouraging him or her to do some organizational writing, such as writing lists or schedules. This is a great activity for developing organizational skills and goal-setting skills.

Help your child to nurture his or her creativity by encouraging him or her to write poetry or song lyrics, descriptions, or short stories.

Try these simple but effective ways to help your child become a better writer. You'll be surprised at how well they work!

You may wish to copy the letter above and send it home with your students.

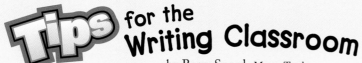 **for the Writing Classroom**

by Barry Sneed, *Master Teacher*

## Literature, Photos, & Writing Prompts

Using literature and photos as writing prompts can jump-start writing tasks in your classroom and stretch your students' imaginations and creativity. I love to share a good read-aloud book with my students and then use it as a starting point for a writing activity. There are several ways to do this.

One of my favorite authors is Robert Munsch, and my students adore all of his books because of their humor and repetitiveness. One of my favorites is *Thomas' Snowsuit*. I read the story, stopping short of the actual ending. My students then go to their seats and write how they think the book will end. We come back together to share our ideas, and then I read the actual ending to the class.

Another way to use a book as a writing prompt is to read one that children may relate to, such as Dr. Suess's *Oh, the Places You'll Go.* Then have your students write in their journals about the different places they'd like to go someday. Books

## Opinion Speech

### Writing Strategies

#### Prewriting

**Gather Ideas**
Think about my opinions on different topics. Write some reasons for my opinions. Choose a topic.

**Organize**
Make a spider map to organize facts for my reasons.

#### Drafting

**Write**
Use my spider map. Write one paragraph about each spider leg.

#### Publishing

**Share**
Give my speech during "Opinion Day" in my class.

#### Editing

**Proofread**
Make sure every sentence has a subject and a predicate.

#### Revising

**Add (Elaborate)**
Add facts to explain my reasons.

**Take Out (Clarify)**
Take out sentences that don't help explain my opinion.

**Note:** A blackline master of the writing process flow chart appears on page T106. You may wish to copy and distribute it to your students.

### MODELED WRITING

**Opinion Speech Writing Mini-Lesson:** You may wish to present the following mini-lesson before the students read the model on Student Page 217. Write the following on the board, chart paper, or an overhead transparency:

Everyone should have a cat. A cat can play with you. It can make you happy. It is fun to watch. A cat is a very beautiful animal. Fish are beautiful, too. A cat is the best pet.

Ask the students what the sentences on the board tell them. [Possible response: They give someone's opinion about having a cat.] Explain that this kind of writing tells what the writer thinks. When the

writing is read aloud, it is an opinion speech. Tell students they will be learning more about writing an opinion speech as they read the chapter in the Student Edition. They will see a model of this kind of writing and learn and practice some strategies for writing their own opinion speech. Write the title "The Best Pet" above the sentences.

Ask the students whether any sentences don't belong. [Possible response: Yes, the sixth sentence is not about cats.] Cross it out. Tell the students that when they write their own opinion speech, they will also revise by crossing out any sentences that don't help explain their opinion.

can be used as writing prompts in as many ways as your imagination can come up with, so pick your favorite books and put them to a whole new use!

Using photographs and pictures is another great way to ignite children's creative ideas and channel them into writing opportunities. I look at garage sales, local library book sales, and discount stores for such things as old calendars, magazines, and even old books. Pictures can be great "writing starters." I have even asked students' families to choose a picture of the family doing something together. The children then write about the picture. You can also use your students' families as a resource for obtaining old magazines and books that they no longer want. Once you have a collection of pic-

tures, hang them in the front of the room and ask students to write a story to explain what is happening in the picture. Depending on the picture you use, this device can be used to practice a variety of writing modes:

- **Narrative:** A picture of a boy fishing can lead to a story about the boy's day.
- **Expository:** A picture of a dog eating can prompt students to write what they know about dogs.
- **Descriptive:** A picture of a field of flowers can lead to a description of the field.
- **Persuasive:** A picture of a hot dog can prompt a child to write about why hot dogs are his/her favorite food.

## Time Management for This Chapter*

| Session | | Session | | Session | |
|---|---|---|---|---|---|
| **1** | Introduce the student guide. Read the model on Student Page 217. Discuss the rubric on Student Pages 218–219. | **6** | Assign *Practice the Strategy Notebook* pages 174–177. | **11** | Read **REVISING: Take Out (Clarify)** (Student Pages 232–233). |
| **2** | Read Student Pages 220–223. Discuss Jonathan's assessment of the model opinion speech. Discuss the information about Jonathan on Student Page 223. | **7** | Read **DRAFTING: Write** (Student Pages 228–229). | **12** | Assign *Practice the Strategy Notebook* page 183. |
| **3** | Read **PREWRITING: Gather Ideas** (Student Pages 224–225). | **8** | Assign *Practice the Strategy Notebook* pages 178–181. | **13** | Read **EDITING: Proofread** (Student Pages 234–235). |
| **4** | Assign *Practice the Strategy Notebook* pages 170–173. | **9** | Read **REVISING: Add (Elaborate)** (Student Pages 230–231). | **14** | Assign *Practice the Strategy Notebook* pages 184–185. |
| **5** | Read **PREWRITING: Organize** (Student Pages 226–227). | **10** | Assign *Practice the Strategy Notebook* page 182. | **15** | Read **PUBLISHING: Share** (Student Pages 236–237). Assign *Practice the Strategy Notebook* pages 186–187. |

*To complete the chapter in fewer sessions, assign the *Practice the Strategy Notebook* pages on the same day the targeted skill is introduced.

## STRATEGIES for Writers Sing-Along CD

You may wish to use the *Strategies for Writers Sing-Along* CD throughout the chapter. See the Appendix in the back of this Teacher Edition for more information.

**WRITER'S HANDBOOK**

Remind students that they can refer to the Writer's Handbook in the back of the Student Edition for more information.

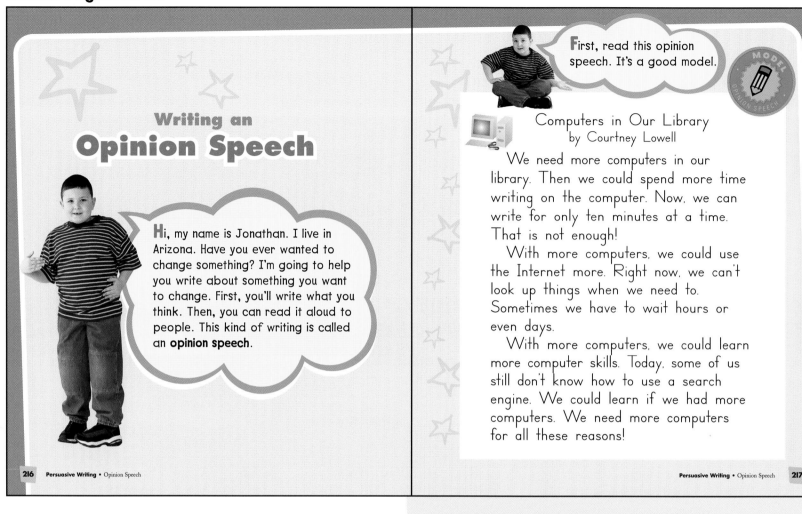

### Writing an
# Opinion Speech

Hi, my name is Jonathan. I live in Arizona. Have you ever wanted to change something? I'm going to help you write about something you want to change. First, you'll write what you think. Then, you can read it aloud to people. This kind of writing is called an **opinion speech**.

First, read this opinion speech. It's a good model.

## Computers in Our Library
by Courtney Lowell

We need more computers in our library. Then we could spend more time writing on the computer. Now, we can write for only ten minutes at a time. That is not enough!

With more computers, we could use the Internet more. Right now, we can't look up things when we need to. Sometimes we have to wait hours or even days.

With more computers, we could learn more computer skills. Today, some of us still don't know how to use a search engine. We could learn if we had more computers. We need more computers for all these reasons!

216   **Persuasive Writing** • Opinion Speech

**Persuasive Writing** • Opinion Speech   217

## Introduce the Genre:
### Opinion Speech

*(Student Pages 216–217)*

Read Student Page 216 with the students. Explain that Jonathan is going to show them how to write an opinion speech. Tell them that they will read his work as a class. They will have a chance to talk about it with a partner and with the whole class. Then they will practice using the same strategies to write their own opinion speech. Ask the students to think of some topics about which they have strong opinions. [Possible responses: when bedtime should be, what to do after school, chores they should or should not have to do]

## Read the Model:
### Opinion Speech

Read Jonathan's words on Student Page 217 with the students. Then read the model of an opinion speech. Ask what makes it a good example of an opinion speech. [Possible responses: It tells what someone thinks. It gives reasons for the opinion.]

Point out that the model contains words that students may not know. You may wish to add these words to your Word Wall and encourage students to refer to the Word Wall as they proofread their own opinion speeches for spelling.

## Meeting Students' Needs:
### Second-Language Learners

Preview the "concept vocabulary" in the speech, such as *computers, Internet, computer skills,* and *search engine.* Draw diagrams as necessary, and pronounce each word several times as you link it to related terms. Then read the speech aloud to the students. On a second reading, students might echo read or read chorally.

### Students Who Need Extra Help

Review the term *opinion* with the students, and then point out the opinion in the speech. Have students read to find the reasons for the opinion. After they have read the speech, have them identify each reason and note where it is stated in the speech.

### Gifted Students

Invite students to identify at least one word, phrase, or sentence that they would give special emphasis to if they were reading the model aloud as a real speech. Have students give reasons for their answers.

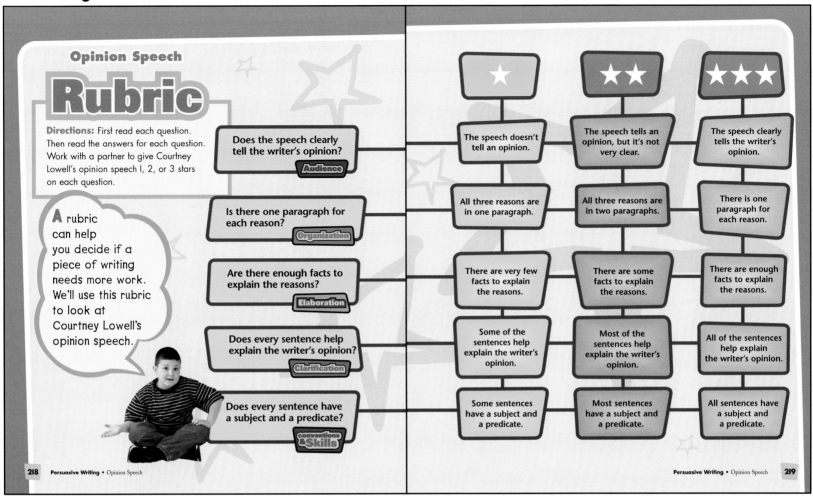

## Using a Rubric

Use the text on Student Pages 220–222 to model the use of a rubric for evaluating a piece of writing. For more information on using a rubric, please see page T21.

### Discuss the Opinion Speech Rubric

*(Student Pages 218–219)*

Read Jonathan's words and the questions on Student Page 218 with the students. Explain that a writer can use these questions to write a good opinion speech. Discuss each question with the students.

**Audience: Does the speech clearly tell the writer's opinion?** The opinion should be stated clearly in the speech. The audience should know what the writer believes.

**Organization: Is there one paragraph for each reason?** The opinion should be supported by reasons. Each reason should appear in a separate paragraph.

**Elaboration: Are there enough facts to explain the reasons?** Facts help explain the reasons and make it easier to understand the opinion.

**Clarification: Does every sentence help explain the writer's opinion?** The speech should stick to the point. It should not contain any information that does not tell what the writer thinks or why the writer thinks it.

**Conventions & Skills: Does every sentence have a subject and a predicate?** Correct grammar makes a speech clear and easy to follow.

Have students evaluate the model opinion speech with a partner, using the opinion speech rubric on Student Pages 218–219. Ask partners to share their evaluations with the whole group.

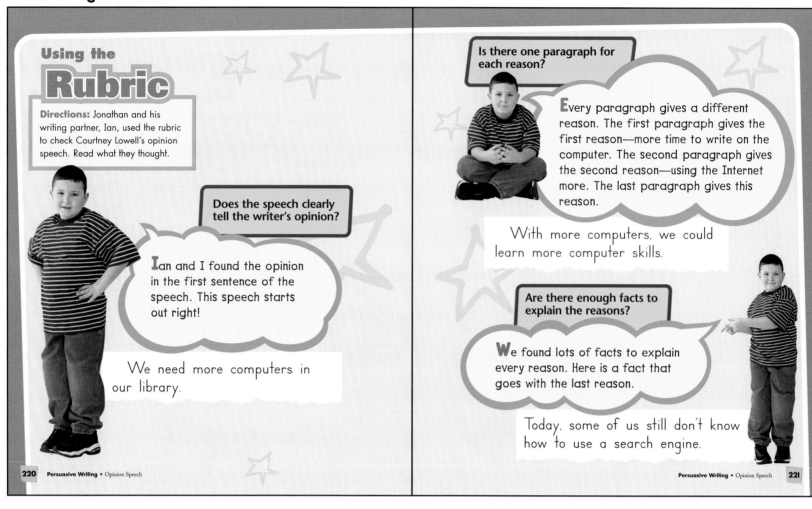

## Using the Rubric to Study the Model

*(Student Pages 220–222)*

Explain to students that now they can see how Jonathan is going to use the questions on the rubric to evaluate the opinion speech.

Read the question in the box on Student Page 220, and then read Jonathan's words. Ask the students whether they agree that the speech begins with an opinion. Read the example sentence.

Read the question in the first box on Student Page 221 with the students. You might want to return to the model on Student Page 217 after reading Jonathan's words and the example sentence. Do students agree that the opinion paper has three paragraphs, one for each reason? Read the question in the second box. Again, you might want to return to the model on Student Page 217 after reading Jonathan's words and the example sentence. Do facts explain every reason?

Read Student Page 222 with the students. Remind them that an opinion speech should not include any sentences that don't help explain the opinion. Remind them also that having a subject and a predicate in every sentence makes it easier for the audience to understand the speech.

## Raising Rubric Awareness Within the School

by Lee Bromberger, *Assessment Specialist*

Efforts can be made to increase rubric awareness internally, as well as outside the school. For example, rubrics from other resources, including non-educational venues such as supermarkets or restaurants, can help teachers focus on the use of rubrics in everyday life.

Setting aside model writings and their accompanying rubrics throughout an entire school year can establish a rubric reference guide. These will offer benchmarks by which teachers can gauge the effectiveness of rubrics, as they become comfortable with implementing them in their classrooms. In addition, other faculty members can use these papers on staff curriculum (i.e., in-service) workdays.

Increasing awareness of rubrics can be as important as the development and implementation of the rubrics themselves. Notification, publication, and discussion of rubrics outside the classroom can go a long way to help assert the validity of rubric evaluation within the classroom.

## Working With a Partner Mini-Lesson:
### Are We Finished?

Help students understand how to work with a partner effectively by giving them some basic tips. You may wish to write these on chart paper and display them where students can readily see them.

Some students may have difficulty making the transition between the end of partner work and the return to their own writing. To ease the transition, students might ask each other, **"Are we finished?"** at the end of each partner session. If both partners agree that they are finished, students may return to individual work. You might want to have students make sure that the materials they will need to continue their individual work are at hand before partner work begins. You may wish to give students a copy of the Working With a Partner Checklist on page T166.

**Model the Tip** Model asking "Are we finished?" by acting out a mock conference with a volunteer partner. After your partner has read his or her paper and you have commented on it, read your paper and allow your partner to comment. Then, ask your partner, "Are we finished?" If the partner says "Yes," proceed to act out getting back to individual work. If the partner says "No," continue to work together until both of you feel that you are finished.

## Jonathan:
### Writer of an Opinion Speech

*(Student Page 223)*

Read the information about Jonathan to learn more about him. Be sure students understand that Jonathan will write his own opinion speech in this chapter. Review the information given about him. Discuss what Jonathan might write about in his opinion speech, based on his favorite sports.

Point out that Jonathan will go through the steps in the writing process (Prewriting, Drafting, Revising, Editing, and Publishing). At each stage, he will use a good writing strategy and explain how he used it. Students should watch for key words, including **Gather, Organize, Write, Add (Elaborate), Take Out (Clarify), Proofread,** and **Share,** to follow the strategies Jonathan uses as he goes through the writing process.

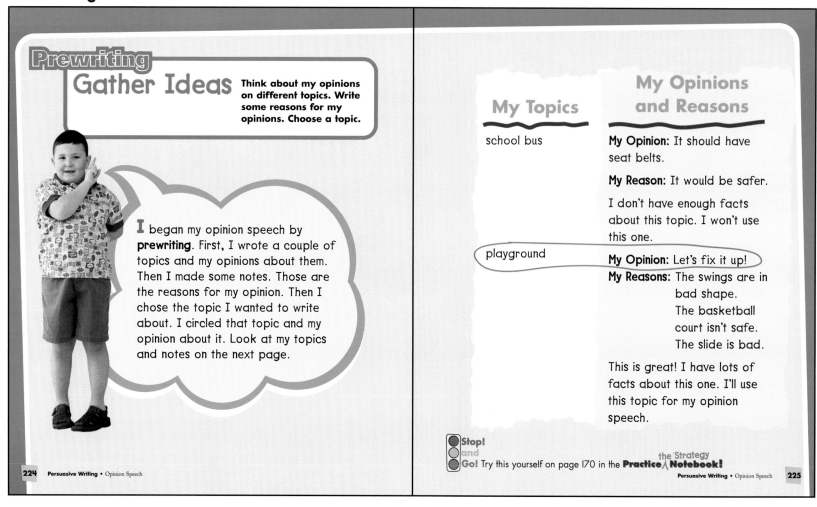

## Prewriting  Gather Ideas

**Strategy: Think about my opinions on different topics. Write some reasons for my opinions. Choose a topic.**

*(Student Pages 224–225)*

Review the term *opinion*. Give students a chance to state an opinion about something they would like to see changed. Then read Jonathan's words with them. Tell the students that in this section Jonathan will explain how he went about writing his opinion speech. He starts by telling how he chose his topic and how he got started on his prewriting. Ask the students to tell what Jonathan did. [Possible response: Jonathan made a list of topics and wrote his opinion about each of them and his reasons for each opinion. Then he chose a topic.]

Point out Jonathan's topics, opinions, and reasons on Student Page 225. Ask students why it is a good idea to start out this way. [Possible response: It helps you think about ideas, choose the best topic, and get your first thoughts down on paper.]

### Practice the Strategy Notebook!

*Practice the Strategy Notebook* page 170 helps students distinguish opinions from statements. Page 171 shows sample notes on a topic for an opinion speech and provides practice in identifying reasons that explain an opinion. After students have completed these two activities, you may wish to have them share their responses.

### Practice the Strategy Notebook!

*Practice the Strategy Notebook* pages 172–173 provide an opportunity for students to list their own ideas for topics, to state opinions about those topics, to choose a topic, and to make notes. You may wish to assign these pages now or after students have completed this chapter in the Student Edition. You may wish to save students' *Your Own Writing* pages and add them to their Work-in-Progress Portfolios.

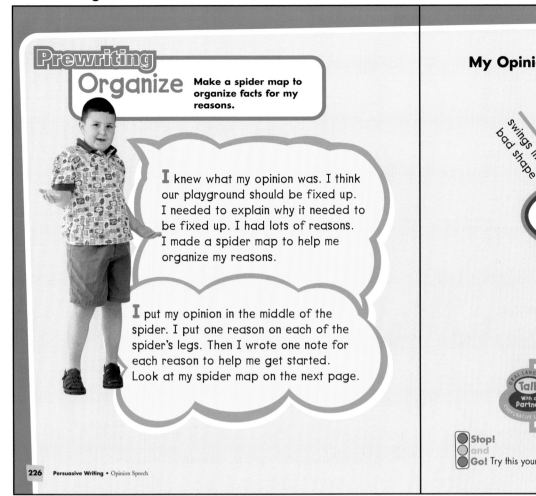

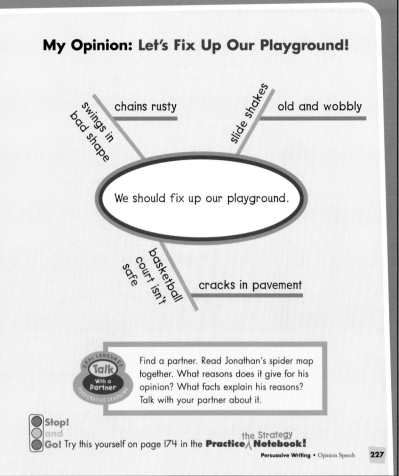

---

# Prewriting Organize

## Strategy: Make a spider map to organize facts for my reasons.

*(Student Pages 226–227)*

Review the term *spider map* with the students. Read Jonathan's words on Student Page 226 with them. Explain that before Jonathan begins his draft, he wants to organize the facts for his reasons. He does this by making a spider map.

Direct students' attention to Jonathan's spider map on Student Page 227. Have students notice where Jonathan writes his opinion. Point out where Jonathan writes his reasons and facts.

Encourage the students to discuss Jonathan's spider map with their partners. Ask the students if Jonathan's spider map seems complete. Does it show the opinion, the reasons, and the facts? Is there more to add? You may wish to discuss the partners' findings as a large-group activity, as well.

**Note:** A spider map transparency is provided in the *Strategies for Writers Transparencies.*

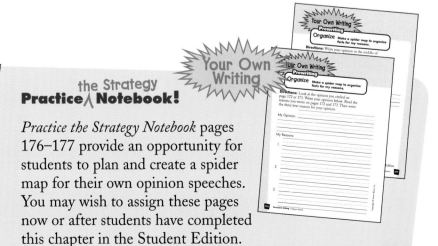

**Practice the Strategy Notebook!**

*Practice the Strategy Notebook* pages 174–175 provide additional practice in understanding how a spider map can be used to organize ideas for an opinion speech. After students have completed this activity, you may wish to have them share their answers to the questions on page 175 with a writing partner.

**Practice the Strategy Notebook!**

*Practice the Strategy Notebook* pages 176–177 provide an opportunity for students to plan and create a spider map for their own opinion speeches. You may wish to assign these pages now or after students have completed this chapter in the Student Edition.

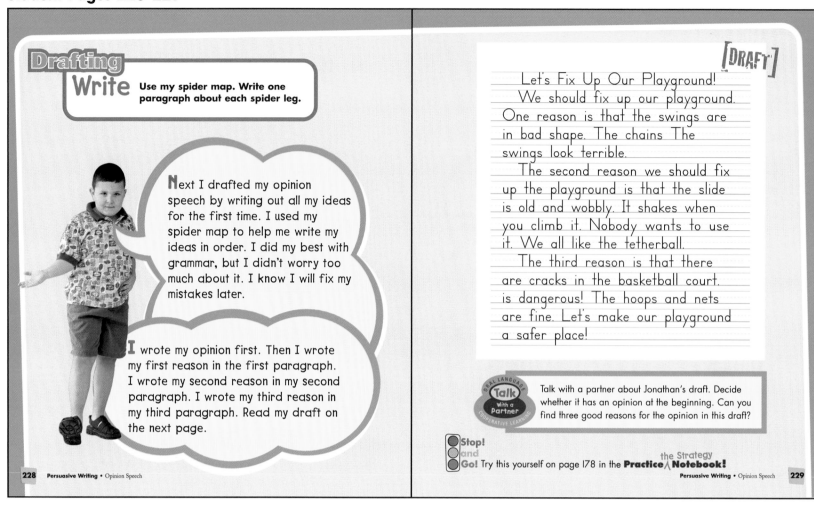

**Drafting Write** — Use my spider map. Write one paragraph about each spider leg.

Next I drafted my opinion speech by writing out all my ideas for the first time. I used my spider map to help me write my ideas in order. I did my best with grammar, but I didn't worry too much about it. I know I will fix my mistakes later.

I wrote my opinion first. Then I wrote my first reason in the first paragraph. I wrote my second reason in my second paragraph. I wrote my third reason in my third paragraph. Read my draft on the next page.

**228** Persuasive Writing • Opinion Speech

[DRAFT]

Let's Fix Up Our Playground!
We should fix up our playground. One reason is that the swings are in bad shape. The chains The swings look terrible.
The second reason we should fix up the playground is that the slide is old and wobbly. It shakes when you climb it. Nobody wants to use it. We all like the tetherball.
The third reason is that there are cracks in the basketball court. is dangerous! The hoops and nets are fine. Let's make our playground a safer place!

**Talk With a Partner** Talk with a partner about Jonathan's draft. Decide whether it has an opinion at the beginning. Can you find three good reasons for the opinion in this draft?

**Stop! and Go!** Try this yourself on page 178 in the **Practice the Strategy Notebook!**

**229** Persuasive Writing • Opinion Speech

---

# Drafting Write

**Strategy: Use my spider map. Write one paragraph about each spider leg.**

*(Student Pages 228–229)*

Review the terms *draft* and *paragraph* with the students, and then read Jonathan's first draft with them. Explain that even though the draft has some mistakes in it, it is a great first try at getting down all the ideas on paper and into paragraphs.

Read the draft on Student Page 229 with the students. Be sure students know that it is important to state the opinion at the beginning of the speech. Ask the students whether Jonathan's speech has one paragraph for each reason. Have students

identify the first paragraph and the first reason, the second paragraph and the second reason, and the third paragraph and the third reason.

Encourage the students to discuss Jonathan's paragraphs. Ask the partners to decide for themselves if Jonathan's speech has an opinion at the beginning and if he wrote a clear paragraph for each reason.

## Practice the Strategy Notebook!

*Practice the Strategy Notebook* page 178 provides students with an opportunity to read another opinion speech draft and to analyze its structure. After students have completed this activity, you may wish to have them share their answers with a writing partner.

## Practice the Strategy Notebook!

*Practice the Strategy Notebook* pages 179–181 provide an opportunity for students to write the draft of their own opinion speech by following the spider map they filled out on page 177. After students have completed this activity, you may wish to have them read their draft to a partner or share their draft in a large-group activity. You may wish to assign these pages now or after students have completed this chapter in the Student Edition.

**T160** **Persuasive Writing** • Opinion Speech

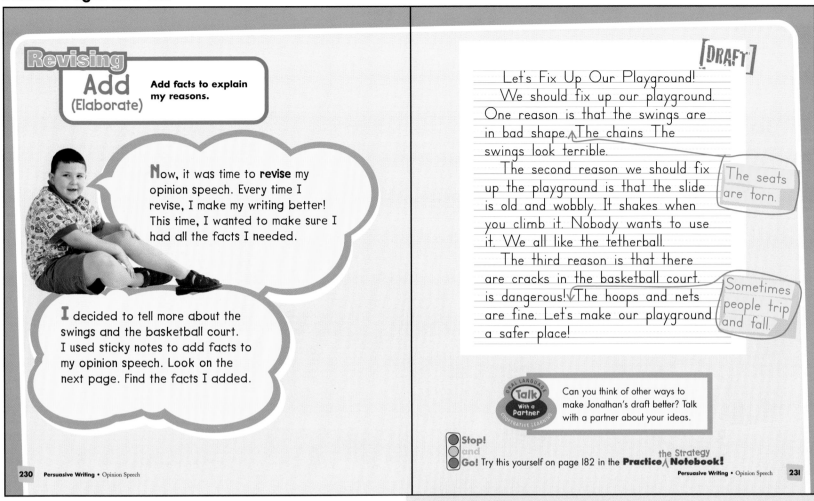

## Revising Add (Elaborate)

**Strategy: Add facts to explain my reasons.**

*(Student Pages 230–231)*

Read Jonathan's words with the students. Review the term *revise*. Explain that when writers revise their work, they change it for the better by adding to it or taking away from it. Explain that one way to revise an opinion speech is to add facts that explain the reasons.

Read Jonathan's revised draft on Student Page 231 with the students. Ask students how Jonathan's revisions have made his paper better. [Possible responses: Telling about the torn seats helps explain why the swings should be fixed up. Saying that sometimes people trip and fall helps the audience understand why the basketball court is dangerous.]

**Note:** *Strategies for Writers* employs the term **Elaborate** in grades 3–8. You may wish to explain to students that *elaborate* means "to add."

Encourage students to talk about Jonathan's revisions with a partner. Did his changes make his opinion speech better? What other changes could Jonathan have made?

## Spelling Strategies:
### Listen for Familiar Small Words

Before students begin the Editing portion of the chapter, you may wish to remind them that checking spelling is an important part of editing their writing. Encourage students to use several strategies to figure out the spellings of new words and hard words. One strategy is to think of or **listen for familiar small words** inside less familiar bigger words. For example, to spell *dangerous*, students can begin with the word *danger*. To spell *safer*, students can begin with the word *safe*.

### Practice the Strategy Notebook!

*Practice the Strategy Notebook* page 182 provides additional practice in revising a draft by adding facts to explain reasons. After students have completed this activity, remind them to use this strategy to revise their own opinion speech.

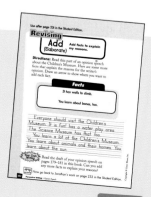

**Persuasive Writing** • Opinion Speech

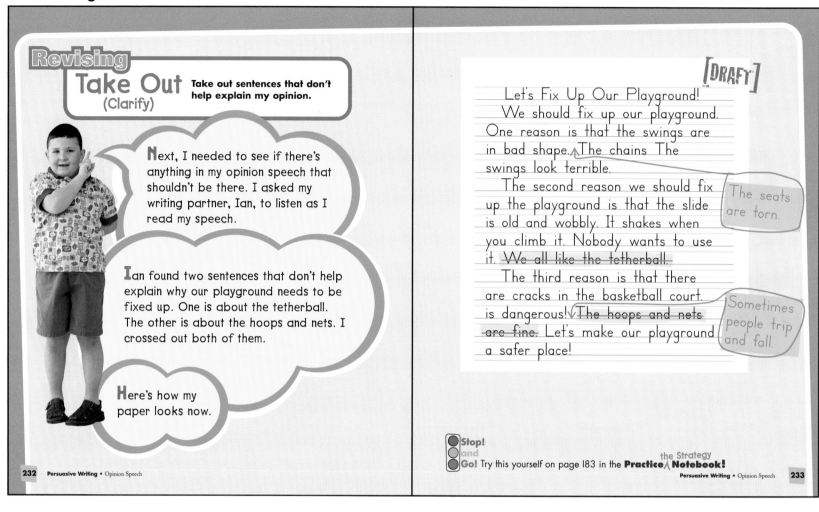

## Revising Take Out (Clarify)

**Strategy: Take out sentences that don't help explain my opinion.**

*(Student Pages 232–233)*

Read Jonathan's words with the students. Explain that another kind of revising is taking out information that doesn't help explain the writer's opinion. Read Jonathan's revised draft with the students. Point out that Jonathan took out the sentence about the tetherball because it didn't help explain his opinion. Ask students why. [**Possible response: The writer is giving an opinion about what needs fixing up. The tetherball doesn't need to be fixed.**] Ask students which other sentence Jonathan crossed out. [**Response: "The hoops and nets are fine."**] Again ask why Jonathan took out this sentence. [**Possible response: The hoops and nets have nothing to do with the writer's opinion that the playground should be fixed up.**]

**Note:** *Strategies for Writers* employs the term **Clarify** in grades 3–8. You may wish to explain to students that *clarify* means "to make clear," usually by taking out what's unnecessary.

## Tips for Successful Conferencing: Interviewing

One option for conferencing is to interview each child. This can be particularly useful as an end-of-the-year informal assessment tool. You might want to choose from among the following questions for an end-of-the-year interview:

- Tell me something you have learned this year about writing.
- How do you think you have changed as a writer this year?
- What can you do better now in your writing than you could a year ago?

You might also ask each child to tell about how he or she uses the writing process.

### Practice the Strategy Notebook!

*Practice the Strategy Notebook* page 183 provides additional practice in revising a draft by taking out information that doesn't help explain an opinion. After students have completed this activity, remind them to use this strategy to revise their own opinion speech.

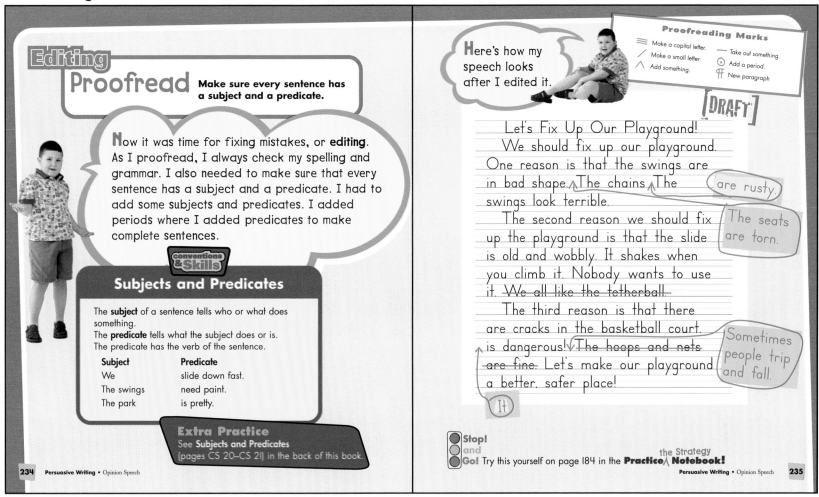

## Editing Proofread

**Strategy: Make sure every sentence has a subject and a predicate.**

*(Student Pages 234–235)*

Be sure students know that *proofreading* means reading to find and fix any problems in spelling, capitalization, punctuation, and grammar.

Read Jonathan's words on Student Page 234 to the students. Remind students that Jonathan always checks his spelling and grammar. Tell students that Jonathan is now going to add missing subjects and predicates. Remind students that using a pencil that writes in a different color helps writers see their revisions. **Note:** You may wish to give students their own colored pencils to edit their writing.

Read the explanation and examples of subjects and predicates on Student Page 234 with the students.

Point out the proofreading symbols chart on Student Page 235 to the students. Explain that these symbols help writers remember what kind of corrections they made, so they can include those corrections in their final copy. You may wish to give students a copy of the Proofreading Marks blackline master on page T136. Read Jonathan's edited draft with the students. Ask them if Jonathan made all the necessary corrections. You may wish to use the corresponding Writing Model for Proofreading Practice Transparency.

## Extra Practice: **Conventions & Skills**
### Student Edition

If your students need more practice in correcting sentence fragments correctly, you may wish to assign Student Pages CS 20–CS 21.

## Conventions & Skills Practice

For more targeted practice related to this skill, see this lesson in the optional *Conventions & Skills Practice Book*:

Lesson 2: Complete Subject and Complete Predicate
Lesson 3: Simple Subject
Lesson 4: Simple Predicate
Lesson 5: Sentence Fragments

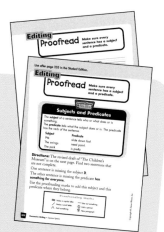

### the Strategy
### Practice∧Notebook!

*Practice the Strategy Notebook* pages 184–185 provide additional practice in editing a draft by correcting sentences that lack either a subject or a predicate. After students have completed this activity, remind them to use this strategy to edit their own opinion speech.

**Persuasive Writing** • Opinion Speech

**T163**

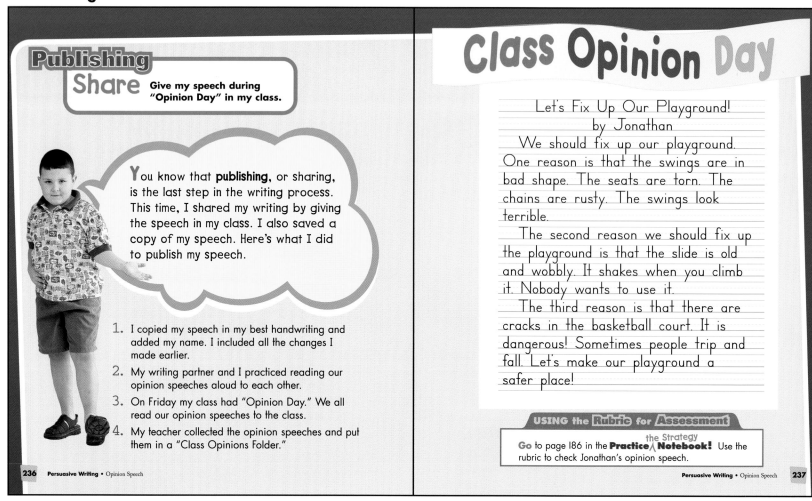

### Publishing Share

Give my speech during "Opinion Day" in my class.

You know that **publishing**, or sharing, is the last step in the writing process. This time, I shared my writing by giving the speech in my class. I also saved a copy of my speech. Here's what I did to publish my speech.

1. I copied my speech in my best handwriting and added my name. I included all the changes I made earlier.
2. My writing partner and I practiced reading our opinion speeches aloud to each other.
3. On Friday my class had "Opinion Day." We all read our opinion speeches to the class.
4. My teacher collected the opinion speeches and put them in a "Class Opinions Folder."

236  **Persuasive Writing** • Opinion Speech

## Class Opinion Day

Let's Fix Up Our Playground!
by Jonathan
We should fix up our playground. One reason is that the swings are in bad shape. The seats are torn. The chains are rusty. The swings look terrible.
The second reason we should fix up the playground is that the slide is old and wobbly. It shakes when you climb it. Nobody wants to use it.
The third reason is that there are cracks in the basketball court. It is dangerous! Sometimes people trip and fall. Let's make our playground a safer place!

**USING the Rubric for Assessment**

Go to page 186 in the **Practice Notebook!** Use the rubric to check Jonathan's opinion speech. *the Strategy*

**Persuasive Writing** • Opinion Speech  237

---

## Publishing Share

**Strategy:** **Give my speech during "Opinion Day" in my class.**
*(Student Pages 236–237)*

Read Jonathan's words to the students. Call on one or more volunteers to explain what *publishing* means. Elicit the ideas of putting written work into final form, incorporating all changes, and sharing.

Remind students that there are many ways to share published writing. Jonathan practiced reading his speech aloud in order to deliver it during "Opinion Day" in his classroom. Other publishing options include posting the speech on a bulletin board, submitting it to the school or local newspaper, and putting it with other speeches for a class magazine. Ask the students why it was a good idea for Jonathan to share his speech in that way. [Possible responses: All the students could listen to it. Jonathan could feel good about his writing by reading it aloud to everyone.]

Read the final copy of Jonathan's opinion speech on Student Page 237 with the students.

Encourage students to talk with a partner about how Jonathan shared his paper. Was it a good way to share writing? How else could Jonathan have shared his writing?

## Using the Rubric

*Practice the Strategy Notebook* pages 186–187 provide a rubric for assessing Jonathan's final opinion speech. Encourage students to work with a partner to evaluate Jonathan's opinion speech by using this rubric. After students have completed this activity, you may wish to have them share the results in a large-group activity.

## Social Studies
## Your Own Writing
### PERSUASIVE

Use what you learned in this unit to write your own opinion paper, opinion speech, or both! Try these ideas.
- Use **Your Own Writing** pages in the *Practice the Strategy Notebook.*
- Pick a topic below, and write something new.
- Choose another idea of your own.

Follow the steps in the writing process. Use the Opinion Paper Rubric on pages 168–169 in the *Practice the Strategy Notebook* or the Opinion Speech Rubric on pages 186–187 in the *Practice the Strategy Notebook* to check your writing.

| Opinion Paper | Opinion Speech |
|---|---|
| • what my community needs <br> • the best way to be a good citizen <br> • the most interesting part of my social studies book <br> • the best place to go in my town, city, or community | • where my class should go on a field trip to learn about history <br> • what should be added to my school to make it better <br> • what should be changed in my city, town, or neighborhood |

portfolio

School–Home Connection

Keep a writing folder. Add **Your Own Writing** pages to your writing folder. You may want to take your writing folder home to share.

## Your Own Writing
## Persuasive Writing for Social Studies

Assign either one or both kinds of opinion writing to the students. Before they begin writing, review key information about each kind. Decide which of the following you wish students to do:

- Choose a topic on this page in the Student Edition.
- Complete one of the Your Own Writing pieces in the *Practice the Strategy Notebook.*
- Come up with a new idea.

## Portfolio/School-Home Connection

Encourage the students to keep a portfolio of their writing.

### Work-in-Progress Portfolio

Remind students to review this portfolio often to revise existing pieces that have not been published. Encourage students to share pieces of their Work-in-Progress Portfolios with family members who can help in editing.

### Published Portfolio

Encourage students to choose pieces from their Published Portfolios to share with family members.

Name _____

_____

My Partner's Name _____

_____

## Working With a Partner Checklist

After working with your partner, check to be sure you have done all of these.

- ☐ **We read our papers to each other clearly and slowly.**
- ☐ **We spoke in soft voices.**
- ☐ **We took turns.**
- ☐ **We were positive.**
- ☐ **We asked good questions.**
- ☐ **We wrote on our own papers.**
- ☐ **We thought about each other's suggestions.**
- ☐ **We listened without interrupting.**
- ☐ **We took notes.**
- ☐ **We are finished.**

You may wish to copy this and give it to your students. See "Working With a Partner Mini-Lessons" throughout this Teacher Edition for information about working with a partner.

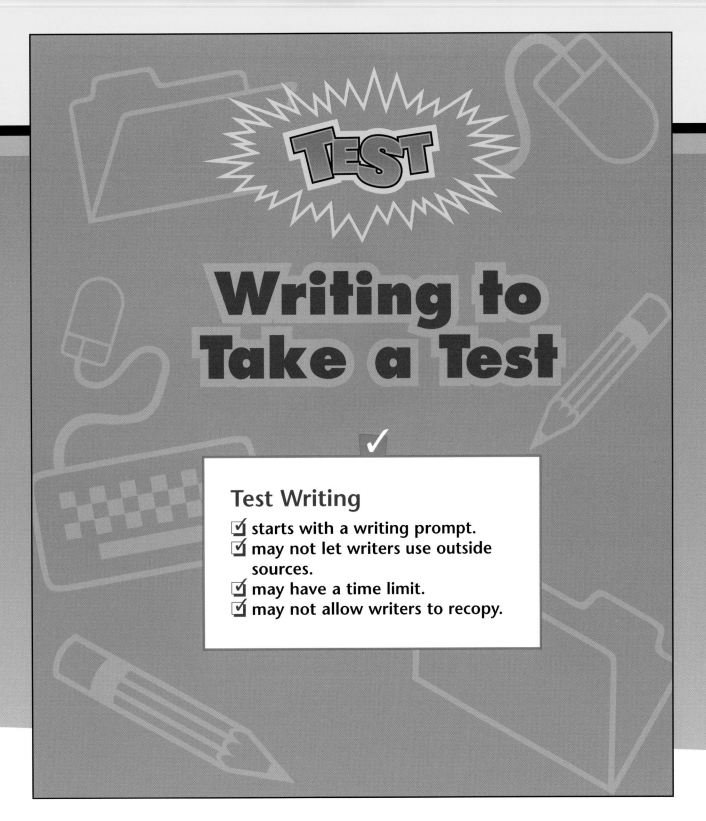

# TEST

# Writing to Take a Test

✓

## Test Writing

- ☑ starts with a writing prompt.
- ☑ may not let writers use outside sources.
- ☑ may have a time limit.
- ☑ may not allow writers to recopy.

## Test Writing

Tell students that writing on a test is a little different from other kinds of writing. Explain that when they write for a test, they must pay careful attention to what they are asked to do. Invite students to recall a time when they had to write an essay for a classroom assignment or for a test.

Read aloud Student Page 239 as students follow along. Tell them that they will be learning special strategies to help them perform well on writing tests of any kind. Explain that these strategies can be used with any kind of writing prompt.

## Books to Share With Students

You may wish to use books from these sets of Zaner-Bloser Literacy to support instruction across the curriculum.

- Reading—Folktales; More Folktales; Biography, Inventors; Biography, Explorers
- Social Studies—Our Economy; Geography; U.S. Landmarks and Symbols
- Science—Life; Earth; Physical
- Math—Working With Numbers

# Tips for the Writing Classroom

by Barry Sneed, *Master Teacher*

## The End of the Year Writing Portfolio Party!

As you approach the end of the school year, it is important to have students self-assess their writing progress from the start of the year, as well as share their assessment with you and with their parents. One way to accomplish this is to invite parents into the classroom for a short (20-30 minute)

"Writing Portfolio Party" (or "Writing Celebration") or whatever title you choose to use. In my classroom, this consists of having students prepare to host their parent(s) or guest(s) for a review of their written work from the first week of school to the present. This review includes samples collected throughout the year.

The first writing sample students have in my classroom is their written response to the prompt given in week one: the poem "Magic Carpet Ride" by Shel Silverstein. We write a response to the very same prompt at the end of the year, and students are then asked to compare the two responses, a

## Test Writing

### Writing Strategies

#### Prewriting

**Gather Ideas**
Carefully read the writing prompt. Make a list of interesting topics. Pick one.

**Organize/Plan My Time**
Make a story map to tell who was in the story, what the problem was, and what happened.

Check my story map against the Scoring Guide.

#### Drafting

**Write**
Use my story map. Write sentences to tell what happened at the beginning, middle, and end, and how the problem was solved.

#### Revising

**Add (Elaborate)**
Add details to make the story and characters more interesting.

**Take Out (Clarify)**
Take out sentences that don't help tell what happened.

#### Editing

**Proofread**
Make sure every sentence begins with a capital letter and ends with correct punctuation and has a subject and a predicate.

**Note:** A blackline master of the writing process flow chart appears on page T106. You may wish to copy and distribute it to your students.

### Modeled Writing

**Writing on Demand Mini-Lesson:** You may wish to present the following mini-lesson before the students read this chapter in the Student Edition. Explain to students that sometimes people are asked to write for tests and for other reasons. They may not have much time to prepare for this kind of writing. This is called **writing on demand**.

Ask students to call out some topics for writing a story. Write these on the board as the students are calling them out. Explain that when writing for a test, the students will be given a topic and a set of instructions. This is called a **writing prompt**.

Explain that in this chapter, students will learn how to read and understand writing prompts, as well as some strategies for doing well on writing tests. They will read a model and practice strategies for a practice writing test.

Tell students that writing on demand is a lot like other kinds of writing. They can use the same strategies that they used for writing stories, essays, and reports. Remind students that they should follow the steps of the writing process when writing for a test.

comparison they share at the Writing Portfolio Party. Other written samples come from the weekly writing conference that I hold with students on their Super Reader Day. (See "Tips for the Writing Classroom," Unit 2, Ch. 2.) Students also fill out a survey on how they feel about many aspects of writing, including how they see themselves as writers.

After writing invitations to our guests for the Writing Portfolio Party, I role-play a Portfolio Party conference for the class. (I play the student, while a child in class plays my mom or dad.) In this way, students will get an idea of how to approach their roles on that day.

When the big day arrives, we schedule the party for the last half hour of the day so parents attending can simply take their students home when they are done. Students present their writing samples, explain their survey and feelings toward writing (which includes their own ideas on their strengths and weaknesses as a writer), and share their writing goal(s) for the next school year. (Cookies and inexpensive punch are available on a table for parents and guests after the conferences are done.) It is always great to see and share in the parents' responses to their child's running of a conference at his/her desk, and a fun and educational time is had by all!

## Time Management for This Chapter*

| Session | | Session | | Session | |
|---------|---|---------|---|---------|---|
| **1** | Introduce Writing to Take a Test. Read Student Page 239. | **6** | Read **PREWRITING: Gather Ideas** (Student Pages 250–251). Assign *Practice the Strategy Notebook* pages 188–193. | **11** | Read **REVISING: Take Out (Clarify)** (Student Pages 264–265). Assign *Practice the Strategy Notebook* page 203. |
| **2** | Introduce the student guide. Read Student Pages 240–243. | **7** | Read **PREWRITING: Organize** (Student Pages 252–253). | **12** | Read **EDITING: Proofread** (Student Pages 266–267). |
| **3** | Read Student Pages 244–245. Discuss the Scoring Guide. Read and discuss the writing model. | **8** | Read **PREWRITING: Organize** (Student Pages 254–255). Assign *Practice the Strategy Notebook* pages 194–197. Read Student Pages 256–259. | **13** | Read **EDITING: Proofread** (Student Pages 268–269). Assign *Practice the Strategy Notebook* pages 204–205. |
| **4** | Read Student Pages 246–247. Discuss the application of the Scoring Guide to the writing model. | **9** | Read **DRAFTING: Write** (Student Pages 260–261). Assign *Practice the Strategy Notebook* pages 198–201. | **14** | Review the Test Tips (Student Pages 270–271). Assign *Practice the Strategy Notebook* pages 206–207. |
| **5** | Read Student Page 248. Discuss the last two elements of the Scoring Guide. Read the information about Danielle on Student Page 249. | **10** | Read **REVISING: Add (Elaborate)** (Student Pages 262–263). Assign *Practice the Strategy Notebook* page 202. | **15** | Assign one of the writing prompts for a practice writing test (Student Page 272). |

\* To complete the chapter in fewer sessions, assign the *Practice the Strategy Notebook* pages on the same day each strategy is introduced.

## STRATEGIES for Writers Sing-Along CD

You may wish to use the *Strategies for Writers Sing-Along* CD throughout the chapter. See the Appendix in the back of this Teacher Edition for more information.

## WRITER'S HANDBOOK

Remind students that they can refer to the Writer's Handbook in the back of the Student Edition for more information.

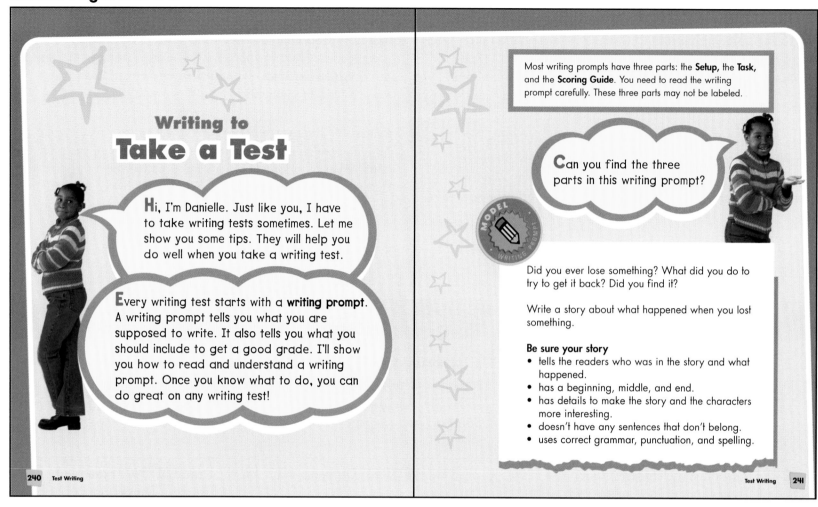

## Introduce the Writing Prompt:
### Narrative Writing

*(Student Pages 240–241)*

Read Student Page 240 with the students. Explain that on a writing test, the writing assignment is called a *writing prompt,* because it prompts or nudges the writer in the right direction. Tell students that a writing prompt is a set of directions. It will help students know exactly what to do to get a good grade on a writing test. Introduce the student guide and explain that Danielle will help them learn about writing for a test.

## Discuss the Writing Prompt:
### Realistic Story

Read Student Page 241 with the students. Explain that the parts of the writing prompt are not usually labeled. Tell students that the Setup part of a writing prompt will usually have a set of questions or an example of something. Tell them that the Task part of a writing prompt will usually tell them to write something. Then explain that the Scoring Guide part of a writing prompt will give more information about the Task. Read aloud the model writing prompt and help students to find the Setup, the Task, and the Scoring Guide.

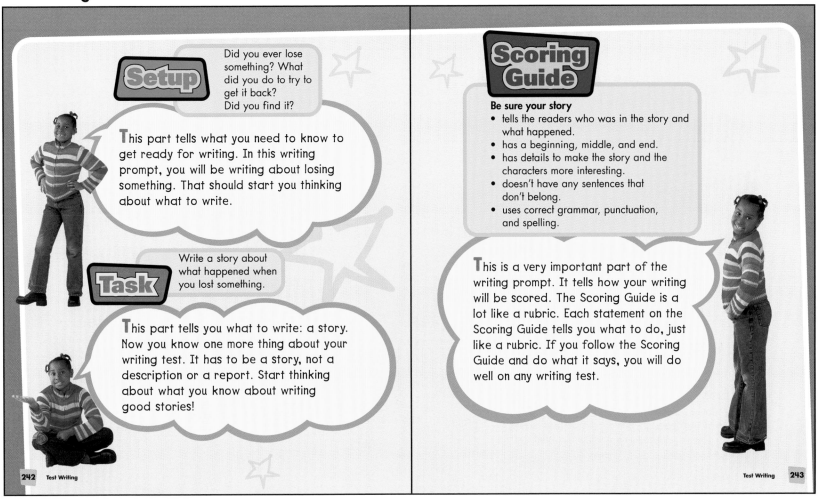

## Studying the Writing Prompt

*(Student Pages 242–243)*

### Setup

Explain that the Setup gives writers information they need to help them understand the assignment. Read Danielle's words on Student Page 242 with the students. Point out the Setup part of the writing prompt on Student Page 242.

### Task

Point out that the Task part of the writing prompt tells students exactly what the writing assignment is. Read Danielle's words on Student Page 242 with the students. Point out the Task part of the writing prompt on Student Page 242.

### Scoring Guide

Point out that an important part of the writing prompt is the Scoring Guide. This part tells writers exactly what they should include in their writing. Remind students that in other parts of the book they have used rubrics. Students should understand that a Scoring Guide is similar to a rubric. Read Danielle's words on Student Page 243 with the students. Point out the Scoring Guide part of the writing prompt on Student Page 243.

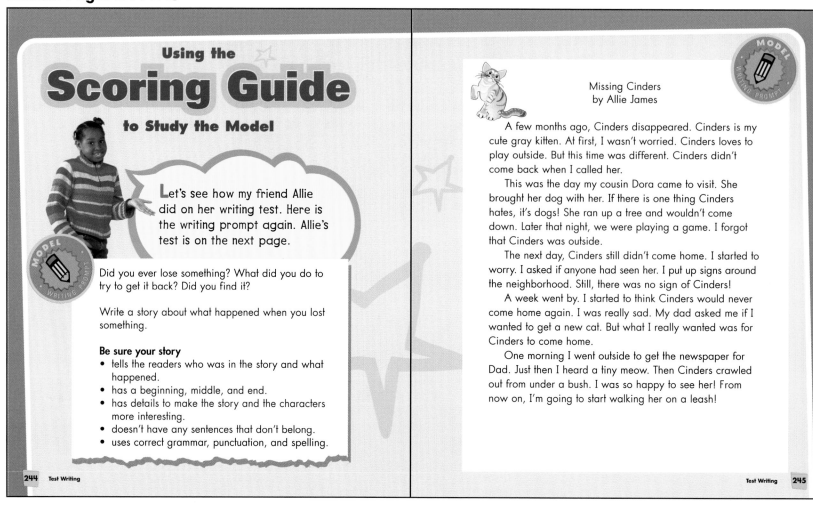

## Using the Scoring Guide to Study the Model

*(Student Pages 244–245)*

Read Danielle's words aloud, or ask a volunteer to read them. Point out that the Scoring Guide does not use key words like **Audience, Organization, Clarification, Elaboration, or Conventions & Skills,** which they have seen in rubrics. These words have been added in the Student Edition to help students understand the Scoring Guide. Still, the Scoring Guide tells readers what to look for in each of these areas. The Scoring Guide shows the main things that the person scoring Allie's test will look for in her writing.

A complete rubric based on this Scoring Guide is found on Student Pages 206–207 in the *Practice the Strategy Notebook.* You may wish to introduce the rubric at this time.

## Read the Model:
### Writing Prompt Response

Explain to the students that the model in this chapter is a story written for a writing test. Allie used the writing prompt on Student Page 244 to write the story. Explain that Danielle will show them how to use the Scoring Guide as they decide how well Allie did on her test. Read "Missing Cinders" with the students.

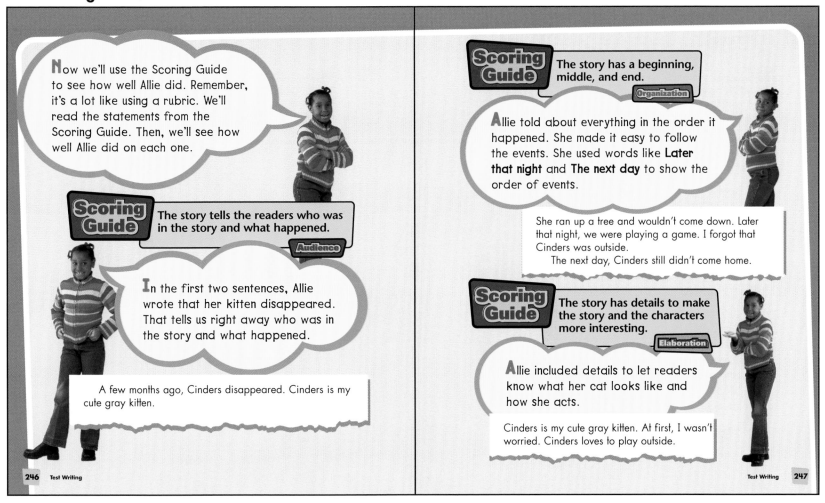

## Using the Scoring Guide

*(Student Pages 246–248)*

Be sure students understand that each highlighted statement comes from the Scoring Guide. Explain that each section on white paper shows a part of Allie's writing. Danielle, the student guide, is using this part of Allie's writing as an example.

Read Student Page 246 with the students. Discuss the text. Ask students whether they agree that Allie's story tells the readers who was in the story and what happened.

Read Student Page 247 with the students. Discuss the text. Ask students whether they agree that Allie's story has a clear beginning, middle, and end, and that it has details that make the story and the characters interesting.

Read Student Page 248 with the students. Discuss the text. Ask students whether they agree that Allie's story doesn't have any sentences that don't belong. Point out that Allie's story uses correct grammar, punctuation, and spelling.

## Avoiding Rubric Pitfalls

by Lee Bromberger, *Assessment Specialist*

Effective rubrics guide students and teachers by giving clear expectations for various levels of performance. Avoiding the following pitfalls will help ensure the successful use of rubrics.

**Using rubric criteria that are unclear or vague.** Failure to make clear distinctions when developing the rubric criteria leads to assessment difficulties. For example, classifying homophone errors as spelling errors, and not usage errors, can lead to confusion. Similarly, rubric criteria that are vague (e.g., "The paper is good.") are difficult to implement successfully.

**Failing to review the rubric with students before it is used.** Students need to know the expectations in the rubric, even if they have had input into the rubric's development.

**Failing to consistently use rubrics as a routine part of the class.** Students need to see the role that rubrics will play in the class curriculum. If rubrics become a once-in-a-while diversion, as opposed to a staple of assessment, students will fail to consider them as invaluable assets to help them improve the quality of their work.

## Meeting Students' Needs:
### Second-Language Learners

Make a photocopy of the writing prompt model response for each student. As you or a volunteer reread the model aloud, have students underline any words that are not familiar. Then use role-playing, pantomimes, or pictures to help students acquire the unfamiliar vocabulary.

### Students Who Need Extra Help

Have students recall the main characters and main events of Allie's story. You may wish to write on the board a blank story map like the one on *Practice the Strategy Notebook* pages 196–197. This will help them understand that any personal narrative has characters, a problem, and a beginning, middle, and end.

### Gifted Students

Have students think of other ways that Allie could have made sure that her cat did not get lost. Then challenge them to find other things Allie could have done to try to find Cinders.

## Danielle:
### Writer for a Test

*(Student Page 249)*

Read the information about Danielle on Student Page 249. Be sure students understand that Danielle will write her own story for a writing test in this chapter.

Point out that Danielle will go through the steps of the writing process (Prewriting, Drafting, Revising, and Editing). At each step, she will use a good writing strategy and explain how she did it.

**Note:** The student writer in this chapter is not from a specific state because writing tests are given throughout the United States.

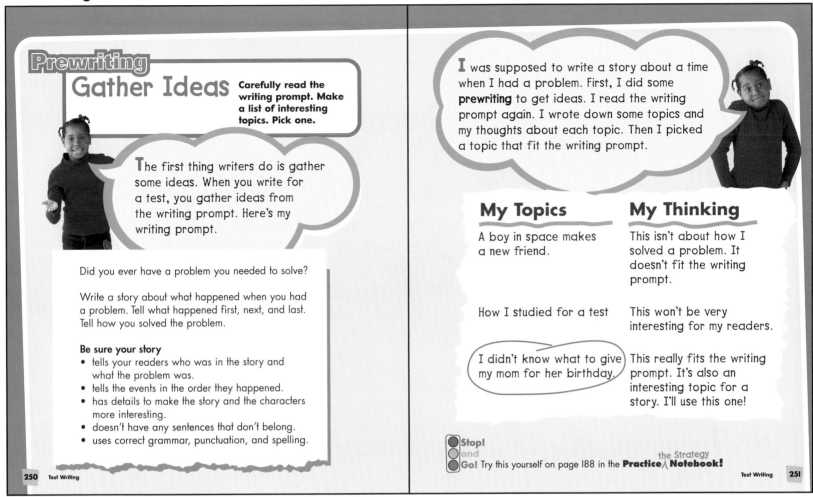

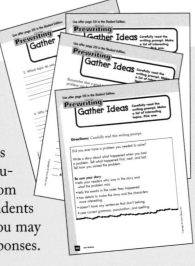

Use after page 250 in the Student Edition.

## Prewriting — Gather Ideas

**Strategy: Carefully read the writing prompt. Make a list of interesting topics. Pick one.**

*(Student Pages 250–251)*

Read Danielle's words on Student Page 250 with the students. Explain that Danielle is now going to write for a test using a writing prompt which is a lot like the one Allie used. Read the new writing prompt aloud. Ask students to put a finger on the Task, the part of the prompt that tells what they should write. Ask a student to read that part aloud. [Response: **Write a story about what happened when you had a problem.**]

Have students brainstorm some topics that would fit the prompt. List a few of these on the board. Then briefly discuss each one to decide whether it tells a story about a problem the student had.

Read Danielle's words on Student Page 251. Then read Danielle's notes. Explain that "My Thinking" shows how Danielle decided which topic would be good for the assigned prompt. Encourage students to discuss whether they agree.

### Practice the Strategy Notebook!

*Practice the Strategy Notebook* pages 188–191 give students the opportunity to practice gathering ideas from another writing prompt. After students have completed these activities, you may wish to have them share their responses.

### Practice the Strategy Notebook! — Your Own Writing

*Practice the Strategy Notebook* pages 192–193 give students the opportunity to gather ideas from a writing prompt for their own practice test. You may wish to assign these pages now or after students have completed this chapter in the Student Edition. You may wish to save students' *Your Own Writing* pages and add them to their Work-in-Progress Portfolios.

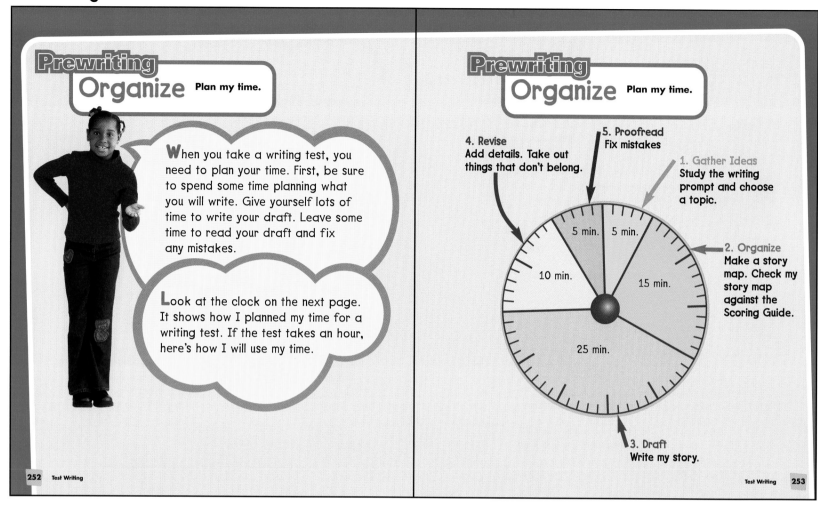

## Prewriting Organize

**Strategy: Plan my time.**

*(Student Pages 252–253)*

Explain to students that when they take a writing test, they need to leave time for each step in the writing process. Thinking about the total amount of time they have will help them figure out how much time to spend on each part.

Read Danielle's words on Student Page 252 with the students. Then look at the clock on Student Page 253. Discuss the amount of time Danielle uses for each step. Point out that she spends about half the total time drafting her story. Remind students to take enough time to gather ideas and organize their papers, so their writing makes sense.

The following chart may help students plan their time if less than one hour is given for a writing test. You may wish to copy and display this chart for the students.

| Total Test Minutes | 30 | 40 | 60 |
|---|---|---|---|
| 1. Study the prompt and choose a topic. | 5 | 5 | 5 |
| 2. Organize ideas. | 5 | 8 | 15 |
| 3. Write a draft. | 10 | 15 | 25 |
| 4. **Revise:** Add details. Take out parts that don't belong. | 5 | 7 | 10 |
| 5. **Edit:** Fix mistakes. | 5 | 5 | 5 |

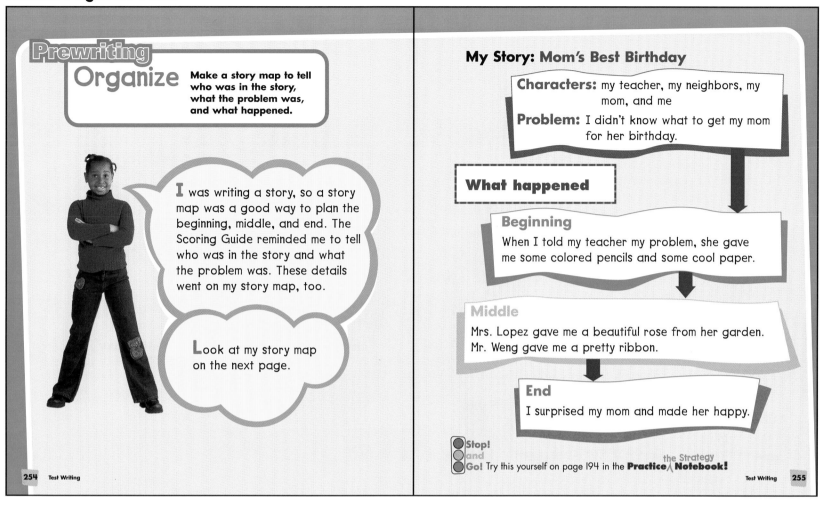

**Prewriting**

## Organize

Make a story map to tell who was in the story, what the problem was, and what happened.

I was writing a story, so a story map was a good way to plan the beginning, middle, and end. The Scoring Guide reminded me to tell who was in the story and what the problem was. These details went on my story map, too.

Look at my story map on the next page.

254    Test Writing

**My Story: Mom's Best Birthday**

**Characters:** my teacher, my neighbors, my mom, and me

**Problem:** I didn't know what to get my mom for her birthday.

**What happened**

**Beginning**
When I told my teacher my problem, she gave me some colored pencils and some cool paper.

**Middle**
Mrs. Lopez gave me a beautiful rose from her garden. Mr. Weng gave me a pretty ribbon.

**End**
I surprised my mom and made her happy.

**Stop! and Go!** Try this yourself on page 194 in the **Practice the Strategy Notebook!**

Test Writing   255

---

**Prewriting** Organize

**Strategy:** Make a story map to tell who was in the story, what the problem was, and what happened.

*(Student Pages 254–255)*

Before reading the pages, ask students different ways they have organized their ideas in the past as they prepared to write stories. Tell students that Danielle uses a story map to organize her ideas. Remind them that a story map is a good way to plan ideas for a story. Remind students that they have seen another story map on Student Page 159 and that they have practiced using a story map in their own writing. Read Student Pages 254 and 255.

**Note:** A story map transparency is provided in the *Strategies for Writers Transparencies*.

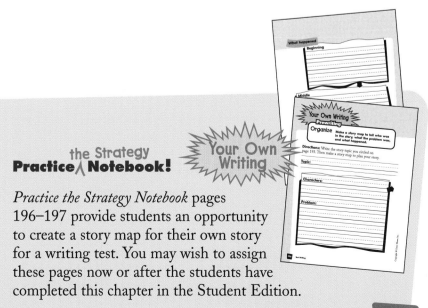

**Practice the Strategy Notebook!**

*Practice the Strategy Notebook* pages 194–195 provide students an opportunity to create a story map for a practice writing test. After students have completed this activity, you may wish to have them share their story maps with a partner or in a large-group activity.

**Practice the Strategy Notebook!**

*Practice the Strategy Notebook* pages 196–197 provide students an opportunity to create a story map for their own story for a writing test. You may wish to assign these pages now or after the students have completed this chapter in the Student Edition.

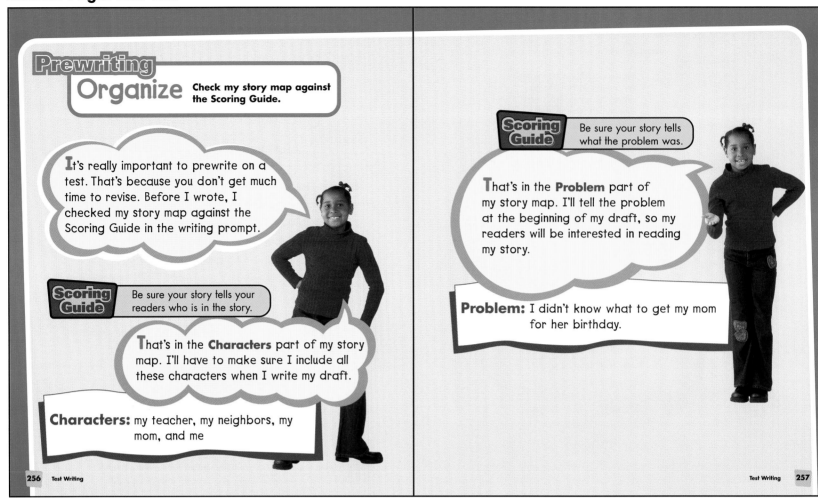

## Prewriting Organize

**Strategy: Check my story map against the Scoring Guide.**

*(Student Pages 256–257)*

Tell students that it is important to keep checking the Scoring Guide to make sure they stay on track. Have them turn back to the Scoring Guide on Student Page 243 to point out how the story map addresses these main points. Read Student Pages 256–257 with the students. Point out that each section of Danielle's story map matches specific sections of the Scoring Guide. That way, she knows that she's doing what she needs to do to get a good grade on her writing test.

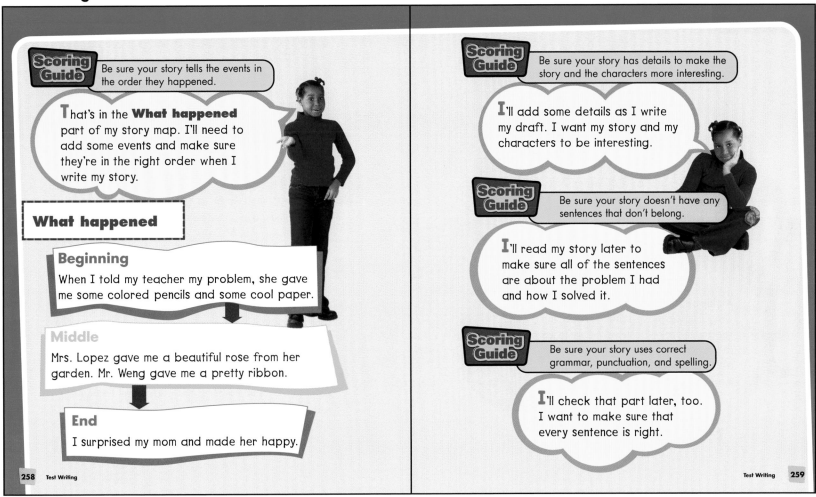

**Scoring Guide** Be sure your story tells the events in the order they happened.

That's in the **What happened** part of my story map. I'll need to add some events and make sure they're in the right order when I write my story.

**What happened**

**Beginning**
When I told my teacher my problem, she gave me some colored pencils and some cool paper.

**Middle**
Mrs. Lopez gave me a beautiful rose from her garden. Mr. Weng gave me a pretty ribbon.

**End**
I surprised my mom and made her happy.

258  Test Writing

**Scoring Guide** Be sure your story has details to make the story and the characters more interesting.

I'll add some details as I write my draft. I want my story and my characters to be interesting.

**Scoring Guide** Be sure your story doesn't have any sentences that don't belong.

I'll read my story later to make sure all of the sentences are about the problem I had and how I solved it.

**Scoring Guide** Be sure your story uses correct grammar, punctuation, and spelling.

I'll check that part later, too. I want to make sure that every sentence is right.

Test Writing  259

## Prewriting  Organize

**Strategy: Check my story map against the Scoring Guide.**

*(Student Pages 258–259)*

Read Student Pages 258–259 with the students. Continue to compare the story map with the Scoring Guide.

Point out that Danielle can't cover every part of the Scoring Guide in her story map. She will make sure to remember those parts of the Scoring Guide as she writes, revises, and edits her story.

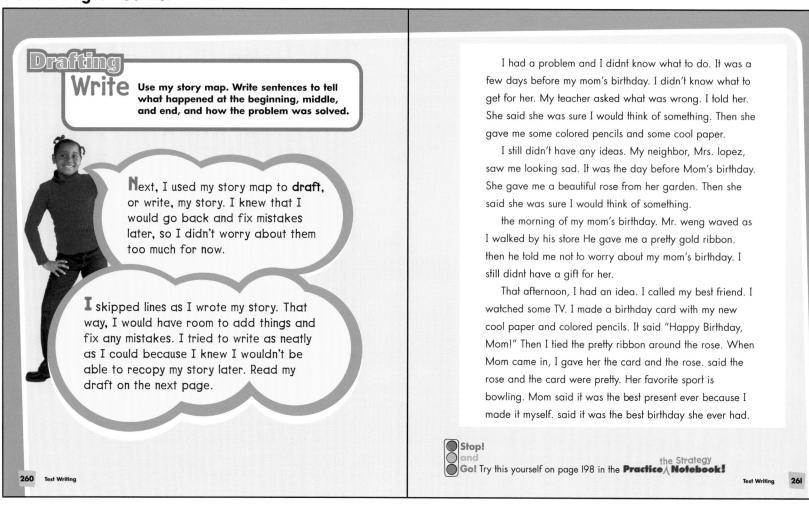

# Drafting Write

**Strategy:** Use my story map. Write sentences to tell what happened at the beginning, middle, and end, and how the problem was solved.

*(Student Pages 260–261)*

Explain that on a writing test, students will most likely not have time to recopy their writing. For this reason, it is important that they write neatly. Also point out that if the person scoring their writing cannot read it easily, the score may be lower. If students have plenty of room, suggest that they skip lines.

Read Danielle's words on Student Page 260, and then read the draft of Danielle's story on Student Page 261. Ask students if they think any parts are unclear or if they like any particular parts.

Explain that students may notice some mistakes because this is a draft, not a final piece of writing. Danielle will correct these mistakes during the Editing step.

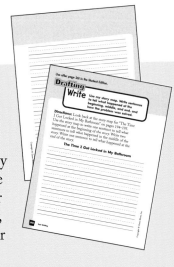

## the Strategy
## Practice ∧ Notebook!

*Practice the Strategy Notebook* pages 198–199 give students an opportunity to practice using a story map to write the important events in a story. After students have completed this activity, you may wish to have them read their drafts to a partner.

## the Strategy
## Practice ∧ Notebook!

*Practice the Strategy Notebook* pages 200–201 give students an opportunity to write a draft of their own story using the story map they created on pages 196–197. You may wish to assign these pages now or after students have completed this chapter in the Student Edition.

## Revising
### Add (Elaborate)

**Add details to make the story and characters more interesting.**

**O**n a test, I can't talk with my writing partner, so I always reread my story to myself. The Scoring Guide says to include details that make the story and the characters interesting. I decided to add more details about the pencils and paper and how my teacher knew I had a problem. I also added a detail about Mr. Weng.

**I** can't use sticky notes on a writing test, so I used proofreading marks to add my details. I'm glad I skipped lines when I wrote my draft!

262  Test Writing

---

I had a problem and I didnt know what to do. It was a few days before my mom's birthday. I didn't know what to get for her. My teacher asked what was wrong. I told her.
I must have looked kind of sad.
She said she was sure I would think of something. Then she gave me some colored pencils and some cool paper.
green and blue     with silver and gold designs

I still didn't have any ideas. My neighbor, Mrs. lopez, saw me looking sad. It was the day before Mom's birthday. She gave me a beautiful rose from her garden. Then she said she was sure I would think of something.

the morning of my mom's birthday. Mr. weng waved as I walked by his store. He gave me a pretty gold ribbon.
Mr. Weng is a decorator.
then he told me not to worry about my mom's birthday. I still didnt have a gift for her.

That afternoon, I had an idea. I called my best friend. I watched some TV. I made a birthday card with my new cool paper and colored pencils. It said "Happy Birthday, Mom!" Then I tied the pretty ribbon around the rose. When Mom came in, I gave her the card and the rose. said the rose and the card were pretty. Her favorite sport is bowling. Mom said it was the best present ever because I made it myself. said it was the best birthday she ever had.

**Stop!**
**and**
**Go!** Try this yourself on page 202 in the *Practice* **the Strategy** **Notebook!**

Test Writing  263

---

## Revising Add (Elaborate)

**Strategy: Add details to make the story and characters more interesting.**

*(Student Pages 262–263)*

Explain to students that adding details to a story makes the story more interesting by helping readers picture story events and the characters. Read Danielle's words on Student Page 262 and the draft of her story on Student Page 263. Ask students if they think the changes Danielle has made help them picture story events more easily.

**Practice** **the Strategy** **Notebook!**

*Practice the Strategy Notebook* page 202 gives students an opportunity to practice adding details to make a story more interesting. You may wish to have them discuss other details that could be added to make the story and characters more interesting.

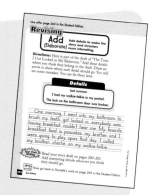

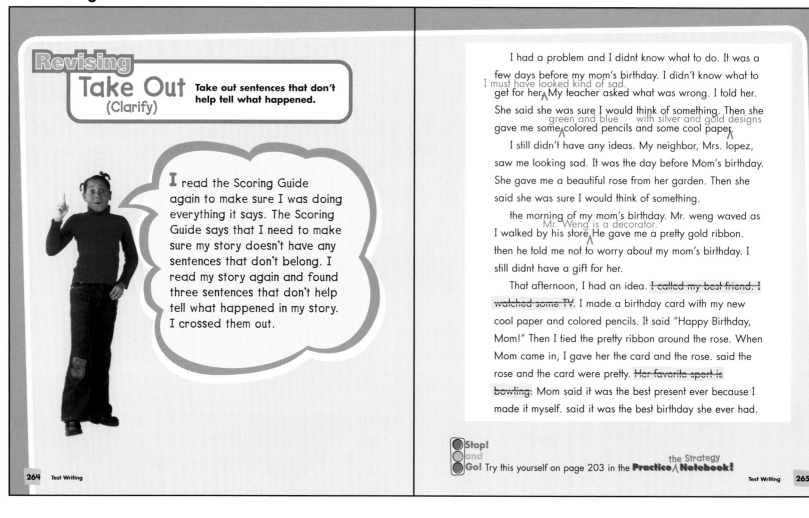

# Revising Take Out (Clarify)

**Strategy: Take out sentences that don't help tell what happened.**

*(Student Pages 264–265)*

Remind students that the Scoring Guide tells them that their story shouldn't have any sentences that don't belong. Explain that readers will be confused by any details that do not tell about what happened in the story. Read Danielle's words on Student Page 264 with the students. Then call attention to the changes she made in the final paragraph of her draft on Student Page 265. Have students discuss why these sentences were deleted.

### the Strategy
### Practice ∧ Notebook!

*Practice the Strategy Notebook* page 203 gives students an opportunity to practice finding and crossing out sentences that do not belong. You may wish to have students work with partners. When students have completed this activity, you may wish to have them share their findings with the whole group.

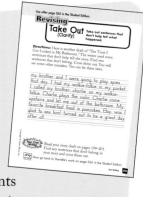

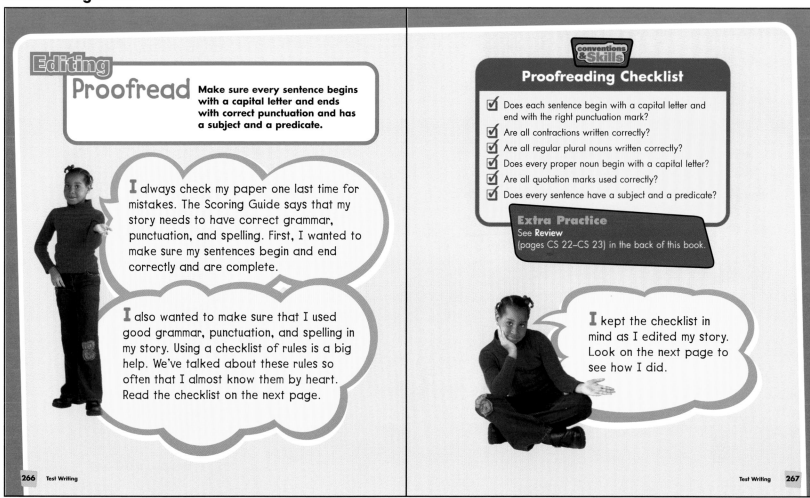

## Editing Proofread

**Strategy: Make sure every sentence begins with a capital letter and ends with correct punctuation and has a subject and a predicate.**

*(Student Pages 266–267)*

Explain to students that on a writing test, it is important to take a final look at their writing to look for errors in grammar, punctuation, and spelling.

Read Danielle's words on Student Page 266, as well as the Proofreading Checklist on Student Page 267. Remind students that Danielle is going to check to be sure her sentences are capitalized and punctuated correctly and that they are complete.

**Note:** You may also wish to use the corresponding Writing Model for Proofreading Practice Transparency.

## Extra Practice: **Conventions & Skills**
## Student Edition

If your students need more practice in capitalization, punctuation, and writing complete sentences, you may wish to assign Student Pages CS 22–CS 23.

## Conventions & Skills Practice

For more targeted practice related to this skill, see these lessons in the optional *Conventions & Skills Practice Book*:

Lesson 2: Complete Subject and Complete Predicate
Lesson 5: Sentence Fragments
Lesson 6: Sentences That Tell
Lesson 7: Sentences That Ask
Lesson 8: Telling or Asking Sentences
Lesson 9: Sentences That Command
Lesson 10: Sentences That Show Strong Feelings
Lesson 41: Capitalizing the First Word in a Sentence
Lesson 47: Writing Sentences Correctly

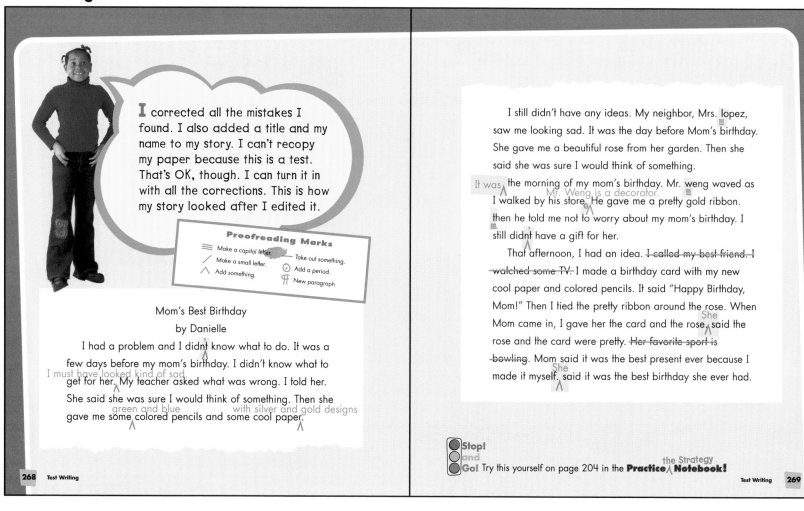

## Editing Proofread

**Strategy:** **Make sure every sentence begins with a capital letter and ends with correct punctuation and has a subject and a predicate.**

*(Student Pages 268–269)*

Point out the proofreading marks and make sure students understand their meaning and how to use them in their own writing. Read Danielle's words on Student Page 268 with the students. Remind students that she is now going to correct any mistakes in her draft.

Read the edited version of Danielle's story on Student Pages 268–269 with the students. Discuss Danielle's corrections with the students.

## Using the Rubric

*Practice the Strategy Notebook* pages 206–207 provide a rubric based on the Scoring Guide in this chapter. You may wish to have students use the rubric to assess Danielle's story.

### Practice the Strategy Notebook!

*Practice the Strategy Notebook* pages 204–205 give students an opportunity to use proofreading marks to correct errors in grammar, punctuation, capitalization, and spelling in a practice story. You may wish to point out to students that they may need to add missing words to some of the sentences.

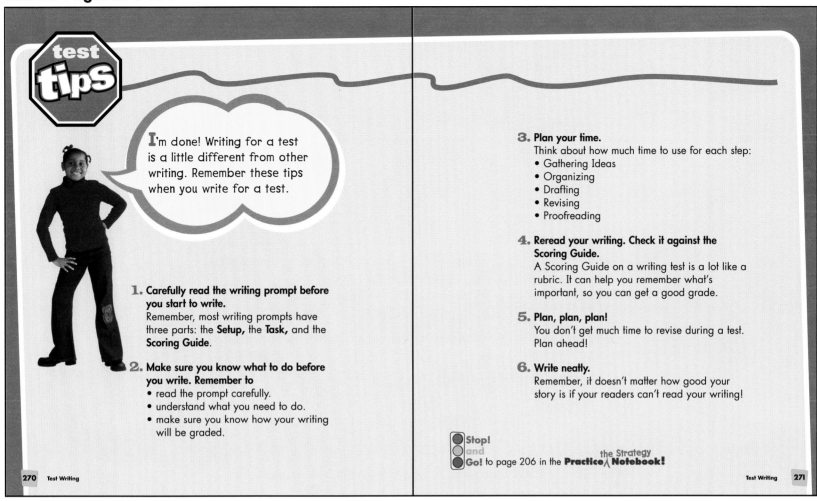

**test tips**

I'm done! Writing for a test is a little different from other writing. Remember these tips when you write for a test.

**1.** **Carefully read the writing prompt before you start to write.**
Remember, most writing prompts have three parts: the **Setup,** the **Task,** and the **Scoring Guide.**

**2.** **Make sure you know what to do before you write. Remember to**
• read the prompt carefully.
• understand what you need to do.
• make sure you know how your writing will be graded.

**3.** **Plan your time.**
Think about how much time to use for each step:
• Gathering Ideas
• Organizing
• Drafting
• Revising
• Proofreading

**4.** **Reread your writing. Check it against the Scoring Guide.**
A Scoring Guide on a writing test is a lot like a rubric. It can help you remember what's important, so you can get a good grade.

**5.** **Plan, plan, plan!**
You don't get much time to revise during a test. Plan ahead!

**6.** **Write neatly.**
Remember, it doesn't matter how good your story is if your readers can't read your writing!

**Stop! and Go!** to page 206 in the **Practice** the Strategy **Notebook!**

270   Test Writing

Test Writing   271

## Test Tips

Read Student Pages 270–271 with the students. Explain that these tips will help them do well on writing tests.

Try out the tips you practiced in this unit. Choose one of the ideas below or come up with your own idea. Then take your own writing "test." Pretend this is a real test. Give yourself one hour to finish all of the steps. Use one of these ideas.

Write a story about a problem you had and how you solved it.

OR

Write a story about a time you had a lot of fun.

OR

Write a story about the first time you tried something new.

**Be sure your story**

- tells the readers who was in the story and what happened.
- has a beginning, middle, and end.
- has details to make the story and the characters more interesting.
- doesn't have sentences that don't belong.
- uses correct grammar, punctuation, and spelling.

portfolio

School-Home Connection

Keep a writing folder. Add **Your Own Writing** pages to your writing folder. You may want to take your writing folder home to share.

272   **Test Writing**

## Your Own Writing
## Test Writing

Assign one of the writing prompts to the students. Before they begin to write, review important points about test writing.

**Note:** A rubric is not provided for students in testing situations in all states. For that reason, this chapter includes a Scoring Guide rather than a rubric. The Scoring Guide appears as a fully developed rubric on pages 206–207 in the *Practice the Strategy Notebook*. You may wish to have students use this rubric to assess their response to the writing prompt.

## Portfolio/School-Home Connection

Encourage students to keep portfolios of their writing. You may also wish to duplicate and distribute the School-Home Letter included in this unit.

## Work-in-Progress Portfolio

Remind students to review this portfolio often to revise existing pieces that have not been published. Encourage students to share pieces of their Work-in-Progress Portfolios with family members who can help in editing.

## Published Portfolio

Encourage students to choose pieces from their Published Portfolios to share with family members.

## School–Home Connection

Dear Family,

Over the next few weeks, your child will be learning a new kind of writing—how to write for a test. Many state assessments and standardized tests such as achievement tests now require students to write essays. For this reason, we will take time this year to help your child learn some specific skills for writing on a test.

Six basic tips for students are outlined in *Strategies for Writers*.

1. *Carefully read the writing prompt before you start to write.*

   The writing prompt is the assignment that students are given on a writing test. Most prompts include the Setup, the Task, and the Scoring Guide.
   The Setup gives background information.
   The Task tells exactly what the writer is supposed to do.
   The Scoring Guide tells how the writing will be scored.

2. *Make sure you know what to do before you write.*

   This part of the lesson teaches students to identify the parts of the prompt and reminds them to check the Scoring Guide as they write.

3. *Plan your time.*

   In tests with a limited amount of time for writing, students need to organize their time so that they can address each step of the writing process: **Gathering Ideas, Organizing, Drafting, Revising,** and **Proofreading**.

4. *Reread your writing. Check it against the Scoring Guide.*

   The Scoring Guide is much like the writing rubrics your child has been using all year. Checking it during writing helps the student stay focused on what is important.

5. *Plan, plan, plan!*

   Because time for revising is limited during a writing test, planning during the Prewriting step is very important.

6. *Write neatly.*

   This reminder is important because the people who score the students' writing must be able to read it easily.

   Help your child prepare for writing tests by following these six steps. By developing these habits, your child can relax and even enjoy writing for a test.

You may wish to copy the letter above and send it home with your students.

# conventions & Skills

Do you need some more practice with the editing skills you worked on in this book? Use the activities in this section to get more practice. Complete each activity on a separate sheet of paper.

## Table of Contents

**Conventions & Skills**  CS 1

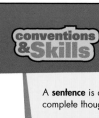

## Conventions & Skills

### Capitalizing and Punctuating Sentences

A **sentence** is a group of words that tells a complete thought.

### Review the Rule

Begin each sentence with a capital letter. End each sentence with a period (unless the sentence asks a question or shows strong feelings).

### Practice

Number your paper 1.–20. Read each sentence. Rewrite the incorrect sentences. Put in any missing capital letters and periods. If a sentence is correct, write **Correct** after the number.

1. We go to the pool
2. our mom watches us.
3. My brother jumps into the pool
4. the water is cold
5. I get in slowly.
6. I put just my feet in first
7. then I get my legs wet.
8. next, I get my arms and body wet
9. My head is the last part to go into the water.
10. now I am all wet.
11. my brother splashes me.
12. I want to splash him back.
13. He swims away from me
14. I don't swim after him
15. soon I will learn to swim
16. I don't know how to yet
17. then I will chase my brother
18. I will swim fast.
19. we will have lots of fun in the pool
20. the pool is a great place.

### Apply

Copy this paragraph on your paper. Add capital letters and periods where they are needed.

> Meg learned to swim. First, she learned to put her face in the water Next, she learned to float. then she learned to kick. Finally, she learned how to use her arms. now, Meg can swim across the pool

---

Answers appear below.

### Practice

1. We go to the pool.
2. Our mom watches us.
3. My brother jumps into the pool.
4. The water is cold.
5. Correct
6. I put just my feet in first.
7. Then I get my legs wet.
8. Next, I get my arms and body wet.
9. Correct
10. Now I am all wet.
11. My brother splashes me.
12. Correct
13. He swims away from me.
14. I don't swim after him.
15. Soon I will learn to swim.
16. I don't know how to yet.
17. Then I will chase my brother.
18. Correct
19. We will have lots of fun in the pool.
20. The pool is a great place.

### Apply

Meg learned to swim. First, she learned to put her face in the water. Next, she learned to float. Then she learned to kick. Finally, she learned how to use her arms. Now, Meg can swim across the pool.

## Parts of a Friendly Letter

A **friendly letter** is written to someone you know. You can tell a story in the letter. A friendly letter has five parts.

### Review the Rule

- The **heading** gives your address and the date. It has three lines.
  The first line is your street address.
  The next line is your city, state, and zip code.
  The last line is the date.
- The **greeting** begins with *Dear*. It ends with the name of the person you are writing to and a comma.
- The **body** is the main part of the letter. It is made up of sentences. It can tell a story.
- The **closing** is a word or two words like *Love, Your pal,* or *Your cousin.* The closing begins with a capital letter and ends with a comma.
- The **signature** is your name, written by you.

CS 4   Conventions & Skills • Parts of a Friendly Letter

### Practice

Number your paper 1.–5. Read the letter below. Write the name of each numbered part.

**1.** 12 Elm Street
   Durbin, ND 54321
   May 21, 20- -

**2.** Dear Keith,

**3.** Yesterday, we got a new house! First, we looked at a lot of homes. Then my parents talked it over. Finally, they bought one on Shady Lane. It's great! I'll give you my new address soon.

**4.** Your buddy,

**5.** Joe

### Apply

This friendly letter is all mixed up. Rewrite it correctly. You can use Joe's letter above to help you.

> August 6, 20–
> Your friend, Chris
>
> We got a cat yesterday. First, we went to an animal shelter. We saw lots of cats there. Then we picked out Franny. Last, we took her home.
>
> Dear George,
> Miami, FL 43210
> 123 Palm Ave.

Conventions & Skills • Parts of a Friendly Letter   CS 5

---

Answers appear below.

### Practice

1. heading
2. greeting
3. body
4. closing
5. signature

### Apply

123 Palm Ave.
Miami, FL 43210
August 6, 20—

Dear George,

   We got a cat yesterday. First, we went to an animal shelter. We saw lots of cats there. Then we picked out Franny. Last, we took her home.

   Your friend,
   Chris

## Writing Sentences Correctly

Sentences must begin with a **capital letter**. A sentence can **tell something**. A sentence can **ask a question**. A sentence can **show strong feelings**.

### Review the Rule
- Begin every sentence with a capital letter.
- Put a period (.) after telling sentences.
- Put a question mark (?) after asking sentences.
- Put an exclamation point (!) after sentences that show strong feelings.

### Practice

Number your paper 1.–20. Read each sentence. Rewrite incorrect sentences so they start with capital letters and end with the correct punctuation. If a sentence has no errors, write **Correct**.

1. My dad takes me to the store
2. What should we buy to eat
3. I love to shop
4. we buy food for the week.
5. dad likes lots of fruit.
6. He buys things for salad.
7. I pick out two kinds of yogurt.
8. mom wants fish and meat
9. Do you think the fruit smells good
10. buying cereal is my job.
11. Which cereal should we buy this week
12. I buy Puff Pops.
13. Next, we pick out bread
14. Dad gets two cartons of milk.
15. I ask for some juice.
16. the basket is so heavy!
17. How long will it take to check out
18. we leave the store
19. We fill up the car with bags.
20. I am glad to go home

### Apply

Read the paragraph below. Write the paragraph correctly on a separate piece of paper by adding capital letters and correct punctuation.

We go to Scali Bakery. What makes it smell so good inside There are all kinds of breads. there are rows of cookies, too. Near the window are many kinds of cakes. some of them are for birthday parties. All of them look so good

---

Answers appear below.

### Practice

1. My dad takes me to the store.
2. What should we buy to eat?
3. I love to shop!
4. We buy food for the week.
5. Dad likes lots of fruit.
6. Correct
7. Correct
8. Mom wants fish and meat.
9. Do you think the fruit smells good?
10. Buying cereal is my job.
11. Which cereal should we buy this week?
12. Correct
13. Next, we pick out bread.
14. Correct
15. Correct
16. The basket is so heavy!
17. How long will it take to check out?
18. We leave the store.
19. Correct
20. I am glad to go home.

### Apply

We go to Scali Bakery. What makes it smell so good inside? There are all kinds of breads. There are rows of cookies, too. Near the window are many kinds of cakes. Some of them are for birthday parties. All of them look so good!

 **Contractions**

A **contraction** is made up of two words put together. Some letters from the two words are left out. An apostrophe (') takes the place of the missing letters.

## Review the Rule

| Two words | Take out | Add apostrophe | Contraction |
|---|---|---|---|
| can + not | the **no** in **not** | ' | can't |
| did + not | the **o** in **not** | ' | didn't |
| do + not | the **o** in **not** | ' | don't |
| does + not | the **o** in **not** | ' | doesn't |
| it + is | the **i** in **is** | ' | it's |
| they + are | the **a** in **are** | ' | they're |

## Practice

Number your paper 1.–20. Read each sentence. Write the words in parentheses as a contraction.

1. (I will) show you my pet.
2. (It is) a goldfish.
3. (Is not) she pretty?
4. She (cannot) talk.
5. She (does not) run.
6. She (has not) ever laughed.
7. (She is) a great pet, though.
8. (Do not) you want one?
9. (You will) get one, too.
10. (You are) going to love it.
11. (I have) got two pet frogs.
12. (He is) Danny.
13. (She is) Frannie.
14. (They are) cute.
15. Danny (does not) jump a lot.
16. (He is) not happy.
17. My mom (did not) want me to get them.
18. Mom says frogs (are not) good pets.
19. A frog (should not) be in a little bowl.
20. (It is) happier in a big pond.

## Apply

Correct any contractions that are not written correctly. Write the paragraph with the correct contractions on a separate piece of paper.

My fish tank doe'snt have any goldfish. Its' full of sharks instead! Theyre small silver sharks that cant hurt you. At first, I did'nt want to get them. Now I dont' want any other kind of fish!

---

Answers appear below.

## Practice

1. I'll
2. It's
3. Isn't
4. can't
5. doesn't
6. hasn't
7. She's
8. Don't
9. You'll
10. You're
11. I've
12. He's
13. She's
14. They're
15. doesn't
16. He's
17. didn't
18. aren't
19. shouldn't
20. It's

## Apply

My fish tank doesn't have any goldfish. It's full of sharks instead! They're small silver sharks that can't hurt you. At first, I didn't want to get them. Now I don't want any other kind of fish!

conventions & Skills

## Plural Nouns

A **plural noun** names more than one person, place, or thing. In most cases, add *-s* to a noun to make it plural. Add *-es* to nouns that end in *x, ch, s,* or *sh*. Don't use an apostrophe (') to make a noun plural.

### Review the Rule

| One | | Plural Noun | One | | Plural Noun |
|---|---|---|---|---|---|
| student | + s | students | fox | + es | foxes |
| town | + s | towns | bench | + es | benches |
| tree | + s | trees | crash | + es | crashes |

### Practice

Number your paper 1.–20. Write the plural of each noun.

1. storm
2. sand
3. dress
4. home
5. girl
6. brush
7. root
8. hall
9. box
10. couch
11. boy
12. trip
13. planet
14. star
15. stone
16. apple
17. pen
18. car
19. team
20. truck
21. letter
22. pencil
23. dish
24. ax
25. top
26. wrench
27. flower
28. tree
29. flash
30. paper

### Apply

Read the paragraph below. Look for errors in plural nouns. Write the paragraph correctly on a separate piece of paper.

We look at the weather map. Weather map's show frontses. A front is the place where cold air meets warm air. Weather reporterss use frontses to predict the weather. Sometimes, reportes for the same area are different. That is because many different thingses change the weather.

CS 10 Conventions & Skills • Plural Nouns

Conventions & Skills • Plural Nouns CS 11

Answers appear below.

### Practice

1. storms
2. sands
3. dresses
4. homes
5. girls
6. brushes
7. roots
8. halls
9. boxes
10. couches
11. boys
12. trips
13. planets
14. stars
15. stones
16. apples
17. pens
18. cars
19. teams
20. trucks
21. letters
22. pencils
23. dishes
24. axes
25. tops
26. wrenches
27. flowers
28. trees
29. flashes
30. papers

### Apply

We look at the weather map. Weather maps show fronts. A front is the place where cold air meets warm air. Weather reporters use fronts to predict the weather. Sometimes, reports for the same area are different. That is because many different things change the weather.

**Periods, Question Marks, and Exclamation Points**

A sentence can make a statement, ask a question, give a command, or express strong feelings. It begins with a **capital letter** and ends with a **punctuation mark**.

### Review the Rule

Begin every sentence with a capital letter. Use a period to end a statement. Use a question mark to end a question. Use an exclamation point to end a sentence that shows strong feelings.

### Practice

Number your paper 1.–20. Read each sentence. If the sentence is punctuated correctly, write **Correct**. If the sentence has a mistake in punctuation, write the sentence correctly on your paper.

1. How many continents does Earth have.
2. Did you know Earth has seven continents.
3. I can name all seven of them.
4. They are Africa, Antarctica, Asia, Australia, Europe, North America, and South America.
5. That's amazing?
6. Do many people live in Asia.

7. Most of the people on Earth live in Asia.
8. How interesting that is!
9. Is Australia a continent or an island!
10. What a question you ask?
11. Australia is both a continent and an island.
12. If you live in the United States, you live in North America?
13. On what continent would you find Egypt?
14. Egypt is in Africa.
15. What is the coldest continent!
16. Antarctica has the coldest weather of all?
17. Did you know that most of that continent is covered in ice.
18. Boy, am I glad we don't live there!
19. Europe has many people in it.
20. Can you find it on a map?

### Apply

Read the paragraph below. Look for mistakes in punctuation. Write the paragraph correctly on a separate piece of paper.

Our class is learning about continents? Did you know that continents move. That's amazing. Sometimes they crash into each other. Is that how mountains form. Many mountains were formed that way.

---

Answers appear below.

### Practice

1. How many continents does Earth have?
2. Did you know Earth has seven continents?
3. Correct
4. Correct
5. That's amazing!
6. Do many people live in Asia?
7. Correct
8. Correct
9. Is Australia a continent or an island?
10. What a question you ask!
11. Correct
12. If you live in the United States, you live in North America.
13. Correct
14. Correct
15. What is the coldest continent?
16. Antarctica has the coldest weather of all.
17. Did you know that most of that continent is covered in ice?
18. Correct
19. Correct
20. Correct

### Apply

Our class is learning about continents. Did you know that continents move? That's amazing! Sometimes they crash into each other. Is that how mountains form? Many mountains were formed that way.

**Proper Nouns**

A **proper noun** is the name of a person, place, or thing. A proper noun begins with a capital letter.

## Review the Rule

Begin a person's first and last names with a capital letter.

| | | |
|---|---|---|
| Bill Green | Sally Chang | Chris Johnson |

Begin place names with capital letters.

| | | |
|---|---|---|
| France | Lincoln School | Elm Road |

Begin the names of specific things, like days, months, and holidays, with a capital letter.

| | | |
|---|---|---|
| Monday | January | Labor Day |

## Practice

Number your paper 1.–20. If a proper noun in the sentence does not begin with a capital letter, write the proper noun correctly. If the proper noun already begins with a capital letter, write **Correct**.

1. We went to the Smith Library.
2. It is on market street.
3. We went there on friday.
4. It was the first day of march.
5. Mrs. cole showed us where to find fairy tales.
6. Matt likes books about hansel and gretel.
7. Nicki likes books about peter pan.
8. I showed a book about four hens to tom.
9. He showed me a book of stories from Mexico.
10. May took out a book of stories from china.
11. Mr. blake is the librarian.
12. He read us stories told by Neil Philip.
13. The stories came from a place called arabia.
14. One of them was about a man named ali baba.
15. He had a brother named kasim.
16. Ali Baba was poor, and his brother was rich.
17. One day, ali baba met forty thieves.
18. I liked the story, and so did bobby.
19. Later, amy checked the book out of the library.
20. I will check it out in april.

## Apply

Read this paragraph. Find all proper nouns that are not written correctly. Write the paragraph correctly on a separate piece of paper.

My friend, paul, told me a story that comes from africa. It is about a spider. The spider's name is anansi. He loves to trick everybody! The stories are funny. Sometimes the spider gets into trouble. You can find the stories at the wilson library. It is open every day but sunday.

---

Answers appear below.

## Practice

1. Correct
2. Market Street
3. Friday
4. March
5. Cole
6. Hansel and Gretel
7. Peter Pan
8. Tom
9. Correct
10. China
11. Blake
12. Correct
13. Arabia
14. Ali Baba
15. Kasim
16. Correct
17. Ali Baba
18. Bobby
19. Amy
20. April

## Apply

My friend, Paul, told me a story that comes from Africa. It is about a spider. The spider's name is Anansi. He loves to trick everybody! The stories are funny. Sometimes the spider gets into trouble. You can find the stories at the Wilson Library. It is open every day but Sunday.

## conventions & Skills — Quotation Marks

**Quotation marks (" ")** show where the words someone says begin and end.

### Review the Rule

Use quotation marks to show where a speaker begins talking and where he or she stops talking.

• Ms. Neal said, **"**I will read you a story.**"**

• **"**What is it about?**"** asked Bob.

### Practice

Number your paper 1.–20. Rewrite all incorrect sentences by adding the missing quotation marks. If a sentence is correct, write **Correct** after the number.

1. Ms. Neal said, This story is about a dog and a bone.

2. She said, "It is a good story.

3. She began, "A dog was carrying a bone."

4. Then she said, "It looked into a lake."

5. What did the dog see?" asked Katie.

6. "It saw a dog in the water carrying a bone!" Ms. Neal answered.

7. The dog said, That dog has a bone, too!

8. It looks better than my bone," the dog added.

9. Nolan asked, What happened?"

10. Ms. Neal laughed.

11. She said, "The dog dropped the bone!

12. Jenna asked, "Why?"

13. He wanted the other bone," said Ms. Neal.

14. Ms. Neal added, "But now the dog had no bone at all!"

15. "Is that a fable? asked Terry.

16. Yes, answered Ms. Neal.

17. I know the lesson! shouted Rico.

18. "What is it? asked Ms. Neal.

19. Rico said, "Don't want what someone else has."

20. That's great! said Ms. Neal.

### Apply

Add quotation marks wherever they are needed and rewrite this fable on your paper.

A boy saw candy in a jar. He asked his mother, May I have some?
She said, You may have a little.
The boy put his hand in and grabbed lots of candy. Then he couldn't get his hand out.
My hand is stuck! he cried.
The lesson is that a little at a time is better than none at all.

---

Answers appear below.

### Practice

1. Ms. Neal said, "This story is about a dog and a bone."

2. She said, "It is a good story."

3. Correct

4. Correct

5. "What did the dog see?" asked Katie.

6. Correct

7. The dog said, "That dog has a bone, too!"

8. "It looks better than my bone," the dog added.

9. Nolan asked, "What happened?"

10. Correct

11. She said, "The dog dropped the bone!"

12. Correct

13. "He wanted the other bone," said Ms. Neal.

14. Correct

15. "Is that a fable?" asked Terry.

16. "Yes," answered Ms. Neal.

17. "I know the lesson!" shouted Rico.

18. "What is it?" asked Ms. Neal.

19. Correct

20. "That's great!" said Ms. Neal.

### Apply

A boy saw candy in a jar. He asked his mother, "May I have some?"

She said, "You may have a little."

The boy put his hand in and grabbed lots of candy. Then he couldn't get his hand out.

"My hand is stuck!" he cried.

The lesson is that a little at a time is better than none at all.

## Subjects and Predicates

The **subject** of a sentence tells who or what does or is something. The **predicate** of a sentence tells what the subject does or is.

### Review the Rule

Every sentence needs both a subject and a predicate.

| Subject | Predicate |
|---------|-----------|
| My favorite food | is noodles. |
| The bread | bakes in the oven. |

### Practice

Number your paper 1.–20. Write **S** if the underlined words are the subject. Write **P** if the underlined words are the predicate.

1. My friend Jen eats with us.
2. My dad makes hamburgers.
3. We eat potatoes, too.
4. A big salad is part of the meal.
5. I drink milk with my meal.
6. Jen has a glass of water.
7. One big hamburger is enough for me!
8. Jen's family invites me to dinner.
9. Her mother makes pasta.
10. The noodles taste great.
11. Red sauce covers them.
12. I dip a big piece of bread in the sauce.
13. The tomato sauce is hot.
14. It tastes a little spicy.
15. A big plate of spaghetti is just right for me.
16. That much spaghetti is too much for Jen.
17. Jen's mom offers us dessert.
18. We are both too full.
19. I say thank you.
20. My stomach feels full and happy.

### Apply

Find any sentences in this paragraph that are missing a subject or a predicate. Write the paragraph correctly on a separate piece of paper. You will have to add some words.

My favorite snack is cheese and crackers. taste great together. Whole wheat crackers. Sometimes I have a big glass of milk, too. fills me up fast. I like to have my snack when I get home from school.

---

Answers appear below.

### Practice

1. S
2. P
3. P
4. S
5. P
6. S
7. S
8. S
9. P
10. S
11. S
12. P
13. P
14. P
15. S
16. P
17. P
18. S
19. P
20. S

### Apply

Answers will vary. Possible responses appear below.

My favorite snack is cheese and crackers. They taste great together. Whole wheat crackers are my favorite crackers. Sometimes I have a big glass of milk, too. It fills me up fast. I like to have my snack when I get home from school.

## Subjects and Predicates

The **subject** of a sentence tells who or what does or is something. The **predicate** of a sentence tells what the subject does or is.

### Review the Rule

Every sentence needs both a subject and a predicate.

| Subject | Predicate |
|---------|-----------|
| The children | like the swings. |
| They | are new and shiny. |

### Practice

Number your paper 1.–20. Write **Subject** if the underlined words are the subject. Write **Predicate** if the underlined words are the predicate.

1. Big Tree Park <u>is on Pine Street</u>.
2. <u>The park</u> has a new playground.
3. <u>My friends</u> like the slide there.
4. They <u>go down it all day long</u>!
5. The park <u>has great swings, too</u>.
6. <u>They</u> are brand new.
7. <u>Maria</u> swings high on them.
8. Rob <u>loves the tire swings</u>.
9. The hopscotch board <u>is always busy</u>.
10. <u>The pond</u> is nearby.
11. <u>People</u> can't swim there.
12. <u>Ducks</u> like it, though.
13. We <u>run up and down on poles and bars</u>.
14. Rope bridges <u>shake under us</u>.
15. Rope ladders <u>hold our weight</u>.
16. <u>My friend Mike</u> spent all day there.
17. <u>We</u> play for hours.
18. <u>My dad</u> takes us to the park often.
19. Mike's older sister <u>drives us there once a week</u>.
20. <u>I</u> feel happy at that park!

### Apply

Read this paragraph. Find any sentences that are missing a subject or a predicate. Write the paragraph correctly on a separate piece of paper.

Some parents wanted a new playground for us. Held a meeting. Asked us for ideas. One weekend we all built it together. Many parents, children, and other volunteers. It was fun to do. Now we have a great playground.

---

Answers appear below.

### Practice

1. Predicate
2. Subject
3. Subject
4. Predicate
5. Predicate
6. Subject
7. Subject
8. Predicate
9. Predicate
10. Subject
11. Subject
12. Subject
13. Predicate
14. Predicate
15. Predicate
16. Subject
17. Subject
18. Subject
19. Predicate
20. Subject

### Apply

Answers will vary. Possible responses appear below.

Some parents wanted a new playground for us. The parents held a meeting. They asked us for ideas. One weekend we all built it together. Many parents, children, and other volunteers helped. It was fun to do. Now we have a great playground.

**Review**

**Proofreading Checklist**

☑ Does each sentence begin with a capital letter and end with the right punctuation mark?

☑ Are all contractions written correctly?

☑ Are all regular plural nouns written correctly?

☑ Does every proper noun begin with a capital letter?

☑ Are all quotation marks used correctly?

☑ Does every sentence have a subject and a predicate?

## Practice

Number your paper 1.–20. Rewrite each incorrect sentence to correct errors in grammar, capitalization, or punctuation. Add any missing subjects or predicates. If a sentence has no errors, write **Correct**.

1. I love birthday parties
2. morgan brought pretty balloons.
3. played games.
4. all my friends were there.
5. My pet kitten, henry.
6. Sam blew out the candles
7. We ate chocolate cake.

8. he wished for some book's.
9. Everyone brought a present.
10. opened a present.
11. Sam jumped up and down.
12. the present was a book.
13. We clapped our hands
14. the book was about animals.
15. It had many pictures.
16. had a red ribbon.
17. Sam opened the next present.
18. the box had another book inside.
19. Everyone laughed
20. was the same book.

## Apply

Copy this thank-you note on your paper. Add any missing subjects or predicates. Correct any errors in grammar, capital letters, or punctuation.

Dear sam,

the party was great  I thank you for asking me. I had a fun time  The chocolate cake. I hope you like the book. My teacher helped me pick it out. knows about bookss.

Your friend,

max

---

Suggested answers appear below.

## Practice

1. I love birthday parties.
2. Morgan brought pretty balloons.
3. We played games.
4. All my friends were there.
5. My pet kitten, Henry, took the ball.
6. Sam blew out the candles.
7. Correct
8. He wished for some books.
9. Correct
10. Sam opened a present.
11. Correct
12. The present was a book.
13. We clapped our hands.
14. The book was about animals.
15. Correct
16. One present had a red ribbon.
17. Correct
18. The box had another book inside.
19. Everyone laughed.
20. It was the same book.

## Apply

Some answers will vary. Possible response appears below.

Dear Sam,

The party was great. I thank you for asking me. I had a fun time. The chocolate cake was really good. I hope you like the book. My teacher helped me pick it out. Mrs. Jones knows about books.

Your friend,

Max

# Writer's Handbook

## Table of Contents

**Student Pages HB 2–HB 3**

## Prewriting
### Gather Ideas

#### Brainstorming

Brainstorming is saying things as you think of them. You can do this alone or with a writing partner. You can also do this in a small group. Let's say you are going to write a report about an animal. How do you pick an animal? Maybe you have a pet. Maybe you read a book about animals. Maybe you went to the zoo. Start naming some animals. Take turns if you are working with others. Write down the animals you say. One of them might become a good topic for your report.

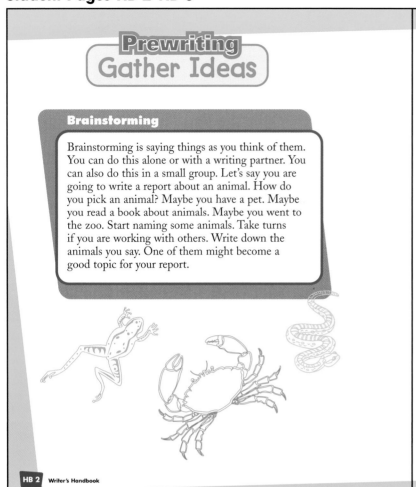

#### Daydreaming/Doodling

Daydreaming is letting your mind wander. Pick a quiet place. Then ask yourself a question that gets you wondering. Here are some good questions to ask.
- "What will I be when I grow up?"
- "What would it be like to live under the sea?"
- "Is there life in outer space?"

Let your imagination take over. You might be surprised at the good ideas that come to you.

Doodling is another word for drawing. Start with a pencil and some clean paper. Draw anything you think of. Look at your doodles. One of them could be a great idea for your next writing project.

---

**Student Pages HB 4–HB 5**

#### Interviewing

An interview is a conversation. Talk to people who know about your topic. You can talk to family members or to other people. If you want to write about baking a cake, talk to someone who bakes. It could be someone in your family or it could be a baker in your town. Ask questions. Listen to people's answers and stories and jot down some notes. It's a good idea to take your parents with you when you talk to other adults.

#### Favorite Books, Movies, and TV Shows

- What books do you like?
- What movies and shows do you watch?

Do you like books about make-believe animals?
Try writing a story about a dragon.

Do you like movies about space?
Try writing about a space trip.

Do you like TV shows about kids?
Try writing a story about you and your friends.

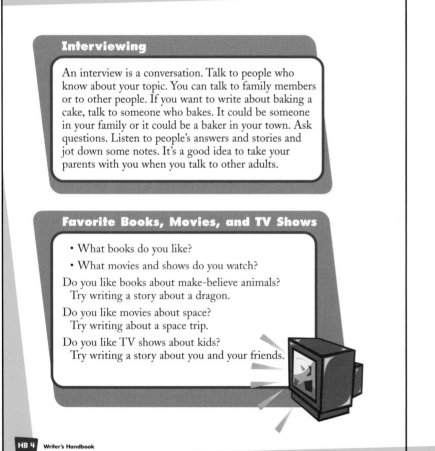

My Topic: Lizards
What I know:
- have scales
- animals
- green

#### Lists

Lists are good tools for all kinds of things. We make lists to shop. We make lists for chores. We make lists to remember things. Writers make lists, too. A list can tell you what you already know about your topic. A list can help you figure out what you need to know. Write a list of things you already know about your topic. Then write a list of things you don't know. Find out the things you need to know. Put them together with what you already know. Now you have everything you need for writing.

What I don't know:
- what they eat
- where they live
- what kinds there are

### Notes

Notes are good tools for jotting down information. You can take notes from books or articles. You can take notes from interviews. Write down the important parts. Keep your notes short. Write clearly because you will need to read your notes later. You can use paper or note cards. Leave two lines between your notes on paper. This makes the notes easier to read. It also leaves room for more notes. Use one note card for each note. You can even use note cards in different colors. Keep your notes in one place. That way you can find them when you need to use them for your writing.

## Prewriting Organize

### Storyboard

Use a storyboard to plan a story. A storyboard shows the events of a story in order. This storyboard shows the events of a story about a boy's first swimming lesson.

Topic: My First Swimming Lesson

HB 6   Writer's Handbook

Writer's Handbook   HB 7

### Five Senses Chart

Use a five senses chart to plan a description or a report. A five senses chart tells how something looks, sounds, tastes, feels, and smells. This five senses chart organizes information for a descriptive paper about a neighborhood market.

| Subject of My Paper: The Super T | | |
|---|---|---|
| I can **see** | • mangoes and kiwis<br>• strings of chili peppers | • herbs<br>• spices |
| I can **hear** | • people talking<br>• music playing | • cash register beeping |
| I can **taste** | I can't taste anything at the Super T unless I buy it. | |
| I can **touch** (feel) | • mangoes and kiwis | • chili peppers |
| I can **smell** | • mangoes and kiwis<br>• chili peppers | • herbs<br>• spices |

### Venn Diagram

Use a Venn diagram to plan a description of two things or a compare-and-contrast paper. A Venn diagram shows how two things are the same and different. This Venn diagram organizes information for a compare-and-contrast paper about goldfish and frogs.

**Goldfish**
• orange
• breathe in water
• can't walk on land
• are quiet

**Both**
• animals
• swim
• can be pets

**Frogs**
• brownish green
• can breathe air
• can hop and leap
• croak

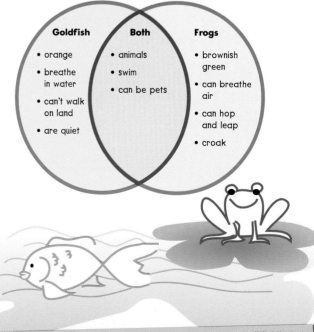

HB 8   Writer's Handbook

Writer's Handbook   HB 9

## Story Map

Use a story map to plan a story. A story map tells who is in the story. It tells what the problem is. Finally, it tells what happens in the story and how the problem is solved. This story map shows the beginning, middle, and end of a fable about two sisters.

## Order Chain

Use an order chain to plan a how-to paper or a report. An order chain tells steps in order. This order chain shows the steps of making a jigsaw puzzle for a how-to paper.

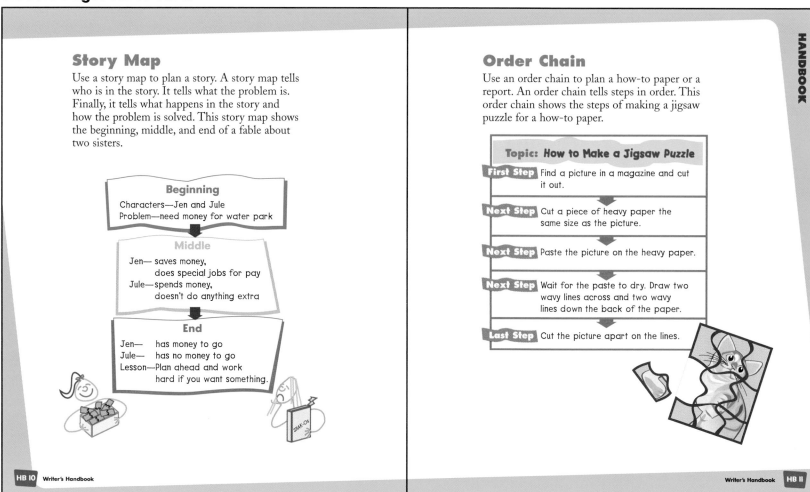

**Beginning**

Characters—Jen and Jule
Problem—need money for water park

**Middle**

Jen— saves money,
 does special jobs for pay
Jule—spends money,
 doesn't do anything extra

**End**

Jen— has money to go
Jule— has no money to go
Lesson—Plan ahead and work
 hard if you want something.

**Topic: How to Make a Jigsaw Puzzle**

**First Step** Find a picture in a magazine and cut it out.

**Next Step** Cut a piece of heavy paper the same size as the picture.

**Next Step** Paste the picture on the heavy paper.

**Next Step** Wait for the paste to dry. Draw two wavy lines across and two wavy lines down the back of the paper.

**Last Step** Cut the picture apart on the lines.

## Web

Use a web to plan a report, a description, or a story. A web has the topic in the center. It has details around the topic. Sometimes the center of the web has a question. This web helps organize information for a report on clouds. It answers the question, "What are clouds?"

## Spider Map

Use a spider map to plan a report or a description. A spider map has the topic in the spider's "body." It has details on the spider's "legs." This spider map shows why lasagna makes the best meal for a persuasive paper about favorite foods.

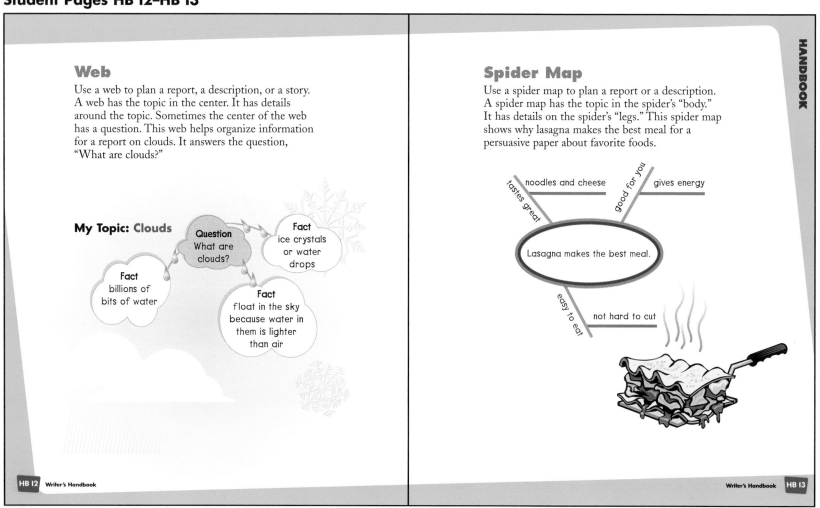

**My Topic: Clouds**

**Question** What are clouds?

**Fact** ice crystals or water drops

**Fact** billions of bits of water

**Fact** float in the sky because water in them is lighter than air

noodles and cheese — tastes great
good for you — gives energy
Lasagna makes the best meal.
easy to eat — not hard to cut

**HANDBOOK**

## Drafting
## Write

### Writing Sentences

A sentence is a group of words that tells a complete idea. Sentences have a subject. The subject is the person or thing doing something. Sentences have a predicate. The predicate is what the subject is doing. Read these two groups of words. Which one is not a sentence?

> Becca ran home.
>
> Raining hard.

The first group of words is a sentence. How can you tell? It has a subject, someone who is doing something—*Becca*. What did Becca do? She ran home. That's the predicate—*ran home*. This is a complete sentence.

The second group of words is not a sentence. Does it have a subject, or a person or thing doing something? No, it doesn't. Does it have a predicate? Maybe *raining* is a predicate. We can't be sure. It is not a complete sentence.

Be sure all your sentences have a subject and a predicate.

### Writing Paragraphs

A paragraph is a group of sentences about the same topic. The first sentence tells the topic. The rest of the sentences tell more about the topic. The first sentence in a paragraph is indented. That means it starts a little to the right.

Read this paragraph.

> I like July best. It is warm in July. My family goes to the lake. We watch fireworks. <u>My best friend likes December.</u> We eat ice cream and drink lemonade. July is my favorite month.

The topic is the main idea of the paragraph. It is in the first sentence. The first sentence is indented. The rest of the sentences tell more about the topic.

Read the underlined sentence. It doesn't tell about the topic. Let's take out that sentence.

> I like July best. It is warm in July. My family goes to the lake. We watch fireworks. We eat ice cream and drink lemonade. July is my favorite month.

Now we have a good paragraph.

---

**HANDBOOK**

### Action Words

Read these two sentences. Which one is more interesting?

> Jake <u>fell</u> to the ground.
>
> Jake <u>tumbled</u> to the ground.

The second sentence is more interesting. The word *tumbled* means the same thing as the word *fell*, but it tells more. The word *tumbled* gives a picture. Try using a special book to find good action words. The special book is called a *thesaurus*. See page HB 18 for information about using a thesaurus.

### Describing Words

Read these two sentences. Which one has more details?

> Emily carried a balloon.
>
> Emily carried a <u>shiny</u>, <u>new</u>, <u>red</u> balloon.

The first sentence doesn't have any details. The second sentence has a lot of details. It tells that the balloon was shiny, new, and red. Describing words tell how something looks, sounds, smells, feels, or tastes. Describing words will make your writing more interesting.

## Revising
## Add and Take Out

### Using a Dictionary

A dictionary is a book of words. It has the spellings and meanings of words. A dictionary is a good tool for writers. It can help you spell words. It can also help you learn new words.

Look inside a dictionary. You will see that the words are in columns. The words go from the top of the page to the bottom. Then the columns go from the left side of the page to the right side. Words in a dictionary are in ABC order. Be sure you understand what words mean and use the right meanings of words when you write.

## Using a Thesaurus

A thesaurus is a special kind of book. It has all kinds of words. A thesaurus has words that mean the same thing. It also has words that mean the opposite. Words in a thesaurus are in ABC order. A thesaurus can help make your writing more interesting. Read this paragraph.

My sister Morgan likes all kinds of fruit. She will eat peaches and pears. She will eat apples, bananas, and grapes. She will also eat plums and oranges. I can't think of any fruit Morgan won't eat.

Does this paragraph seem kind of boring? That's because we used the word *eat* too many times. A thesaurus has many words that mean the same thing as *eat*. You might find the words *munch*, *gobble*, *chomp*, and *nibble* in a thesaurus. Let's use some of those words in place of *eat* in our paragraph. Read the new paragraph on the next page.

My sister Morgan likes all kinds of fruit. She will **munch** peaches and pears. She will **gobble** apples, bananas, and grapes. She will also **chomp** plums and oranges. I can't think of any fruit Morgan won't **nibble**.

Now our paragraph is colorful and rich. Try using a thesaurus when you get stuck with the same word. Use it to learn new words, too.

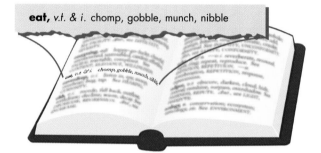

**eat,** *v.t. & i.* chomp, gobble, munch, nibble

---

## Editing
## Proofread

### Sentences

### Capitalization

Every sentence begins with a **capital letter**.

The sun is out today.

### End Marks

Every sentence ends with a **punctuation mark**. Sentences that tell end with a period. **(.)**

We went to the park to play soccer**.**

Sentences that ask a question end with a **question mark. (?)**

Was it hot at the park**?**

Sentences that show strong feelings end with an **exclamation point. (!)**

No, it was a great day**!**

### Subjects and Predicates

A sentence is a group of words that tells a complete thought. A sentence has a **subject** and a **predicate**.

The subject is the "doer" in the sentence. It is the person or the thing that does something.

**Our soccer team** won the game.

The predicate tells what the subject is doing.

Our soccer team **won the game**.

### Quotation Marks

**Quotation marks** separate someone's words from the rest of the sentence. They are used to show conversation in stories.

Jordan said, "I have a baby sister."

## Contractions

**Contractions** are a short way of writing or saying two words. When we put two words together in writing to make a contraction, we use an **apostrophe (')** to replace the dropped letters.

| | | | | | | | |
|---|---|---|---|---|---|---|---|
| do | + not | = don't | | she | + is | = she's |
| can | + not | = can't | | he | + has | = he's |
| will | + not | = won't | | they | + will | = they'll |

### Nouns

**Nouns** are words that name people, places, and things.

A **singular noun** names one person, place, or thing.

| | | |
|---|---|---|
| boy | house | bus |
| girl | town | car |
| box | bench | dress |

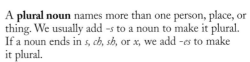

A **plural noun** names more than one person, place, or thing. We usually add *-s* to a noun to make it plural. If a noun ends in *s, ch, sh,* or *x,* we add *-es* to make it plural.

| | | |
|---|---|---|
| boys | houses | buses |
| girls | towns | cars |
| boxes | benches | dresses |

### Pronouns

**Pronouns** take the place of nouns.

| | | |
|---|---|---|
| I | he | she |
| me | it | you |
| we | they | us |

---

## Verbs

**Verbs** are words that show action.

| | | |
|---|---|---|
| play | talk | read |

Some verbs do not show action.

| | | |
|---|---|---|
| is | was | are |

Verbs can show the present, the past, or the future.

| Present | Past | Future |
|---|---|---|
| talk | talked | will talk |
| play | played | will play |

## Adjectives

**Adjectives** describe nouns and pronouns. They tell how something looks, feels, sounds, tastes, and smells.

| | | |
|---|---|---|
| blue | quiet | soft |
| sweet | tall | loud |

## Adverbs

**Adverbs** usually describe verbs. They tell how, when, where, or how much. Many adverbs end with *-ly*.

| | | |
|---|---|---|
| quickly | slowly | nicely |
| carefully | happily | cheerfully |

## Table of Contents

# Using the Mode-Specific Rubrics

Rubrics are central to instruction in *Strategies for Writers*. Each chapter includes a strategy-specific rubric that measures students' performance on the targeted strategies within that chapter.

More general, mode-specific rubrics are included on the following pages. One rubric is included for each of the four writing modes: narrative, descriptive, expository, and persuasive. You may wish to duplicate these rubrics and use them as instruments to assess students' writing within that mode both before (as a pretest rubric) and after (as a posttest rubric) instruction within that mode.

The strands on each of the rubrics are:

**Audience...**meaning the ways in which the writer identifies her audience and keeps that audience in mind as she writes.

**Organization...**meaning the way in which the writer moves from one main idea to the next, carefully presenting supporting information in clear relationship to each main idea.

**Elaboration...**meaning the way the writer adds supporting information to flesh out his writing.

**Clarification...**meaning the way in which the writer makes the meaning clearer by changing words, deleting unnecessary information, and effectively using transitions.

**Conventions & Skills...**meaning the ways in which the writer observes grammar, usage, mechanics, and spelling guidelines.

# Narrative Writing Rubric

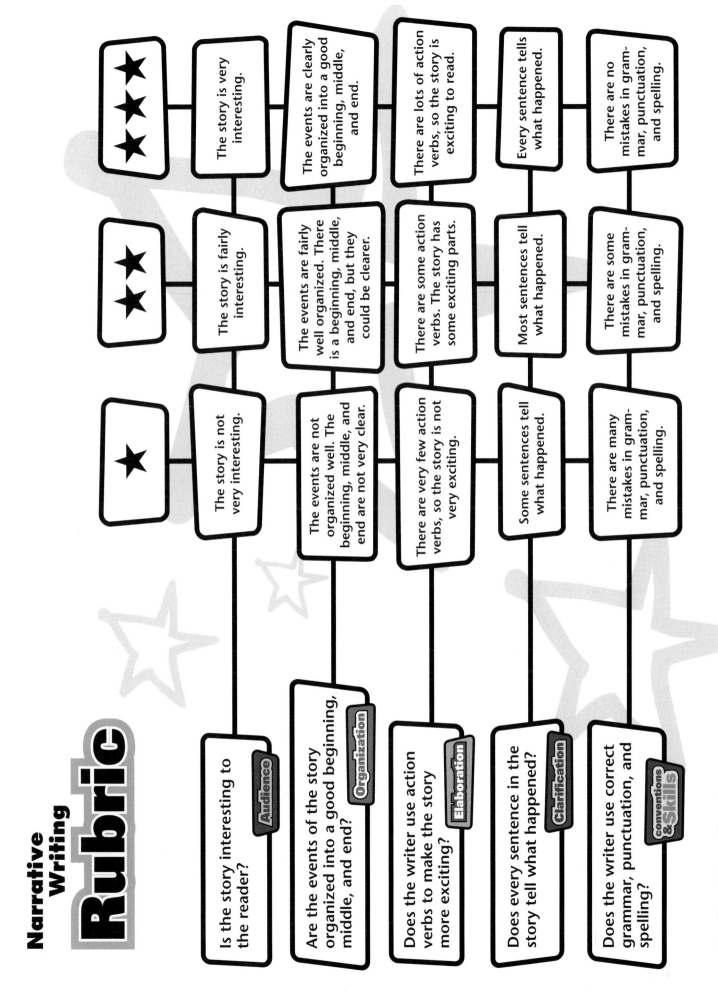

**Is the story interesting to the reader?** — Audience
- ★★★ The story is very interesting.
- ★★ The story is fairly interesting.
- ★ The story is not very interesting.

**Are the events of the story organized into a good beginning, middle, and end?** — Organization
- ★★★ The events are clearly organized into a good beginning, middle, and end.
- ★★ The events are fairly well organized. There is a beginning, middle, and end, but they could be clearer.
- ★ The events are not organized well. The beginning, middle, and end are not very clear.

**Does the writer use action verbs to make the story more exciting?** — Elaboration
- ★★★ There are lots of action verbs, so the story is exciting to read.
- ★★ There are some action verbs. The story has some exciting parts.
- ★ There are very few action verbs, so the story is not very exciting.

**Does every sentence in the story tell what happened?** — Clarification
- ★★★ Every sentence tells what happened.
- ★★ Most sentences tell what happened.
- ★ Some sentences tell what happened.

**Does the writer use correct grammar, punctuation, and spelling?** — Conventions & Skills
- ★★★ There are no mistakes in grammar, punctuation, and spelling.
- ★★ There are some mistakes in grammar, punctuation, and spelling.
- ★ There are many mistakes in grammar, punctuation, and spelling.

**Audience**

Does the writer choose a subject that gets and keeps the reader's attention?

| ★ | ★★ | ★★★ |
|---|---|---|
| The subject doesn't get the reader's attention. | The subject gets the reader's attention but doesn't keep it. | The subject gets the reader's attention right away and keeps it throughout the paper. |

**Organization**

Does the writer use the five senses to describe the subject?

| ★ | ★★ | ★★★ |
|---|---|---|
| The writer doesn't use the five senses to describe the subject. | The writer uses one or two of the five senses to describe the subject. | The writer uses as many of the five senses as possible to describe the subject. |

**Elaboration**

Does the writer use enough descriptive words to make the description interesting?

| ★ | ★★ | ★★★ |
|---|---|---|
| The writer uses very few descriptive words, so the description is not interesting. | The writer uses some descriptive words, so the description is interesting sometimes. | The writer uses lots of descriptive words to make the description very interesting. |

**Clarification**

Does every sentence help describe the subject?

| ★ | ★★ | ★★★ |
|---|---|---|
| Some sentences help describe the subject. | Most sentences help describe the subject. | Every sentence helps describe the subject. |

**Conventions & Skills**

Does the writer use correct grammar, punctuation, and spelling?

| ★ | ★★ | ★★★ |
|---|---|---|
| There are many mistakes in grammar, punctuation, and spelling. | There are some mistakes in grammar, punctuation, and spelling. | There are no mistakes in grammar, punctuation, and spelling. |

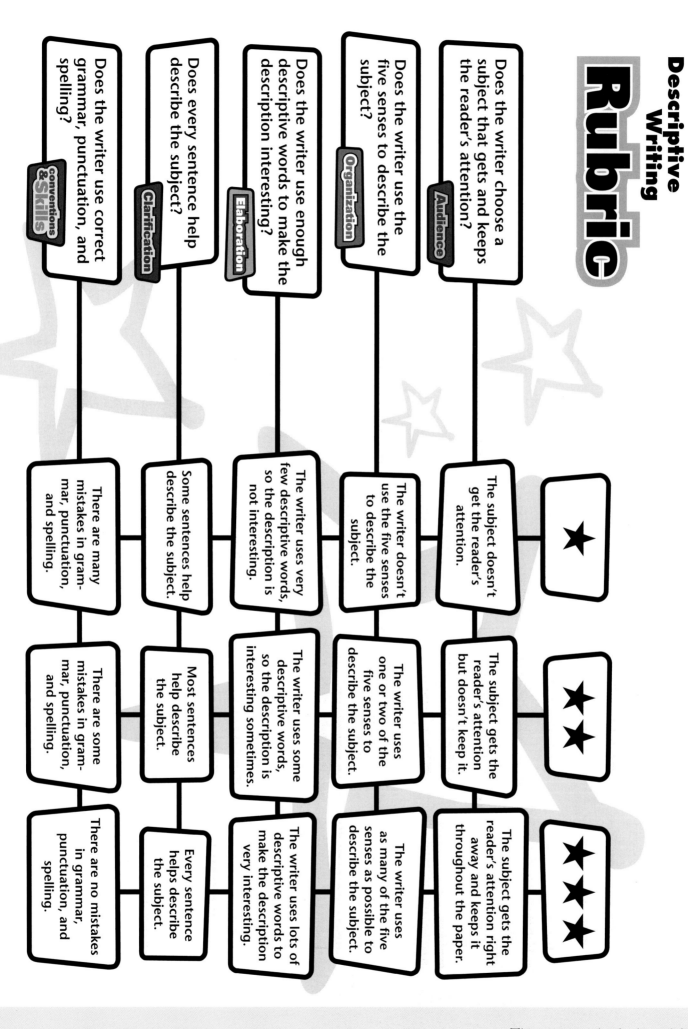

# Expository Writing Rubric

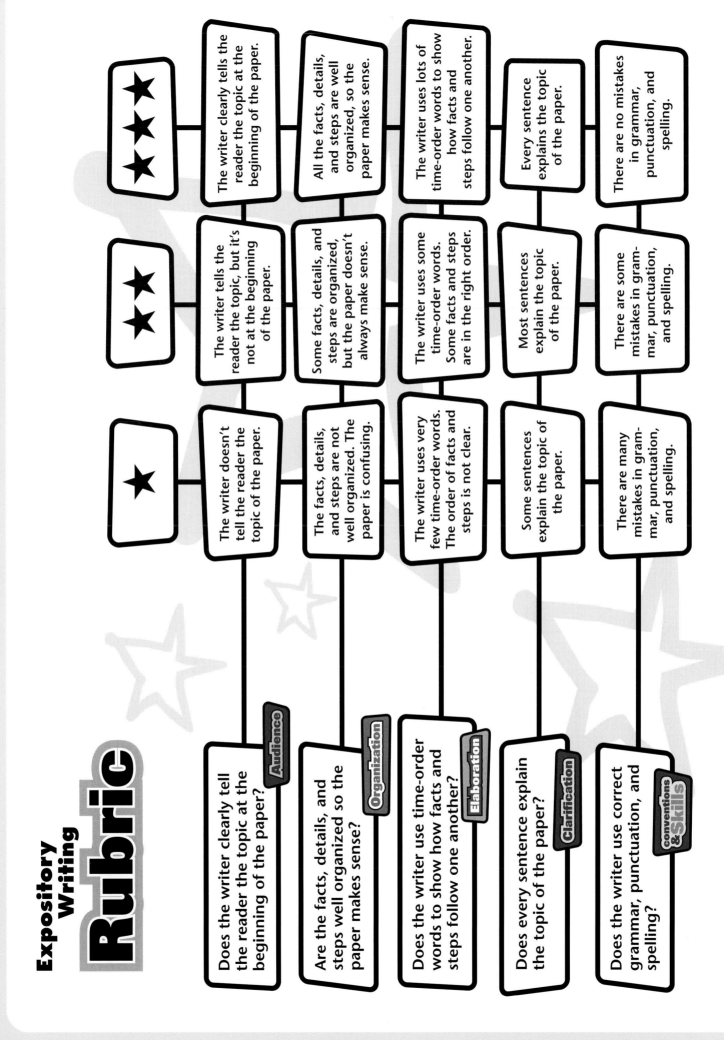

**★★★**

- The writer clearly tells the reader the topic at the beginning of the paper.
- All the facts, details, and steps are well organized, so the paper makes sense.
- The writer uses lots of time-order words to show how facts and steps follow one another.
- Every sentence explains the topic of the paper.
- There are no mistakes in grammar, punctuation, and spelling.

**★★**

- The writer tells the reader the topic, but it's not at the beginning of the paper.
- Some facts, details, and steps are organized, but the paper doesn't always make sense.
- The writer uses some time-order words. Some facts and steps are in the right order.
- Most sentences explain the topic of the paper.
- There are some mistakes in grammar, punctuation, and spelling.

**★**

- The writer doesn't tell the reader the topic of the paper.
- The facts, details, and steps are not well organized. The paper is confusing.
- The writer uses very few time-order words. The order of facts and steps is not clear.
- Some sentences explain the topic of the paper.
- There are many mistakes in grammar, punctuation, and spelling.

**Audience** — Does the writer clearly tell the reader the topic at the beginning of the paper?

**Organization** — Are the facts, details, and steps well organized so the paper makes sense?

**Elaboration** — Does the writer use time-order words to show how facts and steps follow one another?

**Clarification** — Does every sentence explain the topic of the paper?

**Conventions & Skills** — Does the writer use correct grammar, punctuation, and spelling?

# Persuasive Writing Rubric

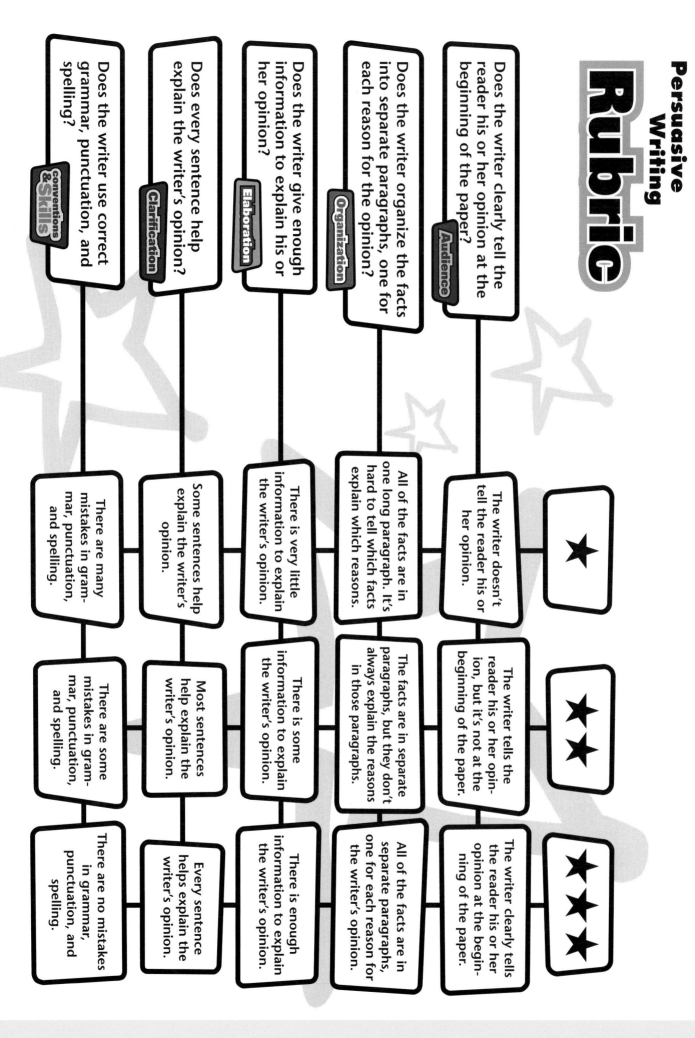

| | ★ | ★★ | ★★★ |
|---|---|---|---|
| **Audience** — Does the writer clearly tell the reader his or her opinion at the beginning of the paper? | The writer doesn't tell the reader his or her opinion. | The writer tells the reader his or her opinion, but it's not at the beginning of the paper. | The writer clearly tells the reader his or her opinion at the beginning of the paper. |
| **Organization** — Does the writer organize the facts into separate paragraphs, one for each reason for the opinion? | All of the facts are in one long paragraph. It's hard to tell which facts explain which reasons. | The facts are in separate paragraphs, but they don't always explain the reasons in those paragraphs. | All of the facts are in separate paragraphs, one for each reason for the writer's opinion. |
| **Elaboration** — Does the writer give enough information to explain his or her opinion? | There is very little information to explain the writer's opinion. | There is some information to explain the writer's opinion. | There is enough information to explain the writer's opinion. |
| **Clarification** — Does every sentence help explain the writer's opinion? | Some sentences help explain the writer's opinion. | Most sentences help explain the writer's opinion. | Every sentence helps explain the writer's opinion. |
| **Conventions & Skills** — Does the writer use correct grammar, punctuation, and spelling? | There are many mistakes in grammar, punctuation, and spelling. | There are some mistakes in grammar, punctuation, and spelling. | There are no mistakes in grammar, punctuation, and spelling. |

Use after page 19 in the Student Edition.

## Prewriting
### Gather Ideas  Make a list of interesting topics. Pick one.

A good topic for a personal narrative
• is about the person writing the story.
• tells what happened to the person.
• is interesting to the reader.

**Directions:** Read the list of topics below. Write a ✓ in front of each topic that would make a good topic for a personal narrative.

_____ 1. the history of the United States

✓ 2. the day I learned to roller-skate

_____ 3. why my school needs more computers

_____ 4. how to ride your bike safely

✓ 5. my trip to the zoo

✓ 6. the best present I ever got

_____ 7. how to plant a flower

_____ 8. cereal makes the best breakfast

✓ 9. the day I met my hero

_____ 10. how to write a song

6   **Narrative Writing** • Personal Narrative

---

Use after page 19 in the Student Edition.

## Prewriting
### Gather Ideas  Make a list of interesting topics. Pick one.

**Directions:** Use the list of topics on page 6 in this book to answer these questions.

1. Which topics on the list would make a good personal narrative? Write the numbers.

   2, 5, 6, and 9

2. Why are those topics good for a personal narrative? Explain why you think so.

   Possible answers: They are about the person writing the story. They sound like stories. They sound interesting to the reader.

3. Which topic do you like best? Write your answer.

   Possible answer: Number 5, my trip to the zoo

4. Why is that topic interesting to you? Write a sentence to tell why.

   Possible answer: I went to the zoo last year.

Go to **Your Own Writing** pages 8–9 in this book.

**Narrative Writing** • Personal Narrative   7

---

## Your Own Writing
### Prewriting
### Gather Ideas  Make a list of interesting topics. Pick one.

**Directions:** Now it's time to find your own topic for a personal narrative. Read and answer the **Questions About Me** to get started. You don't have to answer every question.

**Questions About Me**

1. What have I learned to do?

   Answers will vary.

2. What interesting places have I visited?

3. What was an exciting adventure I had?

4. What story can I tell about myself that others will want to read?

8   **Narrative Writing** • Personal Narrative

---

## Your Own Writing
### Prewriting
### Gather Ideas  Make a list of interesting topics. Pick one.

**Directions:** Think about your answers to the **Questions About Me**. Use your answers to write two topics for a story you could write about yourself.

I could write about

   Answers will vary.

I could write about

   Answers will vary.

Now ask yourself these questions about each topic.

1. Who will read my paper?
2. Will they like this topic?
3. Will this topic make the best story?

Draw a circle around the topic you like best.

RETURN   Now go back to Kyle's work on page 20 in the Student Edition.

**Narrative Writing** • Personal Narrative   9

---

Use after page 21 in the Student Edition.

# Prewriting
## Organize — Make a storyboard to tell what happened.

**Directions:** Below are some notes for a personal narrative called "The Best Present Ever." The writer wants to tell about getting a puppy as a birthday present. Decide which three notes are best to use in the story. Draw a circle around those notes.

☆ My grandmother has three cats.

☆ You can read about the history of dogs in the United States.

☆ ( I picked up my puppy and smiled. )

☆ Pets come in all different sizes, shapes, and colors.

☆ It has rained every day this week.

☆ ( My mom said she had something special for me. )

☆ ( I had to close my eyes when my mom brought me to see my present. )

Copyright © Zaner-Bloser, Inc.

10   *Narrative Writing* • Personal Narrative

---

Use after page 21 in the Student Edition.

# Prewriting
## Organize — Make a storyboard to tell what happened.

**Directions:** In the storyboard below, draw the events you circled on page 10 in this book. Draw the pictures in the right order.

### Topic: The Best Present Ever

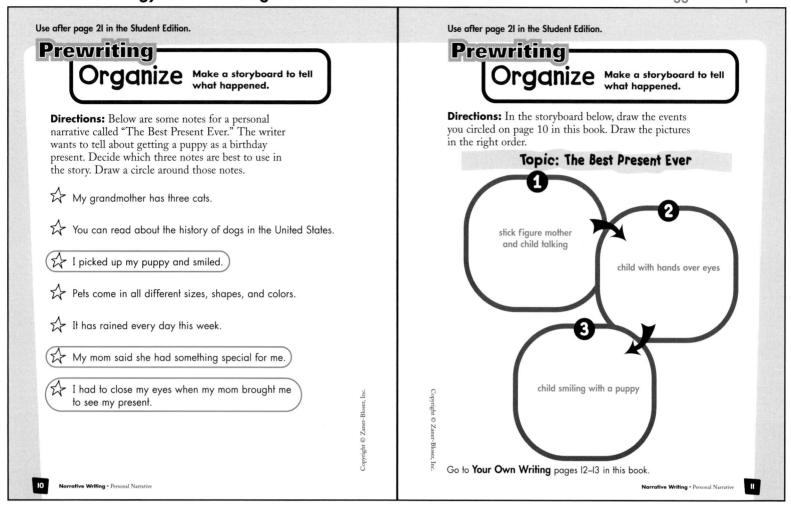

**①** stick figure mother and child talking

**②** child with hands over eyes

**③** child smiling with a puppy

Go to **Your Own Writing** pages 12–13 in this book.

Copyright © Zaner-Bloser, Inc.

*Narrative Writing* • Personal Narrative   11

---

# Your Own Writing
## Prewriting
### Organize — Make a storyboard to tell what happened.

**Directions:** Look at the notes you made on pages 8–9 in this book. Use them to help you make a storyboard. Draw one picture for each event in your notes. Be sure to draw your pictures in the right order on your storyboard.

**My Topic:** _____

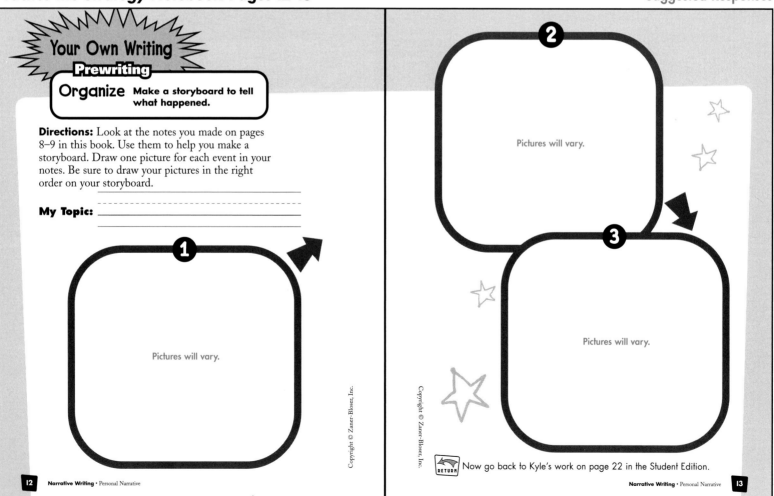

**①** Pictures will vary.

**②** Pictures will vary.

**③** Pictures will vary.

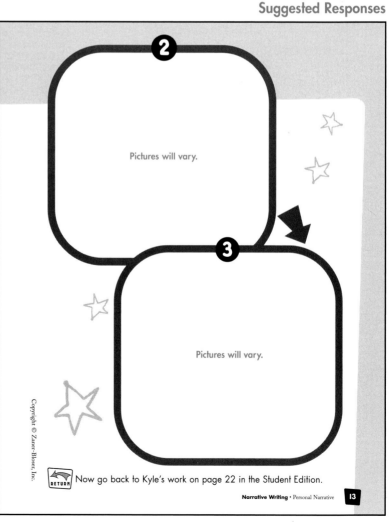

RETURN Now go back to Kyle's work on page 22 in the Student Edition.

Copyright © Zaner-Bloser, Inc.

12   *Narrative Writing* • Personal Narrative

*Narrative Writing* • Personal Narrative   13

---

Use after page 23 in the Student Edition.

## Drafting
### Write Use my storyboard. Write sentences to tell what happened first, next, and last.

**Directions:** Look back at the storyboard for "The Best Present Ever" on page 11 in this book. Read the draft of the story below. Draw a line under the sentence that tells about the first picture in the storyboard. Draw a circle around the sentence that tells about the second picture. Draw a box around the sentence that tells about the third picture. You will see some mistakes. You can fix them later.

The Best Present Ever
I turned seven last month My mom said she had a special present for me. Last year. I got a bicycle. I had to close my eyes. Mom took my hand and led me to the back porch. It's a little cold out there. She told me to open my eyes. I saw a little brown and white puppy. It was wagging its tail and looking at me. my mom said the puppy was for my birthday. I picked it up and smiled and smiled. i hugged my mom. I never got a better present than that

Go to **Your Own Writing** pages 15–17 in this book.

## Your Own Writing
### Drafting
### Write Use my storyboard. Write sentences to tell what happened first, next, and last.

**Directions:** Use this page and the next two pages to write a draft of your own personal narrative. Use your storyboard on pages 12–13 in this book to help you. Be sure to tell events in the right order.

Answers will vary.

## Your Own Writing
### Drafting
### Write Use my storyboard. Write sentences to tell what happened first, next, and last.

Answers will vary.

Answers will vary.

Now go back to Kyle's work on page 24 in the Student Edition.

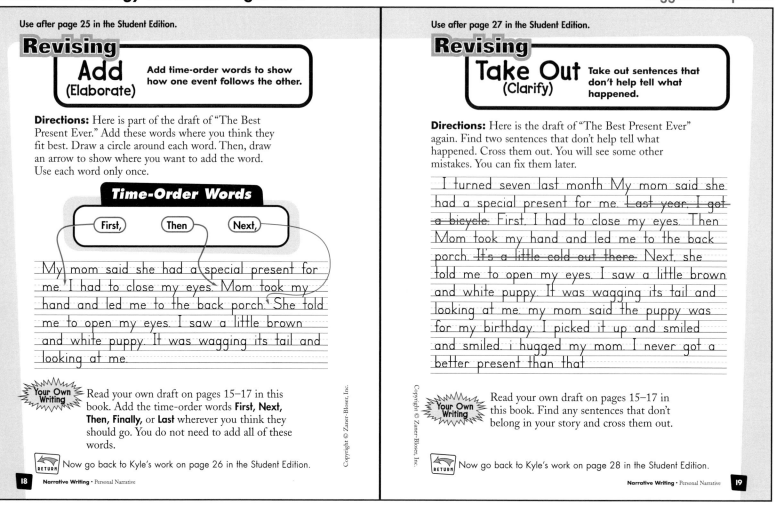

Use after page 25 in the Student Edition.

**Revising**
## Add
(Elaborate)

Add time-order words to show how one event follows the other.

**Directions:** Here is part of the draft of "The Best Present Ever." Add these words where you think they fit best. Draw a circle around each word. Then, draw an arrow to show where you want to add the word. Use each word only once.

**Time-Order Words**

( First, )   ( Then )   ( Next, )

My mom said she had a special present for me. I had to close my eyes. Mom took my hand and led me to the back porch. She told me to open my eyes. I saw a little brown and white puppy. It was wagging its tail and looking at me.

Your Own Writing
Read your own draft on pages 15–17 in this book. Add the time-order words **First, Next, Then, Finally,** or **Last** wherever you think they should go. You do not need to add all of these words.

RETURN
Now go back to Kyle's work on page 26 in the Student Edition.

18 Narrative Writing • Personal Narrative

Copyright © Zaner-Bloser, Inc.

Use after page 27 in the Student Edition.

**Revising**
## Take Out
(Clarify)

Take out sentences that don't help tell what happened.

**Directions:** Here is the draft of "The Best Present Ever" again. Find two sentences that don't help tell what happened. Cross them out. You will see some other mistakes. You can fix them later.

I turned seven last month My mom said she had a special present for me. ~~Last year, I got a bicycle.~~ First, I had to close my eyes. Then Mom took my hand and led me to the back porch. ~~It's a little cold out there.~~ Next, she told me to open my eyes I saw a little brown and white puppy. It was wagging its tail and looking at me. my mom said the puppy was for my birthday. I picked it up and smiled and smiled i hugged my mom. I never got a better present than that

Your Own Writing
Read your own draft on pages 15–17 in this book. Find any sentences that don't belong in your story and cross them out.

RETURN
Now go back to Kyle's work on page 28 in the Student Edition.

Narrative Writing • Personal Narrative 19

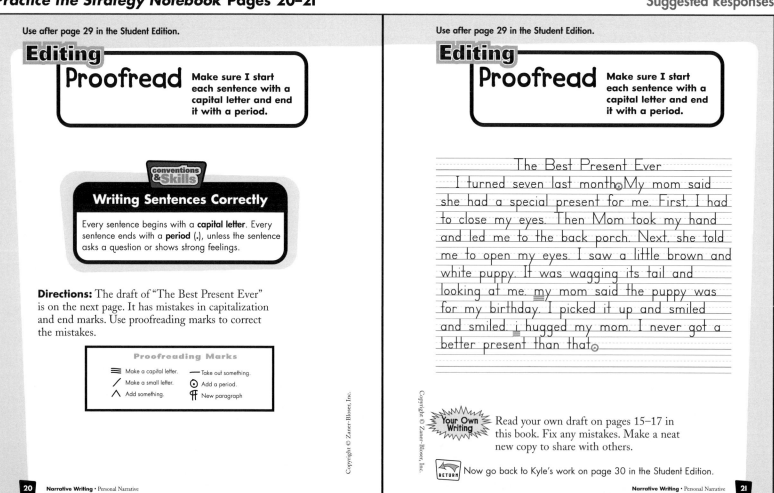

Use after page 29 in the Student Edition.

**Editing**
## Proofread

Make sure I start each sentence with a capital letter and end it with a period.

conventions & Skills

**Writing Sentences Correctly**

Every sentence begins with a **capital letter**. Every sentence ends with a **period** (.), unless the sentence asks a question or shows strong feelings.

**Directions:** The draft of "The Best Present Ever" is on the next page. It has mistakes in capitalization and end marks. Use proofreading marks to correct the mistakes.

**Proofreading Marks**

≡ Make a capital letter.    — Take out something.
/ Make a small letter.      ⊙ Add a period.
∧ Add something.            ¶ New paragraph.

Copyright © Zaner-Bloser, Inc.

Use after page 29 in the Student Edition.

**Editing**
## Proofread

Make sure I start each sentence with a capital letter and end it with a period.

The Best Present Ever
I turned seven last month⊙My mom said she had a special present for me. First, I had to close my eyes. Then Mom took my hand and led me to the back porch. Next, she told me to open my eyes. I saw a little brown and white puppy. It was wagging its tail and looking at me. my mom said the puppy was for my birthday. I picked it up and smiled and smiled. i hugged my mom. I never got a better present than that⊙

Your Own Writing
Read your own draft on pages 15–17 in this book. Fix any mistakes. Make a neat new copy to share with others.

RETURN
Now go back to Kyle's work on page 30 in the Student Edition.

20 Narrative Writing • Personal Narrative

Narrative Writing • Personal Narrative 21

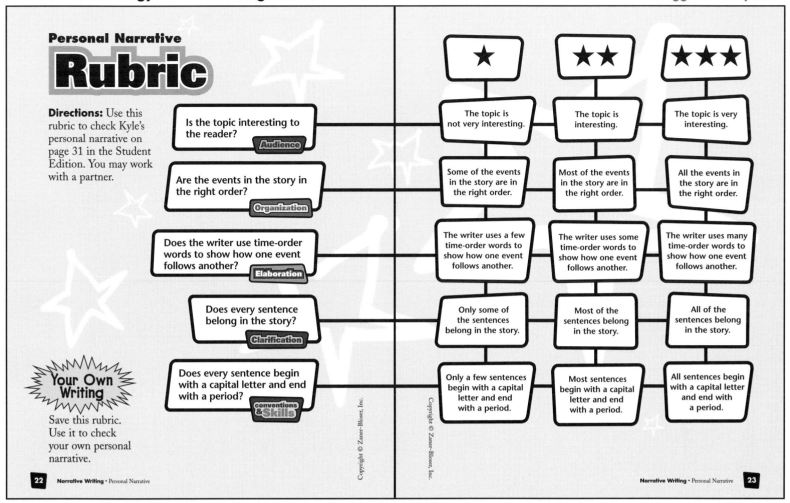

### Personal Narrative
# Rubric

**Directions:** Use this rubric to check Kyle's personal narrative on page 31 in the Student Edition. You may work with a partner.

| Is the topic interesting to the reader? **Audience** |
| Are the events in the story in the right order? **Organization** |
| Does the writer use time-order words to show how one event follows another? **Elaboration** |
| Does every sentence belong in the story? **Clarification** |
| Does every sentence begin with a capital letter and end with a period? **Conventions & Skills** |

**★**
- The topic is not very interesting.
- Some of the events in the story are in the right order.
- The writer uses a few time-order words to show how one event follows another.
- Only some of the sentences belong in the story.
- Only a few sentences begin with a capital letter and end with a period.

**★★**
- The topic is interesting.
- Most of the events in the story are in the right order.
- The writer uses some time-order words to show how one event follows another.
- Most of the sentences belong in the story.
- Most sentences begin with a capital letter and end with a period.

**★★★**
- The topic is very interesting.
- All the events in the story are in the right order.
- The writer uses many time-order words to show how one event follows another.
- All of the sentences belong in the story.
- All sentences begin with a capital letter and end with a period.

**Your Own Writing**
Save this rubric. Use it to check your own personal narrative.

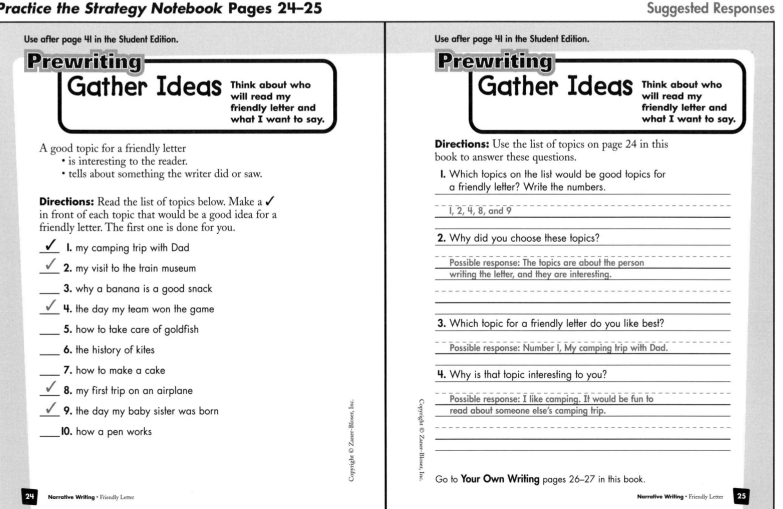

Use after page 41 in the Student Edition.

### Prewriting
# Gather Ideas
Think about who will read my friendly letter and what I want to say.

A good topic for a friendly letter
• is interesting to the reader.
• tells about something the writer did or saw.

**Directions:** Read the list of topics below. Make a ✓ in front of each topic that would be a good idea for a friendly letter. The first one is done for you.

✓ **1.** my camping trip with Dad
✓ **2.** my visit to the train museum
___ **3.** why a banana is a good snack
✓ **4.** the day my team won the game
___ **5.** how to take care of goldfish
___ **6.** the history of kites
___ **7.** how to make a cake
✓ **8.** my first trip on an airplane
✓ **9.** the day my baby sister was born
___ **10.** how a pen works

Use after page 41 in the Student Edition.

### Prewriting
# Gather Ideas
Think about who will read my friendly letter and what I want to say.

**Directions:** Use the list of topics on page 24 in this book to answer these questions.

**1.** Which topics on the list would be good topics for a friendly letter? Write the numbers.

1, 2, 4, 8, and 9

**2.** Why did you choose these topics?

Possible response: The topics are about the person writing the letter, and they are interesting.

**3.** Which topic for a friendly letter do you like best?

Possible response: Number 1, My camping trip with Dad.

**4.** Why is that topic interesting to you?

Possible response: I like camping. It would be fun to read about someone else's camping trip.

Go to **Your Own Writing** pages 26–27 in this book.

## Your Own Writing
### Prewriting
**Gather Ideas** Think about who will read my friendly letter and what I want to say.

**Directions:** Who would like to receive a friendly letter from you? Make a list of people you could write to.

I. _____ Answers will vary. _____

2. _____

3. _____

4. _____

5. _____

6. _____

Read your list above. Draw a circle around the name of the person you would like to write to the most.

## Your Own Writing
### Prewriting
**Gather Ideas** Think about who will read my friendly letter and what I want to say.

**Directions:** Think about some interesting things you have seen or done. List three of them here.

I. _____ Answers will vary. _____

2. _____

3. _____

Read your list above. Think about who will read your letter. Draw a circle around the topic that you think would be most interesting to your reader.

Now go back to Rachel's work on page 42 in the Student Edition.

Use after page 43 in the Student Edition.

### Prewriting
**Organize** Make a storyboard to tell what happened.

**Directions:** Below are some notes for Matt's letter about a camping trip with his dad. Decide which event happened first, next, and last. Number the events in the right order.
Answers may vary. Possible responses appear below.

_2_ cooked dinner

_1_ set up camp

_3_ sat by the campfire

Draw a picture of each event in the right order in the storyboard boxes on these two pages.

**Topic:** My Camping Trip With Dad

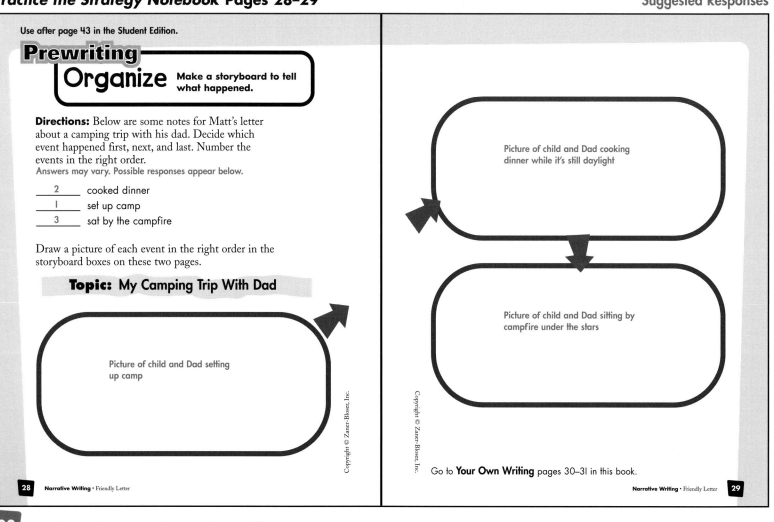

Picture of child and Dad setting up camp

Picture of child and Dad cooking dinner while it's still daylight

Picture of child and Dad sitting by campfire under the stars

Go to **Your Own Writing** pages 30–31 in this book.

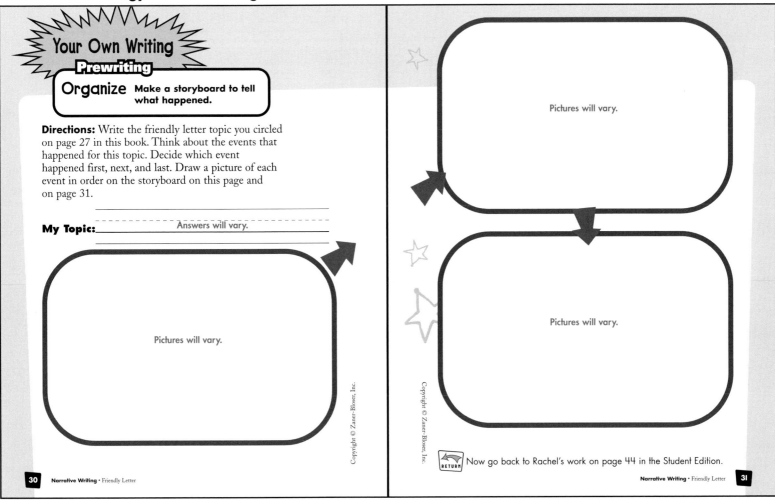

**Your Own Writing**
**Prewriting**

**Organize** Make a storyboard to tell what happened.

**Directions:** Write the friendly letter topic you circled on page 27 in this book. Think about the events that happened for this topic. Decide which event happened first, next, and last. Draw a picture of each event in order on the storyboard on this page and on page 31.

**My Topic:** _____ Answers will vary. _____

Pictures will vary.

Pictures will vary.

Pictures will vary.

Now go back to Rachel's work on page 44 in the Student Edition.

30 **Narrative Writing** · Friendly Letter

31 **Narrative Writing** · Friendly Letter

Copyright © Zaner-Bloser, Inc.

Copyright © Zaner-Bloser, Inc.

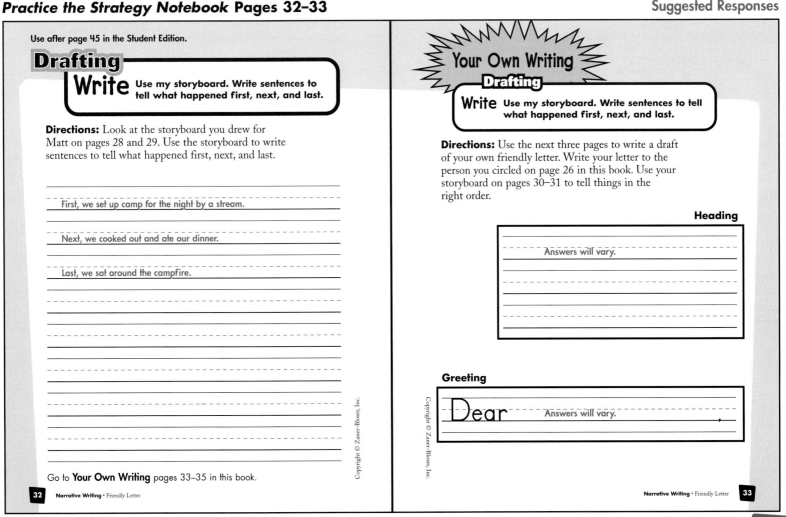

Use after page 45 in the Student Edition.

**Drafting**

**Write** Use my storyboard. Write sentences to tell what happened first, next, and last.

**Directions:** Look at the storyboard you drew for Matt on pages 28 and 29. Use the storyboard to write sentences to tell what happened first, next, and last.

_____

First, we set up camp for the night by a stream.

Next, we cooked out and ate our dinner.

Last, we sat around the campfire.

Go to **Your Own Writing** pages 33–35 in this book.

**Your Own Writing**
**Drafting**

**Write** Use my storyboard. Write sentences to tell what happened first, next, and last.

**Directions:** Use the next three pages to write a draft of your own friendly letter. Write your letter to the person you circled on page 26 in this book. Use your storyboard on pages 30–31 to tell things in the right order.

**Heading**

Answers will vary.

**Greeting**

Dear  Answers will vary.

32 **Narrative Writing** · Friendly Letter

33 **Narrative Writing** · Friendly Letter

Copyright © Zaner-Bloser, Inc.

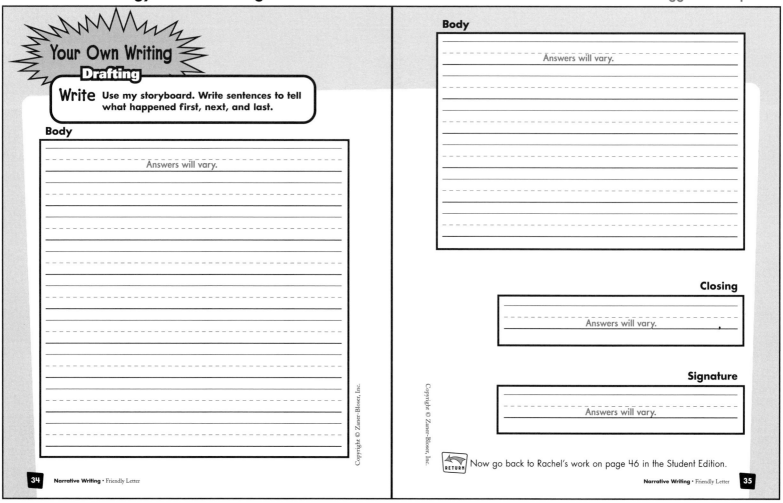

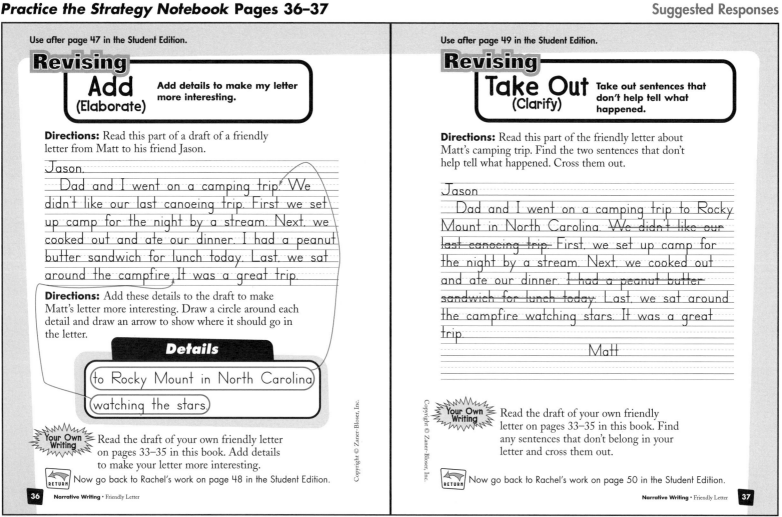

Use after page 51 in the Student Edition.

## Editing
### Proofread
Make sure I wrote all five parts of my friendly letter correctly.

**conventions & Skills**

## Parts of a Friendly Letter

**Heading** →
6 Fair Street
Los Osos, CA 12345
August 6, 2003

Dear Keiko, ← **Greeting**

This is the main part. ← **Body**

**Closing** → Your pal,

**Signature** → Robert

**Directions:** The draft of Matt's friendly letter is on the next page. Matt did not write all five parts of a friendly letter correctly. Find the mistakes. Use the proofreading marks to make changes.

### Proofreading Marks

≡ Make a capital letter.     ✄ Take out something.
/ Make a small letter.        ⊙ Add a period.
∧ Add something.               ¶ New paragraph

Copyright © Zaner-Bloser, Inc.

---

## Editing
### Proofread
Make sure I wrote all five parts of my friendly letter correctly.

Answers may vary.
Possible responses appear below.

16 Clay Street
Columbia, SC 12345

August 4, 20—

Dear Jason,

Dad and I went on a camping trip to Rocky Mount in North Carolina. First, we set up camp for the night by a stream. Next, we cooked out and ate our dinner. Last, we sat around the campfire watching the stars. It was a great trip.

Your friend,

Matt

**Your Own Writing** — Read the draft of your own friendly letter on pages 33–35 in this book. Fix any mistakes. Make a new copy of your friendly letter to share with others.

**RETURN** Now go back to Rachel's work on page 52 in the Student Edition.

Copyright © Zaner-Bloser, Inc.

---

## Friendly Letter
# Rubric

**Directions:** Use this rubric to check Rachel's friendly letter on page 53 in the Student Edition. You may work with a partner.

| | ★ | ★★ | ★★★ |
|---|---|---|---|
| **Is the topic interesting to the reader?** (Audience) | The topic is not very interesting to the reader. | The topic is mostly interesting to the reader. | The topic is very interesting to the reader. |
| **Does the letter tell what happened first, next, and last?** (Organization) | The letter tells some of what happened, but the order is unclear. | The letter tells what happened, but not always in the right order. | The letter tells what happened first, next, and last in the right order. |
| **Does the letter have interesting details?** (Elaboration) | There are few interesting details. | There are some interesting details. | There are many interesting details. |
| **Does every sentence help tell what happened?** (Clarification) | Some of the sentences help tell what happened. | Most of the sentences help tell what happened. | All of the sentences help tell what happened. |
| **Does the letter have all five parts? Are they all used correctly?** (conventions & Skills) | The letter has a few of the five parts. They are not all used correctly. | The letter has most of the five parts. Most of them are used correctly. | The letter has all five parts. They are all used correctly. |

**Your Own Writing** — Save this rubric. Use it to check your own friendly letter.

Copyright © Zaner-Bloser, Inc.

Use after page 65 in the Student Edition.

## Prewriting

### Gather Ideas

Choose a subject to describe. Make a list to tell what I know about it.

**Directions:** Read the list of subjects below. For each subject, write a ✓ in the box if you can see, hear, taste, touch, or smell it. The first one has been done for you.

Answers may vary.

| Subject | See | Hear | Taste | Touch | Smell |
|---|---|---|---|---|---|
| a motorcycle | ✓ | ✓ | | ✓ | ✓ |
| a cloud | ✓ | | | | |
| a toy robot | ✓ | ✓ | | ✓ | |
| an apple | ✓ | | ✓ | ✓ | ✓ |
| a song | | ✓ | | | |

Copyright © Zaner-Bloser, Inc.

42  **Descriptive Writing** · Descriptive Paper

---

Use after page 65 in the Student Edition.

## Prewriting

### Gather Ideas

Choose a subject to describe. Make a list to tell what I know about it.

**Directions:** Look back at the chart on page 42 in this book. Which do you think are the three best subjects for a descriptive paper? Write the name of each subject. Then write a sentence to tell why you think it is a good subject for a descriptive paper.

Subject: _Sample answer: a motorcycle_

_Possible response: You can see, hear, touch, and smell it._

Subject: _Sample answer: a toy robot_

_Possible response: You can see, hear, and touch it._

Subject: _Sample answer: an apple_

_Possible response: You can see, taste, touch, and smell it._

Go to **Your Own Writing** pages 44–45 in this book.

Copyright © Zaner-Bloser, Inc.

**Descriptive Writing** · Descriptive Paper  43

---

## Your Own Writing

### Prewriting

### Gather Ideas

Choose a subject to describe. Make a list to tell what I know about it.

**Directions:** Think of some things you could describe. You could describe a toy, a pet, a car or truck, a place, a food, or something else. Make a list of six things you could describe.

1. _Answers will vary. Students should eventually circle one answer._

2. _____

3. _____

4. _____

5. _____

6. _____

Now choose the subject you would like to write about most. Draw a circle around it.

Copyright © Zaner-Bloser, Inc.

44  **Descriptive Writing** · Descriptive Paper

---

## Your Own Writing

### Prewriting

### Gather Ideas

Choose a subject to describe. Make a list to tell what I know about it.

**Directions:** Write the subject you circled on page 44. Think about how it looks, sounds, tastes, feels, and smells. Make a list of things you know about it. Use as many of the five senses as you can.

Subject: _Answers will vary._

_____

My List: _____

_____

_____

Now go back to Jessica's work on page 66 in the Student Edition.

Copyright © Zaner-Bloser, Inc.

**Descriptive Writing** · Descriptive Paper  45

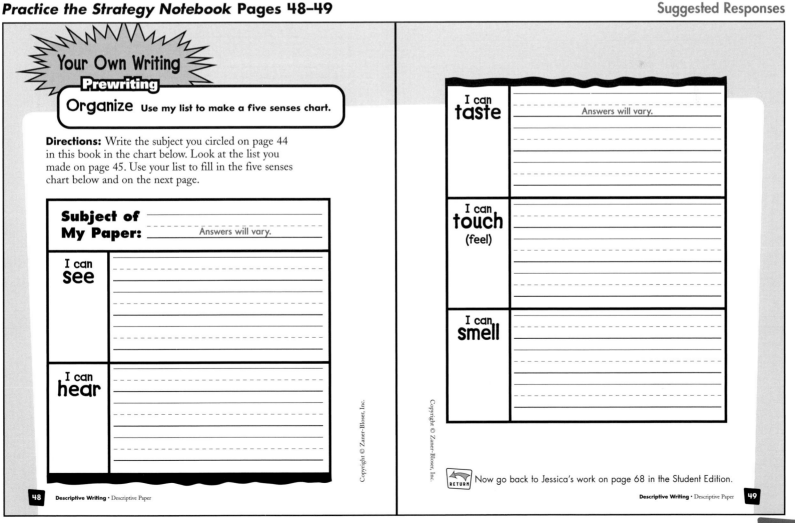

Use after page 67 in the Student Edition.

## Prewriting
## Organize Use my list to make a five senses chart.

**Directions:** Below is one writer's list of ideas for describing a toy robot. Next to each sentence, write whether the sentence helps the reader **see** the robot, **hear** it, **taste** it, **feel** it, or **smell** it.

| Description | Helps Reader |
|---|---|
| 1. The robot has arms and legs. | see |
| 2. It makes a whirring sound. | hear |
| 3. It has green eyes that blink. | see |
| 4. The robot clicks. | hear |
| 5. It is made of hard plastic. | touch and/or see |
| 6. It has a blue head. | see |

46 **Descriptive Writing** · Descriptive Paper

Use after page 67 in the Student Edition.

## Prewriting
## Organize Use my list to make a five senses chart.

**Directions:** Look back at the list of ideas for describing a toy robot on page 46 in this book. Write each idea in the correct place on the five senses chart below.

| Subject: A Toy Robot | |
|---|---|
| I can **see** | arms, legs, green eyes that blink, blue head |
| I can **hear** | whirring sound, clicks |
| I can **taste** | |
| I can **touch** (feel) | hard plastic |
| I can **smell** | |

Go to **Your Own Writing** pages 48–49 in this book.

47 **Descriptive Writing** · Descriptive Paper

## Your Own Writing
### Prewriting
## Organize Use my list to make a five senses chart.

**Directions:** Write the subject you circled on page 44 in this book in the chart below. Look at the list you made on page 45. Use your list to fill in the five senses chart below and on the next page.

| Subject of My Paper: | Answers will vary. |
|---|---|
| I can **see** | |
| I can **hear** | |

| | |
|---|---|
| I can **taste** | Answers will vary. |
| I can **touch** (feel) | |
| I can **smell** | |

Now go back to Jessica's work on page 68 in the Student Edition.

48 **Descriptive Writing** · Descriptive Paper

49 **Descriptive Writing** · Descriptive Paper

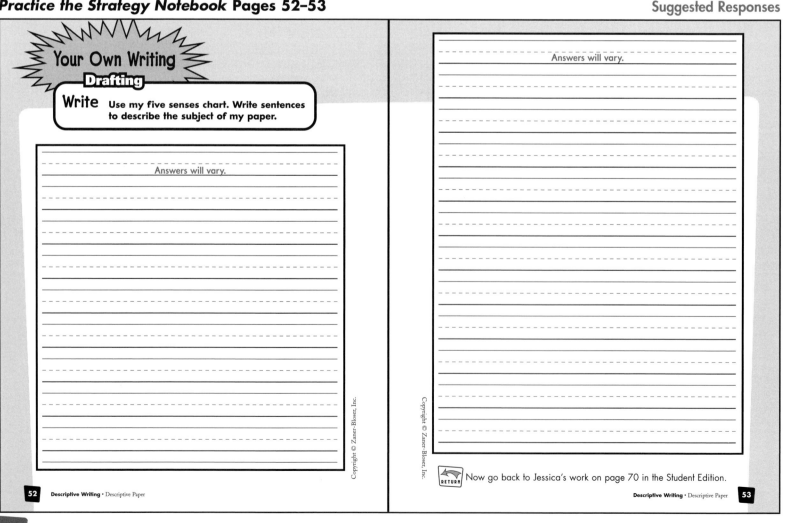

Use after page 69 in the Student Edition.

**Drafting**

**Write** Use my five senses chart. Write sentences to describe the subject of my paper.

**Directions:** Read the five senses chart for a toy robot on page 47 in this book. Use it to write sentences for a descriptive paper about the robot. The first sentence has been written for you.

The toy robot has a blue head and green eyes.

Answers will vary.

Go to **Your Own Writing** pages 51–53 in this book.

50   **Descriptive Writing** • Descriptive Paper

Copyright © Zaner-Bloser, Inc.

**Your Own Writing**

**Drafting**

**Write** Use my five senses chart. Write sentences to describe the subject of my paper.

**Directions:** Use this page and the next two pages to write a draft of your own descriptive paper. Use the five senses chart you made on pages 48–49 in this book to help you.

Answers will vary.

Copyright © Zaner-Bloser, Inc.

**Descriptive Writing** • Descriptive Paper   51

**Your Own Writing**

**Drafting**

**Write** Use my five senses chart. Write sentences to describe the subject of my paper.

Answers will vary.

Copyright © Zaner-Bloser, Inc.

52   **Descriptive Writing** • Descriptive Paper

Answers will vary.

Copyright © Zaner-Bloser, Inc.

RETURN Now go back to Jessica's work on page 70 in the Student Edition.

**Descriptive Writing** • Descriptive Paper   53

Use after page 71 in the Student Edition.

## Revising
## Add
### (Elaborate)
Add describing words to make my paper more interesting.

**Directions:** Read the beginning of one writer's descriptive paper about a toy robot. Then read the describing words in the box. Add these describing words to the draft where you think they belong. Draw an arrow to show where you want to add the words.

Answers may vary.

Pete the Robot
My favorite toy is a robot. his name is Pete. He has a blue head and green eyes. Pete looks like a person with arms, legs, hands, and feet. He wears goggles, a suit, and gloves

### Describing Words
big   silver   red   that blink on and off

**Your Own Writing** Read the draft of your own descriptive paper on pages 51–53 in this book. Add describing words to make your paper more interesting.

RETURN Now go back to Jessica's work on page 72 in the Student Edition.

54   **Descriptive Writing** · Descriptive Paper

---

Use after page 73 in the Student Edition.

## Revising
## Take Out
### (Clarify)
Take out sentences that don't tell about the subject of my paper.

**Directions:** Read this draft of the descriptive paper about the toy robot. Find two sentences that don't tell about the subject. Cross them out. You will see some other problems. You can fix them later.

My favorite toy is a robot. his name is Pete. He has a blue head and green eyes that blink on and off Pete looks like a person with arms, legs, hands, and feet. He wears big goggles, a silver suit, and red gloves I have a stuffed dog with green eyes, too. when Pete lifts his arms, he makes a click. When he walks, he makes a whir. When he bends over, he makes a glug. Dad says I can get a bike for my birthday. Pete is made of hard plastic, so he can crash into things Pete falls over, but he never breaks

**Your Own Writing** Read the draft of your descriptive paper on pages 51–53 in this book. Find sentences that don't tell about your subject and cross them out.

RETURN Now go back to Jessica's work on page 74 in the Student Edition.

55   **Descriptive Writing** · Descriptive Paper

---

Use after page 75 in the Student Edition.

## Editing
## Proofread
Make sure I start each sentence with a capital letter and end it with correct punctuation.

**Directions:** The draft of the descriptive paper about Pete the toy robot is on the next page. It has mistakes in capitalization and end punctuation. Find the mistakes. Use the proofreading marks to make changes.

**conventions & Skills**
### Writing Sentences Correctly
- Every sentence begins with a **capital letter**.
- A sentence that **tells something** ends with a **period**. (.)
- A sentence that **asks a question** ends with a **question mark**. (?)
- A sentence that **shows strong feelings** ends with an **exclamation point**. (!)

**Proofreading Marks**
≡ Make a capital letter.   — Take out something.
/ Make a small letter.   ⊙ Add a period.
∧ Add something.   ¶ New paragraph

56   **Descriptive Writing** · Descriptive Paper

---

Use after page 75 in the Student Edition.

## Editing
## Proofread
Make sure I start each sentence with a capital letter and end it with correct punctuation.

Pete the Robot
My favorite toy is a robot. his name is Pete. He has a blue head and green eyes that blink on and off Pete looks like a person with arms, legs, hands, and feet. He wears big goggles, a silver suit, and red gloves when Pete lifts his arms, he makes a click. When he walks, he makes a whir. When he bends over, he makes a glug. Pete is made of hard plastic, so he can crash into things Pete falls over, but he never breaks

**Your Own Writing** Go back to your own draft on pages 51–53 in this book. Fix any mistakes in capital letters and end punctuation.

RETURN Now go back to Jessica's work on page 76 in the Student Edition.

57   **Descriptive Writing** · Descriptive Paper

---

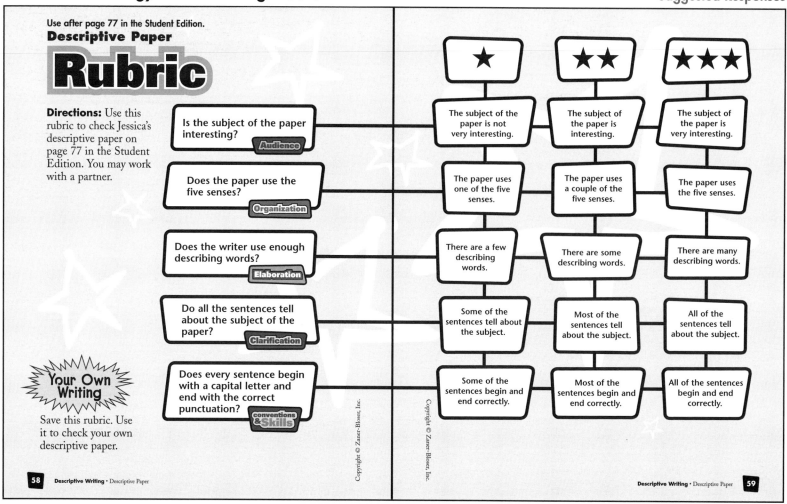

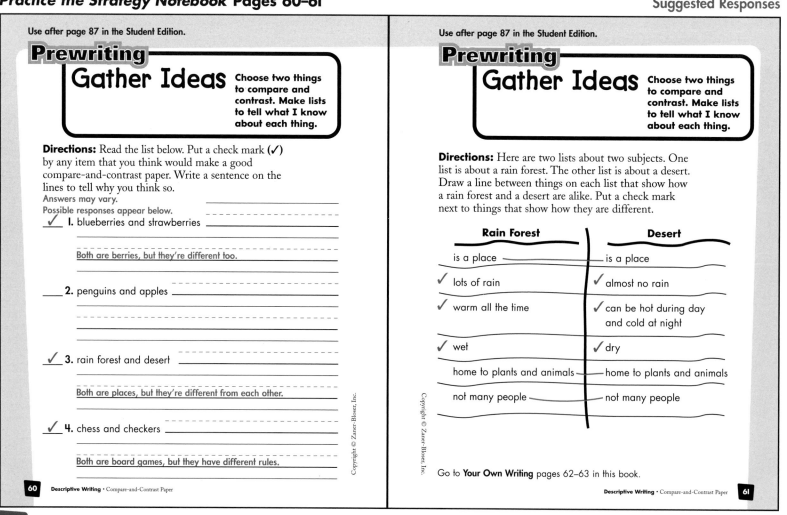

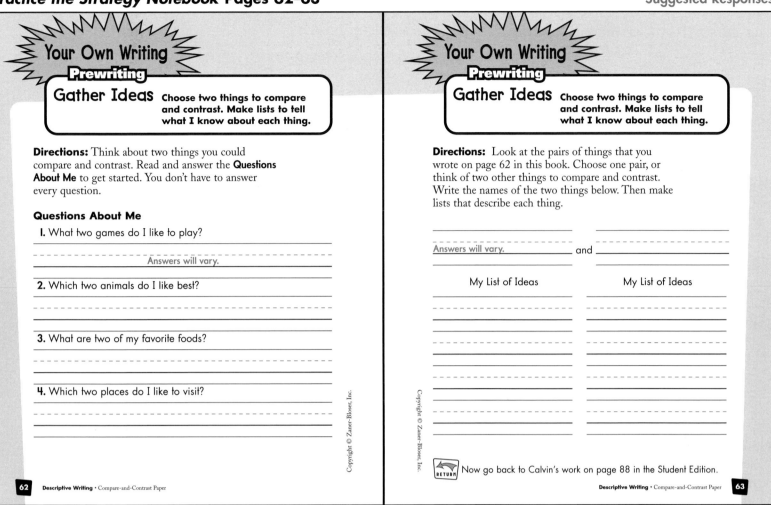

## Your Own Writing
### Prewriting

**Gather Ideas** Choose two things to compare and contrast. Make lists to tell what I know about each thing.

**Directions:** Think about two things you could compare and contrast. Read and answer the **Questions About Me** to get started. You don't have to answer every question.

**Questions About Me**

1. What two games do I like to play?

_____
_____Answers will vary._____

2. Which two animals do I like best?

_____
_____

3. What are two of my favorite foods?

_____
_____

4. Which two places do I like to visit?

_____
_____
_____

Copyright © Zaner-Bloser, Inc.

62   **Descriptive Writing** • Compare-and-Contrast Paper

## Your Own Writing
### Prewriting

**Gather Ideas** Choose two things to compare and contrast. Make lists to tell what I know about each thing.

**Directions:** Look at the pairs of things that you wrote on page 62 in this book. Choose one pair, or think of two other things to compare and contrast. Write the names of the two things below. Then make lists that describe each thing.

_____ and _____
Answers will vary.

My List of Ideas          My List of Ideas

_____    _____
_____    _____
_____    _____
_____    _____
_____    _____
_____    _____

Copyright © Zaner-Bloser, Inc.

Now go back to Calvin's work on page 88 in the Student Edition.

**Descriptive Writing** • Compare-and-Contrast Paper   63

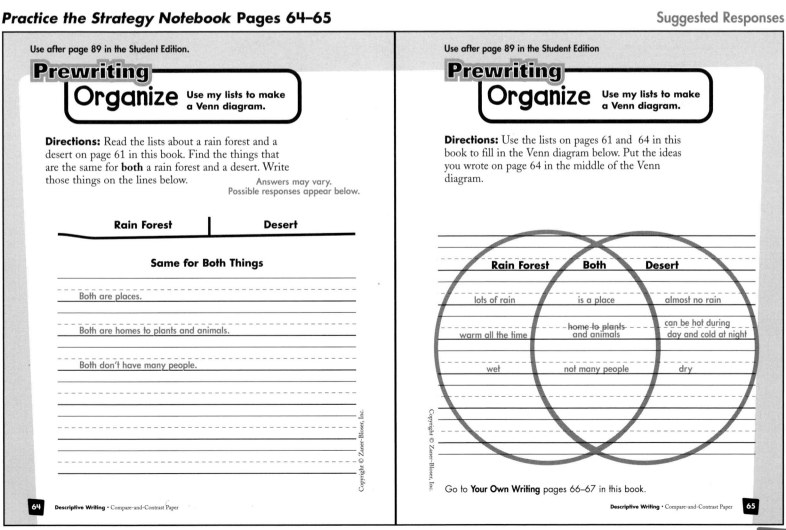

Use after page 89 in the Student Edition.

## Prewriting
### Organize Use my lists to make a Venn diagram.

**Directions:** Read the lists about a rain forest and a desert on page 61 in this book. Find the things that are the same for **both** a rain forest and a desert. Write those things on the lines below.   Answers may vary. Possible responses appear below.

| Rain Forest | Desert |
|---|---|

**Same for Both Things**

_____Both are places._____
_____Both are homes to plants and animals.___
_____Both don't have many people._____
_____
_____
_____
_____

Copyright © Zaner-Bloser, Inc.

64   **Descriptive Writing** • Compare-and-Contrast Paper

Use after page 89 in the Student Edition

## Prewriting
### Organize Use my lists to make a Venn diagram.

**Directions:** Use the lists on pages 61 and 64 in this book to fill in the Venn diagram below. Put the ideas you wrote on page 64 in the middle of the Venn diagram.

| Rain Forest | Both | Desert |
|---|---|---|
| lots of rain | is a place | almost no rain |
| warm all the time | home to plants and animals | can be hot during day and cold at night |
| wet | not many people | dry |

Go to **Your Own Writing** pages 66–67 in this book.

**Descriptive Writing** • Compare-and-Contrast Paper   65

Copyright © Zaner-Bloser, Inc.

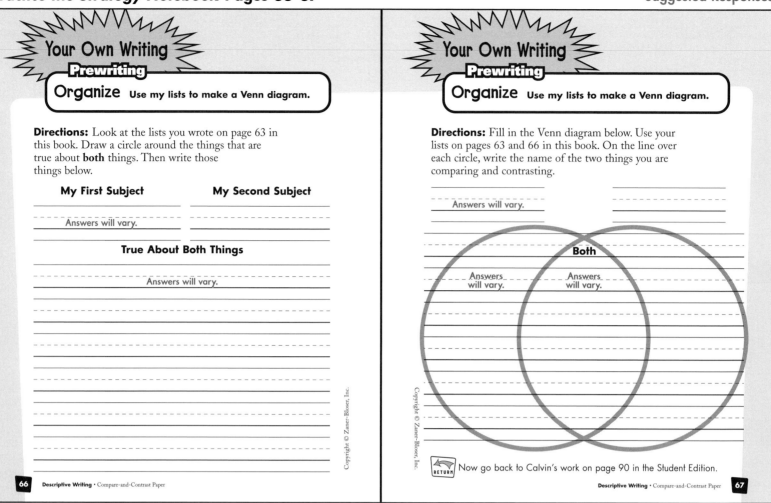

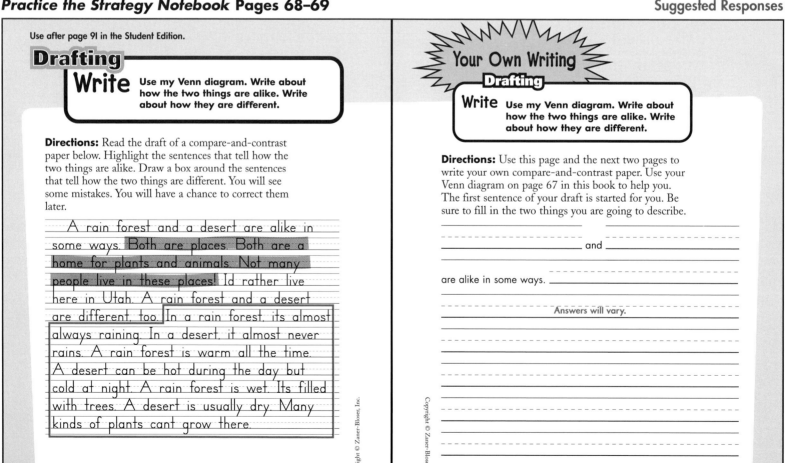

## Your Own Writing

### Drafting

**Write** Use my Venn diagram. Write about how the two things are alike. Write about how they are different.

_____
_____
_____
_____
_____
_____

**Directions:** When you are finished telling how the two things are alike, write this sentence or something like it. ____ **and** ____ **are different, too.** Be sure to fill in the names of the two things. Then tell how the two things are different.

_____
*Answers will vary.*
_____
_____
_____
_____

70  **Descriptive Writing** • Compare-and-Contrast Paper

---

*Answers will vary.*
_____
_____
_____
_____
_____
_____
_____
_____
_____
_____
_____
_____
_____
_____
_____
_____
_____
_____
_____
_____

Now go back to Calvin's work on page 92 in the Student Edition.

71  **Descriptive Writing** • Compare-and-Contrast Paper

---

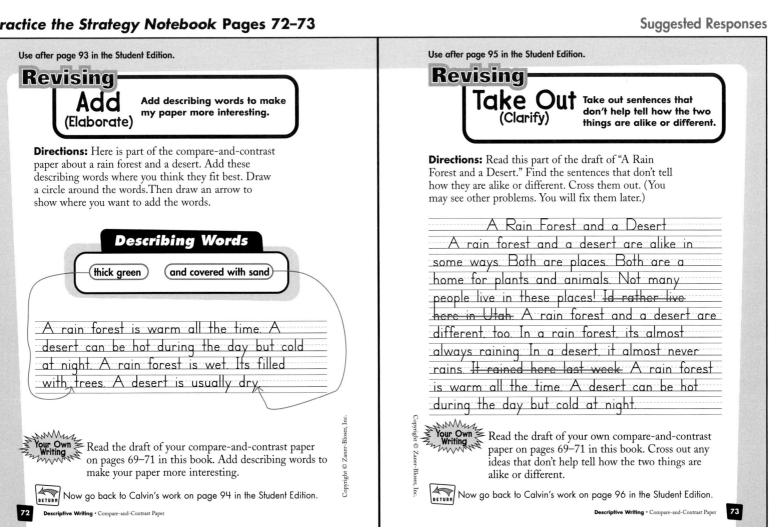

Use after page 93 in the Student Edition.

### Revising

**Add**
(Elaborate)
Add describing words to make my paper more interesting.

**Directions:** Here is part of the compare-and-contrast paper about a rain forest and a desert. Add these describing words where you think they fit best. Draw a circle around the words. Then draw an arrow to show where you want to add the words.

**Describing Words**

( thick green )    ( and covered with sand )

A rain forest is warm all the time. A desert can be hot during the day but cold at night. A rain forest is wet. Its filled with trees. A desert is usually dry.

**Your Own Writing** Read the draft of your compare-and-contrast paper on pages 69–71 in this book. Add describing words to make your paper more interesting.

Now go back to Calvin's work on page 94 in the Student Edition.

72  **Descriptive Writing** • Compare-and-Contrast Paper

---

Use after page 95 in the Student Edition.

### Revising

**Take Out**
(Clarify)
Take out sentences that don't help tell how the two things are alike or different.

**Directions:** Read this part of the draft of "A Rain Forest and a Desert." Find the sentences that don't tell how they are alike or different. Cross them out. (You may see other problems. You will fix them later.)

A Rain Forest and a Desert
A rain forest and a desert are alike in some ways. Both are places. Both are a home for plants and animals. Not many people live in these places! ~~Id rather live here in Utah.~~ A rain forest and a desert are different, too. In a rain forest, its almost always raining. In a desert, it almost never rains. ~~It rained here last week.~~ A rain forest is warm all the time. A desert can be hot during the day but cold at night.

**Your Own Writing** Read the draft of your own compare-and-contrast paper on pages 69–71 in this book. Cross out any ideas that don't help tell how the two things are alike or different.

Now go back to Calvin's work on page 96 in the Student Edition.

73  **Descriptive Writing** • Compare-and-Contrast Paper

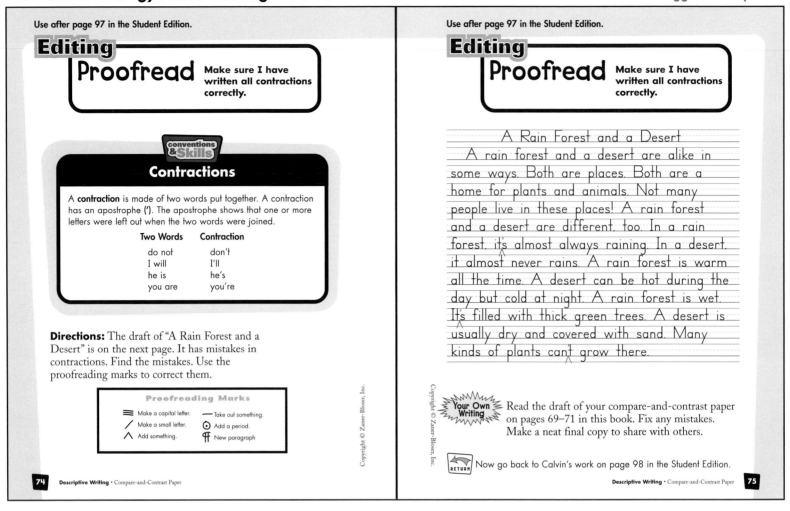

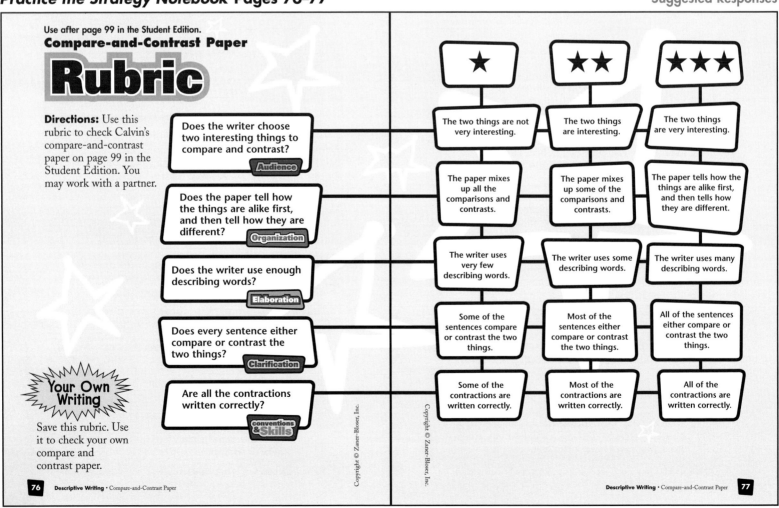

Use after page III in the Student Edition.

## Prewriting
# Gather Ideas

Write two questions I want to answer about my topic. Take notes.

**Topic:** Trees

Here is one question about the topic "trees."

**Question I:** What do trees do for us?

**Directions:** Read these notes for a report about trees. Cross out any notes that don't help answer the question above.

- ~~There is a willow tree near my school.~~

- Trees give us something pretty to look at.

- Trees grow fruit and nuts for us to eat.

- ~~Not all roses are red.~~

- Trees make the air better.

- Trees keep us cool.

Copyright © Zaner-Bloser, Inc.

---

Use after page III in the Student Edition.

## Prewriting
# Gather Ideas

Write two questions I want to answer about my topic. Take notes.

**Topic:** Trees

Here is another question about the topic "trees."

**Question 2:** How do trees grow?

**Directions:** Read these notes for a report about trees. Cross out any notes that don't answer the question above.

- Trees grow by adding wood under their bark.

- The roots get water and food for the tree to grow.

- Wood carries water up and down the tree.

- ~~I camped in a great forest in Maine.~~

- ~~We planted a cherry tree in our backyard.~~

Go to **Your Own Writing** pages 80–81 in this book.

Copyright © Zaner-Bloser, Inc.

---

## Your Own Writing
## Prewriting
# Gather Ideas

Write two questions I want to answer about my topic. Take notes.

**Directions:** Choose a topic for your report. You can choose a famous person, a special place, an animal, or something else that interests you. Write your topic below. Then, write one question you have about your topic. Find a book about your topic. Answer your question by writing notes from the book below.

My Topic: _____ Answers will vary. _____

Question I: _____

My Notes: _____

Copyright © Zaner-Bloser, Inc.

---

## Your Own Writing
## Prewriting
# Gather Ideas

Write two questions I want to answer about my topic. Take notes.

**Directions:** Now, write another question you have about your topic. Answer your question by taking notes from the book on the lines on this page.

Question 2: _____

My Notes: _____

**RETURN** Now go back to Emily's work on page II2 in the Student Edition.

Copyright © Zaner-Bloser, Inc.

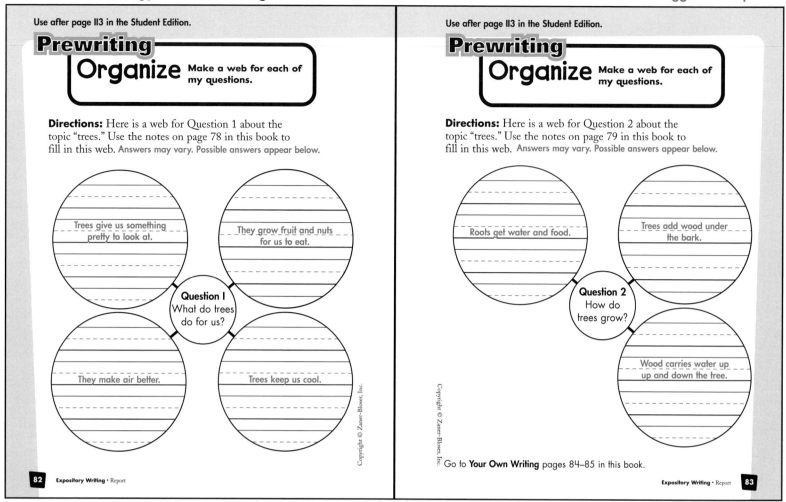

Use after page 113 in the Student Edition.

## Prewriting

### Organize
Make a web for each of my questions.

**Directions:** Here is a web for Question 1 about the topic "trees." Use the notes on page 78 in this book to fill in this web. *Answers may vary. Possible answers appear below.*

- Trees give us something pretty to look at.
- They grow fruit and nuts for us to eat.

**Question 1**
What do trees do for us?

- They make air better.
- Trees keep us cool.

Copyright © Zaner-Bloser, Inc.

82 **Expository Writing** · Report

Use after page 113 in the Student Edition.

## Prewriting

### Organize
Make a web for each of my questions.

**Directions:** Here is a web for Question 2 about the topic "trees." Use the notes on page 79 in this book to fill in this web. *Answers may vary. Possible answers appear below.*

- Roots get water and food.
- Trees add wood under the bark.

**Question 2**
How do trees grow?

- Wood carries water up up and down the tree.

Copyright © Zaner-Bloser, Inc.

Go to **Your Own Writing** pages 84–85 in this book.

**Expository Writing** · Report 83

---

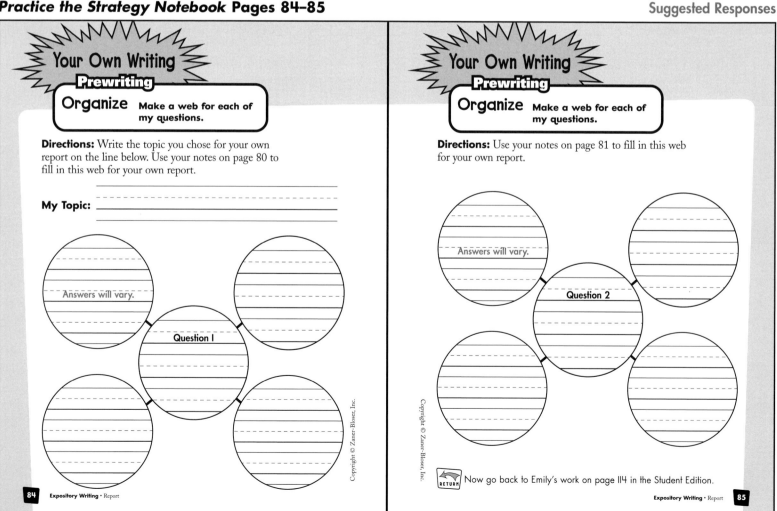

## Your Own Writing
### Prewriting
### Organize
Make a web for each of my questions.

**Directions:** Write the topic you chose for your own report on the line below. Use your notes on page 80 to fill in this web for your own report.

**My Topic:** _____

- Answers will vary.

**Question 1**

Copyright © Zaner-Bloser, Inc.

84 **Expository Writing** · Report

## Your Own Writing
### Prewriting
### Organize
Make a web for each of my questions.

**Directions:** Use your notes on page 81 to fill in this web for your own report.

- Answers will vary.

**Question 2**

Copyright © Zaner-Bloser, Inc.

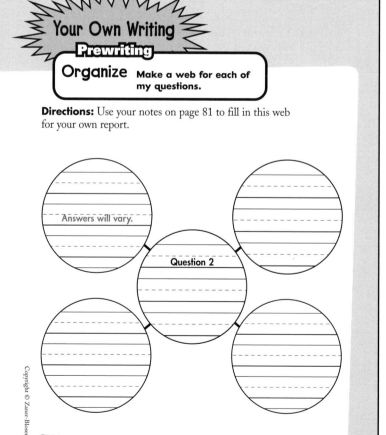

Now go back to Emily's work on page 114 in the Student Edition.

**Expository Writing** · Report 85

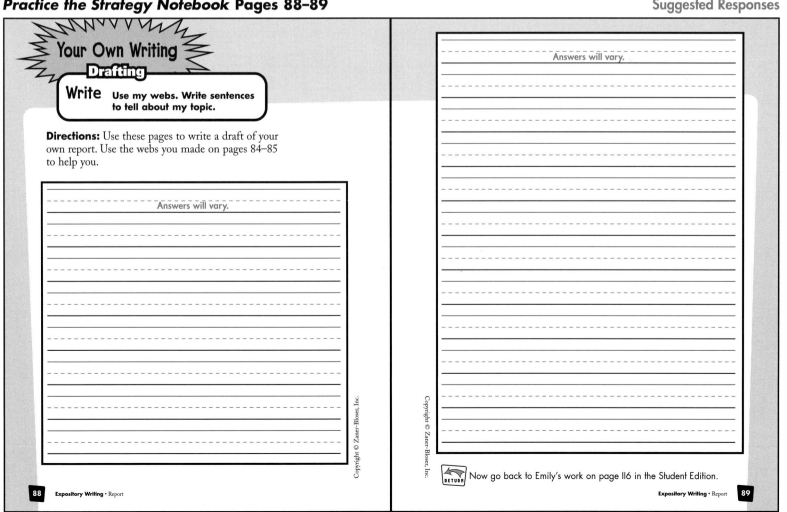

Use after page 115 in the Student Edition.

## Drafting

**Write** Use my webs. Write sentences to tell about my topic.

**Directions:** Use the webs on pages 82–83 in this book to write sentences about the topic "trees." The first sentence is written for you. Answers may vary.

Possible answers appear below.

Trees

Trees are our friends.

They are pretty to look at. Trees keep us cool on hot summer days.

Some trees give us fruit and nuts to eat. Trees grow by adding a

new layer of wood under their bark every year. They use light,

water, and food from the soil to grow. The wood carries water up

and down the tree. The roots find the water and food that the

tree needs.

Copyright © Zaner-Bloser, Inc.

Go to **Your Own Writing** pages 88–89 in this book.

86 Expository Writing • Report

87 Expository Writing • Report

---

## Your Own Writing

### Drafting

**Write** Use my webs. Write sentences to tell about my topic.

**Directions:** Use these pages to write a draft of your own report. Use the webs you made on pages 84–85 to help you.

Answers will vary.

Answers will vary.

Copyright © Zaner-Bloser, Inc.

Now go back to Emily's work on page 116 in the Student Edition.

88 Expository Writing • Report

89 Expository Writing • Report

*Practice the Strategy Notebook* Suggested Responses **T235**

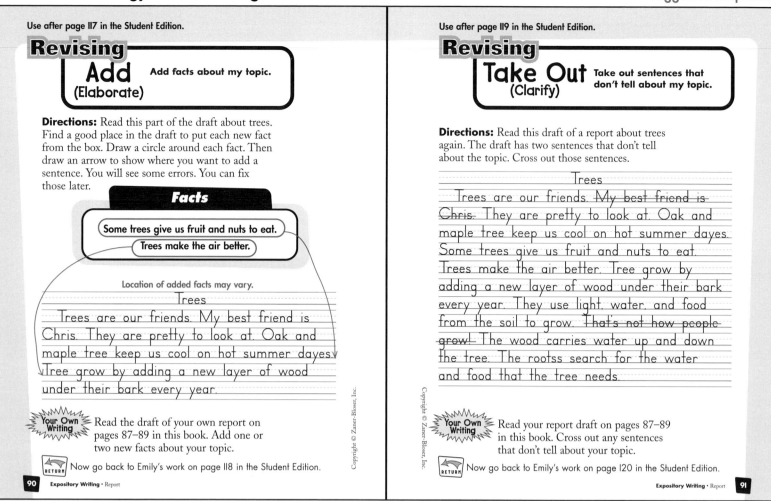

Use after page II7 in the Student Edition.

**Revising**
# Add
(Elaborate)　　**Add facts about my topic.**

**Directions:** Read this part of the draft about trees. Find a good place in the draft to put each new fact from the box. Draw a circle around each fact. Then draw an arrow to show where you want to add a sentence. You will see some errors. You can fix those later.

### Facts
Some trees give us fruit and nuts to eat.
Trees make the air better.

Location of added facts may vary.

Trees

Trees are our friends. My best friend is Chris. They are pretty to look at. Oak and maple tree keep us cool on hot summer dayes. Tree grow by adding a new layer of wood under their bark every year.

**Your Own Writing** Read the draft of your own report on pages 87–89 in this book. Add one or two new facts about your topic.

**RETURN** Now go back to Emily's work on page II8 in the Student Edition.

90　Expository Writing • Report

Use after page II9 in the Student Edition.

**Revising**
# Take Out
(Clarify)　　**Take out sentences that don't tell about my topic.**

**Directions:** Read this draft of a report about trees again. The draft has two sentences that don't tell about the topic. Cross out those sentences.

Trees

Trees are our friends. My best friend is Chris. They are pretty to look at. Oak and maple tree keep us cool on hot summer dayes. Some trees give us fruit and nuts to eat. Trees make the air better. Tree grow by adding a new layer of wood under their bark every year. They use light, water, and food from the soil to grow. That's not how people grow! The wood carries water up and down the tree. The rootss search for the water and food that the tree needs.

**Your Own Writing** Read your report draft on pages 87–89 in this book. Cross out any sentences that don't tell about your topic.

**RETURN** Now go back to Emily's work on page I20 in the Student Edition.

Expository Writing • Report　91

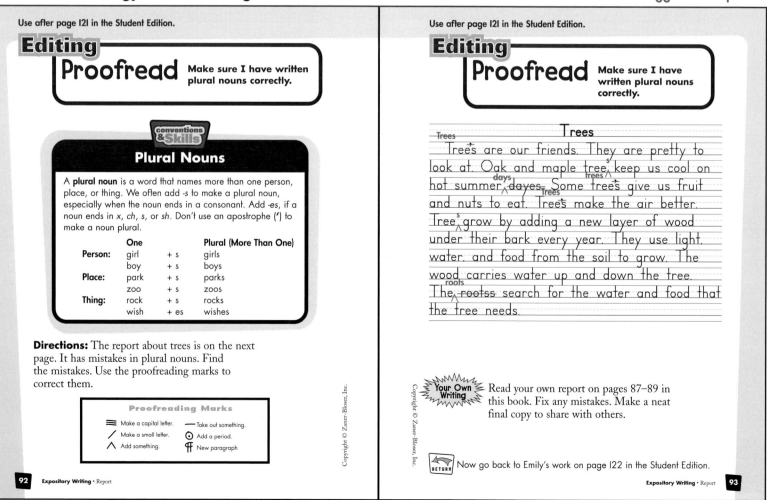

Use after page I2I in the Student Edition.

**Editing**
# Proofread
**Make sure I have written plural nouns correctly.**

**Conventions & Skills**

## Plural Nouns

A **plural noun** is a word that names more than one person, place, or thing. We often add -s to make a plural noun, especially when the noun ends in a consonant. Add -es, if a noun ends in x, ch, s, or sh. Don't use an apostrophe (') to make a noun plural.

|  | One |  | Plural (More Than One) |
|---|---|---|---|
| Person: | girl | + s | girls |
|  | boy | + s | boys |
| Place: | park | + s | parks |
|  | zoo | + s | zoos |
| Thing: | rock | + s | rocks |
|  | wish | + es | wishes |

**Directions:** The report about trees is on the next page. It has mistakes in plural nouns. Find the mistakes. Use the proofreading marks to correct them.

**Proofreading Marks**
≡ Make a capital letter.　— Take out something.
／ Make a small letter.　⊙ Add a period.
∧ Add something.　¶ New paragraph

92　Expository Writing • Report

Use after page I2I in the Student Edition.

**Editing**
# Proofread
**Make sure I have written plural nouns correctly.**

Trees

Trees are our friends. They are pretty to look at. Oak and maple tree(s) keep us cool on hot summer days (dayes). Some tree(s) give us fruit and nuts to eat. Tree(s) make the air better. Tree(s) grow by adding a new layer of wood under their bark every year. They use light, water, and food from the soil to grow. The wood carries water up and down the tree. The roots (rootss) search for the water and food that the tree needs.

**Your Own Writing** Read your own report on pages 87–89 in this book. Fix any mistakes. Make a neat final copy to share with others.

**RETURN** Now go back to Emily's work on page I22 in the Student Edition.

Expository Writing • Report　93

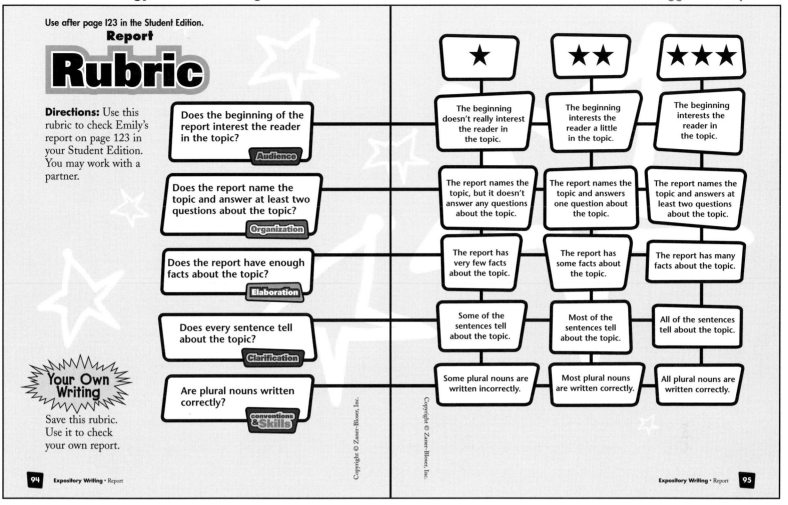

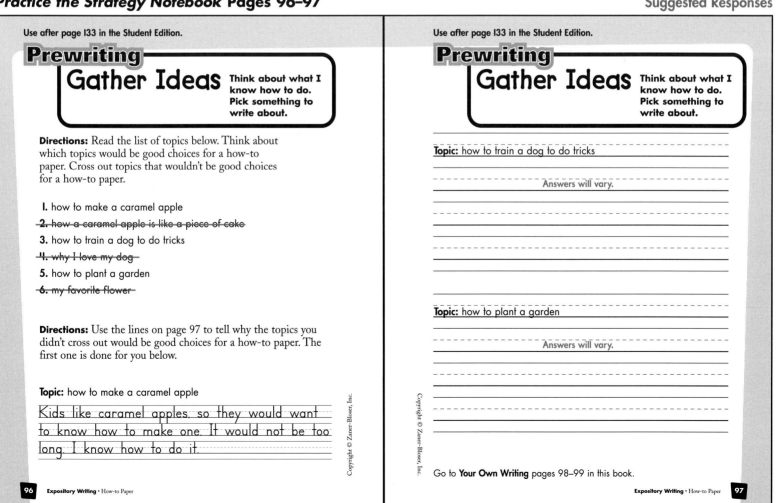

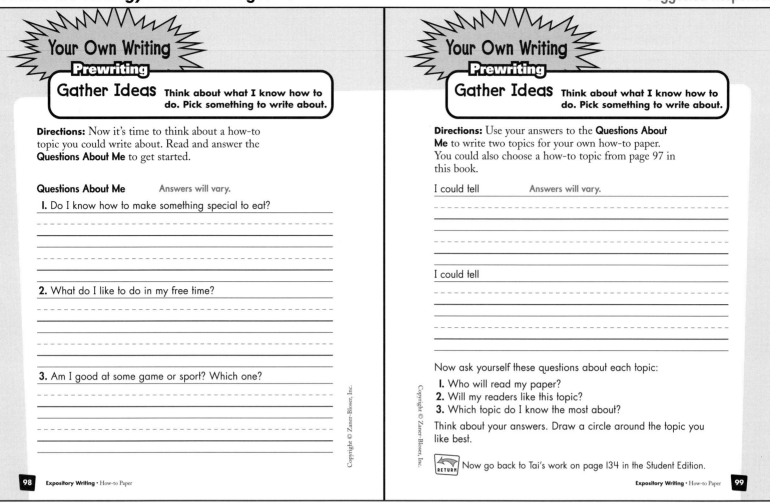

## Your Own Writing
### Prewriting
### Gather Ideas Think about what I know how to do. Pick something to write about.

**Directions:** Now it's time to think about a how-to topic you could write about. Read and answer the **Questions About Me** to get started.

**Questions About Me** Answers will vary.

1. Do I know how to make something special to eat?

2. What do I like to do in my free time?

3. Am I good at some game or sport? Which one?

98 Expository Writing • How-to Paper

Copyright © Zaner-Bloser, Inc.

## Your Own Writing
### Prewriting
### Gather Ideas Think about what I know how to do. Pick something to write about.

**Directions:** Use your answers to the **Questions About Me** to write two topics for your own how-to paper. You could also choose a how-to topic from page 97 in this book.

I could tell Answers will vary.

I could tell

Now ask yourself these questions about each topic:

1. Who will read my paper?
2. Will my readers like this topic?
3. Which topic do I know the most about?

Think about your answers. Draw a circle around the topic you like best.

RETURN Now go back to Tai's work on page 134 in the Student Edition.

Copyright © Zaner-Bloser, Inc.

Expository Writing • How-to Paper 99

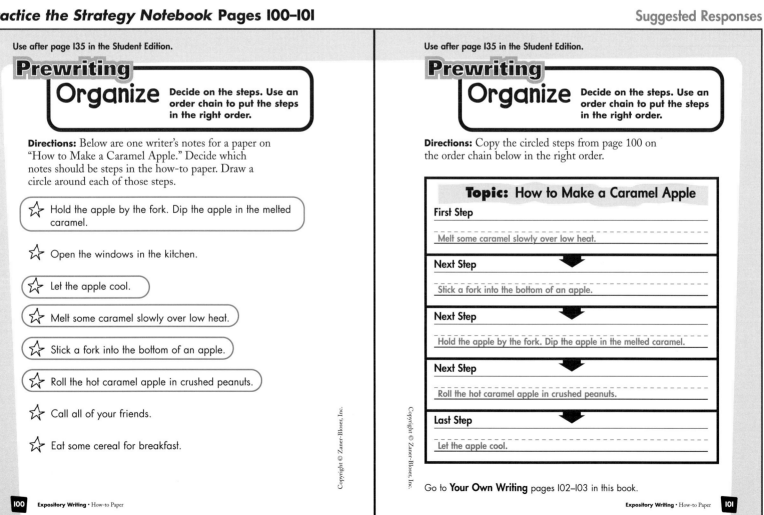

Use after page 135 in the Student Edition.

## Prewriting
### Organize Decide on the steps. Use an order chain to put the steps in the right order.

**Directions:** Below are one writer's notes for a paper on "How to Make a Caramel Apple." Decide which notes should be steps in the how-to paper. Draw a circle around each of those steps.

- ☆ Hold the apple by the fork. Dip the apple in the melted caramel.
- ☆ Open the windows in the kitchen.
- ☆ Let the apple cool.
- ☆ Melt some caramel slowly over low heat.
- ☆ Stick a fork into the bottom of an apple.
- ☆ Roll the hot caramel apple in crushed peanuts.
- ☆ Call all of your friends.
- ☆ Eat some cereal for breakfast.

100 Expository Writing • How-to Paper

Copyright © Zaner-Bloser, Inc.

Use after page 135 in the Student Edition.

## Prewriting
### Organize Decide on the steps. Use an order chain to put the steps in the right order.

**Directions:** Copy the circled steps from page 100 on the order chain below in the right order.

**Topic:** How to Make a Caramel Apple

**First Step**
Melt some caramel slowly over low heat.

**Next Step** ▼
Stick a fork into the bottom of an apple.

**Next Step** ▼
Hold the apple by the fork. Dip the apple in the melted caramel.

**Next Step** ▼
Roll the hot caramel apple in crushed peanuts.

**Last Step** ▼
Let the apple cool.

Go to **Your Own Writing** pages 102–103 in this book.

Copyright © Zaner-Bloser, Inc.

Expository Writing • How-to Paper 101

## *Practice the Strategy Notebook* Pages 102–103

Suggested Responses

# Your Own Writing

## Prewriting

**Organize** **Decide on the steps. Use an order chain to put the steps in the right order.**

**Directions:** Write the topic you circled on page 99 on the line next to **My Topic**. Think about the steps for your topic. Then write your steps in the order chain on these pages. (Use as many of the steps in the order chain as you need. You don't need to use every step.)

**My Topic:** Answers will vary.

**First Step**

Answers will vary.

**Next Step**





**Next Step**

Answers will vary.

**Next Step**

**Last Step**



RETURN Now go back to Tai's work on page 136 in the Student Edition.



## *Practice the Strategy Notebook* Pages 104–105

Suggested Responses

Use after page 137 in the Student Edition.

## Drafting

**Write** **Use my order chain. Write sentences that tell the steps in correct order.**

**Directions:** Use the order chain you filled in on pages 102–103 in this book to write a draft of a how-to paper on how to make a caramel apple. Be sure to write the steps in the right order.

Answers will vary. Possible answers appear below.

Melt some caramel slowly over low heat. Stick a fork in the bottom of an apple. Hold the apple by the fork and dip it in the melted caramel. Roll the hot caramel apple in crushed peanuts. Let the apple cool.

Go to **Your Own Writing** pages 105–107 in this book.





# Your Own Writing

## Drafting

**Write** **Use my order chain. Write sentences that tell the steps in correct order.**

**Directions:** Use the lines on these pages to write a draft of your own how-to paper. Follow the order chain you filled in on pages 102–103 in this book to tell the steps of your how-to paper in the right order.

Answers will vary.

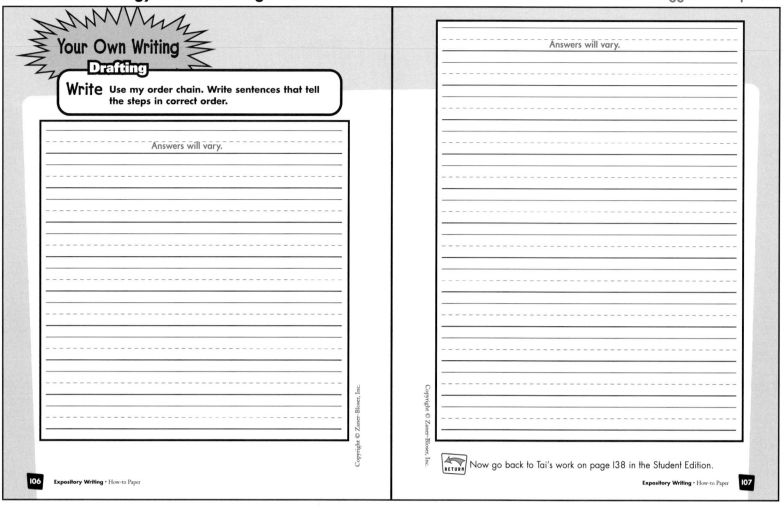

**Your Own Writing**

**Drafting**

**Write** Use my order chain. Write sentences that tell the steps in correct order.

Answers will vary.

Answers will vary.

Now go back to Tai's work on page 138 in the Student Edition.

106  **Expository Writing** • How-to Paper

**Expository Writing** • How-to Paper  107

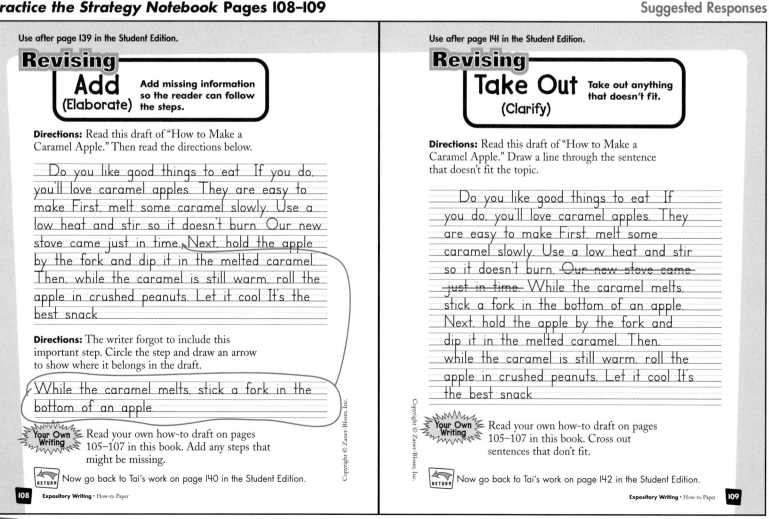

Use after page 139 in the Student Edition.

**Revising**

**Add** **Add** missing information so the reader can follow the steps.
**(Elaborate)**

**Directions:** Read this draft of "How to Make a Caramel Apple." Then read the directions below.

Do you like good things to eat If you do, you'll love caramel apples. They are easy to make First, melt some caramel slowly Use a low heat and stir so it doesn't burn Our new stove came just in time. Next, hold the apple by the fork and dip it in the melted caramel. Then, while the caramel is still warm, roll the apple in crushed peanuts Let it cool It's the best snack

**Directions:** The writer forgot to include this important step. Circle the step and draw an arrow to show where it belongs in the draft.

While the caramel melts, stick a fork in the bottom of an apple

**Your Own Writing** Read your own how-to draft on pages 105–107 in this book. Add any steps that might be missing.

Now go back to Tai's work on page 140 in the Student Edition.

108  **Expository Writing** • How-to Paper

Use after page 141 in the Student Edition.

**Revising**

**Take Out** Take out anything that doesn't fit.
**(Clarify)**

**Directions:** Read this draft of "How to Make a Caramel Apple." Draw a line through the sentence that doesn't fit the topic.

Do you like good things to eat If you do, you'll love caramel apples. They are easy to make First, melt some caramel slowly. Use a low heat and stir so it doesn't burn. ~~Our new stove came just in time.~~ While the caramel melts, stick a fork in the bottom of an apple. Next, hold the apple by the fork and dip it in the melted caramel. Then, while the caramel is still warm, roll the apple in crushed peanuts. Let it cool It's the best snack

**Your Own Writing** Read your own how-to draft on pages 105–107 in this book. Cross out sentences that don't fit.

Now go back to Tai's work on page 142 in the Student Edition.

**Expository Writing** • How-to Paper  109

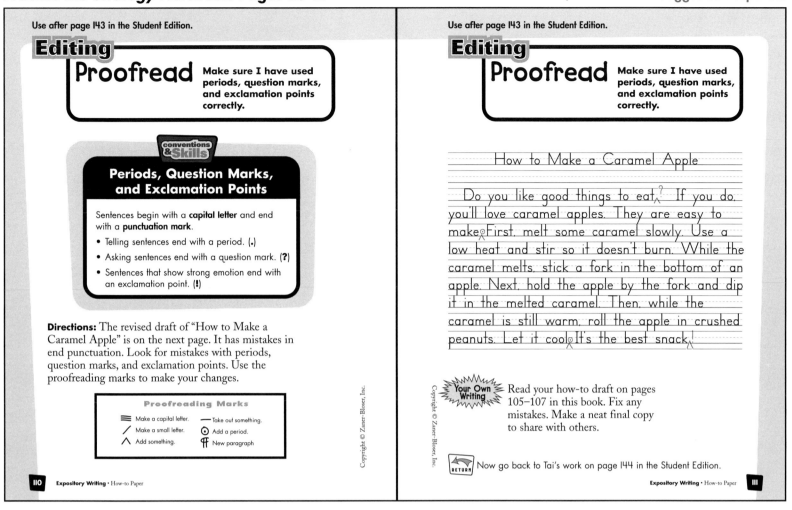

Use after page 143 in the Student Edition.

## Editing
# Proofread
Make sure I have used periods, question marks, and exclamation points correctly.

### conventions & Skills
### Periods, Question Marks, and Exclamation Points

Sentences begin with a **capital letter** and end with a **punctuation mark**.
- Telling sentences end with a period. (.)
- Asking sentences end with a question mark. (?)
- Sentences that show strong emotion end with an exclamation point. (!)

**Directions:** The revised draft of "How to Make a Caramel Apple" is on the next page. It has mistakes in end punctuation. Look for mistakes with periods, question marks, and exclamation points. Use the proofreading marks to make your changes.

#### Proofreading Marks
≡ Make a capital letter.   — Take out something.
/ Make a small letter.   ⊙ Add a period.
∧ Add something.   ¶ New paragraph

110   Expository Writing • How-to Paper

Use after page 143 in the Student Edition.

## Editing
# Proofread
Make sure I have used periods, question marks, and exclamation points correctly.

How to Make a Caramel Apple

Do you like good things to eat? If you do, you'll love caramel apples. They are easy to make. First, melt some caramel slowly. Use a low heat and stir so it doesn't burn. While the caramel melts, stick a fork in the bottom of an apple. Next, hold the apple by the fork and dip it in the melted caramel. Then, while the caramel is still warm, roll the apple in crushed peanuts. Let it cool. It's the best snack!

**Your Own Writing** Read your how-to draft on pages 105–107 in this book. Fix any mistakes. Make a neat final copy to share with others.

RETURN   Now go back to Tai's work on page 144 in the Student Edition.

Expository Writing • How-to Paper   111

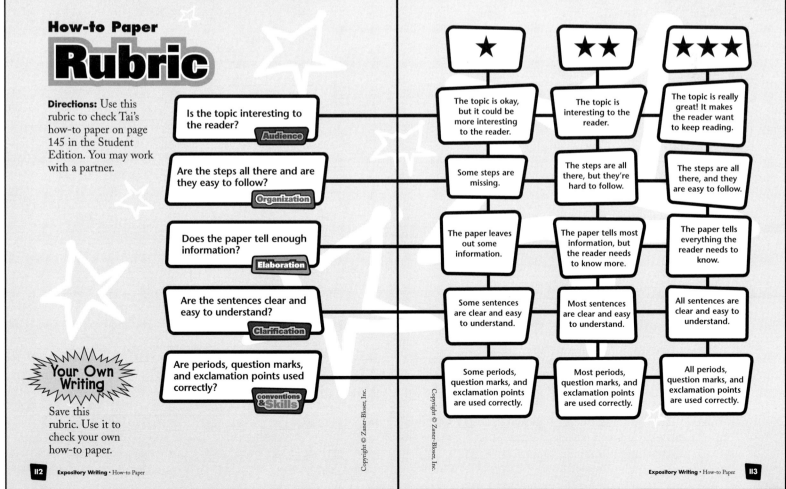

## How-to Paper
# Rubric

**Directions:** Use this rubric to check Tai's how-to paper on page 145 in the Student Edition. You may work with a partner.

| | ★ | ★★ | ★★★ |
|---|---|---|---|
| Is the topic interesting to the reader? **Audience** | The topic is okay, but it could be more interesting to the reader. | The topic is interesting to the reader. | The topic is really great! It makes the reader want to keep reading. |
| Are the steps all there and are they easy to follow? **Organization** | Some steps are missing. | The steps are all there, but they're hard to follow. | The steps are all there, and they are easy to follow. |
| Does the paper tell enough information? **Elaboration** | The paper leaves out some information. | The paper tells most information, but the reader needs to know more. | The paper tells everything the reader needs to know. |
| Are the sentences clear and easy to understand? **Clarification** | Some sentences are clear and easy to understand. | Most sentences are clear and easy to understand. | All sentences are clear and easy to understand. |
| Are periods, question marks, and exclamation points used correctly? **conventions & Skills** | Some periods, question marks, and exclamation points are used correctly. | Most periods, question marks, and exclamation points are used correctly. | All periods, question marks, and exclamation points are used correctly. |

**Your Own Writing** Save this rubric. Use it to check your own how-to paper.

112   Expository Writing • How-to Paper

Expository Writing • How-to Paper   113

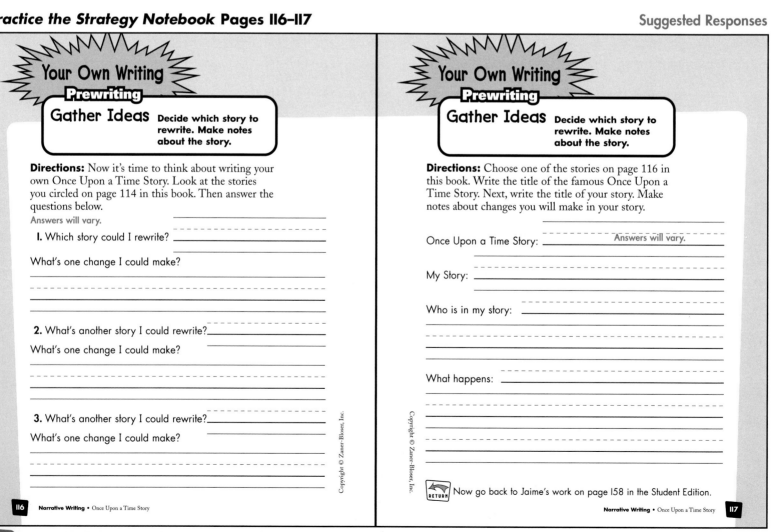

**Practice the Strategy Notebook** Pages 114–115

Use after page 157 in the Student Edition.

## Prewriting
### Gather Ideas
Decide which story to rewrite. Make notes about the story.

**Directions:** Here is a list of Once Upon a Time Stories. You can also add more stories on the lines below the list. Draw a circle around three stories you might like to rewrite. Answers will vary.

"The Fisherman and His Wife"

"Goldilocks and the Three Bears"

"Hansel and Gretel"

"Jack and the Beanstalk"

"Little Red Riding Hood"

"The Old Woman and the Shoe"

"Snow White"

"The Three Billy Goats Gruff"

"The Ugly Duckling"

Answers will vary.

114  Narrative Writing • Once Upon a Time Story

Copyright © Zaner-Bloser, Inc.

---

Use after page 157 in the Student Edition.

## Prewriting
### Gather Ideas
Decide which story to rewrite. Make notes about the story.

**Directions:** Here are some notes for rewriting "The Ugly Duckling." On the left side are notes about this famous Once Upon a Time Story. On the right side are notes showing the changes. Under "The Ugly Zebra," draw a circle around the things that are different.

| Famous Once Upon a Time Story "The Ugly Duckling" | My Story "The Ugly Zebra" |
|---|---|
| ugly duckling | ugly zebra |
| Other ducklings make fun of it. | Other zebras are scared of it. |
| Duckling is lonely and sad. | Zebra thinks it's bad. |
| joins the swans one day | joins the horses one day |
| Duckling finds out it is really a beautiful swan. | Zebra finds out it is really a beautiful horse. |

Go to **Your Own Writing** pages 116–117 in this book.

Narrative Writing • Once Upon a Time Story  115

Copyright © Zaner-Bloser, Inc.

---

**Practice the Strategy Notebook** Pages 116–117

Suggested Responses

## Your Own Writing
### Prewriting
### Gather Ideas
Decide which story to rewrite. Make notes about the story.

**Directions:** Now it's time to think about writing your own Once Upon a Time Story. Look at the stories you circled on page 114 in this book. Then answer the questions below.
Answers will vary.

1. Which story could I rewrite? _____

What's one change I could make? _____

2. What's another story I could rewrite? _____

What's one change I could make? _____

3. What's another story I could rewrite? _____

What's one change I could make? _____

116  Narrative Writing • Once Upon a Time Story

Copyright © Zaner-Bloser, Inc.

---

## Your Own Writing
### Prewriting
### Gather Ideas
Decide which story to rewrite. Make notes about the story.

**Directions:** Choose one of the stories on page 116 in this book. Write the title of the famous Once Upon a Time Story. Next, write the title of your story. Make notes about changes you will make in your story.

Once Upon a Time Story: _____   Answers will vary.

My Story: _____

Who is in my story: _____

What happens: _____

Now go back to Jaime's work on page 158 in the Student Edition.

Narrative Writing • Once Upon a Time Story  117

Copyright © Zaner-Bloser, Inc.

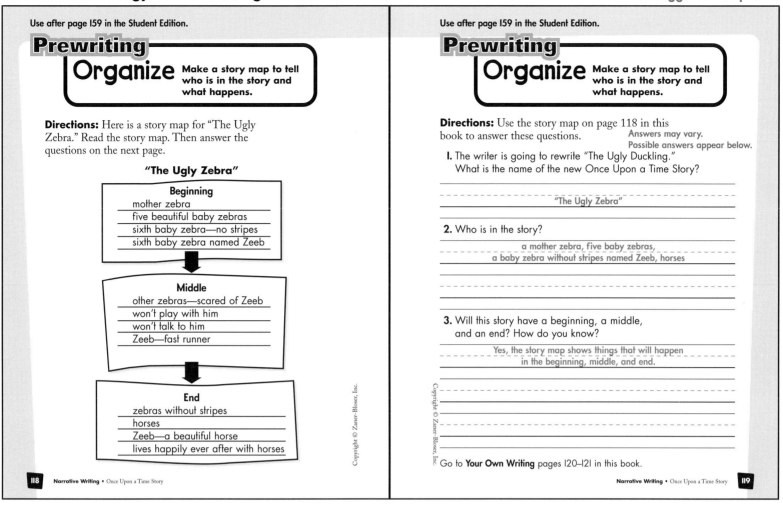

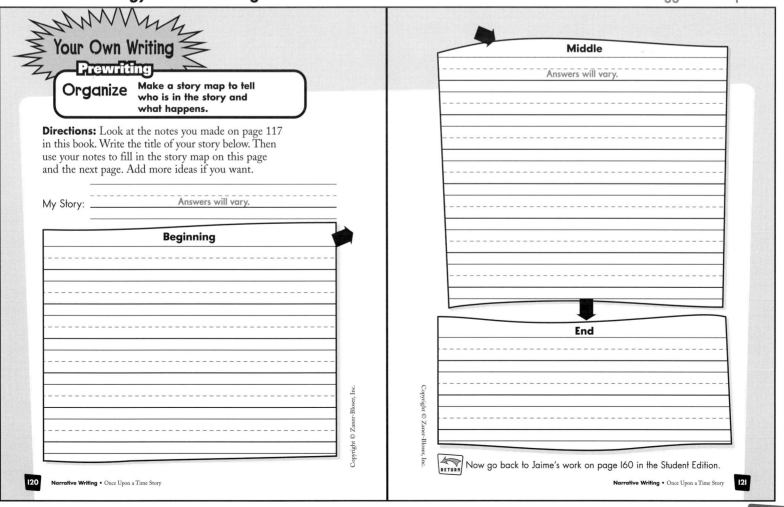

Use after page 161 in the Student Edition.

## Drafting
### Write
Use my story map. Write sentences to tell what happens at the beginning, middle, and end.

**Directions:** Read this draft of the new Once Upon a Time Story. Then answer the questions on the next page. You will see some mistakes. You can fix them later.

The Ugly Zebra

Once upon a time, a mother zebra in africa had six babies. Five of them had black and white stripes. Zebras only live in Africa. One baby had no stripes. His name was zeeb. The other zebras would not play with zeeb. They were scared of zeeb. zeeb was very fast. He was brown. I once saw a zebra in a zoo. One day, zeeb saw some other brown zebras. He went to talk to them. One was named rosie. She told him that they were horses and that he was a horse, too. She wanted him to be with them. zeeb was very glad to finally know who he was. He lived happily ever after with the horses.

## Drafting
### Write
Use my story map. Write sentences to tell what happens at the beginning, middle, and end.

Answers will vary. Possible answers appear below.

**1.** Who is the story about?

The story is about a zebra named Zeeb

**2.** What happened in the middle of the story?

The other zebras would not play with Zeeb.
They were scared of Zeeb.

**3.** What happened at the end of the story?

Zeeb found out he's a horse.

Go to **Your Own Writing** pages 124–127 in this book.

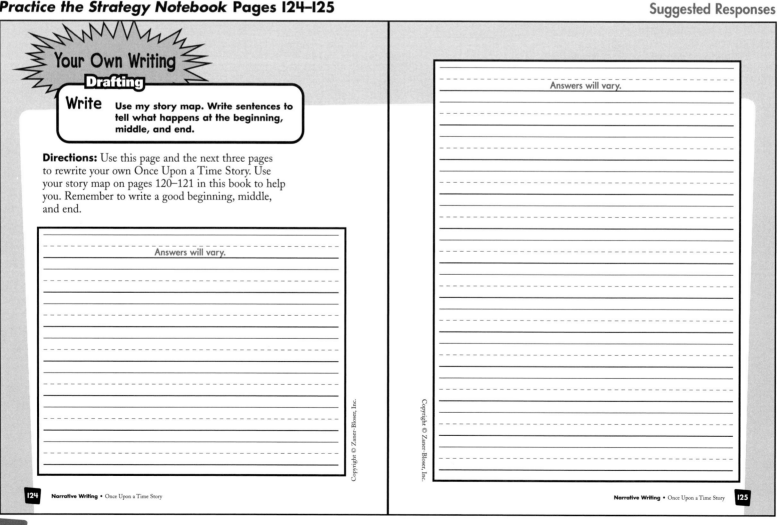

## Your Own Writing
### Drafting
### Write
Use my story map. Write sentences to tell what happens at the beginning, middle, and end.

**Directions:** Use this page and the next three pages to rewrite your own Once Upon a Time Story. Use your story map on pages 120–121 in this book to help you. Remember to write a good beginning, middle, and end.

Answers will vary.

Answers will vary.

## Your Own Writing
### Drafting
**Write** Use my story map. Write sentences to tell what happens at the beginning, middle, and end.

Answers will vary.

Answers will vary.

Now go back to Jaime's work on page 162 in the Student Edition.

---

Use after page 163 in the Student Edition.

## Revising
### Add (Elaborate)
Add action verbs to make the story more exciting.

**Directions:** Read this part of the draft of "The Ugly Zebra." Find the verb **was**. Change it to the action verb **ran**. Be careful! Use **ran** instead of **was** only where it makes sense! Next, find the verb **be**. Change it to the action verb **play**.

They were scared of zeeb. zeeb ~~was~~ <sup>ran</sup> very fast. He was golden brown. I once saw a zebra in a zoo. One day, zeeb saw some other brown zebras. He went to talk to them. One was named rosie. She told him that they were horses and that he was a horse, too. She wanted him to ~~be~~ <sup>play</sup> with them. zeeb was very glad to finally know who he was.

Your Own Writing — Read your draft on pages 124–127 in this book. Add action verbs to your own story.

Now go back to Jaime's work on page 164 in the Student Edition.

Use after page 165 in the Student Edition.

## Revising
### Take Out (Clarify)
Take out sentences that don't fit the story.

**Directions:** Read this part of the draft of "The Ugly Zebra." Two sentences do not fit the story. Draw a line through those sentences.

The Ugly Zebra
Once upon a time, a mother zebra in africa had six babies. Five of them had black and white stripes. ~~Zebras only live in Africa.~~ One baby had no stripes. His name was zeeb. The other zebras would not play with zeeb. They were scared of zeeb. zeeb ran very fast. He was brown. ~~I once saw a zebra in a zoo.~~ One day, zeeb saw some other brown zebras. He went to talk to them. One was named rosie. She told him that they were horses and that he was a horse, too.

Your Own Writing — Read your draft on pages 124–127 in this book. Cross out any sentences that don't fit your story.

Now go back to Jaime's work on page 166 in the Student Edition.

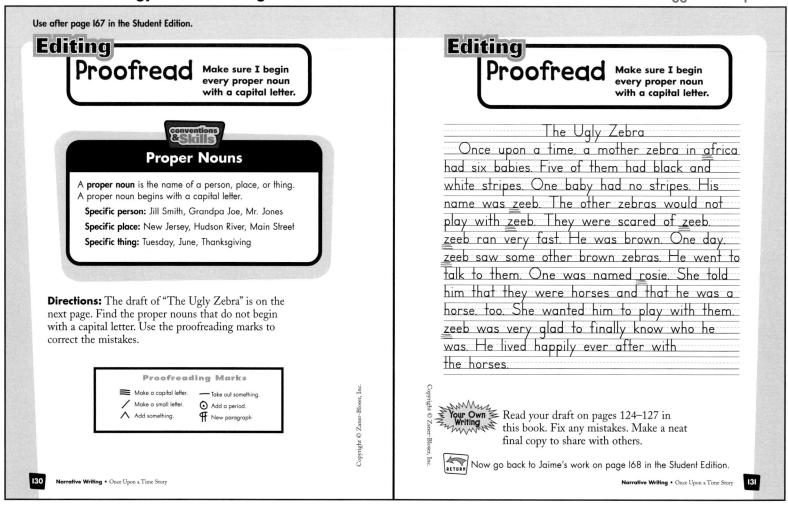

Use after page 167 in the Student Edition.

## Editing
### Proofread
Make sure I begin every proper noun with a capital letter.

**conventions & Skills**
### Proper Nouns

A **proper noun** is the name of a person, place, or thing. A proper noun begins with a capital letter.

**Specific person:** Jill Smith, Grandpa Joe, Mr. Jones
**Specific place:** New Jersey, Hudson River, Main Street
**Specific thing:** Tuesday, June, Thanksgiving

**Directions:** The draft of "The Ugly Zebra" is on the next page. Find the proper nouns that do not begin with a capital letter. Use the proofreading marks to correct the mistakes.

### Proofreading Marks
≡ Make a capital letter.     — Take out something.
/ Make a small letter.     ⊙ Add a period.
∧ Add something.     ¶ New paragraph.

## Editing
### Proofread
Make sure I begin every proper noun with a capital letter.

The Ugly Zebra

Once upon a time, a mother zebra in africa had six babies. Five of them had black and white stripes. One baby had no stripes. His name was zeeb. The other zebras would not play with zeeb. They were scared of zeeb. zeeb ran very fast. He was brown. One day, zeeb saw some other brown zebras. He went to talk to them. One was named rosie. She told him that they were horses and that he was a horse, too. She wanted him to play with them. zeeb was very glad to finally know who he was. He lived happily ever after with the horses.

**Your Own Writing** Read your draft on pages 124–127 in this book. Fix any mistakes. Make a neat final copy to share with others.

RETURN Now go back to Jaime's work on page 168 in the Student Edition.

---

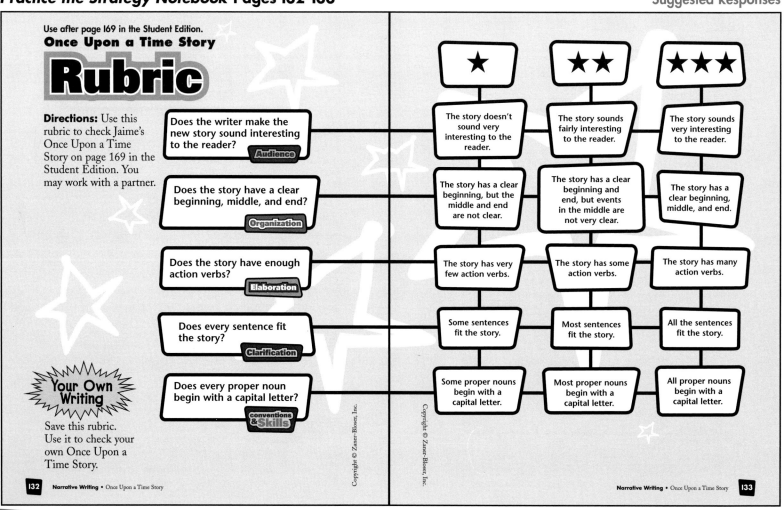

Use after page 169 in the Student Edition.
### Once Upon a Time Story
# Rubric

**Directions:** Use this rubric to check Jaime's Once Upon a Time Story on page 169 in the Student Edition. You may work with a partner.

**Your Own Writing**
Save this rubric. Use it to check your own Once Upon a Time Story.

| | ★ | ★★ | ★★★ |
|---|---|---|---|
| Does the writer make the new story sound interesting to the reader? **Audience** | The story doesn't sound very interesting to the reader. | The story sounds fairly interesting to the reader. | The story sounds very interesting to the reader. |
| Does the story have a clear beginning, middle, and end? **Organization** | The story has a clear beginning, but the middle and end are not clear. | The story has a clear beginning and end, but events in the middle are not very clear. | The story has a clear beginning, middle, and end. |
| Does the story have enough action verbs? **Elaboration** | The story has very few action verbs. | The story has some action verbs. | The story has many action verbs. |
| Does every sentence fit the story? **Clarification** | Some sentences fit the story. | Most sentences fit the story. | All the sentences fit the story. |
| Does every proper noun begin with a capital letter? **conventions & Skills** | Some proper nouns begin with a capital letter. | Most proper nouns begin with a capital letter. | All proper nouns begin with a capital letter. |

Use after page 179 in the Student Edition.

## Prewriting
### Gather Ideas
Decide which fable to rewrite. Make notes about the fable.

**Directions:** Here are two famous fables. Read them. Think about what you would change if you told them in a new way.

### The Goose and the Golden Eggs

A goose started laying one golden egg each day. The farmer was so happy! Then he wanted more. He cut the goose open to get all the eggs at once. There were no eggs inside the goose, and now the goose was gone.

(Lesson: If you try to have everything, you may end up with nothing.)

### Belling the Cat

The mice held a long meeting to decide what to do about the cat. Finally, one mouse had a wonderful idea. "We'll put a bell around the cat's neck so we'll always hear her coming."

Another mouse asked, "Who has the courage to put the bell on the cat?"

(Lesson: Brave talk is easy.)

134　Narrative Writing • Fable

---

Use after page 179 in the Student Edition.

## Prewriting
### Gather Ideas
Decide which fable to rewrite. Make notes about the fable.

**Directions:** Here are some notes for rewriting another famous fable—"The Tortoise and the Hare." A tortoise is a kind of turtle. A hare is like a rabbit. On the left are notes about the famous fable. On the right are notes for rewriting the fable. Draw a line to show which changes on the right match the events in the famous fable on the left. The first one is done for you.

**Famous Fable:**
"The Tortoise and the Hare"

**New Fable:**
"George and Ty"

| Famous Fable | New Fable |
|---|---|
| A race is coming up. | Ty decides he can win the long jump contest. |
| A hare brags that he will win the race. | Lesson: Hard work and practice are better than talk. |
| A tortoise decides she can win. | Field day is coming up. |
| The tortoise goes slowly and wins the race. | George brags that he will win every contest. |
| Lesson: Slow and steady wins the race. | Ty works hard and wins the long jump. |

Go to **Your Own Writing** pages 136–137 in this book.

Narrative Writing • Fable　135

---

## Your Own Writing
### Prewriting
### Gather Ideas
Decide which fable to rewrite. Make notes about the fable.

**Directions:** Now it's time to think about your own fable. Look at the fables on page 134 in this book. Make notes about them, or choose two other fables you know. (You could also pick one from page 134 and one new one.) Then write your answers on the lines below.

Answers will vary.

1. One fable I could rewrite is _____

Here is one change I could make.

_____
_____
_____
_____

2. Another fable I could rewrite is _____

Here is one change I could make.

_____
_____
_____
_____

136　Narrative Writing • Fable

---

## Your Own Writing
### Prewriting
### Gather Ideas
Decide which fable to rewrite. Make notes about the fable.

**Directions:** Choose one of the fables you named on page 136. First, write the title of the famous fable. Next, write the title of your fable. Then make notes about who will be in your fable, what will happen, and the lesson your fable teaches.

Answers will vary.

Famous Fable: _____
_____

My Fable: _____
_____

Who is in my fable: _____
_____

What happens: _____
_____
_____
_____

The lesson: _____
_____
_____

 Now go back to Mina's work on page 180 in the Student Edition.

Narrative Writing • Fable　137

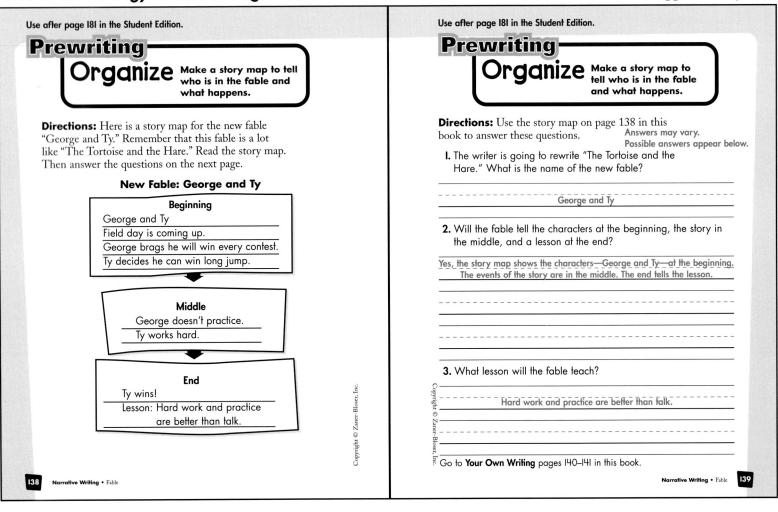

**Prewriting**

**Organize** Make a story map to tell who is in the fable and what happens.

**Directions:** Here is a story map for the new fable "George and Ty." Remember that this fable is a lot like "The Tortoise and the Hare." Read the story map. Then answer the questions on the next page.

**New Fable: George and Ty**

**Beginning**
George and Ty
Field day is coming up.
George brags he will win every contest.
Ty decides he can win long jump.

**Middle**
George doesn't practice.
Ty works hard.

**End**
Ty wins!
Lesson: Hard work and practice are better than talk.

Copyright © Zaner-Bloser, Inc.

**Prewriting**

**Organize** Make a story map to tell who is in the fable and what happens.

**Directions:** Use the story map on page 138 in this book to answer these questions.    Answers may vary. Possible answers appear below.

**1.** The writer is going to rewrite "The Tortoise and the Hare." What is the name of the new fable?

George and Ty

**2.** Will the fable tell the characters at the beginning, the story in the middle, and a lesson at the end?

Yes, the story map shows the characters—George and Ty—at the beginning. The events of the story are in the middle. The end tells the lesson.

**3.** What lesson will the fable teach?

Hard work and practice are better than talk.

Go to **Your Own Writing** pages 140–141 in this book.

Copyright © Zaner-Bloser, Inc.

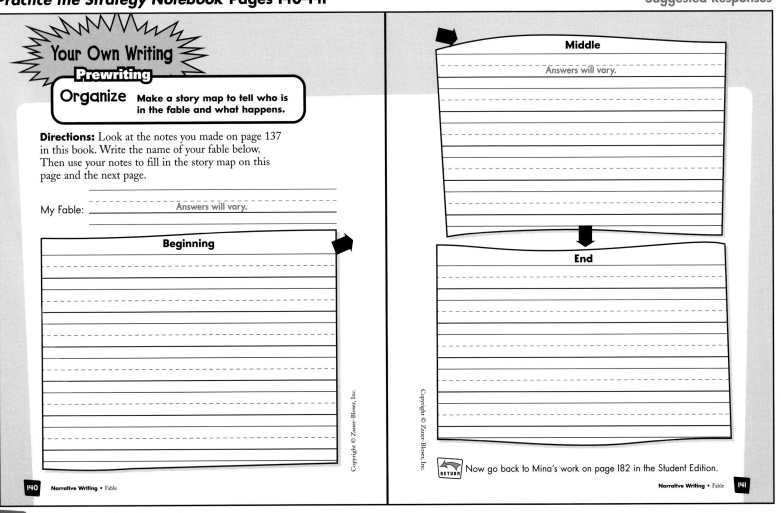

**Your Own Writing**

**Prewriting**

**Organize** Make a story map to tell who is in the fable and what happens.

**Directions:** Look at the notes you made on page 137 in this book. Write the name of your fable below. Then use your notes to fill in the story map on this page and the next page.

My Fable: _____ Answers will vary.

**Beginning**

**Middle**
Answers will vary.

**End**

Now go back to Mina's work on page 182 in the Student Edition.

Copyright © Zaner-Bloser, Inc.

Use after page 183 in the Student Edition.

## Drafting

### Write
Use my story map. Write sentences to tell what happens at the beginning, middle, and end.

**Directions:** Read the draft of "George and Ty" below. Draw a circle around the beginning. Draw a box around the middle. Use a highlighter to show the end. Draw a star beside the lesson.

Field day was coming up. George could run fast and jump high.

He bragged, I will win every contest.
George's best friend was Jimmy.
Little Ty said to his mother, George is not going to win every contest! The long jump is mine!

George never practiced. He was too sure of himself. Ty practiced every day. On some days, he even practiced twice.

Field day finally came. The class went on a trip to Lee Park the week before. George took a big, sloppy leap. Then Ty made a perfect jump. He landed just past George! Practice is more important than talk. ★

Go to **Your Own Writing** pages 143–145 in this book.

Copyright © Zaner-Bloser, Inc.

## Your Own Writing

### Drafting

### Write
Use my story map. Write sentences to tell what happens at the beginning, middle, and end.

**Directions:** Use this page and the next two pages to write the beginning, the middle, and the end of your own fable. Use the story map you made on pages 140–141 in this book to help you. Be sure your fable teaches the reader a lesson at the end.

**My Title:** _____ Answers will vary. _____

**Beginning:** _____

Copyright © Zaner-Bloser, Inc.

---

## Your Own Writing

### Drafting

### Write
Use my story map. Write sentences to tell what happens at the beginning, middle, and end.

**Middle:** _____ Answers will vary. _____

Copyright © Zaner-Bloser, Inc.

**End:** _____

**The Lesson:** _____

RETURN Now go back to Mina's work on page 184 in the Student Edition.

Copyright © Zaner-Bloser, Inc.

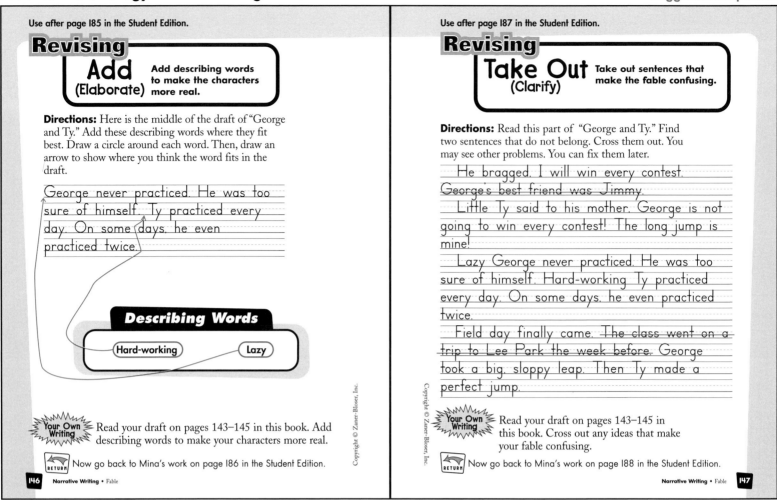

Use after page 185 in the Student Edition.

### Revising
## Add
### (Elaborate)
Add describing words to make the characters more real.

**Directions:** Here is the middle of the draft of "George and Ty." Add these describing words where they fit best. Draw a circle around each word. Then, draw an arrow to show where you think the word fits in the draft.

George never practiced. He was too sure of himself. Ty practiced every day. On some days, he even practiced twice.

### Describing Words
( Hard-working )     ( Lazy )

**Your Own Writing** Read your draft on pages 143–145 in this book. Add describing words to make your characters more real.

**RETURN** Now go back to Mina's work on page 186 in the Student Edition.

146   **Narrative Writing** • Fable

---

Use after page 187 in the Student Edition.

### Revising
## Take Out
### (Clarify)
Take out sentences that make the fable confusing.

**Directions:** Read this part of "George and Ty." Find two sentences that do not belong. Cross them out. You may see other problems. You can fix them later.

He bragged. I will win every contest. ~~George's best friend was Jimmy.~~

Little Ty said to his mother. George is not going to win every contest! The long jump is mine!

Lazy George never practiced. He was too sure of himself. Hard-working Ty practiced every day. On some days, he even practiced twice.

Field day finally came. ~~The class went on a trip to Lee Park the week before.~~ George took a big, sloppy leap. Then Ty made a perfect jump.

**Your Own Writing** Read your draft on pages 143–145 in this book. Cross out any ideas that make your fable confusing.

**RETURN** Now go back to Mina's work on page 188 in the Student Edition.

**Narrative Writing** • Fable   147

---

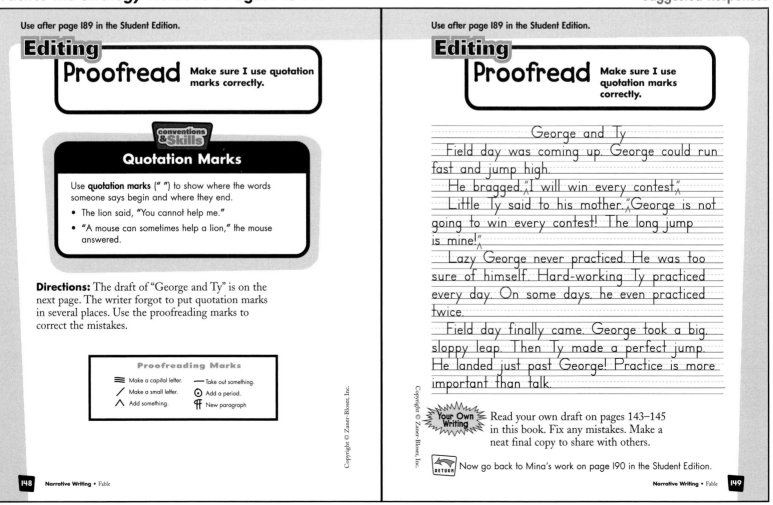

Use after page 189 in the Student Edition.

### Editing
## Proofread
Make sure I use quotation marks correctly.

**conventions & Skills**

### Quotation Marks

Use **quotation marks** (" ") to show where the words someone says begin and where they end.
- The lion said, "You cannot help me."
- "A mouse can sometimes help a lion," the mouse answered.

**Directions:** The draft of "George and Ty" is on the next page. The writer forgot to put quotation marks in several places. Use the proofreading marks to correct the mistakes.

#### Proofreading Marks
≡ Make a capital letter.    — Take out something.
/ Make a small letter.    ⊙ Add a period.
∧ Add something.    ¶ New paragraph.

148   **Narrative Writing** • Fable

---

Use after page 189 in the Student Edition.

### Editing
## Proofread
Make sure I use quotation marks correctly.

George and Ty

Field day was coming up. George could run fast and jump high.

He bragged. "I will win every contest."

Little Ty said to his mother. "George is not going to win every contest! The long jump is mine!"

Lazy George never practiced. He was too sure of himself. Hard-working Ty practiced every day. On some days, he even practiced twice.

Field day finally came. George took a big, sloppy leap. Then Ty made a perfect jump. He landed just past George! Practice is more important than talk.

**Your Own Writing** Read your own draft on pages 143–145 in this book. Fix any mistakes. Make a neat final copy to share with others.

**RETURN** Now go back to Mina's work on page 190 in the Student Edition.

**Narrative Writing** • Fable   149

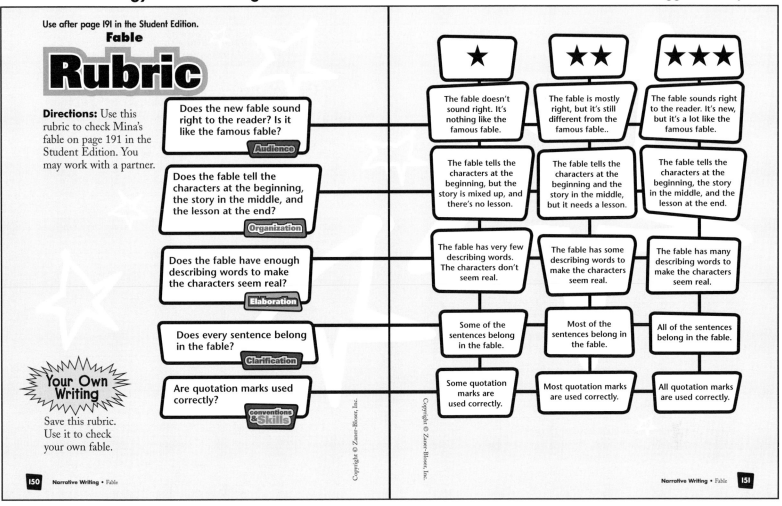

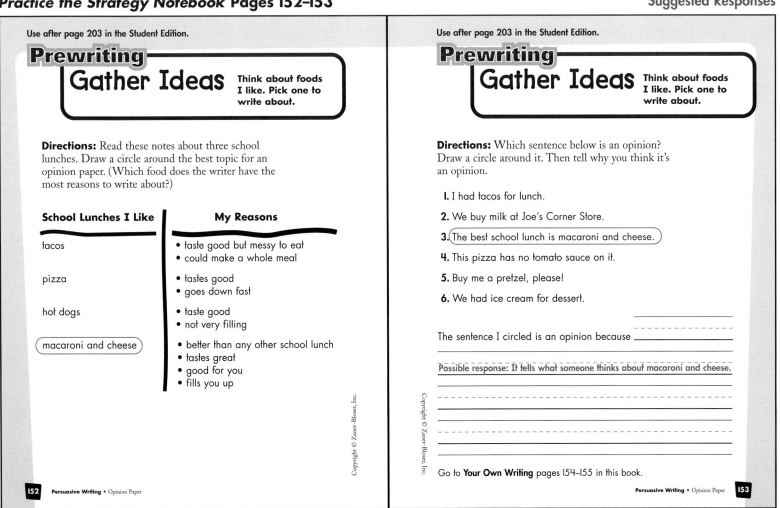

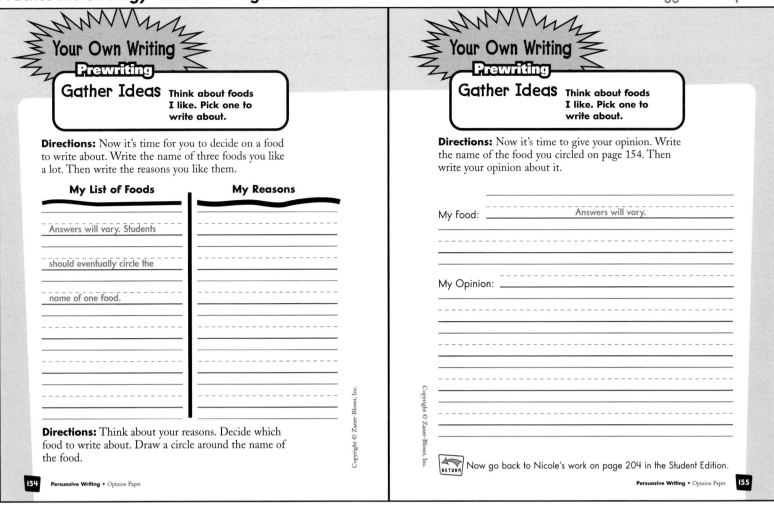

**Your Own Writing**
**Prewriting**
**Gather Ideas** Think about foods I like. Pick one to write about.

**Directions:** Now it's time for you to decide on a food to write about. Write the name of three foods you like a lot. Then write the reasons you like them.

**My List of Foods** | **My Reasons**

Answers will vary. Students
should eventually circle the
name of one food.

**Directions:** Think about your reasons. Decide which food to write about. Draw a circle around the name of the food.

154  Persuasive Writing • Opinion Paper

**Your Own Writing**
**Prewriting**
**Gather Ideas** Think about foods I like. Pick one to write about.

**Directions:** Now it's time to give your opinion. Write the name of the food you circled on page 154. Then write your opinion about it.

My Food: _____ Answers will vary. _____

My Opinion: _____

Now go back to Nicole's work on page 204 in the Student Edition.

Persuasive Writing • Opinion Paper  155

---

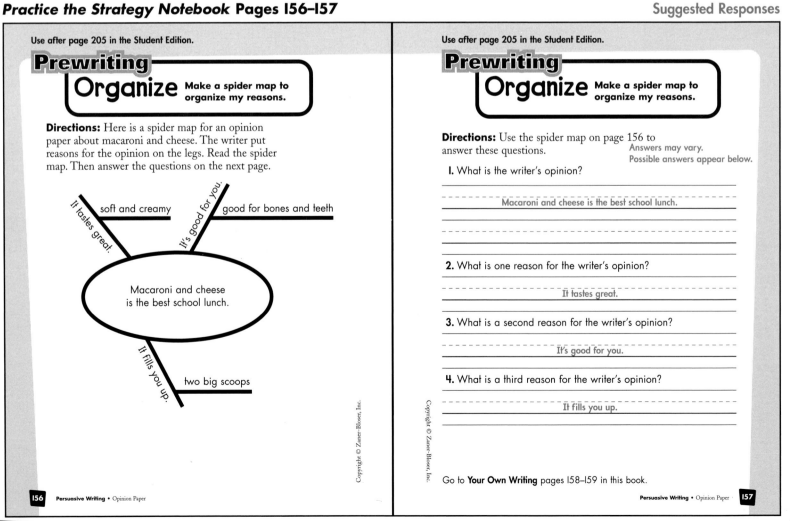

Use after page 205 in the Student Edition.

**Prewriting**
**Organize** Make a spider map to organize my reasons.

**Directions:** Here is a spider map for an opinion paper about macaroni and cheese. The writer put reasons for the opinion on the legs. Read the spider map. Then answer the questions on the next page.

It tastes great.  —  soft and creamy
It's good for you.  —  good for bones and teeth

Macaroni and cheese is the best school lunch.

It fills you up.  —  two big scoops

156  Persuasive Writing • Opinion Paper

Use after page 205 in the Student Edition.

**Prewriting**
**Organize** Make a spider map to organize my reasons.

**Directions:** Use the spider map on page 156 to answer these questions.

Answers may vary.
Possible answers appear below.

1. What is the writer's opinion?

Macaroni and cheese is the best school lunch.

2. What is one reason for the writer's opinion?

It tastes great.

3. What is a second reason for the writer's opinion?

It's good for you.

4. What is a third reason for the writer's opinion?

It fills you up.

Go to **Your Own Writing** pages 158–159 in this book.

Persuasive Writing • Opinion Paper  157

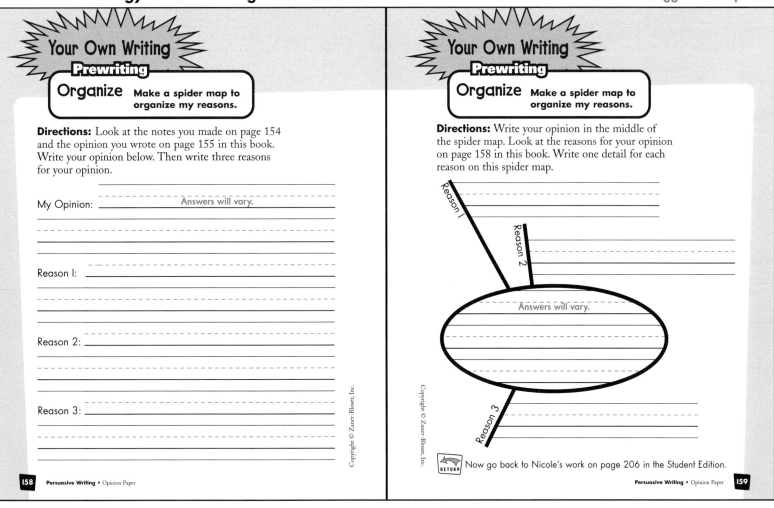

**Your Own Writing**
**Prewriting**
**Organize** Make a spider map to organize my reasons.

**Directions:** Look at the notes you made on page 154 and the opinion you wrote on page 155 in this book. Write your opinion below. Then write three reasons for your opinion.

My Opinion: _____ Answers will vary. _____

Reason 1: _____

Reason 2: _____

Reason 3: _____

Copyright © Zaner-Bloser, Inc.

158   Persuasive Writing • Opinion Paper

**Your Own Writing**
**Prewriting**
**Organize** Make a spider map to organize my reasons.

**Directions:** Write your opinion in the middle of the spider map. Look at the reasons for your opinion on page 158 in this book. Write one detail for each reason on this spider map.

Reason 1

Reason 2

Answers will vary.

Reason 3

Copyright © Zaner-Bloser, Inc.

RETURN Now go back to Nicole's work on page 206 in the Student Edition.

Persuasive Writing • Opinion Paper   159

Use after page 207 in the Student Edition.

**Drafting**
**Write** Use my spider map. Write one paragraph about each spider leg.

**Directions:** Here is the writer's opinion about macaroni and cheese. Look at the spider map on page 156 in this book. Write the writer's reasons for this opinion as sentences on the lines below.

The Writer's Opinion: Macaroni and cheese is the best school lunch.

My Reason 1: _____ It tastes great. _____

My Reason 2: _____ It's good for you. _____

My Reason 3: _____ It fills you up. _____

Go to **Your Own Writing** pages 161–163 in this book.

Copyright © Zaner-Bloser, Inc.

160   Persuasive Writing • Opinion Paper

**Your Own Writing**
**Drafting**
**Write** Use my spider map. Write one paragraph about each spider leg.

**Directions:** Use this page and the next two pages to write a draft of your own opinion paper. Use the spider map you made on page 159 in this book to help you. Use this page for your first paragraph. Write your opinion and your first reason with details.

My opinion: _____ Answers will vary. _____

My Reason 1: _____

Copyright © Zaner-Bloser, Inc.

Persuasive Writing • Opinion Paper   161

**Your Own Writing**

**Drafting**

Write　Use my spider map. Write one paragraph about each spider leg.

**Directions:** Use this page for your second paragraph. Write your second reason with details.

My Reason 2:＿＿＿＿Answers will vary.＿＿＿＿

**Directions:** Use this page for your third paragraph. Write your third reason with details.

My Reason 3:＿＿＿＿Answers will vary.＿＿＿＿

Now go back to Nicole's work on page 208 in the Student Edition.

162　Persuasive Writing • Opinion Paper

163　Persuasive Writing • Opinion Paper

---

Use after page 209 in the Student Edition.

**Revising**

**Add** (Elaborate)　Add details to explain my reasons.

**Directions:** Read this part of a draft about macaroni and cheese. Here are some more details that explain the reasons for the writer's opinion. Put the details in the draft where you think they fit best. Draw an arrow to show where you want to add each detail. You may see mistakes in this draft. You will fix them later.

Locations of details may vary.

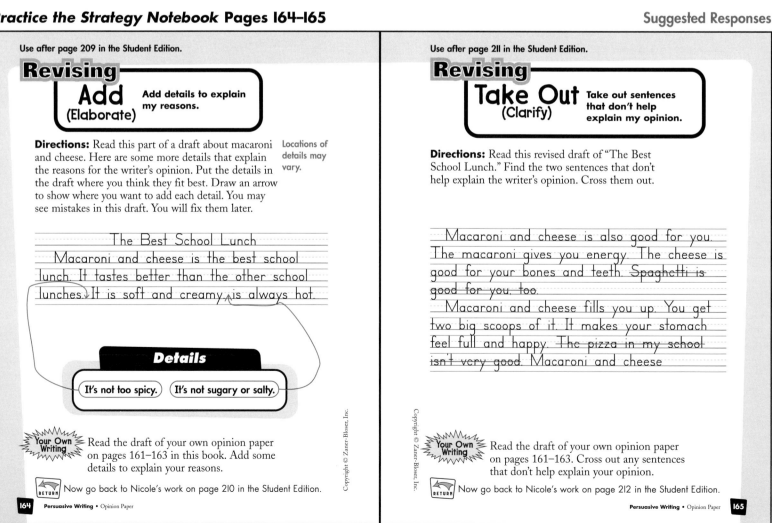

The Best School Lunch
Macaroni and cheese is the best school lunch. It tastes better than the other school lunches. It is soft and creamy. is always hot.

**Details**

It's not too spicy.　It's not sugary or salty.

**Your Own Writing** Read the draft of your own opinion paper on pages 161–163 in this book. Add some details to explain your reasons.

Now go back to Nicole's work on page 210 in the Student Edition.

Use after page 211 in the Student Edition.

**Revising**

**Take Out** (Clarify)　Take out sentences that don't help explain my opinion.

**Directions:** Read this revised draft of "The Best School Lunch." Find the two sentences that don't help explain the writer's opinion. Cross them out.

Macaroni and cheese is also good for you. The macaroni gives you energy. The cheese is good for your bones and teeth. ~~Spaghetti is good for you, too.~~
Macaroni and cheese fills you up. You get two big scoops of it. It makes your stomach feel full and happy. ~~The pizza in my school isn't very good.~~ Macaroni and cheese

**Your Own Writing** Read the draft of your own opinion paper on pages 161–163. Cross out any sentences that don't help explain your opinion.

Now go back to Nicole's work on page 212 in the Student Edition.

164　Persuasive Writing • Opinion Paper

165　Persuasive Writing • Opinion Paper

Use after page 213 in the Student Edition.

## Editing
### Proofread
Make sure every sentence has a subject and a predicate.

#### conventions & Skills
### Subjects and Predicates

The **subject** of a sentence tells who or what does or is something. The **predicate** tells what the subject does or is.

| Subject | Predicate |
|---|---|
| My mother | makes rice and beans a lot. |
| My favorite meal | is rice and beans! |

**Directions:** The revised draft of "The Best School Lunch" is on the next page.

One sentence is missing the subject **It**.

One sentence is missing the predicate **is the best lunch you can buy!**

Use the proofreading marks to add this subject and this predicate where they belong.

#### Proofreading Marks
- ≡ Make a capital letter.
- / Make a small letter.
- ∧ Add something.
- ⎯ Take out something.
- ⊙ Add a period.
- ¶ New paragraph

166 **Persuasive Writing** • Opinion Paper

*Copyright © Zaner-Bloser, Inc.*

## Editing
### Proofread
Make sure every sentence has a subject and a predicate.

The Best School Lunch
Macaroni and cheese is the best school lunch. It tastes better than the other school lunches. It's not too spicy. It is soft and creamy. It's not sugary or salty. It is always hot.
Macaroni and cheese is also good for you. The macaroni gives you energy. The cheese is good for your bones and teeth.
Macaroni and cheese fills you up. You get two big scoops of it. It makes your stomach feel full and happy. Macaroni and cheese

is the best lunch
you can buy!

**Your Own Writing** Read the draft of your own opinion paper on pages 161–163 in this book. Fix any mistakes. Make a neat final copy to share with others.

RETURN Now go back to Nicole's work on page 214 in the Student Edition.

**Persuasive Writing** • Opinion Paper 167

*Copyright © Zaner-Bloser, Inc.*

Use after page 215 in the Student Edition.

### Opinion Paper
# Rubric

**Directions:** Use this rubric to check Nicole's opinion paper on page 215 in the Student Edition. You may work with a partner.

| | ★ | ★★ | ★★★ |
|---|---|---|---|
| Does the paper clearly state the writer's opinion for the reader? **Audience** | The paper doesn't state the writer's opinion for the reader. | The paper states the writer's opinion for the reader, but it's not clear. | The paper clearly states the writer's opinion for the reader. |
| Is there one paragraph for each reason? **Organization** | There is only one paragraph for all the reasons. | There are two paragraphs, but the reasons are all mixed up. | There is one paragraph for each reason. |
| Are there enough details to explain each reason? **Elaboration** | There are few details to explain the reasons. | There are some details to explain the reasons. | There are many details to explain all of the reasons. |
| Does every sentence help explain the writer's opinion? **Clarification** | Some of the sentences help explain the writers opinion. | Most of the sentences help explain the writers opinion. | All of the sentences help explain the writers opinion. |
| Does every sentence have a subject and a predicate? **conventions & Skills** | Some sentences have a subject and a predicate. | Most sentences have a subject and a predicate. | All sentences have a subject and a predicate. |

**Your Own Writing** Save this rubric. Use it to check your own opinion paper.

168 **Persuasive Writing** • Opinion Paper

*Copyright © Zaner-Bloser, Inc.*

**Persuasive Writing** • Opinion Paper 169

Use after page 225 in the Student Edition.

## Prewriting
# Gather Ideas
Think about my opinions on different topics. Write some reasons for my opinions. Choose a topic.

**Directions:** Draw a circle around the sentence that gives an opinion about each topic. Remember, an opinion tells what someone thinks or believes.

### Topic: Bicycles

1. My bike has a mirror and a bell.
2. It is not safe to ride your bike on Main Street.
3. I learned to ride my bike a year ago.

### Topic: My Apartment Building

1. My apartment building is a great place to live.
2. My apartment building is on the corner of Elm Street and Park Road.
3. There are fifty apartments in my building.

### Topic: The Children's Museum

1. You can get into the Children's Museum free on Tuesdays.
2. The Children's Museum is downtown.
3. Everyone should visit the Children's Museum.

Copyright © Zaner-Bloser, Inc.

---

Use after page 225 in the Student Edition.

## Prewriting
# Gather Ideas
Think about my opinions on different topics. Write some reasons for my opinions. Choose a topic.

**Directions:** Read the opinion and the notes below. Draw circles around three notes that would be good reasons to explain the opinion below. Use the lines to write why you think so.

Answers will vary. Possible answers appear below.

My Opinion: Everyone Should Visit the Children's Museum.

It's fun.

Sarah went there last week.

You can learn a lot.

Jamey told me about it.

Everyone will like it.

Go to **Your Own Writing** pages 172–173 in this book.

Copyright © Zaner-Bloser, Inc.

---

## Your Own Writing
### Prewriting
# Gather Ideas
Think about my opinions on different topics. Write some reasons for my opinions. Choose a topic.

**Directions:** Now it's time for you to decide on a topic to write about. Write one topic. Then write an opinion about that topic. Write some reasons for your opinion.

My Topic: _____ Answers will vary.

My Opinion: _____

My Reasons: _____

Copyright © Zaner-Bloser, Inc.

---

## Your Own Writing
### Prewriting
# Gather Ideas
Think about my opinions on different topics. Write some reasons for my opinions. Choose a topic.

**Directions:** Write another topic. Then write your opinion about the topic. Write some reasons for your opinion.

My Topic: _____ Answers will vary.

My Opinion: _____

My Reasons: _____

**Directions:** Draw a circle around the topic you like best. Then draw a circle around the opinion that you wrote for that topic.

  Now go back to Jonathan's work on page 226 in the Student Edition.

Copyright © Zaner-Bloser, Inc.

---

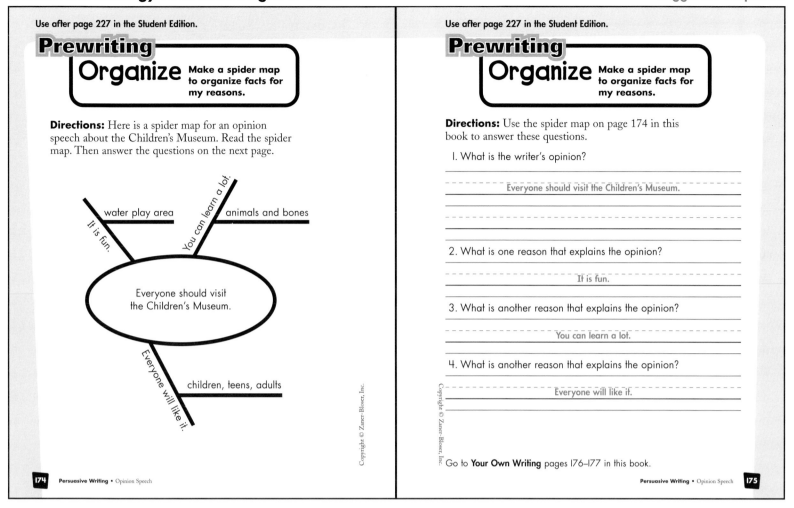

Use after page 227 in the Student Edition.

**Prewriting**

**Organize** Make a spider map to organize facts for my reasons.

**Directions:** Here is a spider map for an opinion speech about the Children's Museum. Read the spider map. Then answer the questions on the next page.

- water play area
- You can learn a lot.
- animals and bones
- It is fun.
- Everyone will like it.
- children, teens, adults

Everyone should visit the Children's Museum.

174  Persuasive Writing • Opinion Speech

Copyright © Zaner-Bloser, Inc.

---

Use after page 227 in the Student Edition.

**Prewriting**

**Organize** Make a spider map to organize facts for my reasons.

**Directions:** Use the spider map on page 174 in this book to answer these questions.

1. What is the writer's opinion?

   Everyone should visit the Children's Museum.

2. What is one reason that explains the opinion?

   It is fun.

3. What is another reason that explains the opinion?

   You can learn a lot.

4. What is another reason that explains the opinion?

   Everyone will like it.

Go to **Your Own Writing** pages 176–177 in this book.

Persuasive Writing • Opinion Speech  175

Copyright © Zaner-Bloser, Inc.

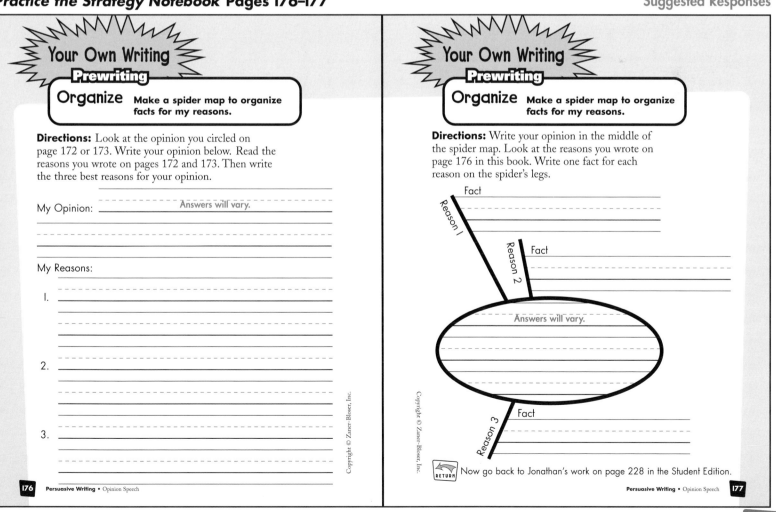

**Your Own Writing**

**Prewriting**

**Organize** Make a spider map to organize facts for my reasons.

**Directions:** Look at the opinion you circled on page 172 or 173. Write your opinion below. Read the reasons you wrote on pages 172 and 173. Then write the three best reasons for your opinion.

My Opinion: _____ Answers will vary. _____

My Reasons:

1. _____

2. _____

3. _____

176  Persuasive Writing • Opinion Speech

Copyright © Zaner-Bloser, Inc.

---

**Your Own Writing**

**Prewriting**

**Organize** Make a spider map to organize facts for my reasons.

**Directions:** Write your opinion in the middle of the spider map. Look at the reasons you wrote on page 176 in this book. Write one fact for each reason on the spider's legs.

- Reason 1 — Fact
- Reason 2 — Fact
- Reason 3 — Fact

Answers will vary.

RETURN Now go back to Jonathan's work on page 228 in the Student Edition.

Persuasive Writing • Opinion Speech  177

Copyright © Zaner-Bloser, Inc.

Use after page 229 in the Student Edition.

## Drafting
### Write
Use my spider map. Write one paragraph about each spider leg.

**Directions:** Here is the writer's opinion about The Children's Museum. Look at the spider map on page 174 in this book. Write each fact for the writer's reasons as a sentence on the lines below.

Writer's Opinion: Everyone should visit the Children's Museum.

Reason 1: It is fun

Fact: _____ It has a water play area. _____
_____

Reason 2: You can learn a lot.

Fact: _____ You can learn about animals and their bones. _____
_____

Reason 3: Everyone will like it.

Fact: _____ Children, teens, and adults all like it. _____
_____

Go to **Your Own Writing** pages 179–181 in this book.

## Your Own Writing
### Drafting
### Write
Use my spider map. Write one paragraph about each spider leg.

**Directions:** Use this page and the next two pages to write the first draft of your own opinion speech. Use the spider map you made on page 177 in this book to help you. Use this page for your first paragraph. Write your opinion and your first reason with facts.

My Opinion: _____ Answers will vary. _____

Reason 1: _____
_____
_____
_____
_____
_____

---

## Your Own Writing
### Drafting
### Write
Use my spider map. Write one paragraph about each spider leg.

**Directions:** Use this page for your second paragraph. Write your second reason with facts.

Reason 2: _____ Answers will vary. _____
_____
_____
_____
_____
_____
_____
_____

**Directions:** Use this page for your third paragraph. Write your third reason with facts.

Reason 3: _____ Answers will vary. _____
_____
_____
_____
_____
_____
_____
_____
_____
_____

Now go back to Jonathan's work on page 230 in the Student Edition.

Use after page 231 in the Student Edition.

## Revising
### Add
### (Elaborate)
**Add facts to explain my reasons.**

Answers may vary. Possible responses appear below.

**Directions:** Read this part of an opinion speech about the Children's Museum. Here are some more facts that explain the reasons for the writer's opinion. Draw an arrow to show where you want to add each fact.

**Facts**

It has walls to climb.

You learn about bones, too.

Everyone should visit the Children's Museum. It is fun! has a water play area. The Science Museum has that, too. You learn a lot at the Children's Museum. You learn about animals and their homes. You learn about the sun.

**Your Own Writing** Read the draft of your opinion speech on pages 179–181 in this book. Can you add any more facts to explain your reasons?

**RETURN** Now go back to Jonathan's work on page 232 in the Student Edition.

Copyright © Zaner-Bloser, Inc.

---

Use after page 233 in the Student Edition.

## Revising
### Take Out
### (Clarify)
**Take out sentences that don't help explain my opinion.**

**Directions:** Read this revised draft of "The Children's Museum." Find two sentences that don't help explain the opinion. Cross them out.

    The Children's Museum

    Everyone should visit the Children's Museum. It is fun! It has walls to climb. has a water play area. ~~The Science Museum has that, too.~~ You learn a lot at the Children's Museum. You learn about animals and their homes. You learn about the sun. You learn about bones, too. ~~You learn about rocks at the Science Museum.~~

    Everyone will like the Children's Museum. It has two floors for children. It has a floor for teens. Even adults find great things to do. The Children's Museum

**Your Own Writing** Read your draft on pages 179–181. Cross out any sentences that don't help explain your opinion.

**RETURN** Now go back to Jonathan's work on page 234 in the Student Edition.

Copyright © Zaner-Bloser, Inc.

---

Use after page 235 in the Student Edition.

## Editing
### Proofread
**Make sure every sentence has a subject and a predicate.**

**Conventions & Skills**

### Subjects and Predicates

The **subject** of a sentence tells who or what does or is something.
The **predicate** tells what the subject does or is. The predicate has the verb of the sentence.

| Subject | Predicate |
|---|---|
| We | slide down fast. |
| The swings | need paint. |
| The park | is pretty. |

**Directions:** The revised draft of "The Children's Museum" is on the next page. Find two sentences that are not complete.

One sentence is missing the subject **It**.

The other sentence is missing the predicate **has something for everyone**.

Use the proofreading marks to add this subject and this predicate where they belong.

**Proofreading Marks**

≡ Make a capital letter.
/ Make a small letter.
∧ Add something.
— Take out something.
⊙ Add a period.
¶ New paragraph

Copyright © Zaner-Bloser, Inc.

---

## Editing
### Proofread
**Make sure every sentence has a subject and a predicate.**

    The Children's Museum

    Everyone should visit the Children's Museum. It is fun! It has walls to climb. It has a water play area.

    You learn a lot at the Children's Museum. You learn about animals and their homes. You learn about the sun. You learn about bones, too.

    Everyone will like the Children's Museum. It has two floors for children. It has a floor for teens. Even adults find great things to do. The Children's Museum has something for everyone.

**Your Own Writing** Read your draft on pages 179–181. Fix any mistakes. Make a neat final copy. Practice reading it aloud.

**RETURN** Now go back to Jonathan's work on page 236 in the Student Edition.

Copyright © Zaner-Bloser, Inc.

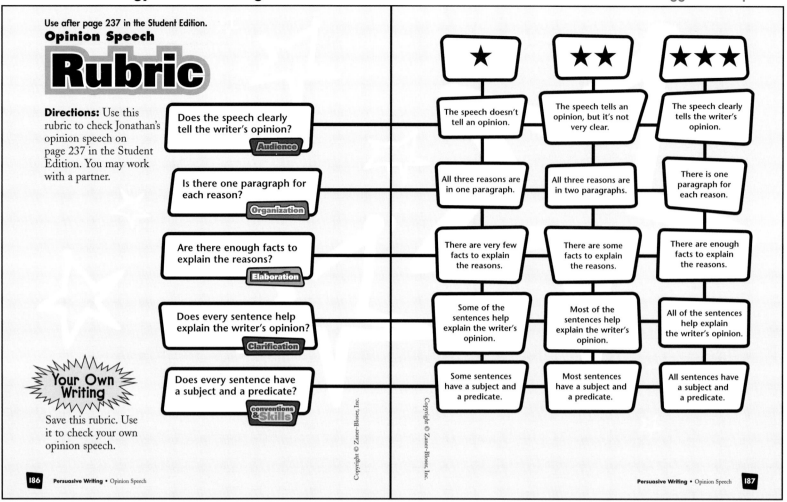

Use after page 237 in the Student Edition.
## Opinion Speech
# Rubric

**Directions:** Use this rubric to check Jonathan's opinion speech on page 237 in the Student Edition. You may work with a partner.

| | ★ | ★★ | ★★★ |
|---|---|---|---|
| Does the speech clearly tell the writer's opinion? **Audience** | The speech doesn't tell an opinion. | The speech tells an opinion, but it's not very clear. | The speech clearly tells the writer's opinion. |
| Is there one paragraph for each reason? **Organization** | All three reasons are in one paragraph. | All three reasons are in two paragraphs. | There is one paragraph for each reason. |
| Are there enough facts to explain the reasons? **Elaboration** | There are very few facts to explain the reasons. | There are some facts to explain the reasons. | There are enough facts to explain the reasons. |
| Does every sentence help explain the writer's opinion? **Clarification** | Some of the sentences help explain the writer's opinion. | Most of the sentences help explain the writer's opinion. | All of the sentences help explain the writer's opinion. |
| Does every sentence have a subject and a predicate? **Conventions & Skills** | Some sentences have a subject and a predicate. | Most sentences have a subject and a predicate. | All sentences have a subject and a predicate. |

**Your Own Writing**

Save this rubric. Use it to check your own opinion speech.

186  Persuasive Writing • Opinion Speech

Copyright © Zaner-Bloser, Inc.

Copyright © Zaner-Bloser, Inc.

Persuasive Writing • Opinion Speech  187

---

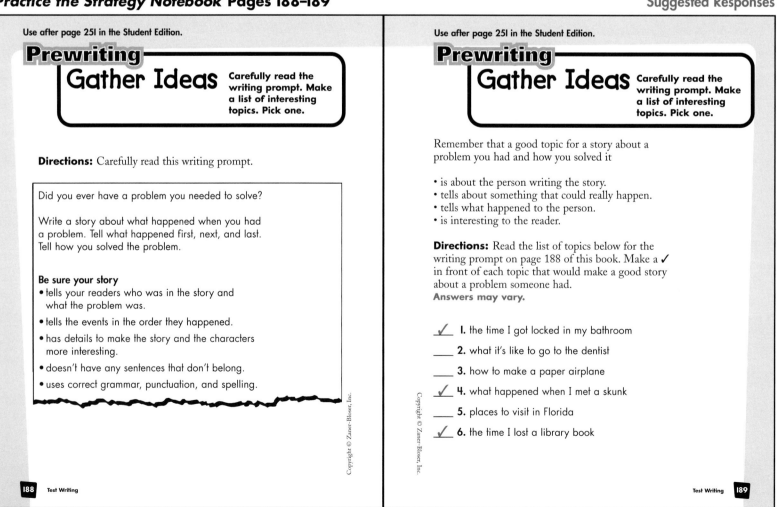

Use after page 251 in the Student Edition.
## Prewriting
# Gather Ideas
Carefully read the writing prompt. Make a list of interesting topics. Pick one.

**Directions:** Carefully read this writing prompt.

> Did you ever have a problem you needed to solve?
>
> Write a story about what happened when you had a problem. Tell what happened first, next, and last. Tell how you solved the problem.
>
> **Be sure your story**
> • tells your readers who was in the story and what the problem was.
> • tells the events in the order they happened.
> • has details to make the story and the characters more interesting.
> • doesn't have any sentences that don't belong.
> • uses correct grammar, punctuation, and spelling.

188  Test Writing

Use after page 251 in the Student Edition.
## Prewriting
# Gather Ideas
Carefully read the writing prompt. Make a list of interesting topics. Pick one.

Remember that a good topic for a story about a problem you had and how you solved it

• is about the person writing the story.
• tells about something that could really happen.
• tells what happened to the person.
• is interesting to the reader.

**Directions:** Read the list of topics below for the writing prompt on page 188 of this book. Make a ✓ in front of each topic that would make a good story about a problem someone had.
**Answers may vary.**

✓ **1.** the time I got locked in my bathroom

____ **2.** what it's like to go to the dentist

____ **3.** how to make a paper airplane

✓ **4.** what happened when I met a skunk

____ **5.** places to visit in Florida

✓ **6.** the time I lost a library book

Copyright © Zaner-Bloser, Inc.

Test Writing  189

---

Use after page 251 in the Student Edition.

## Prewriting

### Gather Ideas
Carefully read the writing prompt. Make a list of interesting topics. Pick one.

**Directions:** Use the list of topics on page 189 in this book to answer the questions on this page and the next page.

1. Which topics on the list would make a good story about how you solved a problem?

<u>Possible answers: numbers 1, 4, and 6</u>

2. Why are those topics good for a story about how someone solved a problem?

<u>Answers will vary. Sample answer: They are all about something that happened to the writer. They are all about solving a problem.</u>

Copyright © Zaner-Bloser, Inc.

190   Test Writing

---

Use after page 251 in the Student Edition.

## Prewriting

### Gather Ideas
Carefully read the writing prompt. Make a list of interesting topics. Pick one.

3. Which topic do you like best?

<u>Answers will vary.</u>
<u>Possible answer: Number 1—the time I got locked in my bathroom</u>

4. Why is that topic interesting to you?

<u>Answers will vary. Possible answer: It really happened to me one time.</u>

Copyright © Zaner-Bloser, Inc.

Go to **Your Own Writing** pages 192–193 in this book.

Test Writing   191

---

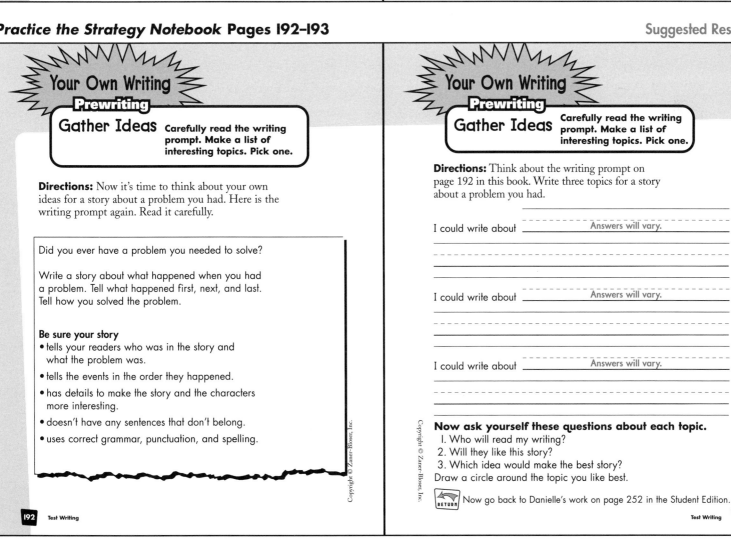

### Your Own Writing
#### Prewriting
### Gather Ideas
Carefully read the writing prompt. Make a list of interesting topics. Pick one.

**Directions:** Now it's time to think about your own ideas for a story about a problem you had. Here is the writing prompt again. Read it carefully.

Did you ever have a problem you needed to solve?

Write a story about what happened when you had a problem. Tell what happened first, next, and last. Tell how you solved the problem.

**Be sure your story**
• tells your readers who was in the story and what the problem was.
• tells the events in the order they happened.
• has details to make the story and the characters more interesting.
• doesn't have any sentences that don't belong.
• uses correct grammar, punctuation, and spelling.

Copyright © Zaner-Bloser, Inc.

192   Test Writing

---

### Your Own Writing
#### Prewriting
### Gather Ideas
Carefully read the writing prompt. Make a list of interesting topics. Pick one.

**Directions:** Think about the writing prompt on page 192 in this book. Write three topics for a story about a problem you had.

I could write about   <u>Answers will vary.</u>

I could write about   <u>Answers will vary.</u>

I could write about   <u>Answers will vary.</u>

**Now ask yourself these questions about each topic.**
1. Who will read my writing?
2. Will they like this story?
3. Which idea would make the best story?
Draw a circle around the topic you like best.

RETURN Now go back to Danielle's work on page 252 in the Student Edition.

Copyright © Zaner-Bloser, Inc.

Test Writing   193

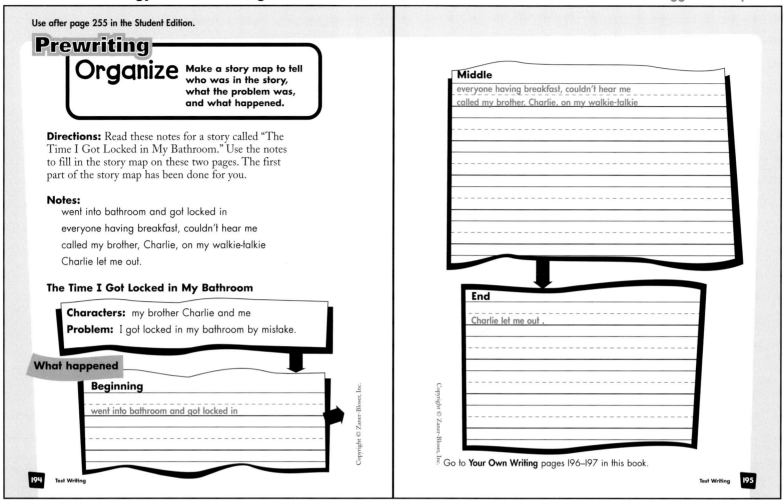

Use after page 255 in the Student Edition.

# Prewriting

## Organize
Make a story map to tell who was in the story, what the problem was, and what happened.

**Directions:** Read these notes for a story called "The Time I Got Locked in My Bathroom." Use the notes to fill in the story map on these two pages. The first part of the story map has been done for you.

**Notes:**
went into bathroom and got locked in
everyone having breakfast, couldn't hear me
called my brother, Charlie, on my walkie-talkie
Charlie let me out.

**The Time I Got Locked in My Bathroom**

**Characters:** my brother Charlie and me
**Problem:** I got locked in my bathroom by mistake.

**What happened**

**Beginning**
went into bathroom and got locked in

**Middle**
everyone having breakfast, couldn't hear me
called my brother, Charlie, on my walkie-talkie

**End**
Charlie let me out .

Go to **Your Own Writing** pages 196–197 in this book.

Copyright © Zaner-Bloser, Inc.

194  Test Writing

195  Test Writing

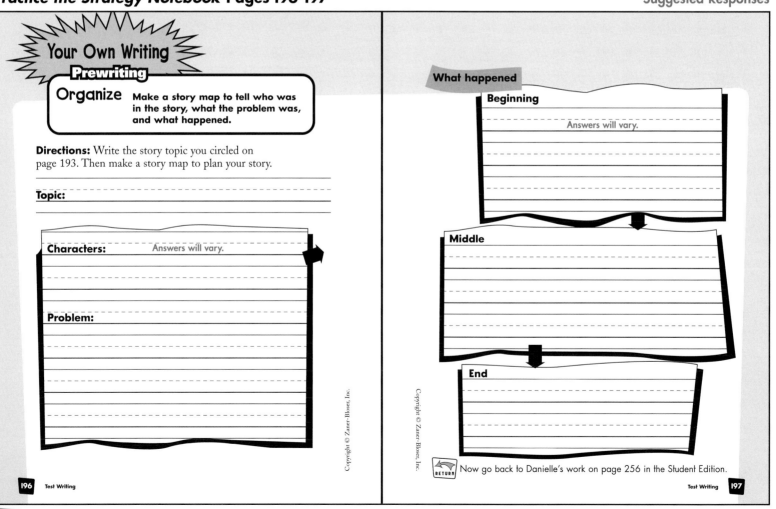

# Your Own Writing
## Prewriting

### Organize
Make a story map to tell who was in the story, what the problem was, and what happened.

**Directions:** Write the story topic you circled on page 193. Then make a story map to plan your story.

**Topic:** _____

**Characters:**    Answers will vary.

**Problem:**

**What happened**

**Beginning**
Answers will vary.

**Middle**

**End**

Now go back to Danielle's work on page 256 in the Student Edition.

Copyright © Zaner-Bloser, Inc.

196  Test Writing

197  Test Writing

Use after page 261 in the Student Edition.

## Drafting
### Write
Use my story map. Write sentences to tell what happened at the beginning, middle, and end, and how the problem was solved.

**Directions:** Look back at the story map for "The Time I Got Locked in My Bathroom" on pages 194–195. Use the story map to write one sentence to tell what happened at the beginning of the story. Write two sentences to tell what happened in the middle of the story. Write one sentence to tell what happened at the end of the story.

**The Time I Got Locked in My Bathroom**

One morning, I went into my bathroom to brush my teeth and got

locked in. Everyone was having breakfast and couldn't hear me. I called

my brother, Charlie, on my walkie-talkie. Charlie came upstairs and let

me out of the bathroom.

Answers will vary.

Go to **Your Own Writing** pages 200–201 in this book.

198   Test Writing        Test Writing   199

---

## Your Own Writing
### Drafting
#### Write
Use my story map. Write sentences to tell what happened at the beginning, middle, and end, and how the problem was solved.

**Directions:** Use this page and the next page to write a draft of your own story about a problem you had. Use your story map on pages 196–197 to help you.

Answers will vary.

Answers will vary.

Now go back to Danielle's work on page 262 in the Student Edition.

200   Test Writing        Test Writing   201

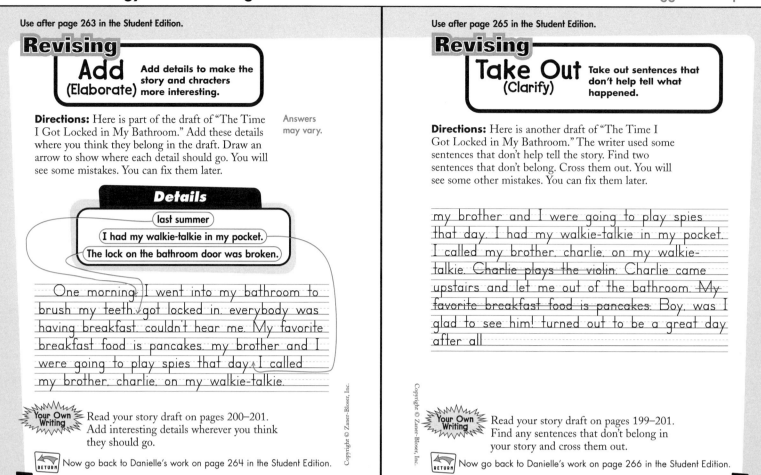

Use after page 263 in the Student Edition.

### Revising
## Add
**(Elaborate)** Add details to make the story and chracters more interesting.

**Directions:** Here is part of the draft of "The Time I Got Locked in My Bathroom." Add these details where you think they belong in the draft. Draw an arrow to show where each detail should go. You will see some mistakes. You can fix them later.

Answers may vary.

**Details**
- last summer
- I had my walkie-talkie in my pocket.
- The lock on the bathroom door was broken.

One morning, I went into my bathroom to brush my teeth. got locked in. everybody was having breakfast. couldn't hear me. My favorite breakfast food is pancakes. my brother and I were going to play spies that day. I called my brother, charlie, on my walkie-talkie.

**Your Own Writing** Read your story draft on pages 200–201. Add interesting details wherever you think they should go.

**RETURN** Now go back to Danielle's work on page 264 in the Student Edition.

202 Test Writing

---

Use after page 265 in the Student Edition.

### Revising
## Take Out
**(Clarify)** Take out sentences that don't help tell what happened.

**Directions:** Here is another draft of "The Time I Got Locked in My Bathroom." The writer used some sentences that don't help tell the story. Find two sentences that don't belong. Cross them out. You will see some other mistakes. You can fix them later.

my brother and I were going to play spies that day. I had my walkie-talkie in my pocket. I called my brother, charlie, on my walkie-talkie. ~~Charlie plays the violin.~~ Charlie came upstairs and let me out of the bathroom. ~~My favorite breakfast food is pancakes.~~ Boy, was I glad to see him! turned out to be a great day after all

**Your Own Writing** Read your story draft on pages 199–201. Find any sentences that don't belong in your story and cross them out.

**RETURN** Now go back to Danielle's work on page 266 in the Student Edition.

203 Test Writing

---

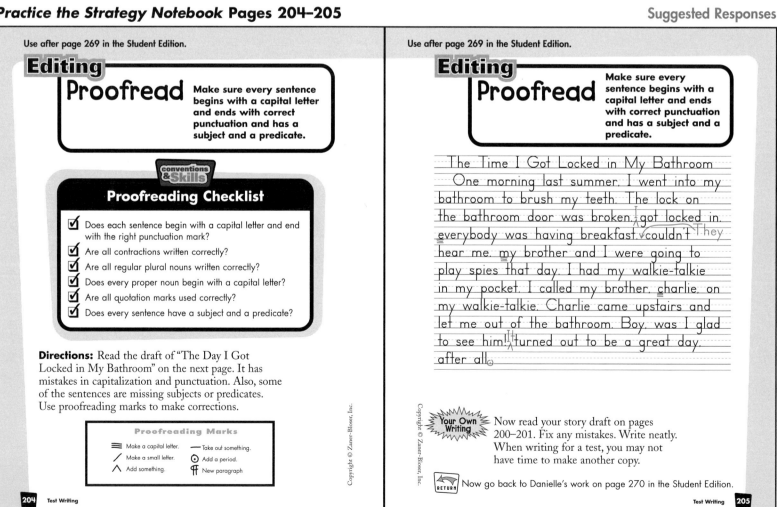

Use after page 269 in the Student Edition.

### Editing
## Proofread
Make sure every sentence begins with a capital letter and ends with correct punctuation and has a subject and a predicate.

**conventions & Skills**

### Proofreading Checklist

- ☑ Does each sentence begin with a capital letter and end with the right punctuation mark?
- ☑ Are all contractions written correctly?
- ☑ Are all regular plural nouns written correctly?
- ☑ Does every proper noun begin with a capital letter?
- ☑ Are all quotation marks used correctly?
- ☑ Does every sentence have a subject and a predicate?

**Directions:** Read the draft of "The Day I Got Locked in My Bathroom" on the next page. It has mistakes in capitalization and punctuation. Also, some of the sentences are missing subjects or predicates. Use proofreading marks to make corrections.

**Proofreading Marks**
- ≡ Make a capital letter.
- / Make a small letter.
- ∧ Add something.
- — Take out something.
- ⊙ Add a period.
- ¶ New paragraph

204 Test Writing

---

Use after page 269 in the Student Edition.

### Editing
## Proofread
Make sure every sentence begins with a capital letter and ends with correct punctuation and has a subject and a predicate.

The Time I Got Locked in My Bathroom
One morning last summer, I went into my bathroom to brush my teeth. The lock on the bathroom door was broken. got locked in. everybody was having breakfast. couldn't hear me. my brother and I were going to play spies that day. I had my walkie-talkie in my pocket. I called my brother, charlie, on my walkie-talkie. Charlie came upstairs and let me out of the bathroom. Boy, was I glad to see him! turned out to be a great day after all.

**Your Own Writing** Now read your story draft on pages 200–201. Fix any mistakes. Write neatly. When writing for a test, you may not have time to make another copy.

**RETURN** Now go back to Danielle's work on page 270 in the Student Edition.

205 Test Writing

---

Use after page 271 in the Student Edition.

**Test Writing**

# Rubric

**Directions:** This rubric was made from the Scoring Guide on page 250 in the Student Edition. Use it to check Danielle's story on pages 268–269 in the Student Edition. You may work with a partner.

**Your Own Writing**

Save this rubric. Use it to check your own writing test.

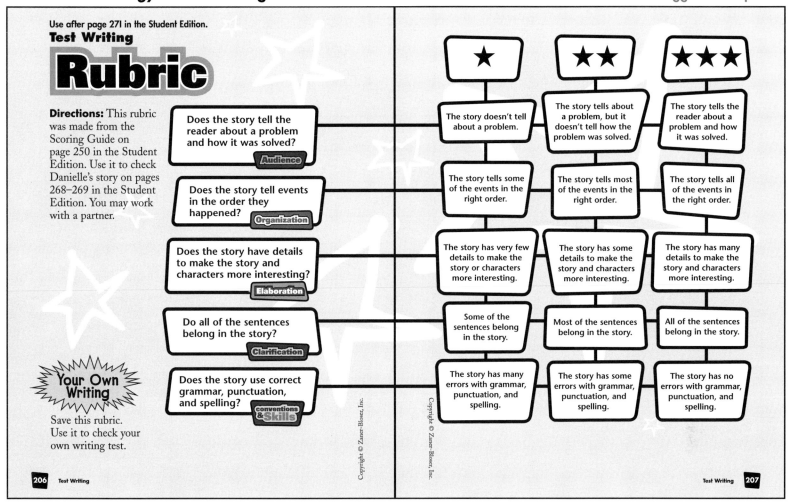

Does the story tell the reader about a problem and how it was solved? **Audience**

Does the story tell events in the order they happened? **Organization**

Does the story have details to make the story and characters more interesting? **Elaboration**

Do all of the sentences belong in the story? **Clarification**

Does the story use correct grammar, punctuation, and spelling? **Conventions & Skills**

★

The story doesn't tell about a problem.

The story tells some of the events in the right order.

The story has very few details to make the story or characters more interesting.

Some of the sentences belong in the story.

The story has many errors with grammar, punctuation, and spelling.

★★

The story tells about a problem, but it doesn't tell how the problem was solved.

The story tells most of the events in the right order.

The story has some details to make the story and characters more interesting.

Most of the sentences belong in the story.

The story has some errors with grammar, punctuation, and spelling.

★★★

The story tells the reader about a problem and how it was solved.

The story tells all of the events in the right order.

The story has many details to make the story and characters more interesting.

All of the sentences belong in the story.

The story has no errors with grammar, punctuation, and spelling.

# STRATEGIES
## for Writers
## Sing-Along CD

All lyrics by Barry Sneed

## With Hand Motions

You may wish to use songs from the *Strategies for Writers Sing-Along* CD as students learn and practice writing strategies for each step of the writing process. This CD uses melodies of familiar children's songs, such as "Mary Had a Little Lamb" and "Row, Row, Row Your Boat," set to lyrics that will help you teach and reinforce important writing skills. The lyrics and optional hand motions for each song on the *Strategies for Writers Sing-Along* CD are provided for you in this section of the Teacher Edition.

## The Lefty Song
(sung to the tune of "Skip to My Lou")

There's a guy on my paper—he lives on the left. (left thumb pointing left)
A guy on my paper—he lives on the left,
A guy on my paper—he lives on the left,
A guy on the left named Lef-ty! (big L with left hand)

I write and my pencil moves to the right. (writing motion to the right)
I write and my pencil moves to the right.
I write and my pencil moves to the right,
Moving away from Lef-ty! (big L with left hand)

I get to the end; I go back again. (jab forward with left index finger,
then point left with left thumb)
I get to the end; I go back again.
I get to the end; I go back again,
Go back again to Lef-ty! (big L with left thumb)

I move down a row and start over again. (down motion with right hand,
then writing motion to the right)
I move down a row and start over again.
I move down a row and start over again,
Moving away from Lef-ty! (big L with left hand)

There's a guy on my paper—he lives on the left. (left thumb pointing left)
A guy on my paper—he lives on the left,
A guy on my paper—he lives on the left,
A guy on the left named Lef-ty! (big L with left thumb)

## The Writing Song
(sung to the tune of "Row, Row, Row Your Boat")

Why, why, why do we write? (shrug)
Tell me why we write.
To communicate, create, or relate, (talking motion with hand)
That is why we write!

How, how, how do we write? (shrug)
Tell me how we write.
With writing tools, ideas, and rules, (writing motion, point to temple,
then hand out with palm open)
That is how we write!

What, what, what do we write? (shrug)
Tell me what we write.
Reports, letters, lists, or stories with twists, (writing motion)
That is what we write!

When, when, when do we write? (shrug)
Tell me when we write.
When we have an idea or a topic that's clear, (circle with hands over head,
like a light bulb)
That is when we write!

Where, where, where do we write? (shrug)
Tell me where we write.
At home or away, at school or at play, (upside-down "V" with arms,
like a roof)
That is where we write!

Write, write, we love to write!
We could write all day.
To communicate, create, or relate, (talking motion)
The things we want to say!

### Writer, Writer...You're A Star!
(sung to the tune of "Twinkle, Twinkle, Little Star")

**Refrain:**   Writer, writer you're a star. (hand up over head with palm open)
Can you tell me what you are? (hand down in front of body with palm up and open)

*1st Verse:*   When I write narrative, I could (writing motion with left hand)
Tell a story that's really good. (OK sign with right hand)

*2nd Verse:*   When I write descriptive, you will find (writing motion)
I paint a picture in your mind. (point to temple with finger)

*3rd Verse:*   When I write ex-pos-i-tor-y, (writing motion)
You get reports and facts from me. (trace a square in air with index finger of each hand)

*4th Verse:*   When I write persuasive, you'll see, (writing motion)
I can make you agree with me. (point forward with index finger,
then thumb to self)

Writer, writer, you're a star. (hand up over head with palm open)
Now I know just what you are! (point forward four times with index finger)

### The Writing Process Hokey Pokey
(sung to the tune of the "Hokey Pokey")

You put your ideas in. (point to head)
You take your ideas out. (thumb out)
You put your ideas in, and you shake them all about.
(point to head, then shake head back and forth)

**Refrain:**
You do the writing process 'til your final
copy's done. (spin around once)
That's what it's all about! (clap three times)

You pick your pencil up. (point index finger of one hand
in air)
You take your paper out. (open palm of other hand,
open upward)
You put your pencil on your paper and you write words
all about.
(place index finger on open palm and move around to
imitate writing)

You put some new words in.
(index fingers point down with both hands)
You take some old words out.
(point back over shoulders with thumbs)
You put some new words in,
(index fingers point down with both hands)
And you move them all about.
(spin hands together in circular motion)

You put your capitals in.
(make "C" with left hand)
You check your spelling out.
(make the OK sign with fingers)
You put your end marks in.
(jab forward with right index finger)
Now you've got it there's no doubt!

You pick your final copy up,
(hands up like an open book)
You put your final copy down,
(hands down, palms down)
You pick your final copy up, and you share it all around.
(hands up with palms open moving side to side)

You did the writing process 'til your final copy's done.
(spin around once)
That's what it's all about! (clap three times)

You do the writing process!
You do the writing process!
You do the writing process!
That's what it's all about! (clap three times)

## The Editing Song
(sung to the tune of "Oh, Dear! What Can the Matter Be?")

**Refrain:**
Oh, dear! (hand to forehead, scanning)
What can the matter be? (shrug)
Oh, dear! (hand to forehead, scanning)
What can the matter be? (shrug)
Oh, dear! (hand to forehead, scanning)
What can the matter be? (shrug)
Writers check their work with care. (shake right index finger)

*1st Verse:*
The first word in a sentence must start with a capital.
(make "C" with left hand)
Be sure your sentences start with a capital.
Sentences must always start with a capital.
Is there a capital there?

*2nd Verse:*
A sentence that tells something ends with a period.
(jab forward with right index finger)
Be sure telling sentences end with a period.
Each telling sentence must end with a period.
Is there a period there?

*3rd Verse:*
A sentence that asks something ends with a question mark.
(trace a question mark in air with index finger)
Be sure asking sentences end with a question mark.
Each asking sentence must end with a question mark.
Is there a question mark there?

*4th Verse:*
The word "I" must be written using a capital.
(thumb pointing to self)
Be sure to write the word "I" as a capital.
"I" must always be written as capital.
Is there a capital "I" there?

*5th Verse:*
A sentence must always have space between the words.
(hands parallel to each other, chopping motion)
Be sure each sentence has space between the words.
Sentences must always have space between the words.
Is there space between words there?

*6th Verse:*
A sentence must always make sense to your audience.
(point to temple with index finger)
Be sure each sentence makes sense to your audience.
A sentence must always make sense to your audience.
Is everything making sense there?

*7th Verse:*
Is there a capital? (make a "C")
Is there a period? (jab forward with right index finger)
Is there a question mark? (trace question mark in air)
Is there a capital "I"? (thumb pointing to self)
Is there space between words? (chopping motion)
Is everything making sense there? (point to temple)

## I'm a Writer Now!
(sung to the tune of "Do Your Ears Hang Low?")

**Teacher's Verse:**
Do your ideas flow? (flowing wave motion with right hand)
Can you make your pencil go? (writing motion)
Can you write a word or two, or a sentence? (one finger up,
then two fingers up, then stretching motion with thumbs and index fingers)
Good for you! (thumbs up sign)
Can you make a final copy that makes sense and isn't sloppy? (trace square
in air with both forefingers)
Are you a writer now? (point "Uncle Sam" style)

**Students' Verse:**
(sung in response)
I can make ideas flow. (flowing wave motion with right hand)
I can make my pencil go. (writing motion)
I can write a word or two, or a sentence. (one finger up, then two fingers
up, then stretching motion with thumbs and index fingers)
Yes, it's true! (OK sign)
I can make a final copy that makes sense and isn't sloppy. (trace square in
air with both index fingers)
I'm a writer now! (point to self with thumb)

## When You Have a Test to Take...
(sung to the tune of "Mary Had a Little Lamb")

**Refrain:**
When you have a test to take, test to take, test
to take…
Don't be afraid, just use your brain. There are
things that you can do.

*1st Verse:*
When you have a test to take, test to take, test
to take…
When you have a test to take, there's no need to
feel blue.
Don't be afraid, just use your brain, use your
brain, use your brain… (point to temple)
Don't be afraid, just use your brain. There are
things that you can do.

*2nd Verse:*
First, are the directions clear, directions clear,
directions clear? (hand to forehead, scanning
motion)
First, are the directions clear? If not, ask your
teacher—that's why she's here!

*3rd Verse:*
Second, take a breath or two, a breath or two, a
breath or two… (both hands up with palms up,
then both hands down with palms down)
Second, take a breath or two. Let your brain
decide just what to do.

*4th Verse:*
Third, look at the test itself, the test itself,
the test itself… (hands open in front of body,
like reading a book)
Third, look at the test itself. Pull what you know
down off the shelf.

*5th Verse:*
Fourth, if something throws you off track,
throws you off track, throws you off track…
(rolling motion with hands)
Fourth, if something throws you off track,
skip it for now, and later, come back!

*6th Verse:*
Fifth, once you have done your best,
done your best, done your best…
(hands dusting off motion)
Fifth, once you have done your best, relax.
Remember it's just one test!

## Writing Modes and Genres

| | LEVEL A | LEVEL B | LEVEL C | LEVEL D | LEVEL E | LEVEL F | LEVEL G | LEVEL H |
|---|---|---|---|---|---|---|---|---|
| Adventure Story | | | | ● | | | | |
| Biographic Sketch | | | | ● | | | | ● |
| Book Report | | | | | ● | ● | | ● |
| Cause-and-Effect Report | | | | | | ● | ● | |
| Character Sketch | | | | ● | | | | |
| Compare-and-Contrast Essay/Paper | ● | ● | | ● | ● | | | |
| Contemporary Story | | | | ● | | | | |
| Descriptive Essay/Paper | | | ● | | ● | ● | ● | ● |
| Descriptive Paragraph | ● | ● | ● | ● | | | | |
| E-mail | | | | | | | ● | |
| Editorial | | | | | | | ● | ● |
| Explanation of a Complex Process | | | | | | | | ● |
| Eyewitness Account | | | | | ● | ● | | |
| Fable | | ● | | | ● | | | |
| Factual Report | ● | ● | ● | | | | | ● |
| Folktale | | | ● | | | | | |
| Historical Fiction/Episode | | | | | | ● | ● | ● |
| How-To Essay/Paper | | ● | ● | | | | | |
| Letters (Friendly/Business) | ● | ● | ● | ● | ● | ● | ● | ● |
| Mystery | | | | | ● | | | |
| Observation Report | | | | | ● | ● | ● | ● |
| Once Upon a Time Story | | ● | | | | | | |
| Personal Narrative | ● | ● | ● | ● | ● | | ● | |
| Persuasive Essay/Paper | | ● | ● | ● | | ● | ● | ● |
| Persuasive Paragraph | ● | | ● | | | | | |
| Persuasive Speech | | ● | | | | | | |
| Realistic Story | | ● | ● | | | | | |
| Research Report | | | | | ● | ● | ● | ● |
| Summary | | | | | | ● | ● | |
| TV Commercial Script | | | | | | | | ● |

## Graphic Organizers

| | LEVEL A | LEVEL B | LEVEL C | LEVEL D | LEVEL E | LEVEL F | LEVEL G | LEVEL H |
|---|---|---|---|---|---|---|---|---|
| Attribute Chart | | | | ● | ● | | | |
| Cause-and-Effect Chain | | | | | ● | ● | ● | ● |
| Character Chart | | | | ● | | | | |
| 5 Senses Chart | | ● | | | | | | |
| 5 W's Chart; 3 W's Chart | | | ● | | | ● | ● | ● |
| K-W-S Chart | | | | | | | ● | |
| Main-Idea Table | | | ● | | | | ● | ● |
| Network Tree | | | ● | ● | ● | ● | | |
| Observation Chart | | | ● | | | | ● | |
| Order-of-Importance Organizer | | | | ● | | ● | ● | |
| Outline | | | | | ● | ● | ● | ● |
| Persuasion Map | | | | | | | ● | |
| Problem-Solution Frame | | | | | | | ● | ● |
| Pros-and-Cons Chart | | | | | ● | | | ● |
| Sequence Chain/Order Chain | | ● | ● | ● | ● | ● | | ● |
| Spider Map | ● | ● | ● | ● | ● | ● | | |
| Storyboard | ● | ● | ● | | ● | | | ● |
| Story Map | | ● | ● | ● | ● | ● | ● | ● |
| Support Pattern | | | | | ● | | | |
| Time Line | | | | ● | | | | ● |
| Venn Diagram | ● | ● | | | | ● | | |
| Web | ● | ● | | ● | | | ● | ● |

| | LEVEL A | LEVEL B | LEVEL C | LEVEL D | LEVEL E | LEVEL F | LEVEL G | LEVEL H |
|---|---|---|---|---|---|---|---|---|
| **Writing Readiness Strategies** | | | | | | | | |
| Alphabet Review | ● | | | | | | | |
| Big Books | ● | | | | | | | |
| Left-to-Right Concept | ● | | | | | | | |
| Letter Recognition | ● | | | | | | | |
| Making Sentences | ● | | | | | | | |
| Making Words | ● | | | | | | | |
| Sound-Letter Correspondence | ● | | | | | | | |
| Top-Bottom Concept | ● | | | | | | | |
| **Writing Strategies** (continued on next page) | | | | | | | | |
| Adding Dialogue/Quotations | | | ● | ● | ● | ● | ● | ● |
| Adding Figurative Language | | | | | ● | ● | ● | ● |
| Adding or Rewriting Details/Facts/Examples | ● | ● | ● | ● | ● | ● | ● | ● |
| Adding Transitions/Signal Words | ● | ● | ● | ● | ● | ● | ● | ● |
| Assessing Personal Experience/Knowledge | | | ● | ● | ● | ● | ● | ● |
| Assessing Personal Interests | | | ● | ● | ● | ● | ● | ● |
| Clear Beginning, Middle, End; Introduction, Conclusion | ● | ● | ● | ● | ● | ● | ● | ● |
| Correcting Sentence Fragments/Run-ons/Confusing Sentences | | ● | ● | ● | ● | ● | ● | ● |
| Deleting Unnecessary or Confusing Information/Wordy Phrases | ● | ● | ● | | ● | ● | ● | ● |
| Determining Audience | ● | ● | ● | ● | ● | ● | ● | ● |
| End Notes, Bibliography | | | | | | | ● | ● |
| Generating Ideas/Statements/Questions | ● | ● | ● | ● | ● | ● | ● | ● |
| Interviewing | | | ● | ● | ● | ● | ● | ● |
| Listing | ● | ● | ● | ● | ● | ● | ● | ● |
| Making Notecards | | | | | | ● | ● | ● |
| Paraphrasing | | | | | | | ● | ● |
| Recognizing and Developing Parts of Genre | ● | ● | ● | ● | ● | ● | ● | ● |

| Writing Strategies (continued) | LEVEL A | LEVEL B | LEVEL C | LEVEL D | LEVEL E | LEVEL F | LEVEL G | LEVEL H |
|---|---|---|---|---|---|---|---|---|
| Recognizing and Using Genre Conventions | ● | ● | ● | ● | ● | ● | ● | ● |
| Reordering Sentences/Paragraphs | | | ● | ● | ● | ● | ● | ● |
| Replacing Vague/Loaded/Cliché Language | | | | ● | ● | ● | | ● |
| Restating Opinion, Purpose | ● | ● | ● | ● | ● | | | |
| Rewriting Unclear/Confusing/Incorrect Information | ● | ● | ● | | ● | | | ● |
| Taking Notes | ● | ● | ● | ● | ● | | ● | |
| Thesis Statement | | | | | ● | | ● | |
| Topic and Detail Sentences | ● | ● | ● | ● | ● | ● | ● | ● |
| Using Appropriate Text Structure | ● | ● | ● | ● | ● | ● | ● | ● |
| Using Appropriate Voice/Tone/Point of View | | ● | ● | ● | ● | ● | ● | ● |
| Using a Thesaurus | | | | ● | ● | | | |
| Using Exact/Precise/Interesting Words | ● | ● | ● | ● | ● | ● | ● | ● |
| Using Graphic Organizers to Generate Draft | ● | ● | ● | ● | ● | ● | ● | ● |
| Using References/Resources | ● | ● | ● | ● | ● | ● | ● | ● |
| Visual Aids/Illustrations | ● | ● | | | ● | ● | ● | |
| Writing Effective Sentences | ● | ● | ● | ● | ● | ● | ● | ● |
| Writing Paragraphs | | ● | ● | ● | ● | ● | ● | ● |
| **Sharing Writing** (continued on next page) | | | | | | | | |
| Author's Circle | | | | ● | | | | |
| Big Books | | | | ● | | | | |
| Mail to Appropriate Person or Publication | ● | ● | ● | ● | ● | ● | ● | ● |
| Multimedia Presentation | | | | | ● | ● | ● | ● |
| Observation Journal | | | | | ● | | ● | ● |
| Part of a Display | | ● | | ● | ● | ● | ● | ● |
| Perform as Play/Newscast/Commercial | | | | | ● | | | ● |
| Post on Website | | ● | ● | ● | | | ● | ● |
| Post on Bulletin Board | ● | ● | ● | | | ● | ● | |
| Present as Speech or Read Aloud | ● | ● | ● | ● | ● | ● | | ● |
| Publish for Class Library | ● | ● | ● | ● | ● | ● | | |
| Publish in Class or School Newspaper/Collection/Magazine/Newsletter/Journal/Diary | | ● | ● | ● | ● | ● | ● | ● |

| | LEVEL A | LEVEL B | LEVEL C | LEVEL D | LEVEL E | LEVEL F | LEVEL G | LEVEL H |
|---|---|---|---|---|---|---|---|---|
| **Sharing Writing** (continued) | | | | | | | | |
| Record on Audiotape | | | ● | | | | | |
| Send as E-mail | | | | | | | ● | |
| Time Capsule | | | | | ● | | | |
| Travel Brochure | | | | ● | | | | |
| **Grammar, Usage, and Mechanics** | | | | | | | | |
| Active and Passive Voice | | | | | | ● | ● | ● |
| Adjectives | | | ● | ● | | | ● | ● |
| Adverbs | | | | ● | | | ● | ● |
| Apostrophes | | | | | | ● | ● | |
| Appositives | | | | | | ● | ● | ● |
| Capitalization | ● | ● | ● | ● | ● | ● | ● | |
| Complete Sentences | ● | ● | ● | ● | ● | ● | ● | ● |
| Contractions | | ● | ● | ● | ● | ● | ● | ● |
| Double Negatives | | | | | ● | | ● | |
| Easily Confused Words/Homophones | | | ● | ● | | ● | ● | |
| Introductory Verbal Phrases | | | | | | | | ● |
| Letters Friendly/Business | ● | ● | ● | ● | ● | ● | ● | |
| Nouns (plural/possessive) | | ● | | ● | ● | | ● | |
| Pronoun Forms/Antecedents | | | ● | ● | ● | ● | ● | ● |
| Punctuation | ● | ● | ● | ● | ● | ● | ● | ● |
| Quotations/Dialogue | | ● | | ● | ● | ● | ● | ● |
| Sentence Patterns | | | ● | ● | ● | ● | ● | ● |
| Sentences: Complex | | | | | | ● | | ● |
| Sentences: Compound | | | ● | | ● | ● | | ● |
| Sentences: Fragments | | | ● | ● | ● | ● | ● | ● |
| Sentences: Run-ons | | | | ● | ● | ● | ● | ● |
| Subject-Verb Agreement | | | ● | ● | ● | ● | ● | ● |
| Verb Forms/Tenses | | | ● | | | | ● | |
| More instruction on grammar, usage, and mechanics can be found in the *Conventions and Skills Practice Book* for each level. | | ● | ● | ● | ● | ● | ● | ● |

# Books on Teaching Writing

Anderson, Carl. *How's It Going?: A Practical Guide to Conferring With Student Writers.* Portsmouth, NH: Heinemann, 2000.

This book offers suggestions on making the most of student conferences.

Avery, Carol. *...And With a Light Touch: Learning About Reading, Writing and Teaching With First Graders.* Portsmouth, NH: Heinemann, 1993.

Avery uses her own experience as a classroom teacher, as well as extensive research, to offer teachers help with everything needed for a writing classroom. This book covers such topics as classroom environment, writing workshop, and assessing and documenting student progress.

Portalupi, JoAnn, and Ralph Fletcher. *Nonfiction Craft Lessons: Teaching Information Writing K–8.* Portland, ME: Stenhouse, 2001.

Divided into chapters for K–2, 3–4, and 5–8, this book presents 25+ one-page descriptions of strategies for aspects of all steps of the writing process, with emphasis on informative writing.

Stead, Tony. *Is That a Fact?: Teaching Nonfiction Writing K–3.* Portland, ME: Stenhouse, 2001.

This book focuses on non-fiction writing in the primary grades. It offers unique and interesting ways to make expository writing fun and accessible to the youngest writers.

Tompkins, Gail E. *Teaching Writing: Balancing Process and Product, 3rd ed.* Upper Saddle River, NJ: Prentice Hall, 1999.

This book contains strong chapters on genres, and one long chapter on strategies, presented in terms of the writing workshop and with the use of student samples.